Economic Capital

Economic Capital

A Practitioner Guide

Edited by Ashish Dev

RISK
BOOKS

Published by Risk Books, a Division of Incisive Financial Publishing Ltd

Haymarket House
28–29 Haymarket
London SW1Y 4RX
Tel: +44 (0)20 7484 9700
Fax: +44 (0)20 7484 9800
E-mail: books@riskwaters.com
Sites: www.riskbooks.com
      www.riskwaters.com

Every effort has been made to secure the permission of individual copyright holders for inclusion.

© Incisive Media Investments Limited 2004

ISBN 1 904339 36 0
ISBN 978 1 904339 36 0

British Library Cataloguing in Publication Data
A catalogue record for this book is available from the British Library

Managing Editor: Sarah Jenkins
Copy Editor: Andrew John
Editorial Assistant: Stephen Fairman

Typeset by Mizpah Publishing Services, Chennai, India

Printed and bound in Spain by Espacegrafic, Pamplona, Navarra

Contents

List of Contributors

Michel Araten is managing director of Global Credit Risk Management at JPMorgan Chase. For the last 12 years he has developed credit risk capital models for global retail, wholesale, and capital markets, and has completed a number of historical studies supporting these models. He joined Chase in 1972 as manager of management science. In 1974, he became group executive in real estate finance and was responsible for high profile work-out problems. In 1980, he was appointed secretary of the Credit Policy Committee. In 1982, he was named director of insurance income products and marketed insurance worldwide and implemented strategies for deregulation opportunities. In 1988, he initiated a mezzanine fund at Chase Investors. In 1990, he returned to real estate finance and developed structured solutions for problem real estate credits. He has been an adjunct lecturer at Columbia University, Fordham Graduate School of Business, and at Polytechnic Institute. He holds a PhD in operations research, an MS in industrial engineering, a BS in chemical engineering, and a BA in liberal arts, all from Columbia University.

Ashish Dev is executive vice president of risk management, at KeyCorp. He is group head of Enterprise Risk Management, which includes economic capital allocations, Basel II coordination, data warehousing, credit underwriting models, strategic analytics and credit portfolio management along with operational risk. As a member of all the three high-level risk committees of KeyCorp viz. ALCO, CREDCO and ORCO, he is involved in decision making in all areas of risk in the bank. Ashish has been the prime mover in establishing enterprise-wide risk-adjusted product pricing and performance measurement and in creating a new credit portfolio management function in the bank. Prior to joining KeyCorp, Ashish was head of quantitative research and analysis in Bank One. Ashish has a PhD in economics and holds the CFA professional designation.

Sebastian Fritz is the head of the Risk Analytics and Instruments Department of the Deutsche Bank Group, responsible for the development of rating and scoring methodologies, pricing tools, portfolio models and operational risk methodology. He has worked in Deutsche Bank's credit risk management division since 1997, in positions such as credit risk instruments analyst and head of rating and pricing tool development. He was previously a research associate at the Gesellschaft fuer

Schwerionenforschung mbH, Darmstadt, Germany. Sebastian gained his physics degree with a minor in computer science and biophysics at the University of Hamburg, and his PhD in heavy ion physics at the Johann-Wolfgang-Goethe-University, Frankfurt.

Jon Frye is a senior economist in the Capital Group at the Federal Reserve Bank of Chicago. In this role he examines economic credit capital models at banking organisations and does research in capital models. His current research interest is the cyclical variation of loss given default and its impact on economic capital. Jon also teaches portfolio risk management at the University of Chicago Graduate Program on Financial Mathematics. Before joining the Fed, he implemented systems for counterparty credit exposure and firm wide Value-at-Risk at large Chicago banks. Dr Frye holds a PhD in economics from Northwestern University.

Michael Gordy is a senior economist in the Research and Statistics Division of the Federal Reserve Board. His current research focuses on the design, calibration and computation of models of portfolio credit risk, and on the adaptation of these models to setting regulatory capital requirements. Michael was the recipient of *Risk*'s 2004 Quant of the Year and GARP's 2003 Financial Risk Manager of the Year, and serves as an associate editor of the *Journal of Banking and Finance*. Michael received his PhD in economics from MIT in 1994 and a BA in mathematics and philosophy from Yale University in 1985.

Michael Kalkbrener is vice president in the Risk Analytics and Instruments department of Deutsche Bank and specialises in developing risk measurement and capital allocation methodologies. His current responsibilities include credit portfolio modelling and the development of a quantitative model for operational risk. Prior to joining Deutsche Bank in 1997, he worked at Cornell University and the Swiss Federal Institute of Technology where he received the venia legendi for mathematics. Michael holds a PhD in mathematics from the Johannes Kepler University Linz. He has published a number of research articles in symbolic computation and mathematical finance.

Nicholas M. Kiefer is the Ta-Chung Liu professor of economics at Cornell University, where he is a member of the graduate field faculties in economics, statistics and hospitality administration. He is widely known for his theoretical and applied contributions in the econometric modelling of duration data, the estimation of dynamic programming models under learning, and financial market microstructure. Kiefer's current research includes applications in financial economics, credit scoring and risk management, consumer trend forecasting, and development of quantitative management techniques for the restaurant and retail industries. He is a

Fellow of the Econometric Society, and a past recipient of the Guggenheim Memorial Fellowship.

David R. Koenig is the executive director and chair of the Board of Directors of the Professional Risk Managers' International Association (PRMIA). He has nearly twenty years of broad managerial and front-line experience in the financial markets and has led the development of three risk management programs. He most recently served as the head of market and institutional credit risk management for US Bancorp Piper Jaffray and has held lead risk management roles for GMAC/RFC and Principal Residential Mortgage, Inc., a subsidiary of the Principal Financial Group. He began his career with the First National Bank of Chicago. David has a masters degree in economics from Northwestern University in Evanston, IL and bachelors degrees in mathematics and economics and a certificate in statistics from Miami University in Oxford, OH, where he was a member of the Pi Mu Epsilon Mathematics, Honor Society.

David Lamb was the head of the counterparty risk analytics group at Citigroup. This group is responsible for the analytics and one-off analysis to determine counterparty exposure across all derivatives products including securities financing and structured products. David is working to improve the measurement of economic capital for these same products and is helping the business start to hedge many of these risks. He has been with Citigroup since 1997 and is a member of the Credit Risk Systems Steering Committee. David has a PhD in theoretical physics from the University of Alberta and has recently moved to join the fixed income derivatives research group at Morgan Stanley.

C. Erik Larson is a senior financial economist in the Risk Analysis Division of the Office of the Comptroller of the Currency (OCC). His present work involves traveling to the largest of our nation's banks and examining the models developed and used by these institutions to measure and manage risk. Larson's research focuses on statistical and econometric issues in the modelling of credit risk and economic capital. Prior to joining the OCC, Larson analysed and developed individual and corporate income tax policy in the Office of Tax Analysis at The Treasury. He also taught courses on probability, statistics, and econometrics while on the faculty of the University of Southern California School of Business Administration, and served as a private consultant, specialising in the development of methods to value financial assets. Larson holds a PhD in economics from Cornell and a BA from Syracuse University.

Ludger Overbeck holds a Professorship of mathematics and its application at the University of Giessen in Germany. His main interests are quantitative methods in finance and risk management and stochastic analysis. Until June 2003, he was head of risk research and development in Deutsche Banks Credit Risk function, located in Frankfurt. Ludger's main responsibilities included development and implementation of the internal group-wide credit portfolio model, the operational risk model and the EC/RAROC-methodology. Ludger holds a PhD in mathematics and habilitations in applied mathematics from the University of Bonn and in economics from the University of Frankfurt.

Wilfried Paus originally started with Deutsche Bank Bremen branch right after school in 1984. After his apprenticeship, he went on to study his favourite subject, pure mathematics, in Bonn and Sydney. Having completed his PhD in 1996, he returned to Deutsche Bank, focusing on credit risk methodology development. Just back in Frankfurt from five years in London, he heads the Economic Capital Methodology and Implementation Team in the bank's Credit Risk Management department.

Tony Peccia is vice president of operational risk and corporate insurance management at the Bank of Montreal. He is responsible for developing, implementing and monitoring the application of emerging best practices in operational risk management, including the proposed new Basel requirements for operational risk practice and regulatory capital. Tony spent eleven years with CIBC in various executive positions, including operational risk management, market risk management, and asset and liability management. Prior to that, he spent ten years at the Royal Bank of Canada holding various positions. Tony has an MBA and a MSc in theoretical physics from McGill University.

Evan Picoult is a managing director and head of the Risk Methods and Analytics Unit within the Risk Architecture Department of Citigroup. Risk Architecture has global responsibility for establishing the risk infrastructure of Citigroup across all of its businesses around the world. The primary function of the Risk Methods and Analytics unit is the development and enhancement of methods for measuring and analysing the risks of the firm, including economic capital. In the past he advised Citibank's Market Policy Committee and its Credit Risk Policy Committee on risk issues. Evan is the North American co-chair of ISDA's Risk Management Committee. He has a PhD in experimental particle physics from Columbia University and an MBA from Columbia University's Graduate School of Business.

Michael Pykhtin is a vice president in the Risk Management Group at KeyCorp in Cleveland, OH. His main responsibility is developing portfolio models of credit risk for capital allocation purposes. Michael has been a regular contributor to *Risk* magazine's Cutting Edge section. He has published articles on capital allocation for securitisations, granularity adjustment for loan portfolios, modelling correlations between default and recovery rates, modelling residual risk in auto leases, analytical methods for multi-factor credit risk models. Prior to joining KeyCorp in 2000, Michael was a researcher in theoretical physics, studying vibrational dynamics at surfaces and interfaces of materials. He holds a PhD degree in physics from the University of Pennsylvania.

Vandana Rao is associate professor in the Business and Economics Division of Indiana University East. She teaches courses in finance, economics and statistics. She has won several teaching awards in the Indiana University system. Her research interests are diverse and range from economic demography to financial institutions. Vandana has worked as a research consultant/project director with community organisations at various levels, including the UNICEF, the Government of India and economic development agencies in the State of Indiana. Vandana has a PhD in economics.

Geoffrey M. Rubin, joined Capital One as director of the Economic Capital Group in 2003. Geoffrey has since coordinated regulatory and economic capital adequacy and managed the internal capital attribution process. Geoffrey previously spent six years at Reis, Inc., a commercial real estate investment and advisory firm, where he headed product development and consulting. In this role, Geoffrey helped a number of lenders develop measures of economic capital for their commercial real estate portfolios. Geoffrey has also worked in Fannie Mae's policy research group and with the overstreet consulting group developing retail credit scoring solutions for credit unions. Geoffrey holds a BA from the University of Virginia and an MA and PhD from Princeton University.

Dirk Tasche is a risk analyst in the banking and financial supervision division of the Deutsche Bundesbank. He specialises in mathematical and statistical aspects of the New Basel Accord. Prior to joining the Bundesbank, Dirk was working in the credit risk management of the Bayerische HypoVereinsbank and as a researcher at Munich University of Technology and at RiskLab Switzerland in Zurich. Dirk received a PhD in mathematics from Berlin University of Technology. He published several papers on statistics, measurement of financial risks and capital allocation.

Ursula Theiler, Risk Training, CEO, is a professional training consultant who is conducting trainings for financial institutions and companies related to bank and risk management. After finishing her degree in mathematics with economics at the University of Ulm, Germany, and

Boulder, Colorado, USA, she was employed as a business customer attendant, credit analyst and risk controller in several large German banks. Ursula holds a doctorate degree from the Banking Business Department of the Ludwig-Maximilians-University of Munich, Germany. Her thesis on "Integrated Risk Return Bank Management" received the dissertation award price 2002 by the German Society of Operations Research. She published different papers on bank applications in risk management.

Gary Wilhite is senior vice president in the Risk Management Group of Wachovia Bank and has been involved with quantitative risk management for more than 11 years with Wachovia and its predecessors. Gary is responsible for commercial loan default probabilities, loss given default, and usage given default rates; the bank's allowance for loan losses; economic capital modelling for commercial and consumer credit; and the credit portion of the bank's Basel efforts. He has made presentations to the RMA portfolio management roundtable, the IACPM, the KMV user group, and the Risk Analysis Division, OCC. Gary has an MBA from the University of Virginia.

Introduction

Ashish Dev

KeyCorp

Economic capital is a measure of risk. It is a single measure that captures unexpected losses or reduction in value or income from a portfolio or business in a financial institution. The risk arises from the *unexpected* nature of the losses as distinct from *expected* losses, which are considered part of doing business and are covered by reserves and income. Economic capital covers all unexpected events except the catastrophic ones, for which it is impossible to hold capital. Economic capital is a common currency in which all risks of a financial institution can be measured, enabling comparison of risk across different risks, across diverse businesses and across different financial institutions. A precise definition of economic capital is not attempted in this Introduction, since such a definition can be found in more than one place in the book.

The most important conceptual distinction between expected loss and unexpected loss is that the expected loss of a portfolio is simply the sum of expected losses for each of the constituent transactions within the portfolio. In that sense, expected loss is similar to variables such as revenue and expense. But the same does not hold true for unexpected loss. Unexpected loss in a portfolio has to take an important additional variable into account: namely, correlation. Correlations can exist between one transaction and another or between one portfolio and another. Typically, correlations are much lower for retail portfolios than for commercial portfolios. Another way of saying this is that retail portfolios are much more diversified than commercial ones. Economic capital models often use the term *granularity* in referring to the proportion that each transaction represents of the portfolio. The extent of underlying granularity has a profound impact on intra-portfolio correlation and consequently on unexpected loss or economic capital.

The term "unexpected loss" is used by practitioners in two different ways. Unexpected loss may be defined as the standard deviation of the portfolio loss distribution. It may also be defined by subtracting the expected loss from the loss level at a high percentile.

A portfolio may have a higher expected loss than another but this does not necessarily imply that it will have a higher economic capital. For example, a highly granular and diversified credit card portfolio may have an expected loss of 4.0% while a commercial real estate portfolio concentrated in a particular region may have an expected loss of 1.0%. The economic capital required to support the credit card portfolio may be less than the economic capital required to support the commercial real estate portfolio.

Since its introduction in sophisticated financial institutions about a decade ago, economic capital has become an important tool for:

❑ measuring and managing risk;
❑ risk-adjusted pricing, so that the bank is adequately compensated for the risk taken;
❑ strategic use and optimum allocation of capital;
❑ performance measurement for shareholder value creation; and
❑ a driver of compensation.

In other words, economic capital now plays a significant role in major functions performed in a sophisticated financial institution, both at the corporate level and at the lines of business. Yet there is a paucity of good literature on economic capital. There are published models on economic capital and occasional papers on applications of economic capital. But it is hard for a practitioner to find an easy source providing both an overview and in-depth understanding. The objective of this book is to fill this void. The subject of economic capital has developed sufficiently that it would be presumptuous to claim this book to be comprehensive. But an attempt has been made to cover a fairly wide range of issues regarding economic capital in the book.

The book is divided into three sections. The first section deals with concepts and applications of economic capital. The second section deals with economic capital methodologies for specific risks pertinent to a financial institution. Mathematical treatment of issues in economic capital methodologies comprises the third section.

The four major categories of risk in a financial institution are credit risk, market risk, counterparty risk and operational risk. Issues relating to economic capital for each of these risks have been covered in the book, though economic capital for credit risk takes the lion's share. Balance-sheet interest rate risk and risks such as strategic risk and reputation risk have not been covered. Balance-sheet interest rate risk is managed at the corporate level through discretionary activities, typically by the use of interest rate derivatives and mortgage-backed investments, coupled with a transfer pricing mechanism. It is the residual risk that is of concern and not the interest rate risk in each transaction or portfolio. This obviates the need for allocating economic capital to each transaction. Risks such as reputation risk are too qualitative to attempt an economic capital calculation.

The chapters in the *first* section, although general for the most part, have a reference to economic capital for credit risk and in particular, credit risk in corporate portfolios. This is no surprise, as some of the models of portfolio credit risk and the concept of economic capital were first developed in the corporate credit world.

Chapter 1 provides a broad introduction to economic capital dealing with all risks relevant to a financial institution. While it introduces economic capital in the special setting of a particular bank, the topics covered provide a conceptual and non-mathematical background for any financial institution.

Chapter 2 addresses the issue of allocation of portfolio economic capital to individual transactions in the portfolio at a conceptual level. The strengths and weaknesses of two well-known approaches of capital allocation to individual transactions have been presented in a simple way with numerical illustrations. These approaches are: risk-contribution approach and tail-risk approach. Chapter 13 addresses the same problem of allocation of portfolio economic capital to constituent sub-portfolios at a much more mathematical level.

Chapter 3 focuses on the inputs to economic capital calculation for wholesale credit portfolios. While some of the results presented are based on data from one particular bank, the chapter provides a broad conceptual framework for credit capital at a practical level. Chapter 4 is concerned with loss-given default or recovery and its modelling and impact on economic capital. Intuitively, in an economic downturn not only are the defaults higher but also the values of the defaulted firms' assets are lower, increasing loss-given default. This issue has been addressed with empirical evidence in both Chapters 3 and 4. Chapter 4 seeks to show how true effects of loss-given default need to be incorporated in an economic capital model.

Modelling of economic capital for credit portfolios comes after and depends on modelling of credit risk. There are three fundamental approaches to modelling credit risk: *intensity-based models*, *structural models* and *empirical models*. Intensity-based models describe default as an unpredictable event and do not assume any economic reason for default. They are based on a stochastic process called intensity of default, which describes the instantaneous probability of default. Correlation between default events is described by the correlation between intensity processes. Empirical models are based on econometric estimation from historical data. Structural models, on the other hand, describe default as an event that arises from the financial situation of the borrower. The first useful structural model of default is described in the seminal work of Merton (1974). Merton assumed that a firm has a stock and a single non-amortising debt obligation. The firm's asset value is described by a geometric Brownian motion. The firm defaults if, at maturity of the debt, the value of the firm's assets falls below the face value of the debt. Stock price in the Merton model is a call option on the firm's assets with the debt face value being the option strike price. Many refinements and extensions of the Merton model have subsequently appeared from both academic and practitioners' perspectives. All of these structural models are based on Merton's framework and are often called Merton-type models.

From the economic capital perspective, the most important adaptation of Merton's model has been done by Vasicek (1987, 1991). Vasicek applied Merton's model to a portfolio of borrowers. As in Merton's model, each borrower is characterised by a lognormal asset value process. A borrower defaults when its asset-value falls below a threshold defined by its liabilities. Correlations between borrowers' defaults arise from correlation between their asset values. Correlations between asset values, in turn, are described by a common dependence of asset returns on a single systematic factor, representing the state of the economy. Thus the asset return for each borrower has a systematic component, reflecting the effect of the economy on the borrower, and an idiosyncratic component, describing fortunes and misfortunes unique for the borrower. Assuming homogeneous portfolio of loans with zero recoveries, Vasicek derived the distribution function for the portfolio loss. The Vasicek model has also been refined and extended to include non-homogeneous portfolios and non-zero stochastic recoveries. The term "Vasicek model" is often used to include these extensions of the original Vasicek model.

To describe different systematic effects for firms belonging to different industries and/or different geographical regions, the single systematic factor in the Vasicek model was replaced by a set of correlated systematic factors. This multi-factor extension of the Vasicek model lies in the foundation of such industry models as KMV's PortfolioManager™ and RiskMetrics' CreditMetrics™. Not all models of portfolio credit risk are of the Merton-Vasicek type (eg, CSFB's Credit Risk Plus™).

Chapter 5 enumerates the applications of economic capital in a financial institution. It argues that the significance of economic capital to a financial institution arises more from these applications than from any theoretical consideration, many of which are possible only with the advent of economic capital methodology. It also shows how the concept of economic capital for a financial institution is a departure from the traditional corporate finance approach for industrial organisations.

The chapters in the *second* section of the book address issues related to economic capital for specific risks: namely, retail credit risk, counterparty credit risk, credit risk in securitisation, market risk and operational risk. Each chapter focuses on economic capital methodology for the particular kind of risk and discusses issues specific to that application.

Chapter 6 deals with economic capital for retail credit exposures. The discussion is in the context of credit cards. However, most of the concepts discussed apply equally to any retail portfolio. The three broad methodologies for credit risk capital presented are the ones prevalent in the wider retail world. The difficulties of estimating loss-given default and particularly exposure at default are unique to revolving credit portfolios.

Chapter 7 presents concepts of economic capital methodologies in general as well as economic capital for counterparty credit risk in particular. Credit risk and market risk intersect in the context of counterparty risk. The chapter indicates that the distinguishing feature of counterparty credit risk from credit risk in general is that the magnitude and direction of the exposure is uncertain. This feature necessitates a distinct methodology for calculating economic capital for counterparty risk. The methodology, in all its details, is presented in the chapter both at a conceptual and a practical level. All derivative portfolios require economic capital for counterparty credit risk as well as economic capital for market risk.

Chapter 8 presents conceptual issues and recent models of credit risk in securitisation tranches. It emphasises the fact that credit risk in a securitisation tranche cannot be modelled in the same way as credit risk in bond or loan portfolios. It also shows that rating of a tranche alone is not enough to compute economic capital attributable to the credit risk in that tranche. On average, highly rated (eg, AAA, AA) senior tranches require significantly less economic capital than similarly rated corporate bonds, while lowly rated junior tranches require significantly more economic capital than similarly rated bonds (eg, BB, B). The chapter describes a couple of models developed recently that address credit risk in securitisation tranches in an appropriate manner. These two models form the foundations of the ratings-based approach and the supervisory formula approach respectively in capital adequacy for securitisation in Basel II (see BIS, 2004).

Chapter 9 is on economic capital for market risk. It describes qualitatively the issues involved in calculating regulatory as well as economic capital for market risk. The most common methodology is to compute value-at-risk (VAR) for the portfolio at a horizon and level of confidence suitable for oversight on trading and then scale the VAR to reflect an annual horizon and a level of confidence corresponding to the desired insolvency standard of the institution. A normal distribution of changes in market value of a portfolio is a reasonable assumption. It is relatively easy to derive the scaling factors under this assumption and that of random walk.

Then the calculation of economic capital rests on the calculation of VAR.

Chapter 10 addresses economic capital for operational risk. It is the discussion around the formulation of Basel II capital adequacy rules that led to a measurable definition of operational risk. While several financial institutions have been allocating economic capital for operational risk prior to that, the methodologies left a lot to be desired. Therefore, unlike other economic capital methodologies, economic capital for operational risk goes hand in hand with the Basel II framework for measurement and management, including precise delineation of the scope of operational risk.

The *advanced measurement approaches* (AMA) constitute the centre-piece of Basel II operational risk capital. As the name suggests, AMA does not refer to a single approach or model, but rather refers to a collection of models that share certain guiding principles, namely incorporating information of (1) internal data, (2) external data, (3) scenario analysis and (4) internal control environment and business environment. AMA models are to be analytic and the capital measure is to reflect a soundness standard comparable to a one-year holding period and a 99.9th percentile confidence interval. As such, AMA provides an appropriate framework to discuss and develop economic capital methodologies for operational risk.

The actuarial technique of modelling the frequency and severity of operational loss events separately is a good starting point. The two are then combined using simulation, or other techniques, to arrive at an aggregate loss distribution. This is typically the analytic core of an economic capital model for operational risk and is known as the *loss distribution approach*. There is an obvious analogy between this loss distribution approach and credit risk modelling. Event frequency is analogous to default and severity is the complement to recovery.

However, scarcity of internal historical loss data necessitates the incorporation of external data and construction of scenarios in order to model frequency and severity. Furthermore, the recognition that operational losses depend on internal controls (in relation to the surrounding business environment), which change with time, necessitates building an explicit dependence of the losses on the state of controls. The "art" of operational risk economic capital consists in estimating the future unexpected loss conditioned on observables, such as historical losses, historical and current state of controls and accumulated institutional knowledge about potential operational risks. The chapter on operational risk economic capital outlines an AMA-type model, emphasising the aspects related to incorporating information from the controls and business environments.

The *third* section of the book is mathematical. While a strong quantitative background is needed to follow the mathematics, others may find it useful to ignore the derivations and think intuitively about the results presented in these chapters. The issues raised in the chapters in this section are fundamental to the concept of economic capital and risk-adjusted measures.

The main objective of Chapter 11 is deriving a theoretically sound risk-adjusted performance measure. It formally introduces the principle of coherent measures of risk and examines profitability measures such as risk-adjusted return on capital and economic profit added from this perspective. The drawbacks of those measures are examined and a new profitability measure based on the capital asset pricing model is introduced.

Chapter 12 provides the fundamentals of an asymptotic single risk factor framework, which has since become the basis of the Basel II internal ratings based (IRB) approach (see BIS, 2004). General closed-form asymptotic expressions for portfolio VAR and its allocation to individual exposures are derived for the asymptotic single-factor case. According to this allocation, exposure-level capital depends only on properties of the exposure and does not depend on the portfolio composition. This property of the asymptotic single risk factor framework allows ratings-based allocation of capital and paves the foundation for Basel II IRB approach. Going beyond the asymptotic case, the chapter also discusses capital adjustment for undiversified idiosyncratic risk, widely known as *granularity adjustment*.

Chapter 13 looks quantitatively at three established portfolio risk measures: standard deviation, VAR and expected shortfall. Each of these risk measures has its own "native" definition of risk contribution: *covariance-based* risk contribution for the standard deviation measure, *quantile-based* risk contribution for the VAR measure and *shortfall-based* risk contribution for the expected shortfall measure. The chapter argues that using a risk contribution with a "non-native" risk measure (eg, the highly popular covariance-based allocation with VAR risk measure) is likely to lead to counterintuitive results.

A new class of coherent risk measures called *spectral risk measures* is introduced in Chapter 14. Spectral risk measure is a natural extension of the expected shortfall measure. Expected shortfall can be represented as an arithmetic average of portfolio VARs at all levels above the chosen confidence level. It can be thought of as a weighted average of portfolio VARs at all levels between zero and one, with the weight function being equal to zero below the confidence level and being equal to one divided by the insolvency probability above the confidence level. A spectral risk measure is a weighted sum of portfolio VARs at levels between zero and one, with an *arbitrary* weight function satisfying certain conditions. This chapter is an attempt at generalising the theory and modelling of economic capital.

Chapter 15 develops a broad framework for validating an economic capital model. With the introduction of Pillar 2 of Basel II (see BIS, 2004), validation has surfaced as an important issue. Validations are at two levels: validation of the inputs and validation of the ratings or capital models. Not much work has been done in this area. Developing a broad framework, within the parameters of which practitioners and regulators can discuss validation issues, is topical.

The international Basel II capital adequacy rules for financial institutions have been finalised in 2004 (see BIS, 2004). The most important objective of the Basel II capital adequacy rules is to better align minimum regulatory capital requirements to the true risk of the portfolios of the regulated institution. The capital adequacy rules under the present Basel I Accord are more or less "one-size-fits-all". The second important aspect of Basel II is to allow banks to use internal assessments of risk (up to an extent) to come up with their minimum capital adequacy. The internal economic capital methodologies, developed over the last ten years, enable measurement and assessment of risk in all areas of a financial institution and to attribute it to business units, portfolios and transactions. Under Basel II, regulatory capital will be determined by the very same inputs that go to determine internal economic capital of a bank, while an individual bank's internal economic capital formulas may be slightly or substantially different from the regulatory capital formulas. Thus, Basel II has not only affected a steady convergence of regulatory and economic capital but has also been a catalyst in development of economic capital methodologies, particularly for securitisations and operational risk.

The significance of economic capital to a financial institution does not arise from regulatory requirements. Use of economic capital is a prerequisite for good risk management. It is also an essential tool for overall bank management for shareholder value maximisation. The applications of economic capital related in various parts of the book, particularly Chapters 1 and 5, amply illustrate this point. In its initial years, economic capital and its application were limited to large sophisticated institutions. However, in recent years the concept of economic capital is steadily spreading to other financial institutions, perhaps under competitive pressure. It is hoped that the contents of this book will be of value to practitioners, as the use of economic capital becomes more prevalent among financial institutions at large.

REFERENCES

BIS, 2004, "International Convergence of Capital Measurements and Capital Standards: A Revised Framework", Basel Committee on Banking Supervision (referred to as Basel II), June.

Merton, R., 1974, "On the Pricing of Corporate Debt: The Risk Structure of Interest Rates", *Journal of Finance,* **29,** pp. 449–70.

Vasicek, O., 1987, "Probability of Loss on Loan Portfolio", KMV Corporation.

Vasicek, O., 1991, "Limiting Loan Loss Probability Distribution", KMV Corporation.

Section 1

Economic Capital:
Concepts and Applications

Background on Economic Capital*

John S. Walter**

Bank of America

Institutions using *economic capital methodology* have coined the term to distinguish it from other measures of capital adequacy – in particular, regulatory and accounting concepts of capital. The term *economic* also encapsulates an ambition, like that of the dismal science, to describe and measure on a consistent basis the range of phenomena that drive a bank's risk/return decisions. A consistent and comprehensive economic model accomplishes two goals:

1. It provides a common currency of risk that management can use to compare the risk-adjusted profitability and relative value of businesses with widely varying degrees and sources of risk.
2. It allows bank management and supervisors to evaluate overall capital adequacy in relation to the risk profile of the institution.

With increasing dialogue among practitioners, regulators, and academics, best practices have gradually emerged, setting standards for calculation in most aspects of economic capital. Advances continue, especially in the areas of operational risk and consumer credit risk, but the overall field has matured to the point where supervisors have begun, with the upcoming implementation of the New Basel Capital Accord, to adopt and codify the industry's best practices in the regulatory capital framework.

*This chapter is reprinted with permission of RMA – The Risk Management Association, www.rmahq.org. The article originally appeared in an issue of The RMA Journal.
**The author thanks Neil Caverley for his invaluable assistance and helpful comments.

MARKET VALUE DEFINITION OF RISK

Over the past decade, economic capital has steadily progressed toward market value models. Most commercial portfolio frameworks have by now discarded first-generation economic capital models based only on default risk, although these models persist in some cases for consumer portfolios. Given the goal of ensuring capital adequacy for a certain level of solvency, the volatility of market value is the best measure of a bank's risk and therefore its capital requirement.

Ultimately, shareholders are interested in the total return on their investment in the bank's stock and its risk in market value terms. They compare the return earned on their investment to a required return based on its risk. Bondholders also care about market values. The value of their fixed-income investment is a function of the credit spread of the bank, the level of interest rates, and the expected cash flows of the debt. Since both stockholders and bondholders evaluate their investments based on market values, management should evaluate its opportunities with the same market value discipline. Defining risk in market value terms reinforces this discipline by aligning the interests of business managers with those of shareholders and bondholders.

The values of debt and equity are intimately related, as they are both derivative claims on the underlying assets of the company. According to the Merton model, the equity of a firm is equivalent to a call option on the firm's value, with the debt being the strike price. The equity holders have the option to "buy" the firm's assets and any other value of the franchise by repaying the debt. Equity holders will not exercise this option and will default on their obligation to the debt holders if the total asset and franchise value falls significantly short of the amount owed to creditors. The firm's leverage in market value terms (ie, the difference between the market value of assets and the book value of liabilities) and the volatility of its market value are therefore the primary determinants of a company's default probability and required credit spread. The measure of risk that drives both the value of debt and equity, then, is the volatility of asset values.

The distinction between a market value-based measurement of risk and an accounting earnings-based measurement of risk is important. Given the need to maintain a low likelihood of default, a high credit rating, and the resulting ability to finance the firm's activity, the most relevant measure of risk for determining capital adequacy is the volatility of a bank's market value.

Just as a bank's overall capital requirement is driven by the volatility of its market value, capital allocations to the bank's individual activities should depend on the contribution of each to the overall market value volatility. However, since most bank businesses do not mark their portfolios to market, risk managers cannot directly track the volatility of market values; rather, model-driven estimates of market value volatility or even the volatility of earnings must serve as surrogates.

ACCOUNTING FOR DIVERSIFICATION

For an economic capital model to apply for the entire bank as well as its individual activities, it must consider not only the volatility of market value for each activity, but also how that value changes with respect to that of all other activities. The logic for this diversification adjustment is straightforward: The less cyclical exposures generate diversification benefits for the bank as a whole that enable the bank to operate with less equity capital. A capital allocation based on risk contribution confers this benefit to business activities that enhance diversification, thereby encouraging their growth. Omitting this effect would clearly overstate the risk of the bank.

Finance theory tells us that investors' required returns are a function of nondiversifiable risk. One of the primary goals of the economic capital framework is to measure and compare business performance across activities with widely varying degrees of risk. SVA (shareholder value added) is calculated by comparing each business's return to the bank's cost of equity. Because the bank's cost of equity is based on systematic risk, the risk measure used for SVA calculation must be based on risk contribution rather than based on stand-alone risk. Otherwise, a second process would be required to determine differentiated costs of equity for each business.

Strictly speaking, the risk contribution approach outlined above measures the exposure to internally undiversified risk rather than truly systematic or undiversifiable risk. However, when this approach is used by large diversified financial institutions, any differences in the theoretical cost of equity after adjusting for risk contribution of individual businesses are likely to be well within the measurement error of the risk measures themselves.[1]

CAPITAL ADEQUACY

For capital adequacy purposes, the overriding goal of allocating capital to individual businesses is to determine the bank's optimal capital structure – the amount of equity that is required to maintain the bank's internal standard of solvency (ie, target credit rating) given the overall level of risk. This process involves estimating how much the risk of each business contributes to the total risk of the bank, and hence to the bank's overall capital requirement.

Ultimately, the *economic* capital based on risk should be compared to the *actual* capital held by the bank. A sensible risk-based capital adequacy framework should match the measured risk with the financial resources available to cover that risk. The financial resources available to cover the total amount of losses over a given horizon include not only book capital, or common equity, but also loan loss reserves and income generated during the period.

Banks consider expected or average level of loss to be a cost of doing business. Margins on loan products, for example, are set at a level sufficient to cover operating costs as well as expected loss and to provide a favourable return on capital. As a result, expected loss is not included in the measurement of risk, but is thought of as a direct charge against current period earnings.

To determine capital adequacy, best practice institutions measure capital based on *unexpected loss*, or volatility around expected loss, and compare their estimate of required capital with financial resources available to cover unexpected loss – common equity and loan loss reserves. Since expected loss is covered by future margin income, *expected loss* is not included in the measurement of economic capital. Likewise, future margin income is excluded from the financial resources available to cover losses.

PERFORMANCE MEASUREMENT

For performance evaluation purposes, risk-adjusted return on capital (RAROC) systems assign capital to businesses as part of a process to determine the risk-adjusted rate of return and, ultimately, the SVA of each business. The objective in this case is to measure a business's contribution to shareholder value after fully adjusting for risk, and thus to provide a basis for strategic planning, ongoing performance monitoring, product pricing, and tactical portfolio management decisions.

The RAROC for each business is its net income divided by its required economic capital. Often, the calculation adjusts *accounting net income* to replace *provisions* with *expected loss* and to remove timing distortions inherent to the accounting process. If the RAROC is higher than the cost of equity – shareholders' required rate of return – then the business is creating value for shareholders.

RAROC is a clear and consistent indicator of profitability. However, the exclusive use of RAROC or any rate of return to evaluate performance can discourage profitable investments. A rate of return does not measure how much value an activity creates or destroys; it only indicates its rate of profitability. To maximise shareholder wealth a bank must undertake any new project that, over its expected life, yields a RAROC that exceeds the cost of capital. Managers rewarded solely on RAROC are likely to reject value-increasing projects that will lower their average return.

To avoid this problem and create the right investment incentives, a bank should evaluate performance according to the SVA of a business. SVA is calculated by subtracting the cost of equity capital from the operating earnings of the business. Like RAROC, SVA uses economic capital as the "currency" for risk and therefore allows comparison of activities with varying risk characteristics. It overcomes the limits of RAROC by incorporating the size of the investment, not just its rate of return.

Rewards to managers should depend on the incremental improvement in SVA rather than its absolute value. This levels the playing field, encourages turnarounds of poorly performing businesses, and avoids rewarding the inheritance of a highly profitable operation.

ECONOMIC CAPITAL AT BANK OF AMERICA

Bank of America defines risk as volatility in the firm's market value. The key elements of this definition are its comprehensiveness and its emphasis on market value rather than earnings. Bank of America calculates risk in four major categories – credit, country, market, and business – but the particular categorisation is less

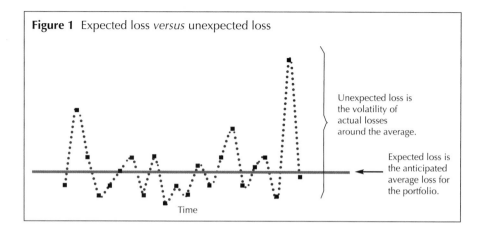

Figure 1 Expected loss *versus* unexpected loss

Unexpected loss is the volatility of actual losses around the average.

Expected loss is the anticipated average loss for the portfolio.

Time

important than its guiding principle: There must be "a place for everything, with everything in its place."

Capitalisation and confidence levels

Two estimates describe a bank's risk profile: expected loss and unexpected loss. As illustrated in Figure 1, expected loss is the average rate of loss expected from a portfolio. If losses equaled their expected levels, there would be no need for capital. Unexpected loss is the volatility of losses around their expected levels. Unexpected loss determines the economic capital requirement.

To prevent insolvency, economic capital must cover unexpected losses to a high degree of confidence. Banks often link their choice of confidence level to a standard of solvency implied by a credit rating of A or AA for their senior debt. The historical one-year default rates for A firms and AA firms are approximately 10 and 3 basis points, respectively. These target ratings therefore require that the institution have sufficient equity to buffer losses over a one-year period with confidence levels of 99.90% and 99.97% (see Figure 2).

Bank of America's reference points for the allocation of economic capital are a target rating of AA and the related 99.97% confidence level for solvency. This confidence level requires that economic capital be sufficient to cover all but the worst three of every 10,000 possible risk scenarios with a one-year horizon. To ensure consistent treatment and the unbiased evaluation of

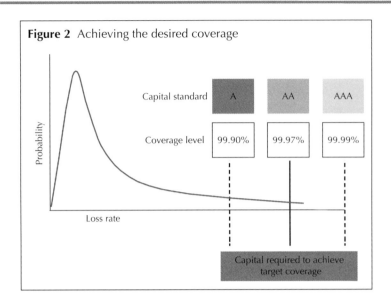

Figure 2 Achieving the desired coverage

businesses, the bank applies this common standard to all businesses and risk categories.

Risk contribution

The theory underlying the economic capital framework requires each portfolio's capital allocation to reflect its "contribution" to the volatility of the bank's market value as opposed to its own stand-alone volatility. The calculation therefore includes both the stand-alone volatility of an exposure and its correlation with value changes for the rest of the portfolio. As long as correlation is less than perfect, the capital allocation will be less than what would be necessary if the activity were a standalone business. This approach will not only capture the diversification benefit to the overall firm of holding a portfolio of risks, but it will also allocate that benefit to the individual activities that contribute to the diversification.

The calculation of risk contribution as opposed to stand-alone risk is also necessary for the aggregation of capital across businesses. A bottom-up approach, including the diversification effect, allows the aggregation of capital at several levels and in various dimensions without distorting the results. For example, a customer relationship manager may evaluate the capital required across all businesses and types of transaction for the customer.

Credit risk

All businesses with borrower or counterparty exposure receive capital for credit risk, or the risk of loss due to borrower defaults or deteriorating credit quality. For commercial portfolios, credit risk capital is calculated for individual loans. For consumer portfolios, the large number of loans makes it cost-effective to calculate credit risk only down to the "risk segment" level. Risk segments are homogenous groups of loans based on product, credit score, delinquency status, and other attributes.

Several factors determine the credit risk capital requirement. The most important are the exposure amount, the borrower's default probability, the estimated loss given default, the remaining tenor, and the correlation to other exposures in the portfolio.

The Bank of America credit risk capital model measures the default risk using an analytic formula for correlated binomial events. The model calculates the volatility of loss for an exposure based on estimates of the expected value and volatility of three factors: exposure given default, loss given default, and the binomial default indicator (yes or no).

Like that of many other institutions, the system relies on a portfolio risk model. Portfolio effects, such as correlation and capital multipliers, are determined by applying the Moody's KMV Portfolio Manager™ software to the total credit portfolio, including both consumer and commercial assets. This approach accounts for the specific portfolio composition, diversification, and concentrations of the institution. Implementation of the model across a wide range of applications requires the estimation, using the Portfolio Manager results, of marginal correlation factors based on product, location, market segment, industry, and credit quality. Capital multipliers, which scale the volatility contribution to the capital requirement, are determined in a similar fashion. The Bank of America model uses capital multipliers based on credit quality in order to capture the varying shape of the loss distribution for different segments and adapt to changes in portfolio composition between model updates.

The portfolio risk model also is used to set the capital requirement for migration risk. Migration risk is estimated by comparing the capital requirement based on market value changes with that based only on default risk. The migration risk component is a function of remaining term and credit quality.

Country risk

Country risk is the risk of loss – independent of the borrower's financial condition – on foreign exposures due to government actions. Causes of these potential losses include foreign exchange controls, large-scale currency devaluation, and nationalisation of capital investments. Country risk is attributed to all businesses with international exposures.

Country risk capital is driven by the sovereign default probability and the borrower's conditional probability of default given a country event. Internal country risk ratings are used to determine the sovereign default probability. The conditional likelihood of default varies within three main categories: transfer exposures, local currency exposures, and trade exposures.

Country and credit risk are similar concepts, so the country risk approach closely parallels the method for default risk. The treatment of borrower concentration is different, however. The total amount of unexpected loss for the country, instead of for each borrower, drives the concentration effect.

Market risk

Market risk is the risk of loss due to changes in the market values of the bank's assets and liabilities caused by changing interest rates, currency exchange rates, and security prices. It arises from outright positions in securities or derivative transactions, structural interest rate risk, and private equity investments. Bank of America estimates market value-at-risk (VAR) on a global level and for each of its trading desks using a historical simulation approach. The economic capital assignment is based on the contribution of each trading desk to the global VAR during the quarter. Before the allocation of capital, the daily VAR contribution is scaled to a one-year horizon and 99.97% confidence level to ensure consistency with other capital allocations. A traditional variance/covariance VAR model, using the historical volatilities and correlations of venture capital and stock market indices, is used to determine the capital requirement for the bank's equity portfolio. For interest rate risk, a Monte Carlo model simulates interest rate scenarios, their effects on cash flows, and ultimately the market value of equity.

Business risk

Business risk is the risk of loss from non-portfolio activities. These activities include origination, servicing, distribution, trust, asset management, and the activities of any other fee-driven businesses. This category is one of the few where risk measurement is not yet market-value based. Business risk comprises two categories: operational risk and strategic risk.

Bank of America measures operational risk using a loss distribution approach (LDA), where operational risk is the risk of loss due to inadequate or failed internal processes, people, and systems or due to external events. The bank uses the Basel categorisation, which divides operational risk into seven subcategories. The model's foundation is a database containing our internal history of operational loss events and their financial consequences. Publicly disclosed industry data, scaled for relative differences in size and quality of controls, supplements the internal data where it is insufficient for statistical models. The LDA model relies on estimates of frequency and severity distributions for each risk category and a Monte Carlo engine to combine them into an aggregate loss distribution, incorporating insurance deductibles and program limits.

Strategic risks and general economic risks, such as those relating to competition, operational leverage, product and technological obsolescence, and business strategy and execution, must also be covered in a comprehensive capital allocation framework. The bank uses a top-down approach for measuring strategic risk, which is based on the volatility of non-portfolio earnings for each business. Non-portfolio earnings are the net income for each business adjusted to remove the effects of credit risk, country risk, market risk, and operational risk.

Recognising the historical nature of both of the above methods, Bank of America's business risk model also includes a qualitative adjustment to reflect changes in the control environment and inherent risk of the business over time. A self-assessment process that evaluates exposure to reputation, execution, people, processing, technology, legal, regulatory, and external risks determines this qualitative adjustment.

Intangible assets

In addition to the capital assignment for operational and strategic risks, Bank of America also includes a capital assignment for goodwill and other intangible assets. The capital assignment for intangibles largely reflects the considerable regulatory capital penalty for these assets. As opposed to the other components of capital, the capital assignment for intangible assets is motivated by their regulatory burden.

Inter-risk diversification.

Capital requirements are determined separately for each of the above risk categories. However, the worst possible losses due to credit risk, market risk, country risk, and business risk are not likely to occur simultaneously. Simple addition of the capital requirements implies perfect correlation across risk categories, which is an incorrect and extremely conservative assumption. Rather than lower the capital requirements within the individual models by using lower confidence levels or other parameter adjustments, Bank of America explicitly measures the inter-risk diversification effect.

A correlation matrix for losses in each risk category is the backbone of this approach. The model treats correlation estimates based on historical data conservatively. The application of the correlation matrix creates an offset to the capital requirements for the individual risk categories and reduces the bank's overall economic capital requirement.

SUMMARY

Over more than a decade, the methods employed by financial institutions to calculate economic capital have advanced to encompass nearly all areas of risk, including operational and strategic risks. They have expanded beyond accounting-based principles to consider the volatility of market values. Looking ahead, improved technology, increasing amounts of better-scrutinised data, and research by both professionals and academics will continue to drive advances in the field.

The New Basel Capital Accord has increased awareness and confirmed the importance of economic capital by adopting and codifying some of the practices of the industry. This convergence of regulatory capital to economic capital should not stifle further innovation and improvements. Economic capital will continue to evolve to suit the needs of the industry as a powerful tool for performance evaluation and capital adequacy.

1 Less diverisified (not always smaller) institutions would need to carefully evaluate the use of a single cost of equity in their SVA calculations. If they use a standalone risk measurement approach, a single cost of equity would not be correct from a financial perspective. If they use risk contribution, it may or may not work, depending on the specifics of their portfolio.

2

Volatility and Capital: Measures of Risk

Gary Wilhite

Wachovia

We work in a risky business: actions we take have uncertain outcomes; investments we make have uncertain returns. We are particularly concerned about outcomes that are not as profitable as we expect them to be. High credit losses, revenue gaps, unanticipated expenses or investment declines lead to shortfalls in earnings – disappointing shareholders and lowering a bank's stock price. Extreme losses could even deplete a bank's equity and lead to default.

That a bank experiences some credit losses is not of itself risk. If one knew with certainty what those losses would be, they could include that amount in their pricing just as they cover other known costs. The problem is that losses are uncertain.

One can, however, state the amount of loss they expect. *Expected loss* (EL) is the mean value (probability-weighted average) of all the possible losses their portfolio could experience (see Figure 1). EL is *not* the most likely event. The nature of credit losses is that they are often relatively low, with an occasional period of much higher losses, generally associated with a recession. The possibility of high losses, although small, pulls the expected value to the right of the most likely outcome, as shown in the first figure.

The uncertainty around EL can be quantified. We have several tools with which to express risk, and each is best at describing a particular aspect of uncertainty.

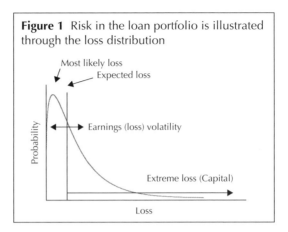

Figure 1 Risk in the loan portfolio is illustrated through the loss distribution

Economic capital (EC) measures the risk of extreme losses and is taken from the bondholders' perspective. A bank holds equity capital as a buffer against unexpected losses. Its capital should be sufficient to protect it from default with near certainty. In the examples, we capitalise the portfolio so that the risk of exhausting capital over 12 months is equal to 0.05%. EC measures how much capital a bank needs to reach this level of protection – its actual equity capital may be higher or lower than the requirement. Economic capital is a measure from the debtholders' point of view.

Earnings volatility measures the year-to-year deviation from expected returns. Shareholders feel the effects of earnings volatility both through the uneven addition of earnings to the bank's capital accounts and through the ups and downs of its share price. For a loan portfolio, one can equate earnings volatility with loss volatility, the variation around EL. Earnings volatility is a measure primarily from the shareholders' point of view.

But debtholders and ratings agencies are interested in earnings volatility, too. A tail event is so unlikely that it is more theoretical than real. That is not to say that one shouldn't use sophisticated analytics to determine the EC needed to support their portfolio. Prudent risk management requires understanding how severe losses may be and ensuring that one has sufficient capital to withstand an extreme event. But the analysis is complex and requires detailed information on the portfolio's makeup – information that debtholders and rating agencies don't have. They cannot observe a tail event – at least one hopes they never have that opportunity.

What they can observe, however, is earnings volatility. Earnings volatility is their window to a portfolio's uncertainty and the risk of default or downgrade.

CAPITAL ALLOCATION

With both measures, adding all the risks together produces a result with less risk than the simple sum of all the individual risks. Diversification reduces risk. (If one had only one or two loans in the portfolio they could lose it all. With a portfolio of many loans, it is essentially impossible to lose it all.) Consequently, the aggregate risk must be *allocated* back to the individual loans in order to describe how each loan contributes to the portfolio's risk.

Not surprisingly, the two most common approaches to capital allocation are based on the two views of risk described above. *Tail risk (TR) allocation* assigns capital to each exposure in proportion to how that exposure contributes to the portfolio's total EC. The designation "tail risk" is used because EC is determined by analysing the tail, or extreme portion, of the loss distribution. *Risk-contribution (RC) allocation* attributes capital in proportion to each exposure's contribution to the portfolio's *unexpected loss* (UL). We define UL as the standard deviation of the loss distribution, a measure of the uncertainty or volatility of losses from one year to another. Since credit losses directly affect earnings, this is equivalent to the earnings volatility from the loan portfolio. RC allocation assigns capital in proportion to each exposure's contribution to earnings volatility. UL is most influenced by the variation of losses across typical periods; tail-risk is determined by the most extreme, atypical periods.

To understand the practical differences between these allocation methodologies, consider that the loan portfolio is made up of a wide range of risks, each with a different risk profile. Some risks contribute relatively more to year-to-year earnings volatility than to the risk of extreme loss and vice versa, as illustrated in Figure 2.

Investment-grade loans rarely experience defaults or losses. The difference in loses between a good year and a bad year is small – there really shouldn't be significant losses from this part of the portfolio even in a bad year. Therefore, these loans contribute little to UL or earnings volatility, and receive little allocated capital with RC allocation. But in a horrible year – the kind of event for which

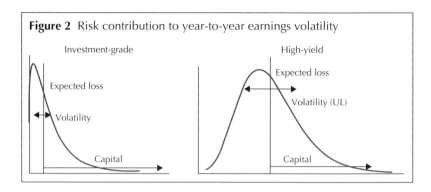

Figure 2 Risk contribution to year-to-year earnings volatility

we hold capital – losses will be many times greater than in a bad year. These loans contribute relatively more to the tail and are allocated more EC when TR allocation is used.

For any group of loans, we can call the ratio of the tail-risk capital for those loans to their UL the *capital multiplier*. Because the extreme loss for investment-grade loans is so much greater than UL, the capital multiplier is large. Said another way, investment-grade loans need more capital per unit of UL than lower-quality loans require.

At the other end of the portfolio, high-yield loans contribute relatively more to earnings volatility than to tail risk. There are usually losses from this part of the portfolio, and the level of losses fluctuates significantly. There's a great deal of difference between a good year, when nearly all loans pay off in full, and a bad year, when there are considerable defaults and losses. Loss volatility from one year to another is high. A horrible year, however, is only a few times worse than a bad year. The losses are already so high in the bad year that it can only get a few times worse in a "tail" year. These loans' contribution to earnings volatility is relatively more than their contribution to tail-risk capital. The capital multiplier for high-yield loans is lower than for investment-grade loans. Each of these loans needs fewer unit of capital per unit of UL than higher-quality loans require.

CAPITAL IN RAROC

The primary use of allocated capital (ie, capital at the loan level) is in RAROC analyses, including pricing/origination, hold/sell decisions, and profitability measurement. RAROC means *risk-adjusted return on capital* and is the return on EC. EC quantifies the returns shareholders require for taking risks and should guide banks to invest in those activities where they earn an acceptable return for their shareholders.

Investments must earn a RAROC at least as high as the shareholders' required return on equity. Returns above the minimum create economic profits, and increasing economic profits enhances shareholder value. For the examples below, we assume the shareholders' required return is 10%, comprising a 5% funding rate (ie, risk-free return) and a 5% risk premium. The economic capital attributed to a loan is intended to adjust results (ie, return on assets) to reflect the returns shareholders require for different levels of risk. If two loans have 10% RAROCs, typical RAROC systems say that shareholders are indifferent between the two uses of their capital – both earn the minimum return they require for taking that level of risk. An important test of a capital allocation methodology, then, is whether or not it produces results that are consistent with the framework. Would shareholders be indifferent to two investments that have the same RAROCs? Do situations with comparable risks have comparable, rational capital levels?

Unfortunately, both TR allocation and RC allocation have limitations. We will look at both and identify their weaknesses so that we can search for solutions.

TR ALLOCATION

It may appear natural to allocate capital in proportion to how much each loan contributes to the bank's overall required capital. Tail-risk allocation produces values similar to marginal capital – the additional capital required when the portfolio takes on another loan. As one adds loans to the portfolio or removes them, total capital changes by an amount approximately equal to the capital allocated to the exposures that have moved into or out of the portfolio.

Consider the two sub-portfolios in the previous examples: one of investment-grade loans, the other of high-yield loans. If capital is allocated by contribution to tail risk, each sub-portfolio holds capital roughly equal to the additional capital needed if it were added to the rest of the portfolio. To simplify the illustration, assume a loss-given default of 100%, so that losses equal the entire defaulted amount. We also assume that there are many loans in each sub-portfolio, and that each is well diversified. This means that each of the loans in each sub-portfolio has received essentially all of the potential benefits of diversification; no significant additional diversification benefits can be achieved by adding either sub-portfolio to a larger portfolio. We capitalise to cover 99.90% of losses.

Table 1 shows the range of losses for the two sub-portfolios. As described above, losses for the investment-grade portion of the portfolio are clustered near zero❶, but these loans are capitalised to handle a much larger loss. The capital multiplier for this sub-portfolio is nearly $10 \times (1.22\%/0.13\%)$❷. The high-yield sub-portfolio has a much wider range of losses❸, but *relatively* less capital is needed to support this portion of the portfolio. The capital multiplier is only $5.6 \times (16.93\%/3.0\%)$❹.

Now suppose the expected return for each sub-portfolio is 10%, the minimum required return. With a few manipulations we can rescale each loss distribution to produce RAROC distributions. As shown in Table 2, one can compute the spread required to produce a 10% RAROC at the expected level of loss for each portfolio❺. In Table 1 we transform this to a return distribution by subtracting the loss distribution values from the nominal return❻. We convert this to a RAROC distribution by dividing each value in the return distribution by the EC attributed to the portfolio. Formulas are shown in Table 2.

The investment-grade loans provide the 10% return on capital with a standard deviation of 11%❼. Expected returns or better are produced 80% of the time❽. There's less than a one-in-ten chance of having a negative return❾. Earnings volatility is quite low. The high-yield sub-portfolio, on the other hand, has an expected RAROC of 10%, of course, but the standard deviation of RAROC is 18%❿. There's more than a 20% chance of a negative return①, more than double the high-quality investments' probability of loss. These loans add far more to earnings volatility than the investment-grade loans add.

Would shareholders be indifferent to these two uses of their capital? No. A rational shareholder would surely prefer a 10% return with little uncertainty to an expected return of 10% with nearly twice the volatility. Shareholders are more concerned with the year-to-year volatility than the fact that each investment has an equal

Table 1 Distribution of losses and RAROCs

	Expected loss (%)	Std Dev (UL) (%)	Allocated capital (%)	Capital multiplier (Cap/UL) (%)	Required spread (%)	Nominal return (%)	Expected RAROC (%)	Std Dev RAROC (%)
Investment-grade								
Losses	0.05	0.13						
RAROC (Tail Risk)			1.22	[2] 9.38	[5] 0.11	0.17	10	[7] 11
RAROC (Risk Contr.)			[3] 0.88	[2] 6.74	0.09	0.14	10	[6] 15
High-Yield								
Losses	3.00	3.00						
RAROC (Tail Risk)			16.93	[4] 5.64	3.85	4.69	10	[10] 18
RAROC (Risk Contr.)			[4] 20.22	[2] 6.74	[5] 4.01	5.02	10	[6] 15

Performance (Percentile)

	10	20	30	40	Median	60	70	80	90	95
Investment-grade										
Losses [1]	0.00	0.00	0.00	0.00	0.00	0.01	0.02	0.05	0.15	0.28
Return distribution (TR) [6]	0.17	0.17	0.17	0.17	0.17	0.17	0.15	0.12	0.02	−0.10
RAROC (Tail Risk)	14.10	14.10	14.09	14.06	13.94	13.54	12.46	[8] 9.69	1.96 [9]	−8.55
RAROC (RC)	0.14	0.14	0.14	0.14	0.14	0.13	0.12	0.08	−0.01	−0.14
RAROC (Risk Contr.)	15.71	15.71	15.70	15.66	15.48	14.93	13.43	9.58 [7]	−1.19	−5.83
High-Yield										
Losses [3]	0.29	0.64	1.04	1.51	2.07	2.76	3.64	4.88	6.98	9.04
Return distribution (TR) [6]	4.40	4.06	3.65	3.18	2.62	1.94	1.05	−0.19	−2.29	−4.35
RAROC (Tail Risk)	26.01	23.96	21.58	18.80	15.49	11.44	6.21	[1] −1.13	−13.53	−25.71
RAROC (RC)	4.73	4.38	3.98	3.51	2.95	2.26	1.38	0.14	−1.96	−4.02
RAROC (Risk Contr.)	23.41	21.69	19.69	17.37	14.60	11.20	6.83	0.69 [6]	−9.69	−19.89

Table 2 Formulas and computations

a) *Capital Multiplier*
UL * Capital Multiplier = Capital

b) *Required Spread*
Expected RAROC% = Expected return%/Capital% return expressed as ROA
Expected return% = Nominal return% – EL%
Nominal return% = Spread% + (Funding rate * Capital%)
Expected RAROC% = (Spread% + Funding Rate * Capital% – EL%) / Capital%
Expected RAROC% * Capital% = Spread% + Funding rate * Capital% – EL%
Spread% = (RAROC% – Funding Rate) * Capital% + EL%

c) *Required Spread for 10% RAROC*

	Required spread (%)	Expected RAROC (%)	Funding rate (%)	Capital (%)	Expected loss (%)	Nominal return (%)	Expected ROA (%)
Tail risk allocation							
Investment-grade	❺ 0.11	10.0	5.00	1.22	0.05	0.17	❻ 0.12
High-Yield	3.85	10.0	5.00	16.93	3.00	4.69	1.69
RC Allocation							
Investment-grade	❺ 0.09	10.0	5.00	0.88	0.05	0.14	0.09
High-yield	4.01	10.0	5.00	20.22	3.00	5.02	2.02

d) RAROC

RAROC = (Spread% – Actual loss% + Funding rate% * Capital%) / Capital%

(extremely low) risk of exhausting capital. We must conclude that TR allocation does a poor job of signalling how shareholders want banks to deploy their capital.

RISK CONTRIBUTION ALLOCATION

We can perform the same analysis with risk contribution (RC) allocation. Losses in Table 1 are again manipulated to get RAROC distributions for the two sub-portfolios. Since the RC method allocates capital in proportion to earnings volatility, the capital multiplier is constant throughout the portfolio. That is, since capital is proportional to RC, the ratio of capital to each loan's contribution to RC is constant and equal to the capital multiplier. With a portfolio capital multiplier of 6.74②, we allocate 6.74*0.13% = 0.88% capital to the investment-grade loans③, and 6.74*3.0% = 20.22% capital to the high-yield loans④.

When we convert to a RAROC distribution, different spreads will be required to produce a 10% RAROC at the expected level of loss for each portfolio. Investment-grade loans receive less capital with RC allocation than they do with TR allocation, and high-yield loans receive more. Consequently, a lower spread will produce an acceptable RAROC for the investment-grade loans, while a higher spread will be needed to reach the minimum RAROC for the high-yield portfolio⑤. We again transform the loss distribution to a RAROC distribution as described above with the new returns and capital levels.

Table 1 shows that with RC allocation both the expected RAROC and the volatility of RAROC are the same for both the investment-grade and high-yield sub-portfolios with the new spreads (10% expected RAROC with 15% volatility)⑥. The risk of experiencing a loss at the sub-portfolio level is more similar with RC allocation than with TR allocation⑦. It is far easier to believe that a shareholder would be indifferent to these two uses of their capital than to the two choices described in the tail-risk section. RC allocation appears to be a better choice for use in RAROC.

REALLOCATION

However, RC allocation can produce some disturbing results. Since RC allocation is not proportional to marginal capital, adding loans to the portfolio changes the total EC by an amount different from the capital attributed to the marginal loans. Normally, the differences are so small that they cause no problems for analysis. But this is not true when there are significant changes in the portfolio concentrated in high- or low-quality assets. Recall that the high-yield sub-portfolio contributes more to earnings volatility than to tail risk. Therefore, because RC allocation distributes capital in proportion to earnings volatility, the high-yield sub-portfolio is allocated more capital than the portfolio needs to support these loans (ie, their tail-risk capital). So, if we remove these loans from the portfolio, *we reduce the need for capital by less than the capital that was allocated to these loans*. The difference will be reallocated to the loans that remain in the portfolio. Since each of the remaining loans now gets more capital, their RAROCs will fall. Loans that may have met the 10% minimum RAROC before the high-yield loans were sold may appear to destroy shareholder value after the high-risk loans are sold. Done this simple way, the result is inconsistent with the objectives of the RAROC approach.

EXPLANATION AND POSSIBLE SOLUTIONS

The reallocation would actually be a quite reasonable result if the RAROC system automatically reacted to changes in volatility in the way finance theory says investors behave. When we remove the high-risk loans from the portfolio, the quality of the remaining portfolio improves, lowering earnings volatility. Since the investor now earns his return with less uncertainty, he will lower his required return on equity (ROE). Higher attributed capital times a lower required return on capital leaves the remaining portfolio about where it was before the loans were sold. This makes sense, since, as we said above, there's no significant diversification benefit from adding the high-yield loans to the rest of the portfolio. The investor's evaluation of the loans (ie, whether they produce a sufficient expected return given the risk) should be about the same whether the high-yield loans are in the portfolio or not.

But many RAROC systems do not reduce the required ROE when the bank removes earnings volatility from their portfolio. A change would come about indirectly, as lower earnings volatility produced a more stable stock price with a lower beta, ultimately resulting in a decision to lower the hurdle rate. At best, this process would take a long time – too long. Even more troubling is that it would reduce the required return on *all* capital, which is unjustified. Why should lower volatility in the commercial loan portfolio, for example, result in a lower required rate of return on capital for the consumer loan portfolio, which may be analysed separately? That portfolio may even be getting riskier, with a shrinking capital multiplier. In that case, reducing the consumer portfolio's required rate of return because the commercial portfolio has shed risk would be exactly the wrong thing to do.

One response would be to adjust the required ROE for both the commercial and consumer portfolios. Within each portfolio, one would continue to use risk contribution to allocate capital and then use the computed ROE volatility for the each portfolio to adjust its required ROE. For example, if the high-yield assets were removed from the illustrative portfolio, capital would be reallocated back to the remaining good loans, but that capital would have to earn a lower required rate of return. The change in the ROE target would affect only the commercial loan portfolio, not the consumer portfolio or other risky activities that receive capital. Likewise, if the credit quality of the commercial loan portfolio deteriorated, its capital rates would rise in response to higher computed ROE volatility. This would happen without an increase in the required return on other risk capital. This makes sense, since changes in the commercial loan portfolio's composition affect neither the level of the bank's other risks nor the shareholders' required return for taking those risks.

Another option would be to attribute capital throughout the bank using a constant capital multiplier linked to the bank's hurdle rate. This approach would likely lead to mismatches between total required capital and attributed EC, which would have to be reconciled. Having significant balances in reconciliation units can be confusing.

Yet another option would be to establish the shareholders' required return as a function of earnings volatility. Economic profit would still be measured as profit less a required return to the shareholder, but this would no longer be a single required ROE multiplied by EC. A few simple computations can equate this approach to adjusted hurdle rates.

Each of these approaches – and additional variations – has pros and cons. Further analyses are needed to determine the approach that best suits the needs of any individual bank.

CONCLUSION

Economic capital is held by a bank to protect itself against extreme, UL. EC is calculated at the portfolio level considering diversification benefits, but to be useful in guiding pricing and portfolio management it must be allocated to individual loans. There are two common measures of risk – loss volatility (called UL) and extreme loss (TR) – and two corresponding capital allocation methodologies. RC allocates EC to individual loans based on how much they contribute to the portfolio's loss volatility, which is equivalent to their contribution to earnings volatility. TR allocation attributes EC to individual loans based on how they contribute to the portfolio's potential for extreme losses.

In general, RC allocation attributes more capital to high-risk loans and less capital to low-risk loans than TR allocation. This discussion shows that RC allocation produces results that are consistent with shareholders' requirements that they be compensated for higher earnings volatility through a higher expected return. Bondholders and rating agencies likewise look for premium earnings to compensate for earnings volatility. TR allocation falls short in linking volatility to a higher required return.

However, RC allocation can produce disconcerting results in a bank's RAROC system if the portfolio's credit quality changes significantly and the hurdle rate is not changed. Likewise, distortions can occur between portfolios if a single, bank-wide cost of equity capital is used without considering each portfolio's contribution to earnings volatility.

3

Conceptual Framework for Economic Capital Models and Required Inputs

Michel Araten

JPMorgan Chase

Credit-risky assets have the potential to result in losses for lenders. Risks of loss need to be assessed so they can be traded off against promised revenues. Credit risk assessments designed to estimate the risks of loss for individual credit transactions are expressed along three dimensions of risk: the likelihood of default, the loss in the event of default, and the exposure at the time of default.

To determine default likelihood, financial-statement and market-based information is evaluated using various forms of models. Models do not have to be quantitative. They can range all the way from expert judgement and rules-based methods to econometric approaches and neural networks. They are oriented towards either directly producing an estimate of default probability or indirectly estimating risk by assigning a rating grade. Rating classifications are designed to distinguish the relative risk of different obligors in an ordinal manner. However, credit capital models require an absolute probability of default (PD) to be assessed for each rating.

To assess loss in the event of default, commonly referred to as loss-given default (LGD), rules-based or more formal models have been developed. LGDs associated with particular transactions are rarely known with certainty and it is important to quantify this potential variability.

To assess the exposure at default (EAD), particularly where borrowed amounts can vary at the discretion of the obligor, analysis of the likelihood of drawdown of any unused commitment or contingent exposure needs to be made.

Multiplying these three parameters together, the expected loss (EL_i) for an individual asset i is

$$EL_i = PD_i \cdot LGD_i \cdot EAD_i \tag{1}$$

Were lenders dealing with only a single transaction, the estimate of the uncertainty of loss for that exposure would be derived in a relatively straightforward manner. Loans either default or they do not, and if they default there may be uncertainty with regard to both the EAD and the LGD. The unexpected loss (UL_i) of an individual exposure is a function of the uncertainty in the outcome for that asset. Default is uncertain, but, since it can be described as a yes/no event, it can be modelled as having a binomial distribution with a variance equal to (PD)(1-PD). While the LGD is also uncertain, historical data or modelling results can give rise to estimates of the standard deviation of LGD (σ_{LGD}) as well as to the form of its probability distribution. Assuming that EAD is constant, then for an individual asset i, the stand-alone UL_i is

$$UL_i = \sqrt{(PD_i)(1 - PD_i)LGD_i^2 + PD_i\sigma_{LGD_i}^2} \tag{2}$$

Lenders assemble portfolios of credit-risky assets, whose aggregate risks are of far lower risk than the sum of the individual stand-alone unexpected losses, assuming they were all perfectly correlated. Lenders put together such portfolios with the objective of risk diversification. It is expected that relatively few borrowers will simultaneously default. However, it is unlikely that risks will be completely independent, as lenders tend to build specialised expertise along various industry and geographic lines, resulting in obligor, industry, and country concentrations. Financial institutions operate at very high levels of leverage under the assumption that they have well-diversified portfolios. Even small variations in risk concentrations can produce large swings in levels of portfolio losses. These swings can produce losses far greater than what would normally be expected and is the source of portfolio risk.

The EL for a portfolio (EL_P) is simply the sum of the EL_i of the individual credit exposures or

$$EL_P = \sum_i EL_i = \sum_i PD_i \cdot LGD_i \cdot EAD_i \qquad (3)$$

The EL of a portfolio cannot be affected by diversification. To determine portfolio-level risk, one needs to specify the extent to which assets may default at the same time, ie, their default or loss correlation (ρ_{ij}).

To assess default correlations, models have been developed that impute correlations based on either structural considerations or market observations. In all instances, correlation estimates are difficult to quantify and are one of the most problematic areas of credit risk needing further research.

The incorporation of default correlations with PDs, LGDs and EADs enables the determination of the possible levels of loss for the portfolio as a whole. Portfolio risk can be expressed in a number of ways, including portfolio UL_P and probabilities that losses could exceed certain critical values. The UL_P is thus

$$UL_P = \sqrt{\sum_i UL_i^2 + \sum_{i,j} \sum_{i \neq j} UL_i UL_j \rho_{ij}} \qquad (4)$$

ECONOMIC CREDIT CAPITAL MODELS

The "required" amount of economic credit capital is determined by analysing the probability distribution of overall loss for the portfolio over a stated horizon, conventionally one year. The criterion for required capital is based on the tolerable amount of loss that the bank feels it can take. Most often, the level of capital is based on the bank's desire to achieve a specific rating target. For example, if a bank wants itself to be rated by the rating agencies as "AA" it will target a probability of loss of 3–5 basis points, which is the conventional default probability assumed for a AA rating.

Once overall portfolio capital is determined, it needs to be assigned to individual exposures based on their contribution to the portfolio standard deviation or based on their contribution to the risk that losses will exceed the capital amount. Capital assessed against individual exposures is an important input into customer and business unit profitability measures.

Economic credit capital models can be divided into those that are based on default only (DO) or on a mark-to-market (MTM) basis. The DO approach deals solely with the default event and assumes that non-defaulting assets maintain their book or par values. These models are justified on the basis of their relationship to balance-sheet and profit-and-loss accounting-related measures. Capital is associated with volatility of accrual-reported income over the coming year. However, the risk that loans with maturities beyond one year may default at a point beyond the horizon also needs to be captured. To that end, a number of approaches can be pursued, including extending the horizon and annualising the results or term-adjusting the capital estimates for individual loans by term-adjusting the default probabilities to their maturity.

In addition to incorporating default losses, MTM models take into consideration shifts in credit quality for the non-defaulting assets and determine whether there is an associated gain or loss in their market value at the end of the horizon. The gain or loss is a function of the contract spread, the required market spread at the horizon, the maturity, and forward default probability or migrated rating. Here, both realised losses associated with defaults and unrealised losses associated with valuation losses for loans maturing beyond the horizon are taken into account. The MTM approach mirrors the volatility of economic results obtained if a portfolio were actually marked to market.

Given the thousands of inputs required for a sophisticated portfolio model, it is not possible to solve for capital requirements analytically. Monte Carlo simulation of the loss distribution is the preferred route. We will concentrate on the inputs that are common to both DO and MTM approaches, recognising that the MTM model also needs market-required credit spreads as a basis for valuing non-defaulted assets.

Default probabilities

Almost all financial institutions use risk ratings to classify the relatively likelihood of default. Rating systems can employ as few as four or five to as many as twenty categories of risk, similar to those used by the major external rating agencies. Ratings are generally divided into a set associated with "investment-grade" credits that correspond to a range of AAA to BBB–. Speculative-grade credits constitute a range between BB+ and C. Banks will often use a numerical scale that maps to these alphabetical grades. The numerical scale will also incorporate "regulatory" grades. Regulatory grades are assigned to two grades for companies that are considered to be "near default" (*special mention* and *substandard accruing*) and two grades for defaulted credits (*substandard non-accruing* and *doubtful*).

For public companies and for those with externally traded debt, models are available to directly estimate PDs from market observations and from financial statements. For many companies, particularly private companies where market information is unavailable, PDs are determined indirectly based on risk ratings.

It is important for a bank to be clear regarding the architecture of its risk rating system, as to whether it is principally designed to reflect "through-the-cycle" (TTC) or "point-in-time" (PIT) conditions. Rating agencies tend to use a TTC approach in assigning ratings. With long-term bond investors in mind, Moody's TTC ratings will "change in response to enduring changes in credit risk. TTC ratings look through temporary changes in credit risk, regardless of whether they are aggregate, industry, or firm-specific in nature" (see Cantor, 2004). Rating agencies strive to avoid rating reversals. As an example, Moody's tracks the frequency of rating changes, the frequency of large rating changes and the frequency of rating reversals. In any given 12-month period, there was only about one rating action for every four issuers and only one out of a hundred issuers experienced a rating reversal (see Cantor and Mann, 2003).

Traditionally, banks have followed rating agencies as far as employing longer-term assessment of risks. Their reasoning was that, once they made a loan, they were forced to hold the loan to maturity or until the borrower paid it off. They were more concerned with assessing a rating over their likely holding period. With the expansion of capital markets to include secondary trading of loans as well as bonds it has become possible for banks to dispose of loans prior to their maturity. In addition, with the advent of credit derivatives, trading and hedging of credit risk has also increased the liquidity of loans in a synthetic manner. As a result, banks have become more conscious of their need to evaluate credit over a shorter time horizon and have begun using a PIT approach to risk rating.

As a consequence of increased trading and hedging of risk for larger borrowers, particularly those with public equity, banks have been forced to develop a consistent risk framework for smaller, private companies, too. Thus, there has been an increase in the number of banks who use a PIT system for both public and private firms.

To support MTM models, market-based assessments of PDs for public companies can be derived from equity prices from sources such as Moody's KMV (Credit Monitor) and RiskMetrics (Credit Grades). These firms employ an option-theoretical structural approach based on a Merton model to relate the firm's market price and volatility of equity in combination with the face amount of debt to estimate how close the firm is to default. The structural approach posits that shareholders have an option to "put" the company back to the debt holders if the asset value of the firm falls below the face amount of debt (the strike price). Since the market values of assets cannot be directly observed, equity values and equity volatilities are translated to asset values and asset volatilities to construct an asset-value distribution. Calibration of historical default experience to "distance-to-default" enables the quantification of default probabilities.

While private companies may not have market-traded equity or publicly rated debt, some banks derive these PDs from PD estimates for public companies. One can map market-based PDs of public companies to their internal or external ratings. The average or median market-based PD associated with a particular rating can then be applied to the private companies. This assumes that the rating system for both public and private companies is based on the same philosophical approach. Banks may find it easier to use a TTC system for both public and private companies, as they can use the external rating for public companies as a calibrating benchmark for their internal ratings. In effect, public companies' PDs are dissociated from their internal ratings but are used to calibrate the PD-rating relationship for private companies.

Some middle-market bankers object to using the market-based PDs for public companies as a basis for assessing current PDs of private companies. Public company PDs tend to be more volatile, moving along with the credit cycle. Middle-market lenders are disturbed by the volatility of these PDs and the implied capital and return volatility for their customers. A more objective basis for calling these market-based estimates into question lies in comparing the actual historical defaults experienced by public versus private companies.

Models to estimate current PDs for private companies can be based on historical financial information with adjustments for current economic conditions and for current market factors observed for companies in the same industry.[1] If these hybrid models are shown to perform well, they will result in a dissociation of PDs from internal ratings for private companies as well as for public companies. However, these models are in their infancy and, until they have been adequately road-tested, internal ratings for private companies will continue to serve as the primary basis for an indirect PD assessment.

Some firms feel that they can assess PIT ratings for both public and private companies by combining current financial information, market-based information, where available, and judgemental assessments. Currently, there are no external PIT rating systems that can be used as reliable benchmarks to calibrate internal ratings. (This is not the case for TTC ratings, where external TTC ratings are often used to calibrate internal TTC ratings.) PIT ratings tend to be more volatile than TTC ratings and it is expected that they will move up and down with the economic cycle and with the current condition of the borrower. PDs associated with a PIT rating system are generally fixed across all rating classes, with the expectation that, as risk changes, the ratings will move up or down into a new fixed PD class. While the relative ratings may reflect relative risk on a current basis, the inability to fix an absolute default probability with a current rating also makes this approach somewhat problematic.

Despite claims by individual institutions that they follow a PIT or a TTC approach, it is difficult to pin them down as to what is their actual horizon for assessing risk. It is likely that different credit personnel in the same institution interpret their rating horizon differently from each other. As a result, these labels can be characterised only as proximate. Regardless of which rating system is chosen, all firms will have a need to validate their PD estimates using historical default information.

To gather historical information on defaults a definition of default must first be agreed. In the case of public debt, default is defined as either (a) the failure to pay principal or interest in a timely manner or (b) a voluntary or involuntary filing for bankruptcy. Note that for these purposes technical defaults, ie, violations of covenants in debt agreements, which may possibly lead to payment default, are not included as default events. Rating agencies compiling statistics on debt that they have rated are usually considered the arbiters of what constitutes a default event. They will also include events of economic default such as a forced exchange of one security for another. Rating histories for public debt are published annually by agencies such as Moody's, Standard and Poor's, and Fitch. Annual and cumulative default statistics are reported for each rating class on a cohort basis. In addition, transition or migration matrices are published showing the percentage of companies whose ratings change from one period to the next, as well as the percentage of companies whose ratings stay the same.

In the case of private debt, banks and other regulated financial institutions will automatically follow regulatory dictums as to when they must cease accruing interest on debt. For commercial debt, this will usually be when payment is 90 days past due. Interest is often paid quarterly and banks are encouraged to cease accruing interest when payment is in doubt, even when the payment is not yet officially past due. One reason for this policy is that, once a loan is placed in a "non-accrual" or "non-performing" state, banks will have to reverse any interest income on their financial statements that has previously been accrued but has not been paid.

Bank financial systems are the beginning point for conducting a historical analysis of defaults. In examining these records, given the thousands of transactions involved, one often finds that a loan may be placed in a non-accrual state in error. On occasion loan payments are credited to the wrong account and, while eventually the error is found and corrected, the loan may have been temporarily designated as being in a non-accrual state. Also, a new loan may have been granted, yet some interest payments due on the old loan have not been completely cleared. Signs of such errors include a loan having a risk rating constituting an acceptable credit, then becoming non-accrual, and within several months returning to an acceptable credit grade. It is thus essential that historical records be carefully examined to exclude all such spurious defaults to avoid an overestimation of the default rate.

A recent study at JP Morgan Chase (JPMC) examined these issues in the process of analysing historical default and migration statistics over a six-year period (see Araten *et al*, 2004). An overall transition matrix is shown in Table 1.

Over the course of this period, JPMC followed a TTC rating philosophy, as can be seen from the relatively large percent of ratings remaining unchanged over a year's period. The column "WR" identifies those borrowers whose ratings were withdrawn. They were customers of the bank at the beginning of the year but were no longer borrowing customers and had no rating at the end of the year. Rating agencies also identify firms with withdrawn ratings and note that these reasons include debt retirement, merger or request not to assign a rating. The proportion of withdrawn ratings observed in the JPMC study is about four times the proportion found in agency studies, illustrating the more dynamic nature of banking relationships. The treatment of withdrawn observations is critical to the calculation of default rates.

In determining the default rate, some agencies such as Moody's will adjust the observed default rate by adding one-half of the "WR" observations to the beginning population of companies and adjusting all of the migration statistics including the default state so that the total percentages add to 100%.

In the case of the JPMC study, a more conservative approach was employed in that all of the withdrawn observations were added to the beginning population with an appropriate adjustment, so that the percentages add up to 100%. From this table we see that the default rates are monotonically increasing across rating classes. We can conclude for this sample that these ratings do reflect an appropriate ordinal ranking of risk.

The observed average one-year default rates can be used to assist in validating a model that assigns risk ratings on a TTC basis. However, it is likely that default rates vary considerably over a cycle, so that it will be necessary to have a fairly long history, even longer than the six years captured here, to validate these assessments. A 3–6-year period is the usual cyclic period and thus only one cycle would be observed here.

Table 1 1-Year-average transition matrix (JPMC 1997–2002)

	Rating	AAA-AA (%)	A (%)	BBB (%)	BB (%)	B (%)	CCC (%)	CC (%)	Default (%)	Total (%)	WR (%)
						Ending risk rating					
Initial risk rating	AAA-AA (%)	91.30	5.62	0.84	1.03	1.11	0.03	0.00	0.08	100.0	14.9
	A (%)	5.98	85.91	5.71	1.67	0.53	0.09	0.03	0.09	100.0	15.4
	BBB (%)	0.66	7.02	84.31	6.96	0.78	0.11	0.05	0.10	100.0	17.2
	BB (%)	0.08	0.58	3.99	89.28	4.81	0.43	0.26	0.57	100.0	20.8
	B (%)	0.12	0.08	0.26	10.95	84.07	1.61	1.06	1.86	100.0	27.6
	CCC (%)	0.00	0.18	0.09	1.99	15.10	63.47	9.13	10.04	100.0	36.1
	CC (%)	0.10	0.10	0.10	1.40	4.60	1.40	74.57	17.72	100.0	40.8
	Total (%)									100.0	22.0

Default rates over a 2–5-year period can also be constructed from the underlying data to develop an observed cumulative term structure of default. Alternatively, the average one-year transition matrix can be multiplied by itself a number of times to yield a cumulative transition and default matrix. In most cases when this operation is performed, statistical tests will reveal that the necessary Markovian properties are not present.

If the rating system was based on a PIT system, then while each year's default rates could be compared to model predictions, averaging these predicted versus actual default rates would also require a somewhat longer time series for validation.

Errors in estimating PDs in an MTM model will result in an initial valuation loss for the portfolio. Capital requirements from that initial MTM value will also be affected depending on the make-up of the portfolio.

LOSS-GIVEN DEFAULT

Estimates of LGD may also be constructed from defaults as reported by external rating agencies, though most of these studies deal with publicly traded debt. The definition of default for LGD purposes should be consistent with the definition used for calculating PDs and the LGD should be based on the exposure at the time of default. Some of the rating agencies report the trading prices of debt approximately a month after the default event. Others determine recoveries obtained in the form of cash and securities following emergence from bankruptcy and discount the recoveries at the contract rate of interest. An analysis of the notional cashflows received post-emergence from bankruptcy versus the market price of debt one month after default can be used to calculate the internal rate of return that the buyers of debt will have received. These have been found to be in the range of 10–20%, depending on economic conditions.

Studies by Altman, Hu and Frye have investigated the degree of dependence of loss severity on the business cycle as measured by either sectoral or overall incidence of default rates (see Altman, Resti and Sironi, 2001; Hu and Perraudin, 2002; Frye, 2000). These studies have found that, when overall default rates are high, recovery rates are negatively impacted. Intuitively, this makes sense, since, when the economy is going through a difficult period, asset values will tend to be depressed. At the same time, new investors in distressed debt, in the underlying assets of the company or in the failed company itself will tend to demand a higher yield on their risky investment during downturns in the economy. When there is an increase in the supply of failed companies, buyers are able to demand a premium yield. Holders of debt also want to quickly clean up their balance sheets and will approve lower prices for the company's assets or for the distressed debt that they hold. Extended periods of time in bankruptcy tend to sap underlying values through payments to lawyers, accountants and advisers.

Rating agencies have collected statistical evidence that shows that recovery rates on different classes of debt depend on seniority and structure. Senior secured debt has the highest recovery rate, followed by senior unsecured and junior debt. Also, recovery rates tend to exhibit relatively high volatilities – on the order of 25%. To estimate recovery rates, it is not only important to gauge the lender's relative rank in the capital structure of the firm, but also to determine the amount of debt above and below that lender's position (see Keisman, van der Castle and Yang, 2000). If there is a relatively small amount of senior debt and a fairly large amount of junior debt, it is likely that recoveries on the senior debt will be at the upper end of the historical range. Alternatively, if there is very little senior debt, recovery rates on junior debt are likely to be enhanced.

Although there exists a fair amount of recovery-rate information on public debt, statistics relative to private bank debt is relatively scarce. Data derived from bank records require extensive clean-up and careful attention to detail. Banks have traditionally kept good records regarding principal losses on defaulted loans as "charge-offs", as this impacts their loan loss reserves. While this information may be sufficient for determining the adequacy of their reserve for loan losses, it is necessary to adjust these charge-offs, or "accounting" losses, to convert them into "economic" losses suitable for capital modelling.

These adjustments require taking into account the timing of cashflows received and incorporating recoveries that may have been received in the form of property or securities. This information must be painstakingly reconstructed from bank records. Other adjustment issues associated with bank LGDs arise where there are multiple facilities to an individual borrower. In the process of working out the defaulted loans, cash recoveries may be arbitrarily attributed to individual facilities without due regard to their relative seniority or collateral strength. It is therefore advisable to aggregate all of the defaulting exposures to an individual borrower and calculate the LGD on a pooled basis. Pooling of exposures will also be required in those situations where not all the facilities default at the same time. There may also be cases when additional money is advanced to the borrower even after default has occurred. For example, these situations can arise in defaulted real-estate construction loans. To maximise the eventual recovery on monies already lent, it is important to advance additional funds to complete the project. Despite being in default, the borrower may be deemed to be in the best position to do so.

Unlike public debt, bank debt is characterised by a highly dynamic relationship between the lender and the borrower. It is often the case, especially in middle-market lending, that, when a borrower is beginning to get into difficulty, the lender will press the borrower to sell assets to reduce leverage. While not yet in default, the borrower will begin to pay down the loan so that, when the company eventually defaults, the exposure will have been considerably reduced. The LGD on the remaining exposure will appear high, yet, when taking into account the exposure at the time that the workout began, the recovery on the original loan will have been substantial. Nevertheless, LGD should still be measured on the basis of EAD and not the exposure at an earlier period.

In measuring LGDs it is important to distinguish between secured and unsecured exposures so that when estimates of LGD are applied in capital models risks of loss can take into account the nature of the facility. However, due to the dynamic nature of the banking relationship and the workout process, a loan, which was originally unsecured, may become secured. That is, as the borrower negotiates with the bank not to press on technical defaults, the bank may obtain collateral in return for forbearance and extending the term of the loan. In other cases, the bank may not fare as well with unsecured loans to other borrowers, so that these loans may remain unsecured all the way through payment default. Therefore, when estimating LGDs for an unsecured loan, one should project the likelihood that a loan will become secured prior to default.

Other cashflow items should include workout costs such as extra staff and legal expenses. In the case of foreclosed real estate, until the property is finally sold, costs of operating the property should also be identified. Recoveries in the form of securities such as warrants or common stock should, if possible, be valued at estimated market when received or at the time of final disposition.

As described earlier, for economic capital modelling we are interested in the "economic" LGD associated with defaulted bank loans, not the "accounting" LGD. Having made the appropriate adjustments to exposure and reconstructed all of the notional recoveries, it is necessary to discount the recoveries to the time of default to determine their present value. The choice of the appropriate discount rate can make a substantial difference in the LGD. Some practitioners feel that the original contract rate on the loan should be used as the discount rate. However, it is clear that there will be few investors in distressed debt that will be satisfied with buying a defaulted loan with highly uncertain recovery prospects at a low yield. Based on experience, a discount rate reflecting the economic return required by investors in distressed assets should be used.

An extensive analysis of recovery rate experience at JPMorgan Chase on almost 4,000 defaulted commercial borrowers over an 18-year period provides a good example of the issues encountered (see Araten, Jacobs and Varshney, 2004). Results of this study were as follows:

❑ average accounting LGD was 27.0%, while economic LGD using a discount rate of 15% was 39.8%. Results varied by business unit (Table 2).
❑ reducing the discount rate to 10% reduced the economic LGD to 36.2%.
❑ the distribution of LGD was highly bimodal with large concentrations close to 0% and 100% with a high standard deviation on the order of the mean.
❑ the workout time until final resolution averaged 2.4 years with significant variability.
❑ LGDs for secured loans averaged 40.9% as compared with 50.5% for unsecured facilities based on a subset of the data, principally from 1990 onwards (Table 3).

Table 2 LGD by business unit (JPMC resolved defaults (1Q82–4Q99))

Business units	Obligor count	Average time-to-resolution (yrs)	Net charge-offs		Discounted LGD	
			Mean (%)	Standard deviation (%)	Mean (%)	Standard deviation (%)
Large corporates (US)	676	3.33	23.8	34.2	41.6	30.9
Large corporates (non-US)	268	2.58	22.9	33.8	37.3	33.2
Real estate	719	2.23	29.8	36.6	42.0	33.7
Emerging markets	394	3.04	25.8	39.5	42.2	35.6
Middle market	1,264	2.15	30.0	40.4	40.3	38.4
Private banking	310	1.66	25.4	40.9	34.5	38.3
Other	130	1.35	15.6	30.1	23.1	28.2
Total	3,761	2.43	27.0	37.9	39.8	35.4

Table 3 LGD by categories of collateral (JPMC resolved defaults (1Q82–4Q99))

Type of secured collateral (primary)	Obligor count	Net charge off		Discounted LGD	
		Mean (%)	Standard deviation (%)	Mean (%)	Standard deviation (%)
Cash & marketable securities	36	23.7	37.1	35.8	33.8
Non-marketable securities	11	15.8	29.7	44.9	54.7
Accounts receivables	126	24.3	34.6	35.1	32.4
Inventory	60	31.9	34.5	40.9	32.2
Accounts receivables & inventory	66	30.9	41.6	41.6	38.6
Fixed assets/machinery & equipment	71	32.1	36.8	42.3	34.2
Mortgages/liens on real property	706	25.0	32.5	39.4	31.2
Blanket lien	120	33.2	34.2	47.2	32.7
Other	83	41.4	48.8	53.0	41.8
Total secured	1,279	27.7	35.3	40.9	33.4
Total unsecured	426	40.3	42.5	50.5	38.1
Total	1,705	30.8	37.2	43.3	34.6

Sample of 1705 borrowers has about 75% of the names coming from 1990 onwards for which special reports were available that enabled differentiation by security type; the remaining 25% comes from the earlier period at one of the heritage firms for which this differentiation was available.

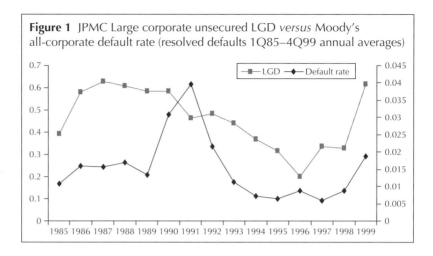

Figure 1 JPMC Large corporate unsecured LGD *versus* Moody's all-corporate default rate (resolved defaults 1Q85–4Q99 annual averages)

As noted earlier, there are well-reasoned arguments as to why the levels of LGD should vary with the business cycle. Figure 1 illustrates the relationship between LGDs on unsecured large corporate exposures at JPMC and Moody's All-Corporate default rates over a 15-year period. A log-linear regression resulted in the following relationship:

$$LGD = 1.16 + 0.16LN \text{ (Default Rate)} \qquad (5)$$

$$(p = .0001), (p = .0069)$$
$$R^2 = 44\% \quad \text{Adjusted } R^2 = 40\%$$

However, for secured exposures, the R^2 was about 2%, showing virtually no correlation. This may in part be due to the bank's ability to monitor and obtain additional collateral as general economic conditions worsen. To incorporate these issues in economic capital modelling it is desirable to link the overall default rates to the LGDs for unsecured credits, but to consider them to be independent for secured credits.

Errors in estimating LGDs will have an important impact on portfolio capital. In a hypothetical portfolio consisting of about 3,000 borrowers, an across-the-board increase in LGDs of 25% will increase capital requirements by about 16%.[4] Other portfolios with different compositions could have different impacts.

EXPOSURE AT DEFAULT

The EAD for public debt is the debt outstanding at any time, as this amount of debt cannot be increased. For amortising debt, a term structure for exposure can be determined that can be related to the PD term structure. Since term loans made by banks are generally prepayable without penalty, sophisticated banks are trying to model the circumstances under which they might be prepaid, such as an improvement in credit spreads or a merger. In most cases, however, banks will assume that the EAD for a term loan is unchanged over the life of the loan.

A more common measurement problem arises when a bank makes a commitment to lend, usually a revolving credit facility, for a certain period of time. In this case, the borrower may draw down on the loan and repay, repetitively. At any time, over the life of the loan, the amount outstanding will range from zero to the full amount of the commitment. The unused commitment will range from zero to the full amount of the commitment, such that the amount used and the amount unused always sum to the commitment.

Capital models require not only assessing the risk of loss associated with the amount drawn, but also the risk of loss associated with the additional EAD arising from a drawdown of a portion of the unused commitment. As noted earlier, in the discussion of LGD, it is possible that the amount drawn can be partially repaid prior to the time of default. For commercial loans, consistent with the practice for term loans, banks generally make the conservative assumption that the drawn portion of the revolving credit will not be prepaid.

We define the loan equivalent amount (LEQ) as the percentage of the undrawn commitment that is expected to be drawn at the time of default. It is clear then that the LEQ of an unused commitment can range from 0 to 100%, while the LEQ of an outstanding loan is conventionally assumed to be 100%.

While it might be conservative to assume that the LEQ of an undrawn commitment is 100%, the ability of banks to structure lending agreements in a such a way as to protect the bank's interests militate against that assumption. In fact, the incorporation of covenants in a lending agreement is specifically designed to reduce the risk that a borrower will draw down on its line just when its credit condition shows a marked deterioration. These covenants are fairly strict for non-investment-grade credits and generally loose for high-investment-grade companies. The latter is certainly true for commercial paper backup lines. Rating agencies will rate commercial paper A1–P1 precisely because backup bank funding lines have few conditions inhibiting a drawdown.

Even where protective covenants exist, there may still be a race between the borrower's ability to draw down on its line and the bank's ability to cut off the line as credit deteriorates. Historical analysis should ideally be based on a classification of the nature and strength of the covenant package to determine the LEQ percentage associated with various classes of covenant. Unfortunately, banks do not keep track of original covenants, much less changes in covenants over the life of a revolving credit, so that it is quite difficult to conduct this historical analysis.

Ratings, however, may serve as proxies for these covenants under the assumption that poorer-rated exposures will have stricter covenants. Other factors that could affect LEQs include the nature of the obligor's business, its access to commercial paper markets, whether there are borrowing-based limits restricting access to the full commitment, the size of the commitment and the current percent utilisation. Since LEQs can be measured at different points in time prior to default, it is important to consider the tenor of the commitment. With long-dated commitments, there is more time for adverse credit migration as well as a greater opportunity and need for a borrower to draw down unused lines.

The results of a six-year study of LEQs associated with revolving credits at JPMorgan Chase were reported (see Araten and Jacobs, 2001). LEQ calculations were made on defaulted facilities based on 1,021 observations on 408 facilities for 399 defaulted borrowers over a 5¾-year period ending in December 2000. While overall LEQs averaged 43%, LEQs showed a significant increase relative to tenor across all ratings categories.[2] One-year LEQs averaged 32%, while five-year LEQs were 72%. As expected, this may be due to a negative rating migration effect and an associated need to draw down on facilities.

LEQs were also found to generally decrease as credit quality worsens, although, unlike the time-to-default relationship, this was not as robust. In general, LEQs for BBBs and better averaged 62%, 48% for grades between BBB– and B+ and 27% for B and worse.

As was the case for LGDs, LEQs exhibited a barbell distribution around 0% and 100% with a standard deviation of around 40%. High LEQs can thus be associated with better-quality credits and with longer-term exposures.[3]

In capital models LEQs have a linear impact on capital requirements. Assuming all LEQs were higher by a given percentage, capital would increase by the same percentage. If LEQs were underestimated for individual exposures so that these now represent higher concentrations than previously assumed, capital could increase disproportionately.

CORRELATIONS

Correlations represent the glue that bonds individual exposures together in a portfolio. If individual assets were uncorrelated, it would be relatively easy to develop a loss distribution for the portfolio. However, it is not only difficult to estimate individual default probabilities for two firms, but it is extremely difficult to estimate the likelihood that their default rates are linked. Since these firms have never been in a state of default, historical evidence will be unavailable. The best that can be done is to infer the default correlations. In developing MTM credit capital models we are not only concerned with the default events but also in changes in credit quality short of default that could result in valuation losses. Therefore, in addition to default correlation, we are also interested in estimating rating change correlations.

There are a number of theoretical approaches. The first is to model joint rating changes directly using historical rating change data. The problem with using credit rating histories is that it assumes that two firms with the same rating would have the same correlation. Thus, two companies in different industries and different countries would have the same correlation as two companies in the same industry and same country as long as they had the same rating.

Another approach is to estimate credit correlations using bond or credit default swap spreads. The difficulty associated with using bond or credit default swap spreads is the lack of a sufficiently long time series of quality data as well as the need to extract default estimates from market spreads.

State-of-the-art approaches involve constructing an option theoretic model of the firm that allows one to develop a time series history of underlying asset values such as provided by Moody's KMV. The changes in the asset values can be decomposed into those factors that are deemed to be systematic and those deemed idiosyncratic. Systematic effects are those related to industry, country and overall market effects, while idiosyncratic effects are peculiar to the company. The proportion of asset-value variation associated with systematic versus idiosyncratic effects is conventionally referred to as the R-square. With asset-value correlations default correlations can be constructed. In addition, asset-value changes can be related to changes in distance to default and to rating changes so that valuation gains and losses can be determined.

While R-squares for public companies can be estimated as described above or proxied from equity correlations, private company R-squares also need to be assessed. These can be estimated based on public company R-square values as a function of the country, industry and size of the company.

Portfolio capital is quite sensitive to R-square estimates. For the hypothetical portfolio referred to earlier, an across-the-board increase in R-squares of 25% will result in an increase in capital of approximately 20%.

SUMMARY

Credit capital models provide the basis for assessing portfolio risk. These models combine the credit characteristics of individual exposures and their correlations with other exposures in the portfolio to produce a probability distribution of loss for the portfolio as a whole. The target level of capital is based on the lending firm's desired rating. Capital can then be assigned to individual exposures to determine whether the risk-adjusted returns of these exposures are above the firm's hurdle rate.

Choices of models include those that only consider default (DO) and are therefore most closely associated with a firm's reported financial statements. Alternatively, an MTM model will parallel a firm's results that recognise both realised and unrealised economic losses in its consideration of risk events.

The key inputs to all capital models consist of PD, LGD and EAD for each of the individual exposures, coupled with their default correlation. Most firms assign ratings to individual obligors as a measure of their relative riskiness. These ratings reflect either a shorter-term view (PIT) or a longer-term view of credit quality (TTC). To derive PDs, an estimate of historical PDs associated with these ratings must be derived, or, if the company has public-traded equity, PDs can be determined from market-based observations. LGDs associated with individual facilities can be estimated as a function of seniority, structure and collateral type based on past historical experience. EADs or LEQs for unused commitments can also be estimated from historical data and have been found to be a function of ratings and tenor. Asset correlations can be derived from market observations and used to determine the degree to which credit-risky assets have large systematic or idiosyncratic risks. Systematic risk tends to increase overall portfolio capital as risky credits are likely to default at the same time.

1   See Moody's KMV RiskCalc 3.0.
2   In an updated internal study covering a longer, nine-year period ending in 2002, a similar average LEQ was obtained.
3   LEQ = 48.36 − 3.49(Facility Grade) + 10.87 (TTD) where Facility Grade corresponds to 1: AAA/AA−, 2: A+/A−, 3: BBB+/BBB, 4: BBB−/BB+, 5: BB, 6: BB−/B+, 7: B/B−, 8: CCC and TTD is time-to-default or maturity in years.
4   As can be seen from Equation (2) even at the standalone UL_i level, UL_i is not linear with LGD since it is the square root of the sum of two terms, while, as can be seen in Equation (1), EL_i is linear with LGD.

REFERENCES

Altman, E. I., A. Resti, and A. Sironi, 2001, "Analyzing and Explaining Default Recovery Rates", ISDA, December.

Araten, M., and M. Jacobs Jr., 2001, "Loan Equivalents for Revolving Credits and Advised Lines", *Journal of the RMA*, May.

Araten, M., et al, 2004, "An Internal Ratings Migration Study", *RMA Journal*, May.

Araten, M., M. Jacobs Jr., and P. Varshney, 2004, "Measuring LGD on Commercial Loans: An 18-Year Internal Study", *Journal of the RMA*, May.

Cantor, R., 2004, Moody's Investor Service, Moody's Corporation and NYU Salomon Center, Inaugural Credit Risk Conference, 19 May.

Cantor, R., and C. Mann, 2003, "Measuring the Performance of Corporate Bond Ratings: Special Comment", Moody's Investor Service, April.

Frye, J., 2000, "Depressing Recoveries", Federal Reserve Bank of Chicago, October.

Hu, Y.-T., and W. Perraudin, 2002, "The Dependence of Recovery Rates and Defaults", Bank of England, 2002.

Keisman, D., K. van de Castle, and R. Yang, 2000, "Suddenly Structure Mattered: Insights into Recoveries from Defaulted Loans", *Credit Week*, pp. 61–7, May.

4

Recovery Risk and Economic Capital

Jon Frye*

Federal Reserve Bank of Chicago

Lenders know that any loan can default. They also know that the default rate of any portfolio can rise. If the default rate rises enough, the portfolio experiences loss. To absorb this possible loss, lenders must have capital.

A second effect can compound the loss. This is the variation in loss-given default (LGD). LGD is the fraction of exposure lost when a loan defaults. Lenders find that, when the default rate rises, the LGD rate tends to rise as well. When we think about possible loss, variation of the default rate is only half the picture. The variation of LGD can be just as important.

This chapter develops a framework for understanding the coordinated rise of the default rate and the LGD rate and their effect on economic capital. Both rates connect to an underlying systematic "risk factor". As will be seen, this brings into being two distributions of LGD. These distributions play distinct roles in the analysis that leads back to economic capital. In this analysis, two pitfalls stem from themes developed earlier, and each leads to an

*The views expressed are the author's and do not necessarily represent those of the management of the Federal Reserve Bank of Chicago or the Federal Reserve System. This chapter benefited immensely from comments by skilled and willing readers. The author thanks Denise Duffy, Craig Furfine, Brian Gordon, Michael Gordy, Paul Huck, David S. Jones, Mark Levonian, Eduard Pelz, Tara Rice, Til Schuermann, and Douglas Stalker. Any errors that remain are the unaided contribution of the author.

understatement of risk. These pitfalls are to ignore a source of systematic risk while measuring LGD and to conflate the two distributions of LGD while estimating expected LGD (ELGD).

LGD AND ELGD

We begin with a simple model of a portfolio containing loans or other products that might default. The definition of default may differ between products, or it may allow discretion in determining whether a default has occurred. At any given time, though, we assume that a particular loan has either defaulted or it has not.

For a defaulted loan, LGD is the proportion of exposure that is lost. LGD is an economic concept; it does not necessarily correspond to the amounts reported under current financial reporting practices. Usually, LGDs take values between zero and one.

This seemingly straightforward definition of LGD contains subtleties that complicate measuring LGD in specific situations. Rather than focus on these, we stay with the broad properties of LGD. We assume that in the absence of default there is neither loss nor potential for gain. Thus, there is no loss due to downgrade and no gain due to upgrade. We also assume that the relevant economic loss can be measured.

Until LGD is measured, it is a random variable. Much of what follows involves an exploration of the distribution of random LGD, but an important observation can be made at the outset.

The observation stems from the definition: for any given loan, LGD is independent of default. Two random variables are independent if knowledge of the value of one of them tells nothing about the value of the other. In this case, the first random variable is the default indicator for the loan. The default indicator equals one in the event of default and equals zero otherwise. The second random variable is LGD. Before default, LGD is thought to have some expected value, distribution, or set of likely values. If the loan in fact defaults, there is no effect on the expected value, distribution or set of likely values – consistent with its name, LGD imagines what happens if default occurs. If the imagined event becomes real, there is no new information; the occurrence of the default has no effect on the distribution of LGD. By definition, LGD is independent of the default event that brings it into being.[1]

The independence of LGD and default allows a simple bit of maths that provides some insight. Credit loss requires a default; then, loss per dollar of exposure equals LGD. Stated symbolically,

$$L = D \cdot \text{LGD} \tag{1}$$

where L is the loss per dollar of exposure and D is the default indicator. Since the factors on the right-hand side are independent, the expectation operator passes through as follows:

$$E[L] = E[D] \cdot E[\text{LGD}] \quad \text{or} \quad \text{EL} = \text{PD} \cdot \text{ELGD} \tag{2}$$

This says that the expected loss on a loan equals its expected default rate (usually denoted "PD" for "probability of default") times the loan's ELGD rate. For example, if a loan has probability of default equal to 5% and ELGD equal to 40%, its expected loss is 2%.

It is important to note the difference between the symbols: LGD is a random variable that has some distribution, and ELGD is the expectation of that random variable. Thus, ELGD is a moment or population parameter, and LGD itself is random. Similarly, PD is the population parameter of the random variable D. It is also important to note that (2) is specific to a given loan. Therefore, the expectation is of the distribution of the LGD of the loan. That distribution depends on the loan's distribution of default, as shown in a later section.

As we have seen, there is independence between an LGD and the default that brings it into being. Correlation does enter the picture, but only at the portfolio level. A given LGD might be correlated with other LGDs or with other defaults. As a practical matter, if in a given year there have been a number of defaults involving a certain kind of collateral, and if the LGD on these defaults has been greater than usual, then it is likely that subsequent defaults involving similar collateral will also produce LGDs that are greater than usual. Separately, an unusually large number of defaults, by itself, might also bring about LGDs that are greater than usual. Thus, "correlated LGD" stems from analysis at the portfolio level. This analysis uses portfolio risk models that provide an estimate of economic credit capital.

ECONOMIC CREDIT CAPITAL

The concept of economic capital quantifies the risk faced by a financial institution over a defined period – usually one year. All types of loss, not just credit loss, are included in the economic capital concept. While keeping this in mind, this chapter analyses economic credit capital but refers simply to economic capital.

Economic capital is analogous to the value-at-risk (VAR) analysis used to control risk on financial trading floors. Like market VAR, economic capital is a high percentile of the loss distribution.[2] This chapter mimics market VAR analysis in another way as well. We assume that the portfolio has its exposures for the entire analysis period. This means there are no deals maturing before the end of the year, and as a consequence there is no reinvestment risk. The risk to the institution is equal to the risk in its current portfolio.

This chapter illustrates economic capital using the 99.9th percentile loss. This means the loss occurring once in a millennium – *if* the model reflects all the elements of reality. But a mathematical model simplifies and stylises reality. Therefore, the nominal percentile is meaningful to the model, but it has a weaker relationship to the reality being modelled. The situation resembles the role of "implied volatility" in option pricing models. Different option pricing models, which stylise the market in different ways, produce different implied volatilities. A given implied volatility has meaning in the context of the model that implies it. In a similar way, the percentile of a loss distribution has meaning in the context of the model that produces the distribution. The probability that the actual portfolio loses more than economic capital could be greater or less than 0.10%.

Still, the loss being estimated is far beyond the loss recorded at the average bank. Therefore, the economic capital model necessarily performs a kind of extrapolation based on a statistical distribution of losses.

This loss distribution depends on so-called "risk factors". In a market VAR model the factors are easily conceived; they are the prices of securities or derivatives that closely resemble portfolio holdings. In an economic capital model, the risk factors are more abstract. They are simply the driving forces behind variations in default and LGD – whatever makes the rates rise and fall. There is no need to interpret the risk factors as transformations of economic data such as GDP, stock prices or interest rates.

ASYMPTOTIC SINGLE-RISK-FACTOR MODELS

The simplest economic capital model employs only a single risk factor that affects other quantities in the model.[3] This risk factor is a random variable that subjects the portfolio to periods of greater or lesser credit loss. We refer to the risk factor as Z and allow it to affect both the default rate and the LGD rate. The Zs affecting different portfolios might be more or less the same, especially if the portfolios are large and well diversified.

A single-factor model is the simplest framework, and it provides the only way to think about the economic capital of a loan without also thinking about the make-up of the portfolio. To see this, suppose there were two risk factors, one that affects obligors based in the US and one that affects obligors based in the UK. Suppose that the obligor of a new loan is based in the UK. If the loan were added to a portfolio of US loans the new loan adds a little diversification, but if it were added to a portfolio of UK loans it adds no diversification. Thus, the risk of the new loan depends on the portfolio it joins. If there are two or more risk factors, the risk of a loan depends on the characteristics of the portfolio. To discuss economic capital without knowing the make-up of the portfolio one must have in mind a single-factor model. Fortunately, single-factor credit models are believed to capture much of the risk seen in multifactor models.

Another assumption is needed to discuss the economic capital of a loan in isolation: within any year, the portfolio is large enough to average away sampling variation. This "asymptotic" assumption can be justified by the law of large numbers. If the portfolio has enough loans, and if the loans are similar enough in exposure amount, the expected rates of default and LGD can be assumed to occur. A given loan may or may not default, but there are enough loans that on average the default rate expected for that year is observed. Similarly, a defaulted loan may have any LGD, but there are enough defaults that on average the LGD rate expected for that year is observed.

Default and LGD vary from year to year because of variation in a single risk factor, Z. The rates of default and LGD are said to be conditioned on Z. A greater value of Z brings about a greater conditionally expected default rate and a greater conditionally ELGD rate. Since Z has an effect on every loan in the portfolio, it is said to be the "systematic" risk factor. This distinguishes Z from the "idiosyncratic" risk factors that contribute sampling noise in a portfolio that is not of asymptotic size.

If Z reflects "stress" conditions – if it is drawn at the 99.9th percentile of its distribution – both the LGD rate and the default rate are at the 99.9th percentiles of their respective distributions. Their product, the loss rate, is at the 99.9th percentile of its distribution as well. We can summarise this by saying that, in a single-factor model, economic capital for a loan equals its stress default rate times its stress LGD rate.

This context readily reveals the potential importance of LGD for economic capital. The stronger the effect of Z on the LGD rate, the greater will be stress LGD, and the greater will be economic capital.

EVIDENCE OF COORDINATED VARIATION

This section examines evidence from Moody's Default Risk Service, which provides the rating history of every Moody's-rated loan or bond. For instruments that default, it provides both the date of the default event and the price of the instrument a few weeks later. The percentage difference between par and the post-default price measures LGD.

The data sample comprises 19 years, 1983–2001. The years are separated into "good" (low-default) years and "bad" (high-default) years. The purpose of separating is to see what happens to LGD when the default rate is high. Therefore, the definition of a bad year is somewhat arbitrary. We take a bad year to mean any year where the default rate is greater than 4%, but some other separator could be used instead. Using 4% identifies four bad years (1990, 1991, 2000 and 2001) that have a total number of defaults approximately equal to the total number of defaults in the 15 good years.

On the LGD side, Moody's observes a "debt type" for each defaulted loan or bond. A debt type designation is rather detailed, for example, one type of loan is "guaranteed senior secured term loan B". There are thousands of debt types in all, but fewer than 100 of them have ever experienced a default. Among these, 49 debt types share a key trait: they have experienced at least one default in a good year and at least one default in a bad year.

For each of these 49 debt types, we calculate the average LGD during good years and, separately, the average LGD during bad years. The averages are plotted in Figure 1.[4] The position of a

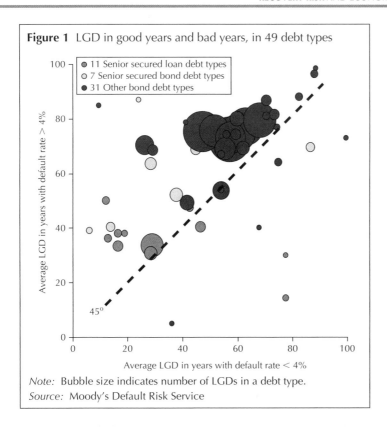

Figure 1 LGD in good years and bad years, in 49 debt types

- 11 Senior secured loan debt types
- 7 Senior secured bond debt types
- 31 Other bond debt types

Average LGD in years with default rate > 4%

Average LGD in years with default rate < 4%

45°

Note: Bubble size indicates number of LGDs in a debt type.
Source: Moody's Default Risk Service

"bubble" reflects the two LGD averages. The size of a bubble reflects the total number of LGDs observed within the debt type. Smaller bubbles represent debt types that have not had many defaults.

Figure 1 provides evidence that default and LGD respond systematically to a common factor. The general pattern is that most of the bubbles appear above the 45-degree line. This means that for most debt types LGD has been greater in high-default years. The exceptions are debt types represented by smaller-sized bubbles. Representing fewer defaults, some of these bubbles may appear below the 45-degree line only by chance. Though the identity of the risk factor remains abstract, Figure 1 suggests that something causes the LGD rate to rise at the same time as the default rate.

MODELLING LGD AND DEFAULT RATES
Returning to the simple model introduced earlier, we tie the default rate and the LGD rate to Z. In other approaches to economic capital

modelling, the default and LGD associated to any particular deal respond to the systematic risk factor.[5] By taking the average within a year, the conditionally expected rates of default and LGD can be derived as functions of Z. These functions have certain common-sense properties regardless of the specifics of the model that brings the functions into being:

❑ the functions are monotonic. Worse conditions produce a greater default rate and a greater LGD rate. We assume without loss of generality that greater Z represents worse conditions; the functions are therefore upward-sloping.

❑ as Z rises without limit, both rates (default and LGD) approach 100%. In the worst imaginable state (collision with a large asteroid, perhaps), all obligors default and all LGDs equal 100%.

❑ as Z falls without limit, both rates approach zero. As long as there is some default and loss, things could always be better.

Rather than focus on the derivation of these functions, and on the complexities of the derivation, this chapter takes a direct approach. We assume that we already have the default rate and the LGD rate as functions of Z. Figure 2 displays the functions we will be using as examples. Both the LGD function and the default function exhibit the properties outlined above. They have not been calibrated to data, but they are useful to show the basics of working with LGD.

To complete the model, we need to specify the statistical distribution of the risk factor Z. The most common assumption, and what

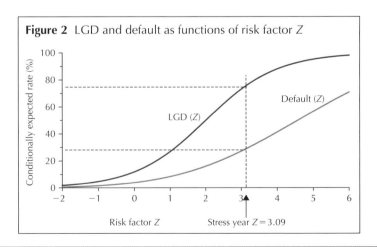

Figure 2 LGD and default as functions of risk factor Z

we will use for purposes of illustration, is that Z follows a standard normal distribution. Thus, each year a random realisation of normal Z implies the default rate and the LGD rate via the functions shown in Figure 2.

The most common realisations of Z are near zero. These imply conditionally expected default rates near 4%. Figure 2 shows that much greater default rates can occur. Weighting all the conditionally expected default rates by their probabilities, the "unconditionally" expected default rate – in other words, PD – equals 5%. Both functions in Figure 2 are quite sensitive to Z. When standard normal Z takes its 99.9th percentile value of 3.09, it produces the stress default rate of 28% and the stress LGD rate of 75%.

LGD DISTRIBUTIONS

Using the "change of variable" technique, one can convert the functions of Figure 2 to probability distributions. That is because the annual rates are monotonic functions of random Z, which has a known probability distribution. The distribution of annual LGD appears in Figure 3. As in any probability distribution, the horizontal axis shows values of the random variable (LGD) and the vertical axis shows the relative frequency of the values.

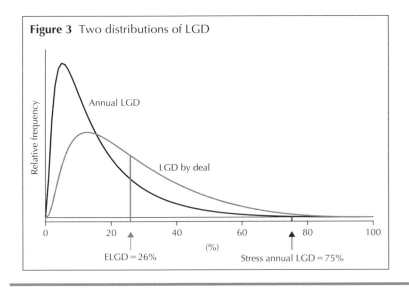

Figure 3 Two distributions of LGD

Figure 3 also shows the distribution of LGD by *deal*, and it is quite different from the distribution of annual LGD. The distribution of LGD by deal depends on both the distribution of annual LGD and the default function.

To begin the derivation, consider an LGD of 32%. About 11% of years have conditionally expected LGD greater than 32%. However, loans with LGD greater than 32% are much more common because the conditions that produce high annual LGD also produce a great many defaulted loans.

When LGD is equal to 32%, Figure 2 shows that Z equals 1.25 and the associated default rate equals 10%. This is twice the "normal" rate of default, which is 5% (and equal, of course, to PD). Therefore, where LGD equals 32% in Figure 3, the distribution of LGD by deal is twice as high as the distribution of annual LGD. Reasoning this way up and down the range of LGD leads to the derivation of the full distribution of LGD by deal.

To better see the difference between the two distributions plotted in Figure 3, imagine having LGDs from defaulted loans in a 10-year period containing nine good (low-default, low-LGD) years and one bad (high-default, high-LGD) year. Though only one year in ten is bad, the bad year produces more than 10% of the defaults. Generalising, bad years have extra weight in determining the distribution of LGD by deal. Since the bad years have large LGDs, the extra weight goes to the right of the distribution.

A different default function in Figure 2 would produce a different distribution of LGD by deal in Figure 3. For example, if default were not sensitive to Z, the default rate equals PD irrespective of Z.

PANEL 1 DERIVING THE DISTRIBUTION OF LGD BY DEAL AT A SINGLE POINT

❑ the normal default rate, PD, equals 5%.
❑ in a year with $Z = 1.25$,
    ❑ the default rate equals 10%, and
    ❑ the annual LGD rate equals 32%.
❑ this says that when LGD = 32%, LGDs are produced at twice the normal rate.
❑ therefore, in Figure 3 where LGD = 32%, LGD by deal has twice the relative frequency of annual LGD.

Table 1 Features of the two LGD distributions

Distribution	Mode (%)	Mean (%)	99.9th percentile (%)
Annual LGD	6	16	75
LGD by deal	13	26	Not useful

In that case, the distribution of LGD by deal is identical to the distribution of annual LGD, instead of being shifted as in Figure 3. In general, though, we assume that default rate is sensitive to Z.

It is not exaggerating to say that a bank lives by the distribution of LGD by deal, but it dies by the distribution of annual LGD. A bank lives by making profitable loans. The pricing for each should include expected loss (EL). As we have seen, the EL for a loan equals PD for the loan times expected LGD of the loan. This expectation uses the distribution of LGD by deal. ELGD is shown in Figure 3 at 26%.

By contrast, a bank dies in an adverse year. In a year when Z is at its 99.9th percentile, loss equals economic capital, which equals the stress default rate times the stress LGD rate. Stress LGD can found from Figure 2, and it is noted in Figure 3. Stress LGD – the 99.9th percentile of annual LGD – equals 75%.[6]

As we have seen, if annual LGD depends on Z, this gives rise to a probability distribution of annual LGD. If, as well, the default rate depends on Z, this gives rise to a distinct distribution of LGD by deal. These two distributions of LGD warrant some observations.

❑ ELGD and stress LGD come from different distributions. ELGD is expected LGD by deal. Stress LGD the 99.9th percentile of annual LGD.

❑ of the two distributions, the distribution of annual LGD is intrinsically simpler. Annual LGD can depend directly on Z. The distribution of LGD by deal, and therefore ELGD, depends on both the distribution of annual LGD and the annual default rate function.

❑ expected annual LGD is less than ELGD. This is because years with greater LGDs contain more LGDs.

❑ using data, the average of annual average LGDs ("time-weighted-average" LGD) tends to understate ELGD. The time-weighted average produces an estimate of expected annual LGD, not of ELGD.

Before moving on it is worth noting that the distributions developed in this section are distributions of conditional expectations. They show systematic risk – the risk created by variation in the systematic risk factor Z. In addition to this, an institution with a finite-sized portfolio has idiosyncratic risk that is essentially the random sampling error around the conditional expectations. Idiosyncratic risk tends to diversify away as the size of the portfolio increases.

CAPITAL MODELS, CAPITAL FUNCTIONS AND ELASTICITY

The above logic produces economic capital for a particular type of loan. In the example, the loan has ELGD = 26% and PD = 5%. These are the so-called unconditional expectations. Both LGD and the default rate vary by year depending on Z, leading to their conditional expectations. Economic capital is the product of the conditional expectations at the stress level of Z. For the above loan, this is 21% = 75% × 28%.

In principle, the same approach provides economic capital for any other type of loan. For a different type of loan, the functions portrayed in Figure 2 are different, leading to different expectations (ie, PD and ELGD) and different stress values. Ideally, the functions result from a statistical estimation process that calibrates the model to default and LGD data, with special attention to the sensitivities to Z. That calibration lies outside the scope of this chapter.

In practice, sampling error has an effect on a bank portfolio. Sampling error, combined with the diversity of characteristics of loans in the portfolio, make the exact distributions like those in Figure 3 difficult or impossible to derive. Therefore, a practical economic capital model takes a different track. It specifies default and LGD functions similar to those in Figure 2, and then performs a Monte Carlo simulation to build up the picture of the distribution of loss. Economic capital for the entire portfolio is found at the desired percentile.

Rerunning the model adding a single loan produces the economic capital for that loan. Generalising for a range of loans, the result can be stated as an economic capital function that depends on the characteristics of loans. The function resembles

$$K = f(\text{PD, ELGD, other characteristics}) \qquad (3)$$

Using the example functions and assuming the asymptotic single-risk-factor model, we found earlier that $K = 21\% = f(5\%, 26\%)$.

An economic-capital function usually states capital at the margin. It tells the effect on capital if a loan of the specified type is added to or removed from the portfolio. Because the portfolio is not "asymptotic" in size and because it depends in practice on more than one risk factor, economic capital in general depends on the other loans in the portfolio. Holding fixed the other loans, a capital function like (3) can always be determined, though it generally cannot be written in closed form because it effectively summarises the output of an extensive Monte Carlo simulation.

The capital function tells the extra capital required when a deal is added to the portfolio, or the capital released when a deal is removed. Often, a bank wants to judge both effects at once, for example, if it contemplates changing the mix of characteristics in its portfolio. The resulting change in capital depends on the sensitivities of the capital function to its inputs.

Sensitivities are most usefully stated as elasticities. Long the bane of introductory economics students, elasticity is a measure of sensitivity resembling slope, but stated in percentage-change terms. It is usually the case that the elasticities of a capital function are more or less constant over some range of inputs. For example, a bank might contemplate exiting a credit having PD equal to 5% and making a similar loan to a credit having PD equal to 2%. Suppose this exchange decreases marginal capital by 50%. Then it probably is the case that an exchange from a loan having PD of 0.5% to one having PD of 0.2% also reduces capital by about 50%.

One elasticity is very readily identified for the asymptotic portfolio: if LGD does not depend on Z, the elasticity of economic capital with respect to ELGD equals 1.0. If expected LGD is no greater in stress conditions than otherwise, the capital function looks like $K = \text{ELGD} \times f(\text{PD})$. The elasticity of capital with respect to ELGD equals 1.0, because if ELGD doubles, capital doubles as well. In the more realistic case where LGD responds to Z, the elasticity of capital with respect to ELGD is generally less than 1.0. A change in ELGD causes a less-than-proportional change in capital.

FIRST IMPLEMENTATION PITFALL: MIS-MEASURING LGD

The foregoing discussion provides a general approach for understanding the effect of LGD on economic capital. The final sections discuss two pitfalls that can be encountered when working with loss data. Either of these pitfalls can lead to a significant understatement of risk.

The first pitfall is to ignore a form of systematic risk while measuring LGD. LGD has been defined as an economic concept, but it must be measured in some way using data that can be observed. Several methods have been put forth.

"Market value" measurements are generally crystallised soon after the default event. They require a financial market willing to bid for the loan soon after it defaults. By contrast, "workout value" measurements wait, possibly for years, for the defaulted contract ultimately to settle in some way. The ultimate cashflows are discounted back to the time of default; LGD is then measured as the proportional difference between the exposure amount and the discounted value of the ultimate cashflows. Intermediate approaches measure LGD at some other time, for example, as soon as the collateral is seized and appraised.

Any of these approaches might result in a workable assessment of economic loss, as long as all systematic effects are properly included. But, when the market and workout approaches are compared in this regard, the workout approach seems more likely to err.

Market-value measurements reflect uncertainty about the ultimate cashflows of the defaulted loan contract. Market participants make an effort to estimate them and to discount them back at risk-adjusted rates. Errors doubtless occur in the valuation process. If the errors are systematic, the evidence produced by market measures of LGD is flawed.

An example of a systematic market pricing error would be if defaulted loans tend to be underpriced in high-default episodes. This would exaggerate LGD while the default rate is elevated; it would overstate risk and economic capital. However, if it is true that markets systematically underprice defaulted loans during high-default periods, a market participant that discovers this fact can make extraordinary returns by buying loans rather than selling them. Therefore, significant deviations of market prices from economic values should be self-correcting to some degree. Without good evidence that defaulted loans have been systematically mispriced, it seems reasonable to assume that market prices reflect an economic valuation process that properly takes into account the systematic influence of the underlying risk factor.

Workout value measurements of LGD discount the ultimate cashflows after they are known. But the cashflows are known only after they are received. Before the cashflows are received, they are unknown and risky. Risk is greater in a high-default period. Greater risk brings with it greater spreads to the risk-free rate. Therefore, during a high-default period the economic discount spread is greater than at other times. The first pitfall is to ignore the systematic variation in spread when discounting the cashflows obtained in the workout process.

A greater discount spread stems from greater systematic risk. In a high-default period, similar obligors are apt to default, and loans with similar collateral are apt to be defaulted; systematic influences are generally more important in a high-default period than otherwise. More broadly, it is more difficult to diversify away from defaulted assets in a high-default period because at that time defaults are more likely to arise for systematic reasons. Still more broadly, during a high-default period a defaulted loan correlates more strongly with the market portfolio, simply because the market portfolio contains more defaulted loans.

If constant spreads are used to discount workout cashflows, the first pitfall taints the LGD data. If those data are used to calibrate a capital model, the model understates risk. It may seem possible, though, to work around the first pitfall. The workaround would attempt to get the discount rate "right on average" without making it cyclically sensitive. Though individual LGDs would be mismeasured, perhaps they could be used in an economic capital model properly calibrated with full regard for systematic risk. The hope would be that, if the mismeasured LGDs produced accurate estimates of ELGD, the economic capital model could still be accurate, if the model were calibrated properly.

The workaround depends on getting the spread "right on average", and this is more difficult than it sounds. Some observations can be made at the outset. First, the right spread is not the original contractual spread on the defaulted loan; it is riskier to hold defaulted loans than to hold other loans. Second, the right spread is not derived from the bank's overall cost of capital; it is riskier to hold defaulted loans than to hold the bank's typical asset. Third, the right spread is not a simple average of the spreads observed through the credit cycle. A greater number of defaulted loans are exposed to the greater discount spreads during a high-default period; the time to resolution may also be longer. Both magnify the effect of the greater spreads observed in high-default periods.

In all, the discount rate used for measuring LGD by the workout method cannot ignore systematic variation in risk. Choosing the right discount rate is subtle and important.

SECOND IMPLEMENTATION PITFALL: MIS-ESTIMATING ELGD

Even if every measured LGD reflects full economic loss, there is a problem with estimating ELGD. The problem is that average historical LGD is a downward-biased estimator of ELGD. A related point was made earlier, namely, that time-weighted average LGD is a downward-biased estimator. The current point cuts deeper. "Default-weighted" LGD is also a downward-biased estimator of ELGD. That is, the average of LGD data is a biased estimator of expected LGD.

The above statement seems to conflict with elementary statistical theory, so an explanation is due. Statistical theory speaks about random sampling. For example, imagine the set of all LGDs experienced in 1,000 years of data. If one LGD is drawn at random, there is a good chance that it comes from a year having a large number of defaults.

The difficulty, when it comes to the real world, is that LGDs are *not* drawn at random. Instead, a few years are drawn at random, and LGDs are sampled intensively from those years. This process is biased against sampling large LGDs. Large LGDs tend to occur in high-default years. These years contain more than an average number of LGDs, but they have only an average probability of being sampled. If the years are sampled randomly, the large LGDs within high-default years tend to be undersampled.

The bias does not occur in the hypothetical case where default does not depend on Z and the expected default rate equals PD in all years. With no systematically high-default years, there is no systematic undersampling of large LGDs. But if default varies systematically, default-weighed average LGD is a downward-biased estimator of ELGD. Fortunately, the bias declines as the sample period extends, and the average is asymptotically unbiased.

The small-sample estimation bias is illustrated in two sets of simulations. Each set of simulations uses a Vasicek default function with PD equal to 0.5%, and each set has an LGD function that produces ELGD equal to 10% and stress LGD equal to 30%. The difference between the two sets is that they use different "asset correlation". Asset correlation controls the degree of systematic variation of default; in terms of Figure 2, greater asset correlation means the default function is steeper. Asset correlation equals 5% in the first set of simulations and 21% in the second.[7] In both sets of simulations, the portfolio is asymptotically fine-grained, so that on each simulation run the conditionally expected rates occur without sampling noise.

Figure 4 shows for each set of simulations the average default-weighted estimator among 50,000 simulation runs. If the average were unbiased, Figure 4 would show lines at 10% throughout. In fact, the upper line, representing the first set of simulations that have asset correlation equal to 5%, shows little departure from 10%. With as few as five years of simulated data, the average estimate equals 9.2%. Though this is slightly less than the true value of ELGD, an error of this size might readily be tolerated.

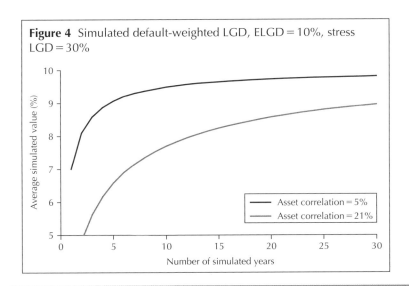

Figure 4 Simulated default-weighted LGD, ELGD = 10%, stress LGD = 30%

The lower line in Figure 4, where asset correlation equals 21%, tells a different story. The average estimate is well below the true value of 10% when the number of years is low to moderate. With five years of data, mean estimated ELGD is about 6.6%. A statistician would use over 150% of the estimated value to create an unbiased estimator of ELGD. With 10 years of data, mean estimated ELGD is about 7.7%; even then, ELGD is 130% of the mean estimated level.

These simulations show that the degree of bias in the default-weighted estimator depends on the value of asset correlation (or on the steepness of the default function in Figure 2). As the number of years increases, the bias in the default-weighted average declines. In any case, the percentage impact of the bias is apt to be greatest for loans having low ELGD.

CONCLUSION

Evidence has shown that, when the default rate is elevated, the LGD rate also tends to be elevated. Tying both rates to a single systematic risk factor, we derive the distributions of the default rate and of annual LGD. The 99.9th percentiles of these distributions provide the stress rates; their product equals economic capital.

Expected LGD, or ELGD, is derived from the distribution of LGD by deal. The distribution of LGD by deal is derived from the distribution of annual LGD and the default rate function.

The economic capital function depends on the characteristics (such as PD and ELGD) of loans that might be added to or removed from the portfolio. The sensitivities of the economic capital function are usefully summarised by the associated elasticities.

Two of the pitfalls of working with LGD data often lead to understatements of economic capital. First, if the effect of systematic risk is ignored when selecting the discount rate for ultimate cashflows, LGD would be understated when risk is high. Extrapolating to a high percentile, the economic capital model would understate risk. Second, if the two distributions of LGD are not kept distinct, average historical LGD would be accepted as a good estimate of ELGD. In fact, average LGD is a downward-biased estimator of ELGD, though the bias declines as the sample period increases.

1 Other variables, such as the value of collateral, may depend on the default event. In addition, LGD may depend on anything but the default event. For example, the reason for default (say, fraud by senior management) may tell something about LGD.

2 An alternative definition of economic capital removes EL from the loss distribution before finding the percentile.

3 This section draws heavily from Gordy (2003).

4 Figure 1 originally appeared in Frye (2003).

5 See, for example, Pykhtin (2003).

6 This observation may be obscured by the thickness of the line used to depict Figure 3.

7 Asset correlation of 5% is estimated in Frye (2000). The level of 21% is a not atypical, following the common practice of equating asset correlation to the correlation of equities or of deleveraged equities; see JP Morgan (1997).

REFERENCES

Frye, J., 2000, "Depressing Recoveries", *Risk*, pp. 108–11, November.

Frye, J., 2003, "A False Sense of Security", *Risk*, pp. 63–7, August.

Gordy, M., 2003, "A Risk-Factor Foundation for Risk-Based Capital Rules", *Journal of Financial Intermediation*, **12**, pp. 199–232.

JP Morgan, 1997, "CreditMetrics", Technical Document, URL: http://www.riskmetrics.com/cmtdovv.html.

Pykhtin, M., 2003, "Unexpected Recovery Risk", *Risk*, pp. 74–8, August.

Schuermann, T., 2004, "What Do We Know about Loss Given Default?" in *Credit Risk Models and Management*, Second Edition (London: Risk Book).

Tasche, D., "The Single Risk Factor Approach to Capital Charges in Case of Correlated Loss Given Default Rates", Working Paper, URL: http://www-m4.mathematik.tu-muenchen.de/m4/pers/tasche/LGD_Charges.pdf.

Vasicek, O. A., 2002, "Loan Portfolio Value", *Risk*, pp. 160–2, December.

5

The Significance of Economic Capital to Financial Institutions

Vandana Rao

Indiana University East

Economic capital (EC) is a relatively new concept. Although some of its roots can be traced to the 1980s, EC was introduced in financial institutions in the 1990s and has evolved into significant practical importance only in the last decade or so. A precise definition will be attempted later in the chapter. As an introduction, EC is a dollar number that serves as a common measure across all types of financial risks and captures the risk of unexpected losses or unexpected reductions in income in a business, a portfolio or a single transaction. EC is necessarily calculated at a portfolio level and attributed to each transaction within the portfolio.

Capital investments in an industrial organisation are on physical plant, machinery and equipment. Therefore, it is relatively easy to assign specific capital investments to particular project or business unit within the corporation. As a result, deriving the capital associated with a project is very tractable. All the focus then falls on deriving the appropriate discount rate for NPV calculation. By contrast, in a financial institution, there is little physical capital investment. Deriving the capital associated with a product or a business unit within the corporation is not trivial. It needs to be explicitly derived by taking stock of the complex risks in the financial instruments associated with the business unit. Financial instruments have complex, uncertain cashflows. Elaborate analytical methodology is required to capture such risks. Risk is best captured in the computation of capital attributable to a product or business unit rather than in the discount rate. This is the genesis of EC and the rationale behind why such a concept is needed for financial institutions. This methodology is also a departure from traditional corporate finance, where the risk of cashflows from a project is reflected in the discount rate.

The need for a concept such as EC has arisen more from practical than theoretical considerations, as financial institutions have tried to address business unit performance at levels below the corporate level performance, price products with adequate compensation for all risk, align business unit managers' objectives to shareholder-value maximisation and take part in active credit portfolio management. The purpose of this chapter is to address each of these applications to illustrate why EC is a necessary tool for financial institutions. In what follows, the next section is a chronology, the three sections following deal with conceptual issues in EC, the next five sections deal with relatively recent applications for which EC has become an essential tool in financial institutions, while the final section concludes the chapter.

BOOK EQUITY, REGULATORY CAPITAL AND EC

From the financing side of a bank, the liability instruments are fairly identifiable. The retail core funding consists of certificate of deposit (term) and indeterminate deposits with coupons ranging from wholly market-indexed to essentially administered coupons. The wholesale non-core funding consists of senior debt and subordinate debt, while the rest of wholesale financing is in the shape of trust-preferred issuance, preferred stock and common stock. In the balance sheet, the last two together constitute book equity. From another perspective, book equity can be categorised as tangible and intangible equity, which is of particular interest to rating agencies.

Till the second half of 1990s, the amount of book equity of most financial institutions was determined by corporate finance considerations only. Attention to reported numbers such as preferred target return on book equity (ROE), tangible-equity-to-tangible-asset ratio and strategies such as potential acquisition and signalling effects of share repurchase were the drivers of how much book equity must be kept (unless book capital fell below regulatory capital). It had no direct relationship to the characteristics (risk profile, term and so forth) of the institution's portfolio. The question of how much capital a bank really needs, given its particular risk profile, could not be answered, even if someone asked. It was the quest for answering this important question that the need for the concept of EC was first felt (see Parsley, 1995).

From the risk measurement side of the bank, EC is for the unexpected losses or unexpected reduction in income. For a long-tailed (say, loss) distribution, extreme events can be associated with significant probability density. The less diversified the portfolio the fatter the tail. These events, although not catastrophic, can cause huge losses for a bank in one year with extremely good performance for many years previous to the bad year. So much so that loss in one or two portfolios can wipe out the entire positive income from the rest of the bank, with depletion of accumulated reserves to boot.[1] Occurrence of such events in some banks in the late 1980s and early 1990s prompted significant interest in understanding tail risk and portfolio diversification in the wholesale credit world. This also prompted the development of the analytical framework from which EC evolved.

Financial institutions (banks and insurance companies in particular) are highly regulated with minimum regulatory capital requirements. Therefore, to the extent that it becomes binding, regulatory capital becomes a constraint. Regulatory capital is based on simplistic formulations and has little correspondence with risk of the portfolios of a bank. This is likely to change with the impending Basel II Accord, which seeks to align regulatory capital to risk more closely than in the present capital accord.[2] Basel II is to take effect in January 2008 and regulatory capital and internal EC are in a path of convergence. Till such time, regulated financial institutions will have to deliberate on the comparison and reconcilement of internally calculated EC with regulatory capital requirements. Given the one-size-fits-all nature of the present accord, the exercise is best done at the corporation level, with product pricing exclusively driven by internal EC.

DEPARTURE FROM STANDARD CORPORATE FINANCE

In corporate finance the risk of investments in different projects is traditionally captured by applying different discount rates to the stream of cashflows from those projects. The discount rate is meant to measure uncertainty in cashflows associated with different projects – the higher the uncertainty, the higher the discount rate. Stated differently, the cost of capital for each project is different depending on the uncertainty of cashflows generated by each project. Also in standard corporate finance, the financing decision can be separated from the investing decision. This implies that the discount rate or cost of capital associated with each project with differing levels of cashflow uncertainty cannot be derived from the observed cost of capital from the financing function of the corporation as a whole.

It is a daunting task to calculate the appropriate discount rate (actual rate percent, not rank ordering) for different projects in an industrial company (see Brealy and Myers, 1996, for a conceptual treatment of the issues involved). The task becomes more difficult when the company is a conglomerate with activities in diverse industries, because the risks are so different. It is perhaps even more difficult for a financial institution (though all its activities are in one industry), because the risks in financial instruments are complex and cover a whole spectrum. In this context, it may be useful to state the ways in which a financial institution differs from an industrial organisation – differences that are particularly relevant in establishing the need for the concept of EC for financial institutions.

Unlike most industrial organisations, capital investment for a financial institution is not on tangible plant, machinery and equipment. The physical assets of a financial institution are a small fraction of its total assets, which consist mostly of financial assets (even for a "bricks and mortar" retail bank). The risk of a bank's primarily financial assets comes from the uncertainty of the complex and often contingent stream of cashflows associated with the financial assets. The broad categories of risks that need to be quantified are credit risk, market risk, prepayment risk, liquidity risk, insurance risk, operational risk and business or strategic risk.[3] The spectrum of risk within each category can be very wide and not easily comparable without a technically sound methodology.

Banks are highly leveraged, with debt-to-equity ratios in excess of 15 to 1, in comparison with industrial firms. Most of the debt liabilities are in the shape of customer deposits, which are insured by the federal government under the deposit insurance programme. This is one reason perceived market risk of a bank stock is much less than the debt-to-equity ratio may imply, everything else being equal. Relatively speaking, a bank is in a position to raise capital rather cheaply. This is less true of other forms of financial institutions.

In an industrial organisation the capital investments are on physical plant, machinery and equipment. It is relatively easy to identify which of the capital investments relate to which project or business unit within the corporation. Therefore, deriving the capital associated with a project is very tractable. All the focus then falls on deriving the appropriate discount rate for NPV calculation. In a financial institution, there is little physical capital investment. Deriving the capital associated with a product or a business unit within the corporation is not trivial. It needs to be explicitly derived by taking stock of the complex risks in the financial instruments associated with the business unit.

In recent years, this departure from the standard corporate finance approach taken by financial institutions and consulting firms while introducing the concept of EC has been applied in the context of non-financial companies as well (see Stein *et al*, 2002; Tierny and Smithson, 2003).

A SINGLE COST PER UNIT OF EC

If all the risks in different portfolios of financial instruments are captured in the measure of EC needed to support the portfolios, then it makes sense to assign all the portfolios identical cost per unit of EC. The corporate cost of equity or the required rate of return on equity that investors require is much easier to determine from market observations in the financing side. This is a single number or rate irrespective of the business unit, portfolio or transaction. The problem of finding the appropriate discount rate for different levels of risk is thus shifted to the problem of finding the appropriate EC. As it turns out, the problem of finding the appropriate EC is complex but can be approached from analytically sound (reasonably) principles using observed price and default data. The same cannot be said of the problem of arriving at an appropriate discount rate.

The most common way of determining the required rate of return for a company's stock is to use the capital asset pricing model (CAPM), which has been prevalent in the finance literature for decades. The following CAPM formula gives the expected or required rate of return, k, for the company's common stock as follows:

$$k = r_f + \beta \cdot \left[E(r_m) - r_f \right] \tag{1}$$

where r_f is the return on a risk-free asset, β is the beta of the stock – a measure of its systematic risk – and $E(r_m)$ is the expected return on the market (say Standard and Poor's 500 index). The term in the [ ] is referred to as the market risk premium. For most US banks, the cost of equity capital calculated using the above formula is between 10% and 15%. The exact rate depends not only on long-term historical observations but also on the current rate environment.

The use of CAPM for calculating the cost of equity capital is analytically simple but is not straightforward when it comes to implementation. Judgement is called for in the estimation of all the three elements: market risk premium, risk-free rate and the institution's beta (see Pettit, 1999 for a detailed exposition of the implementation issues). Clearly, the estimated cost-of-equity number can be different depending on the exact methodology and length of historical data used by the bank. But, once arrived at, the cost of equity is not likely to be a major (and ongoing) management debate in a financial institution. In fact, a single cost of equity capital for all businesses and all products is a boon since all business units are treated equally in this regard.

A PRECISE DEFINITION OF EC AND ITS PRACTICAL DIFFICULTIES

The most widely used definition of EC is the following: *the potential unexpected (US dollar) loss of economic value over one year calculated at a pre-specified confidence level*. The level of confidence is anchored by the desired insolvency standard of the financial institution. Given the desired bond rating of the institution, a probability of insolvency over one year can be determined from historical bond default data. The confidence level is one minus the probability of insolvency. This is sometimes referred to as the debt-holders' perspective (see Hall, 2002).

The definition of EC has similar elements to the definition of the more familiar value-at-risk (VAR), commonly used in the market risk world. But it is pertinent to mention the differences.

First, conceptually the horizon in trading-VAR calculation is the period that is necessary to unwind a position. One day is the most common horizon used for VAR. Conceptually, the horizon in EC calculation is the period over which an institution can rebuild its capital or restructure its capital financing. One year is the horizon that has come to be in common use.

Second, the level of confidence (usually 95%) used in trading VAR calculation is much lower in comparison with the level of confidence used in EC calculation. Most financial institutions have a debt rating of BBB to AA. The corresponding insolvency standard requires the specification of a very high confidence level ranging from 99.5% to 99.97%.

Third, VAR is associated with market risk oversight only. EC has come to play a role in many aspects of a financial institution from pricing to incentive compensation.

In common parlance, a 95% confidence level means that the portfolio value can be expected to go down by the daily VAR (calculated *ex ante*) once every 20 business days or so. A trader or manager used to profit-and-loss volatility can grasp this easily. They expect to see an event reaching the VAR limit once in a while and several times during their tenure. At 99.9% confidence level, EC is to cover annual losses in all years except once in 1,000 years. When managers think about this, they can come to the conclusion that such a rare event may not occur in their whole career. The natural inference is that the business unit is being allocated too much EC. By that logic, so is every other business unit.

Another way of defining EC is more empirical. This is to start from volatility of income or NOPAT (net operating profit after taxes). In corporate finance, risk arises precisely from volatility of cashflows. If a financial institution has reliable historical data and assuming the future will follow the pattern of the past, then the volatility or standard deviation of income can be estimated. EC is then a suitable multiplier of the volatility. Alternatively, an empirical distribution can be fitted to the data and we can go from there.

Unfortunately, reliable historical data over a sufficiently long period are rarely available at the corporation level, let alone at the business unit level. Moreover, many financial institutions change their business mix (and consequently risk profile) significantly as a result of mergers and acquisitions from time to time.

A structural model of EC requires estimation of parameters, which can be done using market information or industry pooled information, and then the loss or value distribution is generated by the model either by analytical means or by Monte Carlo simulation. If an analytically sound structural model is available for the risk in question, it is preferred to a purely empirical model for EC. A pragmatic EC methodology for a diversified financial institution is to utilise the structural model path for all risks (eg, credit risk or market risk) that can be captured by such models and then fall back on the volatility-of-income approach for those risks for which structural models do not exist (eg, fiduciary risk or risk from brokerage business).

SHAREHOLDER-VALUE CREATION

A simple definition of shareholder return for a company is the sum of the dividend yield and the relative price appreciation of the common stock of the company over a specified period. The excess shareholder return by the company over that period is the difference between the shareholder return and the required rate of return. The latter has already been introduced in the section before last. Shareholder value is created as a result of this excess return. However, this simple statement needs to be paraphrased.

First, on the basis of price–earnings ratio, the market seems to reward those companies that have a high excess shareholder return and a high growth of revenue. Thus, while having top-line growth is not enough, shrinking revenue by divestiture in order to increase excess shareholder return is not a good idea, either. Till recently, financial institutions have focused most of their attention to top-line growth, with measures such as return on assets (ROA) and contribution margin as drivers of performance.

Second, much more attention is paid by a financial institution as to how it has performed relative to peers (or to some benchmark) than to shareholder value created by the organisation. This diverts attention to comparisons on several reported measures (some of which are cosmetic rather than economic) instead of attention to shareholder-value creation.

Third, it is likely that there are business units within the financial institution that contribute negatively to shareholder-value creation. Within a limited period of time, it is perfectly legitimate to continue with those business units as long as they reduce the magnitude of their negative contribution (ie, show improvement over time, even though negative) – particularly, if they add significantly to revenue growth.

Finally, the stock price is affected by many factors on which neither the corporate manager nor the business unit manager has any influence. Therefore, particularly for the business units, it is necessary to have a measure that is, by and large, directly influenced by the business unit managers and at the same time is strongly correlated with shareholder-value creation. Stern Stewart's economic value added (EVA) is one such measure. It has been shown that EVA has by far the strongest correlation with market value creation than any other profitability measure such as earnings per share (EPS), net income (NI), ROE or ROA. This is true for financial companies as well as industrial companies (see Uyemura, 1997; Uyemura et al, 1996 for details).

The shareholder-value creation imperative has received attention in financial institutions somewhat later than it did in many industrial organisations. Banks have introduced performance measures similar to EVA such as shareholder-value-added (SVA), economic profit (EP) or economic profit added (EPA) with a view to enhancing shareholder-value creation. Other banks have introduced ratio measures such as RORAC (return on risk-adjusted capital) or RAROC (risk-adjusted return on capital).

We will define single-period EP as simply:

$$EP = NI - k \cdot EC \qquad (2)$$

where NI is net income, k is the required return on equity and EC is economic capital. This is a risk-adjusted measure. The value of the measure is not as much in corporate performance as in business unit performance measurement. It must be obvious to the reader that without a methodology to calculate EC capturing all forms of risk in financial instruments, it is not possible to calculate EP at various levels of a financial institution. Thus the shareholder-value creation imperative in financial institutions needed the concept of EC to precede it. The shift in paradigm from traditional measures to EP or RORAC is intimately tied to the introduction of EC.

The EP formula is for *ex post* measurement. The *ex ante* measure simply replaces NI by expected NI. The ratio measure, single-period return on risk-adjusted capital, is defined as:

$$RORAC = NI/EC \qquad (3)$$

Notice that in the above formula the adjustment for risk has been captured in the denominator (risk-adjusted capital) and not in the numerator. The numerator does have provision for expected losses that may arise particularly from credit risk. But expected losses are considered part of doing a credit business rather than a risk. Also, RORAC is greater than k if EP is positive and vice versa.

EP is derived from accounting results easily available in a financial institution's general ledger, except for EC. EC is, therefore, the only unfamiliar driver of EP. As a result, in the implementation of a new performance system aimed at shareholder-value creation, most of the attention falls on EC.

With the establishment of a comprehensive EC framework, EP can be computed not only for the corporation but also for business units and further down. EP is additive and can be cumulated from one level to the next. Each business unit manager can see the direct connection between their actions and performance and that unit's EP, by and large independent of the performance of other business units. These three properties are not possessed by share price or market value of equity. There is only one share price for the corporation. It is impossible to derive a variable at the business unit level that can add up to the market value of equity. The share price is affected by the performance of all the businesses together as well as exogenous factors beyond the control of the business unit mangers. Hence the value of EP as a performance measure is more at the business unit level than at the corporation level. It helps cascading the shareholder-value creation paradigm down through the organisation.

EC has provided the means for financial institutions to devise a performance measure that leads to shareholder-value maximisation. But that is not enough. Leading institutions have also tied compensation to EP. Such a compensation system has EP as the primary driver, coupled with several other qualitative performance indicators. This helps further aligning managers' objectives to shareholder-value creation.

PRICING FOR RISK AND PRODUCT PROFITABILITY

Of all the applications of EC in a financial institution, pricing every product appropriately to ensure that the institution is getting adequate return for the risk taken is perhaps the most important. A pricing model calculates a break-even price, incorporating accurate funding cost, all-in expense (overhead as well as direct), expected loss provisions and EC.

Pricing of traditional bank products has often been subjective in the past, based on imperfect knowledge of competitors' prices in the geographic region and making a choice to target somewhere in the range of competitors' prices. To this day, many a bank's pricing of retail deposits follows this subjective pattern, except in geographies where the bank is by far the dominant player. In credit products, however, pricing has long taken provision for expected loss into account. What has been lacking is taking into account the EC that is needed to cover unexpected losses. It is appropriate to enumerate here the distinction between expected loss (EL) and unexpected loss.

EL is the mean value of all possible losses the transaction or the portfolio can experience over one year. EL of a portfolio is the sum of the EL of each transaction in the portfolio. EL depends only on the risk characteristics of the transactions. The primary drivers of credit risk in a transaction are many: financial ratios of the obligor (the company to which the credit has been advanced by the financial institution), collateral, guarantees, size of open credit line, etc. But they all collapse to determine three commonly used parameters, namely, PD (probability of obligor default), LIED (loss in the event of default) and LGD (loss-given default) and EAD (exposure at default). The first two are usually expressed as percentages and the last one is obviously a US dollar number.

$$\text{EL (US \$)} = \text{EAD} \cdot \text{PD} \cdot \text{LGD} \qquad (4)$$

$$\text{EL (\%)} = \text{PD} \cdot \text{LGD} \qquad (4a)$$

Unexpected loss of a portfolio cannot be obtained by summing unexpected losses, however determined, of each transaction. Unexpected loss of a portfolio depends on all the risk characteristics mentioned above of all the transactions in the portfolio. But it also depends upon a very important portfolio characteristic – portfolio correlation. When the economy (or a particular sector of the economy) goes bad, not all obligors' fates go together. Default of one obligor does not necessarily mean another one in the portfolio will default at the same time. The portfolio correlation is less than unity. The more diversified the portfolio, the less is the correlation. The lower the correlation, the less is the unexpected loss of a portfolio.

EC, as defined earlier is the potential unexpected (US dollar) loss over one year calculated at a prespecified confidence level.

$$EC = EAD \cdot F(PD, LGD, Correlation; Horizon = 1 \text{ yr},$$
$$Confidence \text{ level}) \tag{5}$$

where F( ) is a complex function. Notice that, generally, EC is not a direct one-to-one function of EL.

Figure 1 illustrates the concepts of EL, unexpected loss and EC for credit risk in a portfolio.

The number and values of the data points are for illustrative purposes only. As mentioned earlier, computing portfolio EC at a very high confidence level empirically is almost impossible, since the amount of consistent historical data necessary is rarely available. The function F( ) is derived from a structural model instead.

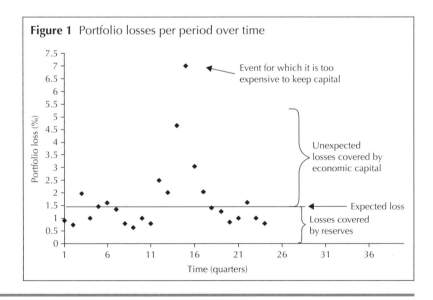

Figure 1 Portfolio losses per period over time

More sophisticated models may capture the interrelationship between default and LGD since recoveries are likely to be lower in bad economic times, when defaults are higher. Notice that LGD = 1 − Recovery. Also LGD in (5) is really expected LGD. A distribution of LGD may be captured in sophisticated models. The functional form F( ) in Equation (5) becomes more and more complex. The correlation in Equation (5) is intra-portfolio correlation. In addition, inter-portfolio correlations (eg, across different industries or geographies, between retail portfolio and wholesale portfolio) may be incorporated in sophisticated EC models.

Product pricing essentially consists of setting fees and coupons in such a way that the RORAC calculated over the life of the product exceeds a break-even rate. The break-even rate can be set at some value equal to or higher than the required return on equity, k. Equivalently, the EP present valued over the life of the product exceeds a break-even value. The break-even EP can be set at some value equal to or higher than zero. Typically, a pricing model allows the user to select reasonable fee and coupon rate combinations that the market is likely to bear and also break even. Any combination of fee and coupon over and above that ensures that the product is profitable to the financial institution in the sense of adding to shareholder value. EC is a major driver of the results of a pricing model but is by no means the only major driver.

CUSTOMER PROFITABILITY

Financial institutions have long been interested in the profitability of an overall relationship or of a customer as a whole and on retaining the best customers. Billions of US dollars have been spent by financial institutions in the US on customer-relationship management systems, which go well beyond profitability. Generally, such investments have not yielded the desired return on investment, for various reasons. One of the less important ones is that customer profitability measures are not fully risk-adjusted. In a highly competitive (pricing) environment, this is a fatal deficiency, at least in the long run.

A commercial or retail customer typically has many different products offered by a financial institution. These products range from loans to deposits to services for a fee. From the perspective of the financial institution, some of these products have credit risk, some have prepayment risk, some have operational risk, some have fiduciary risk, and so on and so forth. In this respect, risk of a relationship is far more complex than the risk of a single product, which is much more tractable.

For customer profitability, therefore, EC as a common measure of risk across such disparate products is essential. It is easy to add or subtract revenues and expenses (and even loan loss reserves) across all such products in a relationship and come up with the traditional customer profitability measure common today. But it is much more difficult to derive measures such as contribution to shareholder value or return on equity for customer profitability, without a well-established EC framework for all important products of the financial institution. In a highly competitive environment, it is likely that a large chunk of customers may appear marginally profitable under the current customer profitability measures while they may actually erode shareholder value.

A MULTI-PERIOD PERSPECTIVE
In dealing with traditional loan and deposit products, the cashflows are primarily coupon payments and principal payments. These payments may occur over several years. For such margin income products, a multi-period perspective and a single-period perspective generate similar results in terms of performance measures. But, in recent years, financial institutions have progressively enhanced their income coming from fees (which are typically one-time rather than recurring cashflows) compared with margin income. The existence of such one-time cashflows in significant proportions makes it imperative to take a multi-period view.

EC has been defined to cover risk of unexpected events occurring over one year. How, then, does it reconcile with multi-period view? It is incorrect to think that recourse to marked-to-market (as against default-only) EC, for transactions with terms in excess of one year, takes care of it. Marked-to-market EC covers losses due to possible migration as well as losses due to default. However, the horizon is still one year.

The multi-period profitability measures can be derived as follows:

$$\text{EPA (multi-period)} = \text{PV(NI)} - k \cdot \text{PV(EC)} \tag{6}$$

$$\text{RORAC (multi-period)} = \text{PV(NI)}/\text{PV(EC)} \tag{7}$$

where PV is present value calculated using k as the discount rate. The relationship, that RORAC is greater than k if EPA is positive, holds only if the discount rate k is used and not some other rate of discount.

Pricing based on EC is an *ex ante* exercise. It must take into account the effects of a single transaction or vintage over multiple periods (say, years). The multi-period EPA may be positive for a product (with significant one-time cashflows) but in one or more of the periods the EPA contribution may be negative. Performance measurement based on shareholder value creation, on the other hand, is an *ex post* exercise. Typically, such performance is of a single manager or a business unit and takes into account the effects, in the period (quarter or year in question), of numerous transactions across several vintages.

It is important to clearly understand the above distinctions between pricing and performance measurement and their ramifications. In the absence of such understanding, discrepancies in measured results will invariably be blamed on the EC methodology. In truth, the EC methodology is usually consistent across both applications. The numbers from the pricing and performance measurement will rarely be the same and there are logical reasons why they differ in many cases. In credit products the difference is particularly significant at the bottom or top of the economic cycle.

ACTIVE CREDIT PORTFOLIO MANAGEMENT AND EC

The loan portfolios of many commercial and retail banks consist of borrowers whose names do not trade publicly. The customers underlying a retail portfolio may have bureau scores available but there is no active market for trading of such portfolios, just as there is no active market for trading of loans to private firms. That is not to say that there is no active securitisation market, eg, of mortgages or credit cards or other retail assets. But most financial institutions view the securitisation market as a source of funding rather than from the perspective of active credit portfolio management.[4]

In recent years active credit portfolio management has become a discipline for financial institutions to go from a buy-and-hold mode to a mode of active repositioning of their overall portfolio credit risk, especially with the development of the credit default swap market. However, a liquid credit default swap market exists only for highly rated names and there is market for private names. Active credit portfolio management is, therefore, mostly restricted to the institutional portfolio consisting of corporates with public ratings and publicly traded stocks. Another offshoot of active credit portfolio management in large financial institutions is the arm's-length separation that is possible between originators on the one hand and portfolio managers on the other. For each name in the institutional portfolio, the observed or implied spreads in the capital markets (bond market, credit default swap market or collateralised debt obligation market) can be used to "transfer-price" the transaction moving from the originator to the portfolio manager.

Financial institutions with assets, for which there is no direct or implied spread observed in the capital markets, cannot easily take part in such active credit portfolio management. A well-developed EC framework (in this instance EC for credit risk) with explicit intra- and inter-portfolio correlations can enable a financial institution to fruitfully participate in active credit portfolio management and, through a mapping, to transfer price credit transactions. The details of such an application are beyond the scope of this chapter.

CONCLUSION

Economic capital is a relatively new concept, which has become prevalent in large financial institutions only in the last decade. In an industrial company, the capital invested in a project is relatively easy to identify. The uncertainty of the cash flows from the project is captured in the appropriate discount rate used to compute net present value. In a financial institution, economic capital takes a departure from this standard corporate finance approach. The economic capital attributable to a product, portfolio or business explicitly incorporates the uncertainty of the cash flows. The discount rate applied is the company's required return on equity, which is the same across all products of different levels of risk. This shift in emphasis from discount rate to capital necessarily requires a complex methodology for calculating economic capital.

The significance of economic capital to financial institutions ultimately comes from its applications. Various applications have been discussed in this chapter to show how economic capital has become a necessary tool for many important functions in a financial institution. These include risk-adjusted pricing and product profitability, shareholder value maximisation, customer profitability and credit portfolio management. Historically, many of these applications actually required economic capital methodology to precede their introduction in financial institutions. This is particularly true at business unit levels below the corporation level.

1   This is not to say that the accumulated equity capital is wiped out – far from it!
2   See introduction (pp. 1–5) in Basel Committee on Banking Supervision (2004).
3   For an exhaustive list and description of types of financial risk, see Porteous *et al* (2003).
4   In fact, a good understanding of the credit risk in securitisation tranches has come about only in the last few years (see Gordy and Jones, 2003; Pykhtin and Dev, 2002, 2003).

REFERENCES

BIS, 2004, "International Convergence of Capital Measurements and Capital Standards: A Revised Framework", Basel Committee on Banking Supervision, June.

Brealy, R. A., and S. C. Myers, 1996, *Principles of Corporate Finance* (New York: McGraw-Hill).

Gordy, M., and D. Jones, 2003, "Random Tranches", *Risk*, pp. 78–83, March.

Hall, C., 2002, "Economic Capital: Towards an Integrated Framework", *Risk*, pp. 33–6, October.

Parsley, M., 1995, "The RORAC Revolution", *Euromoney*, pp. 36–41, October.

Pettit, J., 1999, "Corporate Capital Cost: A Practitioner's Guide", *Journal of Applied Corporate Finance*, **12(1)**, pp. 113–20.

Porteous, B., L. McCulloch, and P. Tapadar, 2003, "An Approach to Economic Capital for Financial Services Firms", *Risk*, pp. 28–31, April.

Pykhtin, M., and A. Dev, "Credit Risk in Asset Securitisations: an Analytical Model", *Risk*, S16–S20, May.

Pykhtin, M., and A. Dev, "Coarse-Grained CDOs", *Risk*, pp. 113–16, January.

Stein, J. C., et al., 2002, "A Comparables Approach to Measuring Cashflow-at-Risk for Non-Financial Firms", *Journal of Applied Corporate Finance*, **13(4)**, pp. 27–40.

Tierny, J., and C. Smithson, 2003, "Implementing Economic Capital in an Industrial Company: The Case of Michelin", *Journal of Applied Corporate Finance*, **15(4)**, pp. 81–94.

Uyemura, D. G., 1997, "EVA: A Top-Down Approach to Risk Management", *Journal of Lending and Credit Risk Management*, **79(6)**.

Uyemura, D. G., C. C. Cantor, and J. M. Pettit, 1996, "EVA for Banks: Value Creation, Risk Management and Profitability Measurement", *Journal of Applied Corporate Finance*, **9(2)**.

Zaik, E., et al., 1996, "RAROC at Bank of America: from Theory to Practice", *Journal of Applied Corporate Finance*, **9(2)**, pp. 83–93.

Section 2

Economic Capital for Specific Risks

6

Economic Capital for Retail Credit Card Portfolios

Geoffrey Rubin*

Capital One Financial Corp

UNIQUE CAPITAL MODELLING CONSIDERATIONS

While credit card portfolios share many characteristics with other retail portfolios – granularity, portfolio size, management techniques – their unique characteristics challenge economic capital modellers. Among the credit card features that impact the assessment of unexpected loss and capital need are the following.

Undrawn credit lines. Credit cards are unique in that both borrower and lender possess options on the undrawn line: borrowers can draw down – and lenders can cancel – the remaining credit line at will. Open credit limit is a key aspect of card utility, with borrowers typically preferring higher limits. Along with rate, features and rewards, credit limit is an important basis for product differentiation. Undrawn line is also a source of backstop funding for distressed borrowers. While drawdown behaviour in advance of default is more complex than "charge to the max", borrowers typically draw on open lines prior to default.

Issuer disposition towards open credit line is more subtle. On the one hand, undrawn lines represent potential future outstandings and earnings. Credit line size is also a source of competition among issuers. Issuers are less sanguine about open-to-buy, of

---

* We want to pay special thanks to Wei Xu for helping formulate many of these observations. The opinions and statements expressed here are ours and not those of Capital One Financial Corp.

course, when it comes to potential loss. Among borrowers headed towards default, undrawn lines are but a source of additional loss. In the face of these competing dynamics, sophisticated line management has become a critical lender competency. If line management is too aggressive, lenders risk driving off customers or suppressing card usage; too liberal and lenders face significant loss exposure among defaulting borrowers. The ability to extend full credit to good borrowers while throttling back lines in the face of mounting borrower duress is a key aspect to controlling both expected and unexpected portfolio loss.

Large profit margin. Margin and fee structure certainly distinguishes many card portfolios from other lending products. Credit cards provide key services as well as funds and customers are willing to pay for the convenience and access they afford. Among subprime and some prime portfolios, in particular, the combination of fees and finance charges yields a higher expected return on outstandings than is typically found in other loan portfolios.

To what extent can margin absorb unexpected credit losses before capital is impaired? This question is relevant for all loan portfolios, but the magnitude of margin makes it particularly germane for some card portfolios. The Basel Committee, for example, acknowledged cards' future margin income as a source of protection against loss in some early drafts of the New Basel Accord. An understanding of margin volatility and correlation with default is the first step towards addressing the impact of margin on capital needs. Decomposing the elements of margin – types of fees and income and their persistence under stressed scenarios – helps identify the margin that lenders might expect when default exceeds expectation.

Specialised portfolio management. As with most retail portfolios, the capital needs of card loans are typically assessed at the pool or segment level rather than the account level. The continuing evolution of data and systems is bringing card management down to ever more granular levels of analysis. For example, FICO (Fair Isaac & Co) scores are being supplanted by proprietary models as the means of segmenting portfolios into tighter, more homogeneous groups for the purpose of loss analysis. As card portfolio management evolves along more specialised lines, the unique tools, techniques and expertise of this field will be reflected in the assessment of capital needs.

High loss-given default. Because most card outstandings are unsecured, lenders typically recover only pennies on every defaulted US dollar. This is not to say that recovery management is a static field – on the contrary, lenders, regulators, legislators and consumer advocacy groups are all heavily invested in this work. We only note that the level and volatility of recoveries has implications for capital need.

Ambiguous loss definition. Even the fundamental exercise of defining loss is a challenge among card portfolios. A mix of principal and accrued interest and fees constitutes legally owed amounts at default, and lenders and regulators have distinct views of the relevance of each for capital need. Card capital modellers must also contend with the timing and happenstance of default. The practices of loan forgiveness, debt conversion and transference, and rigid delinquency bucketing can complicate the analysis of defaulted and non-defaulted loans.

Off-balance-sheet funding. Oddly, the means by which some credit card outstandings are funded has implications for credit risk capital modellers. The extent to which issuers shed credit risk when they sell outstandings into revolving card trusts is an open and complex question.

CREDIT CARD CREDIT RISK CAPITAL MODELS

Credit risk capital modelling for card portfolios has followed similar developments in the larger retail and C&I spaces. Among a handful of approaches, the single-factor default-mode model seems to have gained industry-wide currency.

The single-factor default-mode model

The single-factor default-mode model or the Merton–Vasicek framework is particularly relevant to the assessment of unexpected credit loss among card portfolios. This framework is described in this book and in the Introduction. An important parameter in this framework is asset value correlation (AVC). Later in this chapter, a one-to-one relationship between AVC and loan default correlation (LDC) will be derived. Hence we will refer to this framework as AVC/LDC model. Amongst the reasons this model is applicable to card portfolios.

High portfolio granularity. The AVC/LDC model assumes complete diversification of idiosyncratic loss within loan pools. The accuracy of this assumption is a function of the number of distinct credits.[1] Major card lenders have many millions of account holders on file, and even small subsegments number borrowers in the tens of thousands, so the induced bias of applying this technique to card portfolios is all but eliminated.

Precise segmentation methods. The segmentation of loans into homogeneous risk pools is a necessary step in the estimation of an AVC/LDC model. Most card lenders maintain metrics that facilitate this exercise, yielding pools of loans with similar default likelihoods.

Forward-looking default probabilities. The AVC/LDC model also requires a prospective default probability for existing outstandings. Indeed, scoring models that assess default probabilities are a hallmark of card portfolio management. The tools and techniques for estimating expected card loss are among the most sophisticated and proven of any asset class.

Accrual treatment of outstandings. Card portfolios are typically held to maturity (attrition or default), so the two-state AVC/LDC model – default and no-default – is more immediately applicable than a migration model or other mark-to-market technique. The accounting treatment of expected loss is similarly structured; reserves are typically restricted to those amounts with demonstrable evidence of impairment over the coming year. There is no provision for the partial write-down of a current loan with increasing risk characteristics. Lenders with active portfolio sales programmes notwithstanding, most card lenders will find the two-state AVC/LDC model corresponds to their existing treatment of loss.

The one aspect of the AVC/LDC model seemingly at odds with the card product is the notion of an "underlying asset" or factor that drives default correlation. Identifying the underlying asset for secured products is easy – the market for homes, cars, publicly traded companies and commercial property can be directly assessed. The underlying asset upon which card correlation rests is more ephemeral: perhaps earnings prospects or the larger economy are the "asset" common to card borrowers. Nonetheless, articulation and identification of a precise underlying factor is not critical for model application. The LDC fitting approach dispenses with direct measurement of the common factor by attributing observable loan correlation to this unspecified factor, however conceived.

Beyond its conceptual appeal, the AVC/LDC model is an obvious practical choice. A recent industry study noted that industry participants are increasingly adopting this approach for their retail portfolios, so modelling and data benchmarks are more common.[2] Basel II enshrined this modelling approach for the measurement of regulatory capital need, guaranteeing its future relevancy. The challenges and nuances of this modelling approach are also featured points of debate and conversation among industry trade groups. A growing consensus suggests that this approach might form a universal paradigm for assessing card credit risk capital need. No one suggests that all methodological and estimation issues have been solved, but the AVC/LDC modelling approach is developing into the common language for assessing card credit risk capital needs.

Other models of credit risk capital

Two other effective models of card credit risk capital need are briefly considered here.

Loss variance models. Sometimes referred to as "EL-sigma" (expected loss variance) models, these models fit alternative parameters with data similar to those used in AVC/LDC models. Here, observed segment-level loss volatility parameterises a complete loss distribution for each segment, permitting the analytical derivation of unexpected loss. The capital need for any segment is thus defined by that segment's historical loss experience. These models are relatively easy to implement; stable segments and historical losses are the two primary modelling needs. Difficulties arise when the historical loss distribution is no longer relevant to the segment's future prospects. Changes in underwriting standards, the operating environment, or segment composition can disrupt the historical pattern. The consolidation or bifurcation of product lines, for example, might yield a segment for which no history is available.

Modellers can circumvent this problem by relating the capital need identified for each historical segment to a prominent feature of the segment such as default probability or expected loss. This EL–UL relationship can then be applied to *de novo* segments for which a meaningful estimate of future EL is available. Practically, this approach is very similar to standard AVC/LDC assessment. Circumstances under which they might provide materially different capital estimates are the following.

1. When results are applied to a segment with expected losses outside the range of the estimation dataset

Consider, for example, a lender that adds 20% EL business to a portfolio with historical EL experience in the range of 0–10%. Extrapolating the historically defined EL–UL relationship to this new segment might generate results quite different from an extrapolation of AVC/LDC estimates to this segment. This is particularly true for very high EL segments: AVC/LDC models demonstrate stabilising or even falling unexpected loss as EL increases. The extrapolation of an increasing EL–UL relationship, estimated at low levels of expected loss, will support a different conclusion.

2. When the modeller has a strong prior expectation for AVC or LDC

Mounting card portfolio evidence, for example, suggests that AVCs do not vary substantially across PD bands. This prior expectation casts light on outliers and helps ground an overall AVC–PD relationship. Lacking a similar prior, loss variance mappings depend entirely on the quality of data and estimation.

3. When the components of unexpected loss – stressed default, recovery, and exposure rates – benefit from individual rather than joint estimation

EL-sigma models conveniently subsume the joint behaviour of these loss factors. This is an advantage with stable populations because correlations among PD, LGD and EAD are reflected in model estimates. Individual estimates of the components of loss are more useful when any demonstrate instability. The introduction of new recovery procedures or extension of higher credit limits, for example, will alter LGD and EAD, respectively. In contrast to the AVC/LDC model, these updated parameters are easily incorporated into an EL-sigma model.

Non-parametric models. Rather than estimate specific loss-distribution parameters, models of this type directly assess loss through simulation or similar techniques (see Miller, 1998). Earnings-at-risk (EAR) models exemplify this type of approach.[3] Historical earnings variability might be used to calibrate a relationship between earnings and macroeconomic factors such as personal income, consumer confidence and employment rates. The anticipated distribution of these economic factors then identifies a probability distribution of earnings trajectories, which in turn reveals the severity of earnings impairment at a threshold likelihood. The income statement might also be decomposed into components such as interest income, fee income, interest expense, credit loss, and overhead if each demonstrates a unique historical relationship to the driving economic factors. Card portfolio value-at-risk (VAR) can also be assessed with non-parametric models, though value transitions are difficult to estimate for all but the most actively traded portfolios.

Non-parametric models have a number of attractive features. First, they can address issues beyond credit risk capital need. While unexpected credit loss is certainly an important concept, total earnings and loss are more directly responsible for company performance and insolvency. EAR models incorporate credit loss into this larger assessment of possible earnings and loss. In addition, the behaviour of the various factors comprising overall earnings – revenue streams, credit loss, operational and market risks – is jointly modelled, capturing any correlations among those components. EAR models can answer the big question of overall corporate performance within a single model.

The power of joint estimation is also a hindrance in certain applications. By jointly estimating all risks in a single model, the contribution of each risk type is not easily ascertained. Credit, operational, market and strategic risk capital needs are not only elements of the larger capital equation, but are also important business management metrics. The results and integrity of non-parametric models are also difficult to compare across institutions; lacking common threads such as AVC or other parameters, each EAR model is a unique assessment of complex, company-specific dynamics. The developing dialogue among institutions both public and private cannot easily incorporate non-parametric modelling.

IMPLEMENTING AN AVC/LDC CREDIT RISK CAPITAL MODEL FOR A CREDIT CARD PORTFOLIO

Various practical aspects of AVC/LDC model estimation are briefly considered here. While this is far from comprehensive, capital modellers will likely confront many of these issues in developing an internally estimated AVC/LDC model.

Portfolio segmentation. AVC/LDC models require the segmentation of fitting-sample accounts into homogeneous groups. Homogeneity might be measured along a number of dimensions – size, seasoning, geography, borrower characteristics, management technique – but default probability is the most common basis for partition. Credit-scoring variables are an obvious choice of metric for institutions that score accounts. Some institutions assign accounts proprietary default probability scores, but scores need not have cardinal or absolute meaning: all that is required is a basis for partitioning loans into segments composed of accounts with similar default likelihoods. Segmenting accounts by FICO score, for example, will identify pools of accounts with similar default risk. Delinquency status is another critical determinant of default probability.[4]

Segmenting accounts by default probability sets the stage for a convenient modelling of AVC/LDC as a function of default probability. Just note that some model richness is lost when this single segmentation dimension is employed. For any particular institution, account performance correlation and credit risk capital need might vary meaningfully across segments defined by account management approach or credit risk modelling technique, for example. Segmentation schemes focused exclusively on default probability are the current standard, but future research might fruitfully identify other means of defining homogeneous pools of loans.

Bootstrapping samples. Most credit card modellers will find that their fitting sample – huge numbers of accounts tracked over a relatively short period – lends itself to bootstrapping. Consider, for example, a large lender intending to analyse 10 million accounts on file as of 1 January 2000. Without bootstrapping, only 36 points of observed loss are available for each segment in the period through 31 December 2003.[5] Sample size can be substantially expanded by drawing subsamples from the accounts in each segment. With roughly a million accounts in each segment, hundreds of boot-strapped subsamples of 50,000 accounts can vastly improve estimation precision (see Hall, 1992; Hjorth, 1994).

Measuring default rates. Having defined account segments and constructed data samples, modellers must next calculate observed default rates for the various samples in the segment. One might think this is as simple as calculating the ratio of accounts that default at any point over the subsequent 12 months. Consider a sample of 10,000 accounts on file as of 1 January 2002. If 1,000 of those accounts defaulted between that date and 31 December 2002, one might attach an annual default rate of 10% to this sample.[6] This "unweighted" loss rate might provide an answer different from the "dollar-weighted" loss rate that measures the proportion of initial outstandings, not accounts, that default during this 12-month window. If accounts with larger balances as of 1 January 2002 comprise a disproportionate share of defaults over the sample period, the dollar-weighted loss rate will exceed the unweighted loss rate.[7] The dollar-weighted loss rate is arguably more relevant to capital modelling, though the unweighted loss rate can also be employed if adjustments are made when assessing loss-given default and exposure at default. Lenders are ultimately more concerned about an unexpected increase in the US dollar amount than number of defaults.

The fundamental task of determining when and if an account defaults also merits some discussion. Most modellers use the bank's internal definition of default, a designation typically applied to accounts 120 or 180 days past due or those for which borrower bankruptcy has been confirmed. This designation, or any other that might gain currency (perhaps due Basel II rule interpretations), can be accommodated in the AVC/LDC framework as long as the segmentation scheme properly groups loans by default probability, as defined. Consider loans 150 days past due at the start of analysis. For lenders that do not classify these loans as defaulted, their segmentation scheme should group these loans into the same (high) default-probability segment. That virtually all of these loans will subsequently default over the coming 12 months does not prevent the assessment of the default rate for this segment. Modellers should be careful to analyse as many segments of non-defaulted loans they can – even those severely delinquent – if their definition of default provides for liberal delinquency periods.

Using empirical data to estimate LDC and AVC. The collection of sample loss rates within each segment identifies loan default correlation for each segment through the following equation:

$$\text{LDC} = \left[(\sigma^{2*}n - (\mu^{*}(1 - \mu)))\right]/\left[(\mu^{*}(1 - \mu))^{*}(n - 1)\right]$$

Where: n = sample size

μ = Observed mean of charge off rate of the sample

σ^2 = Observed variance of charge off rate of the sample

LDC can then be translated into AVC through this relationship:

$$N_2[N^{-1}[p], N^{-1}[p], \text{AVC}] - p^2 = (p(1 - p))\,\text{LDC}$$

Where: p = Probability of default

N_2 = Cumulative Bivariate Normal Distribution

N^{-1} = Inverse Normal Distribution

With these data in hand, the relationship between AVC and loss rate across segments can be estimated. Expressing AVC as a function of PD is a key simplifying device for the subsequent analytical derivation of unexpected loss. The evidence: the few publicly available data suggest that AVCs are roughly constant across PD rates. This evidence is hardly conclusive, but most modellers report constant AVCs across their card portfolios, with estimates in the 0.5–2.0% range (see Risk Management Association, 2003; Rosch and Scheule, forthcoming).

Applying the AVC/LDC capital model to the existing portfolio. The estimate of AVC described above figures in the following expression of credit risk capital need:

$$K = N\left[\left(N^{-1}[p] + \sqrt{AVC}\, N^{-1}[RCL]\right)\Big/\sqrt{1-AVC}\,\right] - p$$

Where: K = Capital Ratio
p = Probability of default
RCL = Risk Coverage Level
N = Standard Normal Distribution
N^{-1} = Inverse Standard Normal Distribution

This expression can be applied to any portion of the existing card portfolio, down to the account level, for which reliable PD, LGD and EAD estimates are available. In particular, this expression need *not* be applied to the portfolio segments used in estimating AVC. Whereas AVC fitting-sample data segments should comprise loans with homogeneous default likelihoods, lenders might assess capital need across operating unit or product type segments comprising loans with differing default likelihoods. If institutional decisioning models and risk-adjusted return measures are applied at the business-line level, for example, it makes sense to similarly assess credit risk capital need. The cost of applying the AVC/LDC capital model to non-homogeneous segments is rooted in the concave relationship between PD and capital: the sum total capital requirement for any two homogeneous segments will be less than the capital requirement calculated at the mean PD of a single, combined segment, as shown in Figure 1.

Credit card lenders are typically well equipped to anticipate the PD of their operating segments or accounts. As described earlier, many maintain proprietary models of default likelihood. The burden on these measures is greater here than in the segmenting exercise because the absolute level of PD, rather than the relative difference across segments, is critical. Card lenders can also exploit their

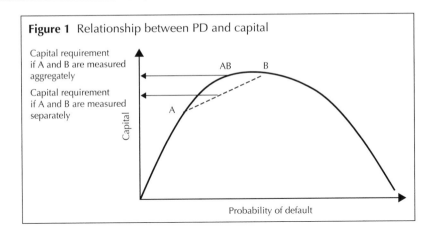

Figure 1 Relationship between PD and capital

accounting reserve calculations in deriving going-forward PD estimates. Accounting reserves are distinct from PD (as acknowledged in the Basel II "excess reserves" framework), but the work that supports reserves designation often considers datasets and loss forecasts that might help assess going-forward PD. Lastly, the lender can calculate capital need along the same segmentation scheme employed when estimating AVC/LDC. If the fitting-sample segments are stable and relevant to company operation, the historical default rate within each segment provides a meaningful measure of going-forward PD.[8]

Estimating loss-given default. Going-forward LGD, the next key parameter in an AVC/LDC model, is more difficult to estimate among card portfolios than for C&I loans. Card recovery accounting practice is the main culprit. Recoveries are typically pooled across accounts and cannot be easily attributed back to particular accounts or segments. Recoveries are also pooled across time, so amounts collected in any period might derive from accounts that defaulted over many previous years, depending upon the length of the collection life cycle. This undermines the use of accounting collections for two related reasons. First, collections in any accounting period, expressed as a percentage of charge-offs in the same period, will be biased by the past charge-off rate. For an institution that recently improved its risk profile, the relatively high past default experience will inflate the amounts collected in the current period and make the current ratio of recoveries to charge-offs an overly optimistic estimate of the recovery rate on accounts that might default in the coming year. Second, recovery pooling obscures the economic value of recoveries from the point of default. The numerator of going-forward LGD should discount the value of any future collections if the modeller wishes to anticipate unexpected economic, rather than accounting, loss.

On the bright side (from a modelling, rather than operating, perspective), card LGDs are so high that simple, conservative estimates can be usefully employed. Even though recovery techniques are growing in sophistication and effectiveness, LGDs of less than 80% are probably rare, particularly during periods of extreme PD duress. The market for recently defaulted paper underscores this point – prices of between five and ten cents per US dollar of defaulted balance typically prevail even during periods of low supply. Overall, credit card LGD modelling is a challenge that will hopefully encourage additional future modelling.

Estimating exposure at default. Estimates of anticipated EAD complete the parameterisation of an AVC/LDC capital model. EAD, a simple calculation for bullet or amortising loans, is complicated by the card open-to-buy feature. As described in the first section, borrowers draw and repay their open credit over time, and lenders can both increase and decrease credit limits. Behind the standard story of credit line usage – that borrowers maximise their draw in advance of default – lies a complex dynamic that might be assessed in a number of ways.

We first note that analysis of exposure should consider total outstandings (principal, accrued interest, and fees), not just principal. Once assessed, fees and finance charges are booked as assets in a manner identical to principal. As such, unexpected fee and finance charge reversals impair equity just as readily as unexpected loss from principal. When accounts slip into default, fee and finance charge reversal should give lenders as much pause as principal loss. US treatment of reserves supports this approach: lenders typically hold both an allowance for loan loss (expected principal loss) and a fee and finance reserve (expected fee and finance reversals). Credit risk capital should cover the unexpected portion of future loss from these two exposures.

The fundamental question of EAD analysis is, How big will an exposure be at the time of default? In practice, this typically distils down to an assessment of expected balance growth among loans that will default at any point in the coming 12 months. Note the subtle distinction between this measure and one that considers balance build in the full 12 months leading up to default. Of those accounts that default in the coming year, some will default tomorrow while others will default 12 months hence. The former have little opportunity to draw additional balance (particularly if they are currently delinquent or have already drawn down their entire open credit). To maintain a consistent AVC/LDC capital framework, modellers should look to measure balance growth for accounts that default at any point over the coming year (or period of analysis), not the typical drawdown in the full year prior to default.

The core EAD dynamic might be modelled as (1) a percentage (greater than one) of current outstandings; (2) the sum of current outstandings and a percentage (between zero and one) of current open-to-buy; (3) a percentage (between zero and one) of current credit limit.[9] When applied to large, stable segments, these approaches tend to yield identical answers. Distinctions arise when the EAD model is applied to smaller segments or when active portfolio management changes drawdown behaviour. Consider "transactors", or accounts that carry zero balance because borrowers repay in full each period. The first EAD modelling approach can handle larger, positive-balance segments with a sprinkling of transactors, but it cannot be applied to individual transactors or pools composed exclusively of transactors.

Each of these models is easily estimated with data on the drawdown experience of a sample of defaulted loans. To estimate the first EAD model, a group of loans that defaulted at some point during a particular three-year period will yield 24 observations by comparing, at the start of each of the first 24 months, the outstanding balances of loans that default over the next 12 months with their balance at default. If capital is to be assigned to operating segments different from those for which historical data are available (or if the segments are non-stationary), EAD might be additionally modelled as function of PD, product type or jurisdiction (bankruptcy laws might impact drawdown behaviour).

What about margin? We noted at the outset that many card portfolios generate substantial margin, even after accounting for expected credit loss and operating costs. To what extent might margin stand in for capital as a means of mitigating unexpected credit loss? The answer draws on both mechanical and conceptual arguments. Mechanically, the correlation between margin and default during periods of extreme duress must be considered. The migration of accounts into default not only increases credit loss but leaves fewer good accounts behind to generate revenues and margin. In the presence of fixed costs and the possible expense of unwinding funding on defaulted assets, it is entirely possible that even the most profitable segments generate little margin in times of high default.

Conceptually, the relevance of margin reflects on the very purpose of capital. If capital is held only to protect creditors against balance-sheet insolvency, margin indeed serves as a first line of defence. Alternatively, capital might be viewed as an instrument to help underwrite the larger management plan. In this paradigm, expected margin is already baked into expectations; any deviation from plan requires a capital plug, so the first US dollar of unexpected credit loss (or margin reduction, for that matter), should be covered by capital. Each institution must resolve – or at least contend with – this issue on its own terms. And remember, card lending maintains no unique claim to this debate; it only brings it to the fore because of its high profitability.

AVC/LDC model implementation and Basel II. The new Basel capital accord bears sufficient resemblance to AVC/LDC modelling to merit quick comment here. In its current form, Basel II dispenses with AVC estimation – AVC is fixed at 4% for qualified revolving exposures. This figure compares favourably to those from most empirical studies (or at least more favourably than earlier versions), though it is perhaps a bit conservative. Until such a time as the Basel II framework permits own estimates of AVC, however, this seems a reasonable approach.

It is in its application that Basel II deviates somewhat from internal card capital models. Basel II seems focused on tying going-forward PD, LGD and EAD estimates to historically demonstrable, longer-term estimates. The Basel II framework also layers conservatism into the assessment of these parameters. Internal economic capital models are able to exploit historical data in a more refined way, supporting estimates of PD, LGD and EAD that best reflect going-forward conditions. One should not make too much of this distinction, though, particularly since regulators may well look for a convergence in approaches and estimates over time. It just bears noting that card capital modellers will need to find a well-balanced means of serving both internal and external capital modelling needs.

THE IMPLICATIONS OF REVOLVING TRUST SECURITISATION ON CARD CAPITAL NEEDS

The prominent place that securitisation occupies in the card capital debate might seem odd to those unfamiliar with the structure of card securitisations. For most asset classes, true sale to a trust or other party includes the full transference of risk. The credit risk capital burden of residential and commercial real estate loans, participations and corporate bonds leaves with these assets when they are transferred to a securitising trust, even if the originating institution is also the master servicer. The unique card securitisation structure makes for a more complex situation. A detailed description of these structures is not possible here, but I highlight two issues fundamental to the assessment of capital need.[10] Very generally, the open question is whether issuers should hold capital against that portion of investors' interest collateralising bonds held by third parties.[11] Two related features of revolving trusts have a bearing on this issue: implicit recourse and early amortisation.

Implicit recourse. It is widely agreed that the transfer of card receivables into a revolving trust constitutes a true sale. The actions of a few bankruptcy courts notwithstanding, there is no legal basis for the issuer to claim beneficial ownership of the investors' interest.[12] Losses incurred among trust collateral are legally required to flow into the structure waterfall. Once they are in the waterfall, there is no legal means of diverting losses back to the issuer. Third-party investors have no explicit recourse to the issuer if losses flow through to their positions.

Some observers worry that issuers might act in a way that provides implicit recourse to investors. Revolving trusts are somewhat unique in that the issuer constantly blends new collateral into the existing trust. Issuers can respond to deteriorating trust performance by substituting higher-quality collateral for failing assets. In this way, the burden of unexpected loss among the investor's interest is shifted back to the issuer. The record on implicit recourse is somewhat ambiguous (see Higgins and Mason, 2003), but, as this issue becomes better understood, the ability of regulated entities to prop up their trusts becomes more remote. Regulators are sensitive to the presence or even appearance of implicit recourse, and the implications of an unfavourable ruling in this regard are severe.[13] And, as described below, issuers have at best a dubious incentive to implicitly support investors.

Early amortisation. Some readers may find the preceding discussion of implicit recourse puzzling: why would a lender want to surreptitiously appropriate losses for which they have no legal responsibility? The answer lies in the early amortisation provision of revolving trusts. If trust performance deteriorates below certain trigger levels, investor principal is repaid on an accelerated amortisation schedule; the trust, in effect, starts to unwind. But, whereas the trust and its issued bonds start receding, the underlying collateral – outstanding credit card balances – does not. As the trust amortises, the issuer must immediately arrange alternative financing for account balances, a highly unattractive prospect for a number of reasons. First, these assets are presumably underperforming if trust performance triggered early amortisation, so financing terms might be onerous. Second, alternative means of financing such as equity issuance, note issuance and deposits are less capital-efficient than securitisation. The lender might be forced to raise capital at precisely the point when "headline" risk is most palpable. Early amortisation heightens issuer funding needs at precisely the moment they are least able to raise additional funds. For this reason, issuers might conceivably go to great lengths – including providing implicit recourse – to avoid triggering early amortisation.

While the danger of early amortisation is real, it is fundamentally a risk of *liquidity*, not *credit*. Unexpected credit loss might help trigger early amortisation, but those losses are shared among the issuer and investors as anticipated by the waterfall structure. Once early amortisation commences, funding, not credit performance, is the issuer's primary concern. In this regard, early amortisation is not dissimilar from other liquidity crises a lender might face.

Liquidity management – funding source diversity, backup lines of credit and a strong capital market presence – not capital, seems the best instrument for addressing the risk of early amortisation. Stated another way, early amortisation is not an insolvency risk if the issuer can obtain alternative funding. In sum, early amortisation provides no rationale for holding credit risk capital against the investor's interest. Credit risk capital must be held if the lender props up the Trust under the spectre of early amortisation, but solid liquidity management and legal trust oversight can disrupt the motivation and means of doing so. Practice in this regard seems split: some institutions calculate credit risk capital need on their entire managed book, while others exclude investor's interest from analysis. Those taking the managed view do so as much for convenience and conservatism, and as a means of representing liquidity risk, as they do for conceptually capturing the credit risk capital needs of off-balance-sheet assets.

CONCLUSIONS AND FUTURE DIRECTIONS

Credit card portfolios are sufficiently unique to require the awareness of capital modellers. Some of the peculiarities of this asset class – undrawn lines, margin, funding issues – were considered here and should be addressed in any capital modelling effort. Various models of unexpected credit loss might be applied to card portfolios, but the AVC/LDC approach is particularly well-suited to this asset class. There is real hope that this modelling approach can form the basis of an industry discourse that yields better data, information, benchmarks, and techniques for capital modellers.

Looking forward, three issues might stimulate additional research in this area. First, the correspondence between internal capital models and Basel II regulatory capital requirements will be a key research focus. Researchers need to reconcile their Basel II and capital models to identify products and portfolios that might drive a wedge between the two. A second issue that requires additional research focus is the risk-transference of off-balance sheet securitisation. While the concepts developed in the fourth section argue that credit risk is transferred in the absence of implicit recourse, the empirical performance of off-balance sheet Trusts might provide additional colour. Finally, researchers might push for a more sophisticated understanding of the role margin plays in capital policy. Addressing these and other outstanding issues will continue the evolution of capital treatment for this unique and complex asset class.

1 Imprecision in the AVC/LDC translation is less than one basis point for segments with 100,000 distinct credits, about 10 basis points for segments with 1,000 distinct credits, and more than 100 basis points for segments with only 100 distinct credits.

2 "Retail Credit Economic Capital Estimation – Best Practices", *The Risk Management Association*, February, 2003. Eight of twelve respondents noted that they use AVC/LDC models and some of the remaining few indicated that they intended to migrate towards this approach in the future.

3 This type of model is developed in Perli and Nayda (2004).

4 A recent industry study, "Industry Practices in Estimating EAD and LGD for Revolving Consumer Credit", Risk Management Association, March 2004, identified FICO scores, proprietary scores, delinquency status, borrower type, product type, seasoning, balance, limit and utilisation as the bases of portfolio segmentation.

5 For each month between January 2000 and December 2002, twelve months of subsequent loss data are available for analysis.

6 One can also measure the proportion of accounts that defaulted over the month of January and then annualise that monthly figure, but temporal card default structure poses difficulties in this regard. In particular, annualised monthly default might differ markedly from annual default rates. Consider accounts in bucket four of a six-bucket delinquency ladder; few of those loans will default in the coming month although a huge portion will default in the coming year. This structure can be accommodated in a careful statistical study, but the measurement of annual default rates is a more natural approach.

7 If loans in the sample were perfectly homogeneous the dollar-weighted and unweighted default rates would be identical. In fact, a comparison of these two default measures can help evaluate the discriminatory power of the segmentation scheme.

8 As described below, Basel II anticipates a convergence among datasets and techniques that support both historical segmenting and forward-looking PD assessment.

9 In "Industry Practices in Estimating EAD and LGD for Revolving Consumer Credit" (March 2004), *the Risk Management Association* suggests that institutions are even split in using the first two methods to model EAD.

10 For a primer on revolving securitisations, see "ABC's of Credit Card ABS", Fitch Investors Service, 1997.

11 The need for issuers to hold capital against seller's interest (the portion of trust collateral still owned by the issuer) and the portion of investor's interest they retain (AIR, recourse, first-loss positions) is less controversial.

12 The case of the LTV Steel Corporation securitisation and a few other trusts are considered in Dill and Accarrino (2002).

13 When regulators determined that NextCard inappropriately defined losses in their trust in a way that suggested recourse, they immediately terminated regulatory capital relief for the investor's interest, setting off a chain of events that led to NextCard's failure.

REFERENCES

Dill, A., and L. Accarrino, 2002, "Bullet Proof Structures Revisited: Bankruptcies and a Market Hangover Test Securitisations' Mettle", Moody's Investors Service, August.

Hall, P., 1992, *The Bootstrap and Edgeworth Expansion* (New York: Springer).

Higgins, E., and J. Mason, 2003, "What is the Value of Recourse to Asset Backed Securities? A Clinical Study of Credit Card Banks", Federal Reserve Bank of Philadelphia, April.

Hjorth, J., 1994, *Computer Intensive Statistical Models* (London: Chapman & Hall).

Miller, R. M., 1998, "A Nonparametric Test for Credit Rating Refinements", *Risk*, August.

Perli, P., and W. Nayda, 2004, "Economic and Regulatory Capital Allocation for Revolving Retail Exposures", *Journal of Banking and Finance*, April.

Risk Management Association, 2003, "Retail Credit Economic Capital Estimation – Best Practices," February.

Rosch, D., and H. Scheule, "Forecasting Retail Portfolio Credit Risk", Forthcoming, *Journal of Risk Finance*.

7

Economic Capital for Counterparty Credit Risk

Evan Picoult; David Lamb

Citigroup; Morgan Stanley

COUNTERPARTY CREDIT EXPOSURE

Economic capital (EC) is a measurement of economic risk from an insolvency perspective. The measurement of EC for counterparty credit risk is conceptually more difficult than it is for a loan portfolio for three reasons: (a) the uncertainty in the future credit exposure, (b) the bilateral nature of counterparty credit exposure (ie, each party to a forward or swap has potential credit exposure to the other) and (c) the challenge of defining the credit value adjustment (CVA) to take into account the effect of market spreads on the market value of a derivative portfolio with a counterparty.

This chapter has five sections: (1) an introduction to issues surrounding the measurement of counterparty exposure and counterparty risk; (2) a description of the method for measuring a counterparty's credit exposure profile on a portfolio basis; (3) a summary of the fundamental issues for measuring EC for a loan portfolio from a potential default-only and a potential loss-of-economic-value perspective; (4) a description of the method for measuring EC for counterparty risk from a potential default-only perspective; (5) a description of the method for measuring EC for counterparty risk from a potential loss-of-economic-value perspective. The last requires the definition of both the unilateral and bilateral measurement of the CVA, a discussion of which definition of the CVA is appropriate in what context and an analysis of how changes in the CVA should be incorporated into the measurement of EC.[1]

INTRODUCTION
Definition of counterparty exposure and risk
Counterparty risk is the risk that the counterparty to a trade or trades could default *before* the final settlement of the transaction's cashflows. An economic loss would occur if the contract (or portfolio of contracts) with the counterparty has a positive economic value at the time of default.

Potential counterparty risk
Like all other forms of credit risk, the precipitating cause of a loss is the risk that an obligor will be unable or unwilling to meet its contractual obligations. The potential credit exposure that a firm may have to each of its counterparties at each future date will depend on the market value of the contracts with the counterparty at that future date, the effect on exposure of any legally enforceable risk-mitigating agreements (such as netting, margin and/or optional early-termination agreements) and some other factors discussed below. The primary distinguishing features of counterparty risk relative to other forms of credit risk is that the magnitude (and the sign) of the credit exposure to a counterparty on any future date is uncertain. It will depend on the market value of the contracts with the counterparty on that future date, which will depend on the potential future state of the market, which cannot be known with certainty today.

The exposure profile is the potential exposure to a counterparty at a set of future dates over the life of the portfolio, measured at a specified confidence level. The potential exposure at any confidence level is best represented as an exposure profile rather than a single number because: (a) the remaining unsettled cashflows with a counterparty will contractually change over time as floating rates are set, options expire and cashflows settle and (b) the potential range or probability distribution of each underlying market rate tends to widen the further out into the future one looks.

The assessment of the potential future exposure is conditional on the current composition of the portfolio, the current state of the market and the volatilities and correlations used in the simulation of future states of the market. Consequently, a counterparty's exposure profile needs to be recalculated on a regular basis (ideally at least once a day) to reflect (a) changes in the composition of the portfolio, (b) material changes in the current level of market rates, (c) material changes in the volatility or correlation assumptions that underlie the simulation.

As a consequence, the measurement of EC for counterparty risk has to begin with a delineation of the measurement of the potential credit exposure to a counterparty over time. There are four reasons for describing the method for measuring counterparty exposure before describing methods for measuring EC for counterparty risk:

❑ the measurement of the credit risk rests on the measurement of credit exposure.
❑ more particularly, one measure of potential credit exposure, the EPE profile, is a useful "loan equivalent" for calculating EC when scaled by the appropriate factor.
❑ the EPE profile is also a key component of the CVA. The CVA is the difference between the risk-free value of a derivative portfolio with a counterparty and the value after taking counterparty credit risk into account. Potential changes in the CVA of each counterparty are a key component of the potential loss of the economic value of the portfolio – ie, a key component of EC from an economic loss perspective.
❑ the portfolio issues involved in calculating the potential exposure of a single counterparty are a subset of the larger portfolio issues in calculating EC across all counterparties.

Types of firms that have counterparty risk

The parties that enter into derivative contracts have a range of characteristics. At two extremes are simple end-users and very large market-makers:

❑ the simplest end-user will enter into one or at most a few derivative contracts to hedge a single market rate (eg, the US dollar–Japanese yen exchange rate). If this firm enters into more than one derivative contract, these contracts will be in a single direction (eg, to hedge the risk of a fall in the yen) for roughly the same tenor.

❑ at the opposite end of the spectrum, a very large derivative market-maker will enter into a multitude of types of OTC derivative contracts (eg, forwards, swaps, options) on a very large set of underlying market rates (eg, yield curves, spot exchange rates, equity indices, specific equities, the credit risk of specific obligors, commodity prices), in different directions (buying and selling), for different tenors, with a large number of counterparties.

❑ market participants may have characteristics that fall in between a simple end-user and the very large derivative market-marker.

As we shall see, the nature of the portfolio of the counterparty is part of the context that needs to be assessed in ascertaining the most appropriate method to measure counterparty exposure and EC for counterparty risk.

Contrasting lending risk and counterparty credit risk

Counterparty credit exposure and credit risk materially differs from loan portfolio exposure in several important respects:

❑ the market value of a forward or swap with a counterparty could potentially be positive or negative, depending on the future state of the market. Consequently, unlike a loan, either party to a forward or a swap could potentially have a credit loss to the other. This complicates the assessment of the proper cost of credit risk, since counterparty risk is often bilateral (ie, depending on the future state of the market, either party could have a credit loss if the other defaulted).

❑ as described above, the magnitude of the current exposure (CE) to a counterparty on a future date will depend on the future state of the market, which we cannot know with certainty today. The potential future exposure to a counterparty can best be described *statistically*, as a potential exposure profile over time, measured at some high confidence level. In contrast, the exposure of a bullet loan is certain.

❑ for a very large derivative market-maker, with multiple counterparties, not every derivative counterparty may have a positive exposure at the same time. For example, some simple end-user counterparties may have transactions that are in offsetting directions to the trades of other end-users (eg, some counterparties may want protection for a decrease in the yen, others for an increase in the yen). In contrast, a bank has credit exposure to all of its loan obligors at the same time.

❑ various types of legally enforceable, risk-mitigating agreements such as netting, margin and/or optional early-termination agreements can materially reduce potential exposure and risk and need to be included in the simulation of these quantities.

MEASURING COUNTERPARTY EXPOSURE

The first step to measure EC for counterparty risk is to identify the method for simulating the potential exposure to each counterparty over time. A second step is to identify the method for measuring the EC for counterparty risk from either a potential default-only or a potential loss-of-economic-value perspective. In essence, the calculation of EC for counterparty risk will require a double *level of simulation:*

❑ the simulation of potential exposure due to the potential changes in market rates; and

❑ the simulation of the types of credit events (eg, default, recovery, changes in the CVA of non-defaulted counterparties) associated with default or the loss of economic value short of default.

Let us begin with a description of a method for measuring the potential credit exposure of a counterparty with multiple transactions.

Current counterparty exposure

The CE or immediate exposure to a counterparty is the current replacement cost of the contracts with the counterparty if the counterparty were to immediately default. For a counterparty with many transaction, CE will be a function of the market value of each contract and the effect of any legally enforceable risk-mitigating agreements with the counterparty, such as netting and margin. Ignoring the effect of margin for the time being, we have:

CE under a *legally enforceable netting agreement* k, summed over all contracts, j, covered by netting agreement k.

$$CE_{\text{netting } k} = \max\left(\sum_j PV_{j,k}, 0\right) \quad (1)$$

Where $PV_{j,k}$ is the current market value of contract j covered by netting agreement k.

CE for contracts with the counterparty *without a legally enforceable netting agreement*, summed over all contracts j not covered by any legally enforceable netting agreement:[2]

$$CE_{\text{no netting}} = \sum_j \max\left(PV_j, 0\right) \qquad (2)$$

A large derivative market-maker may have many contracts with a counterparty, transacted in the same legal jurisdiction (eg, New York to New York) and across legal jurisdictions (eg, Hong Kong to Jakarta). As a result the large set of transactions with a counterparty may entail several separate legally enforceable netting agreements and a set of contracts with no netting agreement. The more general form of CE will then be:

$$CE_{\text{total for counterparty}} = \sum_k \max\left(\sum_j PV_{j,k}, 0\right) + \sum_j \max\left(PV_j, 0\right) \qquad (3)$$

The first summation is across each legally enforceable netting agreement k; the embedded summation is across all contracts, j, covered by netting agreement k; and the last summation is across all contracts without a netting agreement.

The CE can also be reduced by legally enforceable margin agreements. In the US and some other countries, assets posted as margin have a different legal status than more general assets posted as collateral. For example, one of the conditions necessary for a margin agreement to be legally enforceable is that no stay can be placed on the assets posted as margin in the event of counterparty default. As a consequence, assets currently posted as margin (and potentially posted in the future) can be viewed as reducing the current (and potential future) exposure to the counterparty. In contrast, assets posted as collateral are generally viewed as leaving exposure unchanged while reducing risk solely by reducing the loss-given default (LGD).

The cash value of the margin on hand (after taking haircuts into account for non-cash assets) will depend on several factors, such as the frequency with which margin is required to be posted, the magnitude of the threshold above which margin must be posted, the minimum transfer amount and other factors. Let us designate the current cash value of the margin on hand as CCVM.

Let us assume that every margin agreement requires a netting agreement whereas netting agreements can be entered into without a margin agreement. The most general formula for the CE taking margin and netting into account is:

$$CE_{\text{total for counterparty}} = \sum_{m} \max\left(\left(\max\left(\sum_{j} PV_{j,m}, 0\right) - CCVM_{m}\right), 0\right)$$

$$+ \sum_{k} \max\left(\sum_{j} PV_{j,k}, 0\right) + \sum_{j} \max\left(PV_{j}, 0\right) \quad \textbf{(4)}$$

❏ the first set of summations is over all legally enforceable joint margin and netting agreements m.
❏ the second set of summations is over all legally enforceable netting agreements k, without any concurrent margin agreements.
❏ the last summation is across all contracts covered by no netting (or margin) agreement.

Counterparty exposure and potential future replacement cost

To avoid the surprise of a potentially large exposure to a counterparty at a future date, after market rates have dramatically changed, a firm should define and measure its counterparty exposure as a potential exposure profile over the remaining life of the transactions with the counterparty. The need to measure potential exposure over the life of the transactions with the counterparty is most important for longer-tenor OTC derivative contracts that have no margin.

The potential exposure to the counterparty at each future date may be significantly different from the current exposure. As explained above, the potential future exposure is best represented as an exposure profile, measured at some confidence level. The calculation of the exposure profile requires the simulation of the potential value of the current exposure (Equation 4) at a set of future dates. Since the CE at a future date will depend on the state of the market it will tend to have a range of potential values which can best be described statistically.

Naïvely, a value-at-risk (VAR) measurement, as defined for market risk, might seem the best way to measure this potential exposure. However, VAR for market risk normally assumes a static set of market-factor sensitivities and measures the effects on market value of potential changes in market rates.[3] In contrast, the measurement of the potential future credit exposure of a transaction, for a portfolio of transactions with a counterparty, requires that we simulate both the *potential changes in market rates over a long time period* and also the *contractual setting of floating rates, the expiration of options and the settlement of cashflows over time*. Note that the latter is not an attempt to "model trader behaviour" but rather is the modelling of the effect of each transaction's contractual terms and condition over time. Thus, while the measurement of potential counterparty exposure usually does not entail simulating new transactions dynamically, it must simulate the potential changes in sensitivity due to contractual setting of floating rates, expiration of options and settling of cashflows.

In addition, as should be obvious from Equation 4, a robust calculation of a counterparty's potential exposure over time also needs to take into account the effect of all risk-mitigating agreements, such as netting, margin and/or optional early-termination agreements. A robust calculation of potential exposure must therefore also simulate the value of the CCVM of each margin agreement at a set of future dates. In essence, this requires that we simulate the cash value of the margin at hand on each forward date, as if that were the day that the counterparty would be closed out, with collateral being sold and hedges being unwound. This requires that we assume some reasonable "margin period of risk" since the last time margin was posted – ie, the time interval since margin was last posted before the assets posted as margin will be sold and the derivatives with the counterparty replaced in the market.

The two most common ways of measuring potential exposure of a counterparty with multiple transactions are a *simple transaction methodology* and a more precise and sophisticated *portfolio simulation methodology*.

Simple transaction exposure method of measuring counterparty exposure

The best way to represent the potential exposure of each transaction is by the transaction's *exposure profile over time*. A transaction's exposure profile describes its potential replacement cost at a set of future dates, at some confidence level. The exposure profile will tend to vary in magnitude over time, in contrast to the fixed credit exposure of a bullet loan. Because of the number of factors it depends on (the shape of the yield curve, the contracts' detailed specific terms and conditions and so forth), a transaction's exposure profile generally can be precisely calculated only by Monte Carlo simulation.

The simple transaction exposure method defines the counterparty credit exposure of each transaction as the sum of two terms, its current market value and a prudent estimate of its potential increase in the value. The potential increase in value can be expressed either as a time-varying profile over the remaining life of the transaction or, in the simplest method, as a single number (ie, a fixed profile over time). Standardised tables can be defined that approximately represent the potential increase in the value of each transaction per unit of notional principal. Such tables are, of necessity, approximations because they are always derived from the exposure profile of a set of standard transactions calculated under a specific set of plausible market conditions. The terms and conditions of the standard contracts and the assumed plausible market conditions will likely vary somewhat from the actual terms and conditions of the transactions in the portfolio and the actual current state of the market. For example, standardised tables may be calculated by assuming a particular shape of the yield curve that often will differ from the yield curve's current shape.

The simplest transaction exposure method makes the additional approximation of condensing a transaction's time-varying exposure profile into a single number. That number might be the peak or the average of the transaction's exposure profile over time, calculated under some standard conditions, as described above.

In the simple transaction method (whether the potential increase in value is represented by a fixed or a time-varying profile) the total exposure of a counterparty with many transactions is calculated simply as the sum of each transaction's potential exposure. This method is flawed because it ignores portfolio effects.

There are two basic shortcomings inherent in the simple transaction method:

1. Any practical implementation of the simple transaction method will rest on the calculation and firm wide dissemination of tables of the potential increase in the value of each transaction. These tables invariably employ approximations to make them simple to implement, as described above.

2. A more fundamental limitation of the simple transaction exposure method is its inability to accurately *calculate* and *represent* the potential exposure of a portfolio of multiple contracts with a single counterparty. *Under the simple transaction exposure method the total exposure of a portfolio of many contracts with a counterparty is simply the sum of each contract's potential exposure.* There are several flaws in such a calculation of portfolio exposure:

❑ for the simplest transaction exposure method, which reduces the potential exposure to one number, a problem occurs when a counterparty has transactions with different tenors. The peak exposure of each transaction's exposure profile would occur at different times. As a consequence, the sum of each transaction's potential peak exposure, for example, tends to overestimate (sometimes dramatically) the potential peak exposure of the portfolio.

❑ when a counterparty has forwards and derivatives on several underlying market rates, it is unlikely that changes in these market rates will be perfectly correlated. Adding up the potential exposure of each transaction, calculated in isolation, ignores the diversification of having transactions with sensitivity to different market rates.

❑ the counterparty may have done transactions in offsetting directions. Consequently, it may not be possible for all transactions with the counterparty to increase in value at the same time. This is a critically important issue even if there is no netting agreement. For example, for perfectly offsetting transactions, at any future time both transactions will not concurrently have an increase in market value.

❑ the simple portfolio method cannot properly calculate the effect of a netting agreement.

In summary, the exposure profile of a counterparty will tend to be less, and potentially dramatically less, then the sum of the potential exposure of each transaction. The shape of the exposure profile to the counterparty will tend to be very different from the arithmetic sum of the shapes of the potential exposure of each transaction.

For a simple end-user with only a few transactions in the same direction, portfolio diversification is not a material issue. Consequently, the simple transaction method of calculating potential exposure will not be a bad approximation. In contrast, for a large market-marker with many transactions, in either direction, on many underlying market rates, the simple method will be grossly inaccurate. Portfolio simulation is the only accurate method for measuring the potential exposure of such obligors.

Counterparty portfolio simulation method and counterparty exposure profile

Citibank developed a portfolio simulation method for calculating a counterparty's pre-settlement exposure in 1991.[4] The essence of the simulation method is described below:

1. Simulate thousands of scenarios of changes in market factors over time

For each simulated scenario, begin with the current level of market rates. It is necessary to simulate as many market rates as are required to value the contracts in the portfolio. For a large financial firm this may require simulating thousands or tens of thousands of market rates.

Each simulated scenario should consist of a simulation of the potential value of market rates at a set of future dates. For example, start with today's market rates and simulate market rates at each day over the next week, each week over the next month and each month over many years (depending on the types of contracts traded this might be ten or more years).

The simulation of long-term changes in market rates can be done with varying levels of sophistication and subtlety. At a minimum it should take into account the long-term volatilities and correlations of all simulated market rates and should make some explicit assumption regarding the relationship between the expected spot rate at a future date and the current forward rate for that date.

*2. Calculate the potential market value of each transaction
at each future date of each simulated path*

For each simulated path: *calculate the simulated market value of each contract* at the current date and at each future date for which market factors are simulated. The simulated market value at each future date will depend on the revaluation algorithm appropriate to the contract, the contract's terms and conditions, the number of remaining unrealised cashflows of the contract and the particular path over time that market rates had been simulated for that scenario (which will affect how floating rates were set, etc).

*3. Calculate the potential exposure of each counterparty at
each future date of each simulated path*

For each simulated path, at each simulated future date, employ the appropriate aggregation rules (such as described in Equation 4) to transform the simulated market value of each contract into the simulated exposure of the portfolio of transactions with the counterparty. The aggregation rules need to take the legal context into account, including the effect on exposure of any enforceable risk mitigants that have been entered into, such as netting agreements, margin agreements or optional early termination agreements.

4. Calculate the counterparty's exposure profile

The exposure profile of a counterparty is the potential future exposure, calculated at some confidence level at a set of future dates, starting with the current exposure calculated today. The exposure profile is defined in the context of the existing set of forwards and derivatives transacted with the counterparty, the risk-mitigating legal agreements that have been entered into and the assumptions and methods underlying the long-term simulation of changes in market factors. An example of a counterparty's exposure profile is shown in Figure 1. The exposure profile measures the potential exposure of the current set of transactions and assumes no additional transactions with the counterparty. Figure 1 shows a hypothetical exposure profile for a counterparty.

For the purpose of monitoring and limiting the potential credit exposure to a counterparty, the exposure profile should be calculated at a high confidence level, eg, the 99%CL. For other purposes (see below) the EPE profile should be calculated. The EPE profile

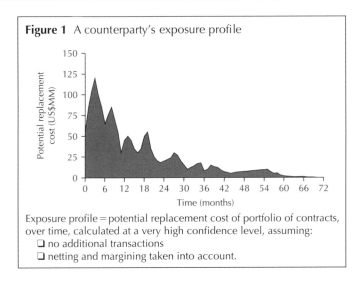

Figure 1 A counterparty's exposure profile

Exposure profile = potential replacement cost of portfolio of contracts, over time, calculated at a very high confidence level, assuming:
❏ no additional transactions
❏ netting and margining taken into account.

is defined as the average positive exposure at a set of future dates t:

$$EPE_t = \text{Expected}\left(\max\left(\text{Exposure}_t, 0\right)\right) \quad (5)$$

where Exposure_t is the simulated exposure at future time t.

EC FOR A LOAN PORTFOLIO
Definition of EC
EC is a measure of risk. It is the potential *unexpected loss (UL) of economic value* of a portfolio or business, over some *long time horizon* (eg, one year), at some *high confidence level* (eg, 99.97%CL). EC can be defined for a *specific risk type* or across the *full range of risk types* of a business. It can be calculated at different organisational levels of a firm on a standalone or marginal basis.

As illustrated in Figure 2, EC is derived from the calculation of the probability distribution of potential loss over some time horizon. Two key features of a loss distribution are the expected loss (EL) and the UL, where UL is defined as the difference between the potential loss at a high confidence level (eg, 99.97%CL) and the EL. EC is the UL measured at a specified confidence level.

EC depends on the shape of the potential loss distribution and the confidence level at which the UL is measured. All other things

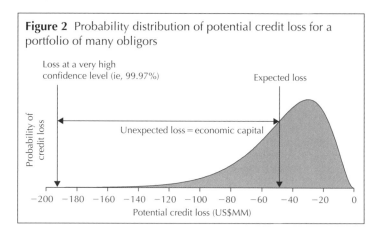

Figure 2 Probability distribution of potential credit loss for a portfolio of many obligors

held constant, the *wider the width of the potential loss distribution* (ie, the more uncertainty in the amount of the potential loss) the *larger will be the EC*. The shape of the potential loss distribution will depend on several things: (a) the type of risk (eg, market risk, loan portfolio credit risk, counterparty credit risk, operational risk), (b) the definition of loss (eg, economic loss vs accounting loss), (c) the time horizon over which the potential loss distribution is simulated (eg, one year, three years, lifetime of portfolio), (d) the degree of *concentration* or *diversification* of risk exposure of the underlying portfolio, (e) the assumptions underlying the simulation of future states of the drivers of potential loss.

EC for loans

Before describing how to measure EC for counterparty risk, it is worth summarising the definition and calculation of EC for lending risk. This will lay a necessary foundation for the discussion of counterparty credit risk and will also enable us to highlight the unique features of EC for counterparty risk by contrasting it with that of loans.

EC for a portfolio of loans can be measured from two different perspectives of loss: a *default-only* perspective or an *economic-loss* perspective. A default-only perspective measures the potential loss due to default and recovery. An economic-loss perspective measures not only the potential loss due to default but also the potential decrease in the imputed market value of the loan portfolio that did not default, from changes in general and idiosyncratic (ie issuer-specific) market spreads.

The observed (or imputed) market value or fair value of a loan will depend on the observed (or imputed) market spread of the obligor and on the base rate (eg, Libor or Treasury). One must, however, differentiate between the fundamental market factors that determine the market value of a loan and the method used to simulate changes in those factors over long time horizons. The simulation of changes in spreads over long periods of time, such as the one-year horizon used to calculate EC, is often segmented into components because long time series of spreads are usually specified as a function of the obligor's credit risk rating. The long-term simulation of obligor spread can thus be generated in terms of:

❑ the simulation of changes in credit rating via a transaction matrix, which includes the simulation of a jump to default;
❑ the simulation of changes in general market spreads for each credit rating; and
❑ the simulation of changes in an obligor's idiosyncratic spread, given the simulated rating and the simulated general spread associated with that rating.

Thus, although market value is driven by spreads, changes in spreads over long periods of time can be simulated as the sum of several components, including ratings, as described above.

To measure the potential loss distribution of a loan portfolio over a one-year horizon, from a *default-only* perspective, one needs to simulate hundreds of thousands of scenarios of potential defaults and recoveries of the loan portfolio over some time horizon, such as a year. For a given time horizon, the width (and hence the EC) of the loss distribution will be driven by several factors:

❑ uncertainty in how many obligors will default over the specified time horizon.
❑ uncertainty in which obligors will default over the specified time horizon. This matters particularly if there is inhomogeneity in the obligor exposures (ie, if some obligors have small exposure and some have very large exposures). The lumpier the portfolio (eg, the more risk concentration in a few obligors), the wider will be the loss distribution.

❑ uncertainty in how much will be lost from each obligor in the event of default. The loss should be simulated from a distribution of potential LGDs for each type of risk mitigant. To avoid a double count, a risk mitigant (such as a legally enforceable netting or margin agreement) that reduces exposure should not also reduce the LGD.

❑ the correlation of default between obligors.

A simple method for simulating the changes in the credit risk (and the default) of each obligor is to model the risk in terms of a component dependent on the general state of the economy and an idiosyncratic component specific to the obligor. In a well-diversified portfolio, with no material concentration of obligor risk, the marginal contribution of the idiosyncratic component of credit risk to total economic risk will decrease as the number of obligors increases. In this model, in the limit of many obligors, the total economic risk (and EC) of the portfolio will depend on one general factor (ie, the state of the economy) and the correlation of each obligor's credit risk to that factor. The default-only component of EC in Basel II is modelled in this way, as the asymptotic limit of a model in which a single common factor drives defaults.

The assumptions underlying the Basel II default calculation (an infinitely diversified portfolio with one common factor driving defaults) is reasonable for a large retail credit portfolio in a single country – ie, a credit card portfolio in the US with tens of millions of obligors, each with small exposures. These assumptions are not reasonable for an international retail portfolio, where there will be a large set of factors (ie, the state of each economy in which the portfolio has exposure) driving defaults, and the size of the portfolio in each country may not be large enough to ignore idiosyncratic risk.

It is most particularly not a reasonable approximation for corporate loan portfolios or portfolios of counterparty credit risk. Such portfolios tend to have most of their credit risk to relatively few obligors (ie, typically most of the exposure is attributable to at most a few hundred, rather than tens of millions, of obligors) and the exposure per obligor is not homogeneous. We will return to this issue below when we discuss the appropriate "loan equivalent" for counterparty risk.

To measure the potential loss distribution of a loan portfolio over a one-year horizon, from an economic-value perspective, one needs to simulate changes in the imputed market value (ie, the fair value) of the loan portfolio over time. For a corporate loan portfolio this will require the simulation of not only defaults and recoveries but also the simulation of potential changes in the economic value of non-defaulted obligors, due to changes in market spreads (general and idiosyncratic).

There are several ways of simulating the potential loss distribution from a default-only perspective or an economic value perspective, which will not be described in this chapter.

EC FOR COUNTERPARTY RISK – POTENTIAL DEFAULT-ONLY PERSPECTIVE

As explained above, the EC for counterparty credit risk is derived from the probability distribution of potential loss, as illustrated in Figure 2.

An essential difference between the potential loss distribution due to lending risk and the potential loss distribution due to counterparty risk is the uncertain exposure of the latter. If the future state of market rates could be known with certainty the credit exposure arising from counterparty risk would be known with certainty. Under that condition, we would have certainty about the magnitude and value of all future cashflows between each counterparty and our firm. Consequently, measuring EC for counterparty credit risk would be no different from measuring it for loans: given our assumed omniscience about future market rates, we would know exactly how much credit exposure (if any) we had to each counterparty at each future time.

Of course, we do not know what the future state of markets will be. However, for each simulated path the market could take over time, we could measure the corresponding exposure (if any) we would have to each counterparty at each future point in time. Consequently, whether we define credit loss from a default-only perspective or a loss-of-economic-value perspective, for each simulated path of market rates over time we can calculate a potential loss distribution for forwards and derivatives using the same principles developed to measure the potential loss distribution of loans. The final total loss distribution due to

counterparty risk would be the sum of the loss distributions calculated over all future states, where each future state is a joint
path over time of the state of the market and the credit state of
the counterparty.

EC for counterparty risk – default only, full simulation
To calculate EC for counterparty risk under a default only perspective we need to follow these steps:

*1. Simulate thousands of paths of changes in market
factors over time*
This step is identical to the first step in calculating a counterparty
exposure profile on a portfolio basis.

*2. For each simulated path of the market, calculate the potential
exposure to each counterparty, at many future dates*
This is identical to the second and third steps in the calculation of
a counterparty's exposure profile on a portfolio basis, as described
above.

*3. For each simulated path of the market, calculate
potential loss by simulating counterparty defaults,
at many future dates*
In more detail, for each simulated path of the market we can generate thousands of simulations of potential defaults and recoveries
of counterparties over time. Each simulation of potential default
would be similar to what is done for lending risk: at each future
date of the simulation we would randomly make a draw to determine how many counterparties were simulated to default and
make another draw to ascertain which counterparties were simulated to default. For each defaulted counterparty a loss could occur
if our firm had a simulated positive exposure to the counterparty
at that point in time. If a default was simulated and the counterparty had a positive exposure we would also simulate the LGD.
The result of tens of thousands of simulations of defaults and
recoveries, for each simulated path of the market, would be a probability distribution of potential loss. Note that, for a given path of
the market, not every counterparty simulated to default will have
a positive exposure.

4. Repeat the simulation of potential defaults and recoveries
for each stimulated path of market rates

By taking into account many potential paths of market rates we introduce another stochastic element into the calculation of the final loss distribution due to counterparty exposure.

5. Calculate the final loss distribution by appropriately aggregating
the potential loss distribution for each simulated future state, eg,
for the joint path over time of market rates and the state of the
counterparty (ie, either no-default or default and recovery)

EC from a default-only perspective would then be derived from the loss distribution by measuring its UL at the appropriate confidence level.

EC for counterparty risk – default-only using loan equivalent

The method of calculating EC for counterparty risk described above is a "full simulation" method in that it entails the *joint simulation* of potential changes in exposure and in default and recovery. One could ask if it is possible to define a "loan equivalent" for EC for counterparty risk. In other words, can we define a *fixed-exposure profile* for each counterparty, such that the EC calculated under the simulation of defaults and recoveries (but without simulating changes in exposure) is identical to the EC calculated under full simulation? Note that this definition of loan equivalent would not require an identical loss distribution, only the same EC at the specified confidence level.

One could ask if the loan equivalent for EC could be defined as the EPE profile of the counterparty (ie, the average positive exposure of the counterparty at a set of future dates). One of the problems of using the EPE is that it ignores the contribution to EC from the uncertainty of the potential exposure. As explained above, all sources of uncertainty in exposure and default increase the width of the potential loss distribution and thus increase the EC. On the other hand, for a large market-maker, not all counterparties will have a positive exposure at the same time. Consequently it is not self-evident how good the EPE is for the calculation of EC – ie, the ratio of the EC calculated with full simulation divided by the EC calculated using an EPE is not obvious.

Two years ago one of the authors of this chapter (Picoult) wrote a proposal to an ISDA working group that recommended that we define a quantity called "alpha", a scaling factor to transform the EPE into a good loan equivalent. Picoult defined alpha as the ratio of two quantities A/B, where:

❑ A = the EC for counterparty risk measured with full simulation, as described above; and
❑ B = the EC for counterparty risk measured assuming a constant exposure profile for each counterparty equal to its EPE.

Picoult proposed that alpha should be measured as a function of various characteristics of a firm's counterparty portfolio, ie, alpha should be measured as a function of:

❑ the effective number of independent counterparties;
❑ the effective number of independent market rates that affect potential exposure;
❑ the default probability of each counterparty; and
❑ the correlation of default across counterparties.

The goal was to see if alpha could be reasonably defined for a typical large derivative market-maker.

Within the ISDA working group, Eduardo Canabarro (then at Goldman Sachs) developed a very efficient simulation method, making use of "stylised transactions", for measuring alpha as a function of the characteristics of the counterparty's portfolio. Tom Wilde (Credit Suisse First Boston) was able to replicate Eduardo's simulation results analytically. Here is a high level summary of our findings (see Canabarro, Picoult and Wilde, 2003):

❑ in the limit of a very large portfolio, with highly diversified exposure to an unlimited number of counterparties and an unlimited number of independent market rates, alpha will equal 1.0 and the EPE is an exact value of the loan equivalent.
❑ for more realistic portfolios of large derivative market-marker, who are have exposure to a large but realistic number of effective counterparties and effective market rates, alpha will equal about 1.10.
❑ for end-users with only a few counterparties and exposure to only one or two market factors, alpha will be higher.

EC for counterparty risk – other issues

The above discussion assumed there was zero correlation between the potential future state of market rates and the probability of a counterparty's defaulting. In general that is a reasonable thing to assume for most derivative transactions. However, under some circumstances the correlation between changes in market rates (potential exposure) and counterparty default are clearly non-zero. Throughout this chapter we have assumed a correlation of zero between default and changes in exposure. A more general treatment would take into account such non-zero correlations into account where appropriate.

EC FOR COUNTERPARTY RISK – POTENTIAL LOSS-OF-ECONOMIC-VALUE PERSPECTIVE

The calculation of the probability distribution of the potential loss of economic value of a corporate loan portfolio entailed the simulation of default, recovery and the potential change in value due to changes in market spreads. The calculation of a similar loss distribution for counterparty credit risk requires the identification of how the market value of a portfolio of derivatives with a counterparty is affected by changes in general and counterparty-specific market spreads.

For many years the derivative portfolios of commercial banks were marked-to-market independent of the credit rating or market spread of the counterparty. For example, a portfolio of US$ Libor interest rate swaps would have been marked-to-market by discounting all future cashflows at Libor, with no adjustment for the credit risk of the counterparty.

In the early 1990s some investment banks began to make a CVA to take into account the counterparty's credit risk (see Sorensen and Bollier, 1994).

$$\text{MV}_{\text{counterparty}\_k} = \sum_j \text{PV}_{\text{risk free, } j} - \text{CVA}_k \qquad (6)$$

where the summation is over all derivative transactions with counterparty k.

The CVA is thus the difference between the risk-free market value of the portfolio of derivatives with the counterparty and the smaller market value that results from taking credit risk into account.

To identify how the CVA should be defined, let us examine the definition of the equivalent CVA for a corporate bond:

The market value of a single corporate bond can be written:

$$\begin{aligned}
MV_{bond} &= MV_{bond,\,risk\,free} - CVA_{bond} \\
&= \sum_m Bond\ cash\ flow_m \times e^{-\left(r_{m,\,risk\,free} \times t_m\right)} - CVA_{bond} \\
&= \sum_m Bond\ cash\ flow_m \times e^{-\left(\left(r_{m,\,risk\,free} + Spread_{bond}\right) \times t_m\right)}
\end{aligned} \tag{7}$$

Therefore, to a first-order approximation, the CVA of a corporate bond is:

$$\begin{aligned}
CVA_{bond} &= \sum_m Bond\ cash\ flow_m \times e^{-r_{m,\,risk\,free}} \times t_m \times Spread_{bond} \\
&= MV_{bond,risk\,free} \times Spread_{bond} \times Duration_{bond}
\end{aligned} \tag{8}$$

where $MV_{bond,\,risk\,free}$ is the risk-free value of the bond, $Spread_{bond}$ is the spread of the bond relative to the risk-free yield to maturity and $Duration_{bond}$ is the duration of the bond.

It has now become industry practice to take a CVA into account when marking-to-market a derivative portfolio. However, as we shall describe below, there is disagreement within the industry, at the current time, about whether the CVA should be defined from on a unilateral or bilateral basis.

Unlike what is done for a bond, the CVA for derivatives cannot be defined and calculated simply by discounting expected future cashflows at a spread to Libor:

❑ the CVA has to take into account not only the current expected future cashflows but the potential future cashflows that could occur if market rates change. For example, in a flat yield curve the expected cashflow of an at-the-market interest rate swap, at each future settlement date, is zero. However the EPE profile at each future date is not zero.

❑ the CVA should be calculated on a portfolio basis, across all transactions with the counterparty, taking all legally enforceable risk mitigating agreements into account.

❑ the CVA needs to deal with the issue of the bilateral nature of counterparty credit risk – eg, each counterparty to a forward or a swap has potential credit exposure to the other.

Unilateral CVA based on loss norms or credit reserve

Following the lead of investment banks, some commercial banks began to calculate an explicit CVA that they defined as the expected historical loss over the life of the counterparty's portfolio. By definition, the EL over the life of the portfolio will equal the sum, over all forward periods, of the product of the EPE in the period times the historical forward loss norm. The historical loss norm is the product of the PD and the LGD for the forward period. This is consistent with how one might calculate a credit reserve to cover expected losses if the portfolio were to be held to maturity, and one assumes that historic losses are a good predictor of future losses.

$$EL = \sum_t EPE_t \times LN_t \times df_t \tag{9}$$

where EPE_t is the expected exposure at the future time t, LN_t is the historic loss normal for the same forward time t, and df_t is the appropriate discount factor. In a simulation framework (with N simulated paths) the EPE_t is literally the expected exposure at future time t reflecting the fact that exposure cannot be negative. For example for a single transaction:

$$EPE_t = \frac{1}{N} \sum_n Max(0, mtm(t)_n). \tag{10}$$

Comparing Equations 8 (CVA of a bond) and 9 (EL of a derivative portfolio), we see that EPE_t corresponds to the market value of the bond in the forward period. This makes sense given our previous discussion of the relation of EPE to the "loan equivalent" of counterparty risk. The α factor introduced in the calculation of the loan equivalent for EC from a default-only perspective is not needed in Equation 9 because we are not concerned in Equation 9 with the variance around the EL. The forward loss norm, LN_t, corresponds to the product of the forward spread times the forward time period. Although they have a similar role in the two formulas, market spreads can be many times larger than historical loss norms, particularly for investment-grade obligors and forward periods not far from today.

A CVA formula for derivatives that is market-based rather than based on historical losses will have a similar structure to Equation 8.

Market-based unilateral CVA

To convert this credit reserve to a credit valuation adjustment one needs to make two adjustments.

❑ instead of using historic volatilities and correlations in calculating EPE_t one should use current market based implied volatilities and correlations.

❑ instead of using historic loss norms one should use current credit spreads.

$$CVA = \sum_k EPEI_k \times Spread_k \times \Delta t_k \times df_k \qquad (11)$$

In Equation 11, $EPEI_k$ is the expected exposure based on implied volatilities and correlations and $Spread_k$ is the current credit spread of the counterparty in the forward time interval Δt_k. This form of CVA is typically referred to as a unilateral CVA due to its one-sided view of the risk. The credit risk the firm takes with the counterparty is part of this adjustment but the credit risk that the counterparty takes with the firm is not.

Bilateral CVA

The bilateral CVA model incorporates both sides of the transaction:

$$CVA_{bilateral} = \sum_k (EPEI_k \times Spread_k - EPEI'_k \times Spread'_k)$$
$$\times \Delta t_k \times df_k \qquad (12)$$

where $EPEI'_k$ is the expected exposure the counterparty has to the firm and $Spread'_k$ denotes the firm's own credit spread in forward interval Δt_k.

In principle, a derivative market-maker could use a unilateral CVA to set the initial terms and conditions of a derivative transaction with a corporate end-user – ie, to ensure that the counterparty credit risk of the corporate end-user was a factor in specifying the transaction's initial terms and conditions. However, a problem would arise in the interdealer/bank market if each party wanted to be compensated for the credit risk it had with its counterparty and if the unilateral CVA was of similar size to or larger than the typical bid–offer spread. If every player demanded to be compensated for the risk they were taking, without regard to the risk their counterparty was taking, the interdealer/bank market would clearly not be as liquid as it is today. Thus, one use of a bilateral CVA is to specify the initial terms and conditions of derivative transactions in the interbank/dealer market. However, it is possible that the primary reason we do have a liquid interdealer/bank market is not because firms actively calculate a bilateral CVA for each deal but because of the widespread use, in that market, of bilateral margin agreements with daily margin calls. Daily margin agreements can so materially reduce counterparty credit risk that the risk can effectively be ignored when specifying a transaction's initial terms and conditions.

Incorporating changes in the CVA into the simulation of EC

Changes in the CVA give rise to changes in the economic value of the derivatives book. Consequently, these changes should also be incorporated in the calculation of EC. As is evident from Equations 11 and 12, there are two drivers of changes in the CVA: (a) changes in basic market rates, which will change the expected exposure profile (the EPEI for the unilateral and both the EPEI and the EPEI' for the bilateral model); (b) changes in spreads (the counterparty's spreads for the unilateral model and both the counterparty's spreads and the firm's spread for the bilateral model).

The most precise calculation of the potential changes in the expected exposure profile would require a double level of simulation: the current expected exposure profile (the EPEI for the unilateral and both the EPEI and the EPEI' for the bilateral model) requires the simulation of thousands of paths of market rates given the current state of the market (and the CE). The potential future value of the expected exposure profile requires the calculation of an expected exposure profile for each potential future state of the market (ie, for each potential future CE, hence a double level of simulation).

To avoid this double level of simulation, one may have to introduce a means of estimating the sensitivity of the EPEI (and the EPEI') to changes in the CE of the portfolio of transactions with the counterparty at a set of future dates. With that sensitivity measurement, calculations of the potential changes in the EPEI (and the EPEI') would be reduced to the calculation of potential changes in the CE, for which we have already described the method of calculation (see above).

More attention has been given to the sensitivity of the CVA to changes in credit spreads and it can probably be argued that the CVA is in general more sensitive to change in credit spreads than to changes in market rates (other than credit spreads).

When calculating EC from a default-only perspective, by using EPE $\times$ α as a loan equivalent, EPE can be defined as a single number: the average *EPE over the next year*. In contrast, when measuring EC from a potential loss-of-economic-value perspective, the effective maturity, M, needs to be taken into account *over the full life of the portfolio* in order to have the ability to calculate the effect of changes in spreads on the economic value of the transactions with the counterparty.

Effective maturity M for a unilateral CVA

One can calculate the effective maturity of a portfolio of derivatives in the following manner. This can be thought of as an effective credit duration.

Unilateral CVA for counterparty

$$\text{CVA} = \sum_{k=1}^{N} \text{EPEI}_k \, \text{Spread}_k \, \Delta t_k \, df_k \tag{13}$$

Sensitivity of CVA to change in forward spread.

$$\Delta\text{CVA} = \sum_{k=1}^{N} \text{EPEI}_k \, \Delta\text{Spread}_k \, \Delta t_k \, df_k \tag{14}$$

Definition of some terms:

$$\overline{\Delta\text{Spread}} = \frac{\displaystyle\sum_{k=1}^{N} \Delta\text{Spread}_k \, \Delta t_k}{\displaystyle\sum_{k=1}^{N} \Delta t_k} \quad \text{(average change in spread over full life)} \tag{15}$$

$$\text{EPEI} = \sum_{k=1}^{1\text{ year}} \text{EPEI}_k \, \Delta t_k \, df_k \quad \text{(EPE over one year)} \quad \text{(16)}$$

Derivation of maturity, M:

$$\Delta\text{CVA} = \sum_{k=1}^{N} \text{EPEI}_k \, \Delta\text{Spread}_k \, \Delta t_k \, df_k$$

$$\equiv \text{EPEI} \, \overline{\Delta\text{Spread}} \, M \quad \text{(17)}$$

Therefore:

General formula for M, taking into account term structure of credit spreads:

$$M = \frac{\displaystyle\sum_{k=1}^{N} \text{EPEI}_k \, \Delta\text{Spread}_k \, \Delta t_k \, df_k}{\text{EPEI} \, \overline{\Delta\text{Spread}}} \quad \text{(18)}$$

$$= \frac{\displaystyle\sum_{k=1}^{N} \text{EPEI}_k \, \Delta\text{Spread}_k \, \Delta t_k \, df_k}{\left(\displaystyle\sum_{k=1}^{1\text{ year}} \text{EPEI}_k \, \Delta t_k \, df_k\right) \left(\dfrac{\displaystyle\sum_{k=1}^{N} \Delta\text{Spread}_k \, \Delta t_k}{\displaystyle\sum_{k=1}^{N} \Delta t_k}\right)} \quad \text{(19)}$$

If one assumes parallel shifts in the spread curve this simplifies to

$$= \frac{\displaystyle\sum_{k=1}^{N} \text{EPEI}_k \, \Delta t_k \, df_k}{\left(\displaystyle\sum_{k=1}^{1\text{ year}} \text{EPEI}_k \, \Delta t_k \, df_k\right)} \quad \text{(20)}$$

and it simplifies to perhaps the obvious answer if one assumes constant time buckets

$$= \frac{\displaystyle\sum_{k=1}^{N} \text{EPEI}_k \, df_k}{\left(\displaystyle\sum_{k=1}^{1\text{ year}} \text{EPEI}_k \, df_k\right)} \quad \text{(21)}$$

Effective maturity M for a bilateral CVA

The sensitivity of the bilateral CVA to changes in the counterparty's spread and/or to changes in one's own firm's spread is given by:

$$\Delta CVA_{\text{bilateral}}$$

$$= \sum_k \frac{\partial CVA_{\text{bilateral}}}{\partial Spread_k} \Delta Spread_k + \sum_k \frac{\partial CVA_{\text{bilateral}}}{\partial Spread'_k} \Delta Spread'_k$$

$$= \sum_k (EPEI_k \times \Delta Spread_k - EPEI'_k \times \Delta Spread'_k) \times \Delta t_k \times df_k$$

$$= M \times EPEI \times \overline{\Delta Spread} - M' \times EPEI' \times \overline{\Delta Spread}' \qquad (22)$$

Where in analogy to the definition of M in Equation 18, M' can be defined as:

$$M' = \frac{\sum_{k=1}^{N} EPEI'_k \Delta Spread'_k \Delta t_k df_k}{EPEI' \overline{\Delta Spread}'} \qquad (23)$$

Let us measure how the effective maturity, defined as in Equation 18, is modified under a bilateral CVA relative to its magnitude under a unilateral CVA. In analogy to Equation 18 we define:

$$M_{\text{bilateral}} = \frac{\Delta CVA_{\text{bilateral}}}{EPEI \times Spread} \qquad (24)$$

Therefore:

$$M_{\text{bilateral}} = M - \frac{\sum_{k=1}^{N} EPEI'_k \, \Delta Spread'_k \, \Delta t_k \, df_k}{\left(\sum_{k=1}^{1\,\text{year}} EPEI_k \, \Delta t_k \, df_k \right) \left(\dfrac{\sum_{k=1}^{N} \Delta Spread_k \Delta t_k}{\sum_{k=1}^{N} \Delta t_k} \right)} \qquad (25)$$

Equation 25 describes how the unilateral Maturity, M, is modified under a bilateral CVA.

If for simplicity one allows only for parallel shifts in the credit spread and assumes equally sized time buckets then this can be rewritten as

$$M_{\text{bilateral}} = \frac{1}{\sum\limits_{k=1}^{1\text{year}} \text{EPEI}_k \, \Delta\text{Spread}_k \, df_k}$$

$$\times \left(\sum_{k=1}^{N} \text{EPEI}_k \Delta\text{Spread}_k \, df_k - \sum_{k=1}^{N} \text{EPEI}'_k \, \Delta\text{Spread}'_k \, df_k \right) \quad (26)$$

The effect of the bilateral model relative to the unilateral model on the effective maturity M of the counterparty's portfolio will depend on the relative size of the product (EPEI $\times$ ΔSpread) to the product (EPEI' $\times$ ΔSpread') and the correlation of changes in the counterparty's and one's own firm's spread.

❑ if changes in the counterparty's spread are highly correlated with changes in the firm's own spread and if EPEI and EPEI' are similar in magnitude (such as would be the case with daily margining) then the bilateral M will be much smaller than the unilateral M.
❑ if (EPEI $\times$ ΔSpread) > (EPEI' $\times$ ΔSpread') then the value of M for the two models will not differ by much.
❑ if changes in the counterparty's spread are highly correlated with the firm's then there will be a reduction in the effective maturity, even if EPEI $\neq$ EPEI'. If however the spreads are not highly correlated, the effective maturity may be larger due to the resultant increase in the width of the loss distribution. This is true even though it is always true that the bilateral CVA is smaller than the unilateral CVA.

Hedging changes in the CVA

Because of the impact to a firm's profit and loss, it is natural to ask how one would go about hedging changes in the value of the CVA. This also facilitates a deeper understanding of both the unilateral and bilateral models.

Looking at the unilateral CVA, which is also the first term of the bilateral CVA, one sees there are sensitivities to the level of market rates, the implied volatility associated with those market rates and the counterparty's credit spread. In the simple case of a single interest rate swap with a single counterparty this term can be hedged by entering into a default swap and an interest rate swaption with a different counterparty. For a par swap the magnitude of the sensitivities to changes in the CVA would be split roughly half and half between the two.

Hedging the second term of the bilateral model is much less intuitive and less obvious. The analogous hedges would be to sell an interest rate swaption and sell protection on one's own firm. Of course one cannot sell protection on oneself, so we must look to some other means of realising the value implied by the second term of the bilateral CVA. If one does not find a means of realising this value, the use of the bilateral CVA would imply putting an unrealised asset on one's balance sheet that will decline in value to zero with certainty. Although this approach seems to have been recently advocated by FASB (2003) and was also deemed correct by the IRS, it seems extremely aggressive and wrong from a commonsense point of view.[5]

One possible means of justifying this value is through possible benefits of funding that can be realised and are implied by the expected liability that drives this term. The argument is that if one has a hedged book the presence of this potential liability will give rise to an equally sized asset. The goal is to have this asset give rise to decreased funding costs. This asset could be seen in one of two different forms, depending on how the book is hedged: it could be in the form of (a) cash if the hedge is with a margined counterparty or (b) a receivable if it is not. The cash portion can immediately be a source of funding for the firm. The receivable could also provide a similar benefit if one is somehow able to get it funded either through the issuance of a double-default paper (both the counterparty and the firm would have to default for the holder of this chapter to have a loss) or some other means. It is therefore assumed that the treasury function of the firm should be willing to pay for this anticipated funding benefit. On the one hand, this approach, if instituted naïvely, would put the treasury function at risk if realised funding benefits turned out to be very different from anticipated risk-neutral funding benefits. On the other hand, the treasury unit appears to be the true "owner" for the entire second term of the bilateral model because it may naturally want to hedge appropriately for any differences between risk-neutral implied funding benefits and what funding benefits are actually realised.

The key issue is that a bank should not use the bilateral CVA until and unless it has a definite process in place for realising the value of its potential liability to its counterparty. Without such a process, the bank will be putting an asset on its books that of necessity will eventually be worth zero.

1 The authors wish to acknowledge very fruitful discussions with Eduardo Canabarro (currently at Lehman Brothers) on the topic of bilateral and unilateral CVA. The views expressed herein however are entirely those of the authors. The authors also want to make it clear that the papers referenced in the chapter are not a complete list of the most relevant references to the topics under discussion.

2 Implicit in the formula for the CE of contracts without a netting agreement is the assumption that in default, the court would "cherry-pick" the contracts of the defaulted counterparty. That is, require performance by the non-defaulted counterparty on all derivative contracts that were assets to the defaulted counterparty (ie negative value to the non-defaulted counterparty) while treating the contracts with positive value as contingent claims settled in bankruptcy.

3 A VAR measurement requires two components: (a) a representation of the sensitivity of the portfolio to changes in market factors (ie market rates) and (b) the simulation of potential changes in these market factors. The market sensitivity of a linear portfolio may be represented by a set of single factor sensitivities, one sensitivity for each underlying market factor that the value of the portfolio depends on. In contrast, a convex portfolio needs to be represented by a set of one-dimensional (or two-dimensional) grids of factor sensitivities, with a one or two-dimensional grid of sensitivities for each underlying market factor (or relevant pair of market factors) that the value of the portfolio depends on. See for example, Evan Picoult, 1997, "Calculating Value At Risk with Monte Carlo Simulation", in *Risk Management for Financial Institutions* (London: Risk Publications). The same essay with a minor change regarding BIS rules appears in two other books by Risk Publications: *Monte Carlo* (1998) and *Internal Modeling and CAD II* (1999).

4 The portfolio method of calculating pre-settlement credit exposure and the representation of exposure as a portfolio exposure profile were developed in 1991 by David Lawrence and Evan Picoult with critical technical assistance from Byron Nicas. See D. Lawrence and E. Picoult, 1991, "A New Method for Calculating Pre-Settlement Risk", *The Tactician* 4(3), internal Citibank publication; D. Lawrence, 1995, in *Derivative Credit Risk: Advances in Measurement and Management* (London: Risk Publications); E. Picoult, 1996, "Measuring Pre-Settlement Credit Risk on a Portfolio Basis", in *Risk Measurement and Systemic Risk*, Proceedings of a Joint Central Bank Research Conference, November 1995, Board of Governors of the Federal Reserve System.

5 Bank One Corporation vs Commissioner of Internal Revenue; 120 T C No 11, Docket Nos 5759–95, 5956–97. Filed 2 May 2003. United States Tax Court.

REFERENCES

Canabarro, E., E. Picoult, and T. Wilde, 2003, "Analysing Counterparty Risk", *Risk*, pp. 117–22, September.

FASB, 2003, No 1201-100, "Exposure Draft, Proposed Statement of Financial Accounting Standards, Fair Value Measurements", June.

Sorensen, E. H., and T. F. Bollier, 1994, "Pricing Default Swap Risk", *Financial Analysts Journal*, pp. 23–33, May–June.

8

Economic Capital for Securitisations

Michael Pykhtin

KeyCorp

Securitisation is pooling of financial assets and issuing claims on cashflows generated by those assets in the form of marketable securities. These securities are generally known as asset-backed securities (ABS). Assets in the pool are usually some form of debt, and, depending on the nature of the debt, there are different names for ABS:

❑ *first mortgages:* mortgage-backed securities (MBS) and collateralised mortgage obligations (CMO);
❑ *consumer loans other than first mortgages:* ABS; and
❑ *bonds and commercial loans:* collateralised debt obligations (CDO).

The financial institution that originally owns the assets is called *originator.* Typically, the originator does not issue ABS. Instead, it sells the pool of assets to a special-purpose vehicle (SPV) – a company set up specifically for the purpose of the transaction. The SPV, which is usually rated AAA, is needed to protect ABS from default of the originator. The SPV issues notes backed by the cashflows from the pool of assets (hence the name ABS), sells them to investors and uses the proceeds of the sale to pay the originator for the assets.

Since different investors have different risk preferences, the SPV issues notes of different risk classes. Different risk classes are created by prioritisation of the pool cashflows. The most standard prioritisation scheme is simple subordination (which we will consider in this chapter), when notes of a given risk class receive contractual payments only after all notes of less risky classes are paid. In other words, less risky (more senior) notes are protected from losses in the pool by a cushion of more risky (more junior) notes. In a securitisation with simple subordination, a given risk class is called a *tranche*. The notionals of all tranches in a securitisation sum up to the pool notional. The most subordinated tranche, called the *first loss piece*, is often kept by the originator to enhance the credit quality of the notes sold to investors. Notes sold to investors are usually rated by rating agencies.

In this chapter, we will discuss models of economic capital (EC) for securitisations and their implications.

MODELS OF EC

Securitisations have become a major tool of funding and risk management for banks. However, while several models for loan and bond portfolios were developed in the banking industry in the second half of 1990s, assessing portfolio credit risk associated with securitisations lagged far behind.[1] For example, a common approach to allocating EC to rated securitisation tranches was to assign the same capital as to a bond with the same rating. Indeed, notes of a securitisation tranche strongly resemble bonds: they have principal, contractual maturity, receive interest payments and are rated by credit agencies. But does a tranche rated Ba carry the same risk as a bond rated Ba? The answer is no, and even a crude analysis can show why.

Loss on a bond comes from default of a single borrower, while loss on a tranche comes from defaults of many borrowers in the underlying pool. Therefore, a large portion of idiosyncratic risk is diversified away in a tranche. Hence a tranche carries much more systematic risk than a bond, and one cannot use the same sensitivity of loss to the systematic factors (for example, asset correlation) as one would use for bonds. Another fundamental distinction between tranches and bonds is the degree of dependence between default and loss-given default (LGD) drivers. In the case of bonds, this dependence is relatively weak and assumed nonexistent in most industry models.[2] In the case of tranches, both default and LGD of a tranche are driven by the same variable – the loss in the underlying pool. Thus, portfolio credit risk models developed for loan and bond portfolios are not directly applicable to securitisation tranches, and a Ba tranche may require very different EC than a Ba bond.

A dedicated model is necessary to adequately describe portfolio credit risk associated with securitisations. Such a model must relate loss on a tranche to losses on other assets in the portfolio. Loss on a tranche is uniquely determined by the loss in the underlying pool via contractual distribution of payouts, known as *cashflow waterfall*. The structure of this waterfall can be quite complicated, depending on timings of pool defaults and recoveries as well as principal and interest payments. To take into account all this complexity, one needs to simulate pool cashflows dynamically and then apply the waterfall to generate losses on a tranche.[3] To make the model analytically tractable, some simplifying assumptions are necessary.

The need of an analytically tractable portfolio model of credit risk associated with securitisation tranches became urgent with the development of the New Basel Capital Accord (known as Basel II). Since the inception of the current Basel Accord (now known as Basel I) in 1988, banks have learned to use inconsistencies in the old accord to reduce regulatory capital requirements without reducing the actual economic risk they are taking. To discourage such practice, known as regulatory arbitrage, it was necessary to bring the regulatory capital in Basel II in line with the underlying risk. A portfolio model that is simple enough to provide closed-form results, but rigorous enough to adequately describe the economic risk of securitisations, was needed to accomplish the task.

Two such models have been developed recently: by Pykhtin and Dev (2002, 2003) and by Gordy and Jones (2003). Both models are consistent with the asymptotic single-risk-factor (ASRF) framework – the foundation of the Internal Ratings Based (IRB) approach in Basel II – as they consider a tranche being held in an asymptotically fine-grained portfolio driven by a single systematic risk factor.[4] Both models found their application in the Basel II rules for securitisations (see paragraphs 538–643 in Basel Committee, 2004): Pykhtin and Dev's model was used in calibrating the ratings-based approach (RBA) by Peretyatkin and Perraudin (2003), while the supervisory formula approach (SFA) is based on Gordy and Jones's model. Even though the RBA and the SFA were calibrated to different models, this does not necessarily lead to inconsistency between the two approaches, as was shown by Gordy (2003b). He was able to map the parameters of one model to the parameters of the other so that the resulting capital requirements were approximately equal.

ASRF FRAMEWORK

Portfolio EC is usually defined as the q-th percentile of the portfolio loss distribution (ie, a level of loss such that portfolio loss does not exceed it with probability q). Then, this portfolio EC is allocated to individual assets according to certain rules (see, for example, Bluhm, Overbeck and Wagner, 2002). The asset EC obtained this way can be interpreted as the asset's contribution to the portfolio risk. Generally, while asset expected loss (EL) depends only on the characteristics of the asset itself, its contributory EC additionally depends on properties of the portfolio where the asset is held. Gordy (2003a) has shown that the only case when the asset EC is independent of the portfolio composition is when (a) the portfolio is infinitely fine-grained (ie, its largest exposure represents a negligible fraction of its total exposure) and (b) the portfolio losses are driven by a single systematic risk factor. These two conditions constitute the ASRF framework. Under the first condition, all the idiosyncratic risk in the portfolio is diversified away and the asymptotic portfolio loss equals the EL conditional on the systematic risk factors.[5] The second condition makes the portfolio loss to be a deterministic monotonic function of the single systematic factor. Therefore, the portfolio EC equals its EL conditional on the systematic risk factor being equal to its qth $((1 - q)$-th) percentile when the loss is an increasing (decreasing) function. Due to the linearity of the expectation operator, contributory EC of an asset is nothing but the EL on this asset conditional on the appropriate value of the systematic risk factor.

The ASRF framework can be applied to any asset in the portfolio, including securitisation tranches. We assume that a securitisation tranche is held in an infinitely fine-grained portfolio of assets. The exposure to the tranche represents a negligible fraction of the total portfolio exposure, so that the portfolio remains infinitely fine-grained after inclusion of the tranche. The losses in the portfolio are driven by a single systematic risk factor Z having standard normal distribution. We will interpret this systematic factor as the state of the economy: higher values of Z corresponding to strong economy and lower values corresponding to weak economy. This interpretation makes portfolio EL conditional on Z a decreasing function of Z. Under the ASRF assumptions, Gordy's arguments are applicable to any asset, including securitisation tranches. Therefore, if we denote the stochastic one-year loss on a tranche by U, the tranche EC is

$$EC_q = E\left[U|Z = z_{1-q}\right] \tag{1}$$

where $z_{1-q} = N^{-1}(1 - q)$ is the $(1 - q)$-th percentile of the standard normal distribution.

Equation (1) is the starting point for both Pykhtin–Dev and Gordy–Jones models. Both models consider pool losses over a one-year horizon. Only losses of principal are taken into account. We will denote the probability that the pool loss rate (ie, the loss as a fraction of the pool notional) L will exceed level l by $G(l)$. This complementary distribution function is related to the more conventional distribution function $F(l) \equiv \Pr[L \le l]$ via $G(l) = 1 - F(l)$ and is a non-increasing function of the pool loss rate defined on the interval $[0, 1]$. Since the loss cannot exceed the pool notional, the relation $G(l) = 0$ always holds. The value of the complementary distribution function at $l = 0$ is determined by the probability of exactly zero loss in the pool: $G(0) = 1 - \Pr[L = 0]$. For credit pools, this probability is always positive and $G(0) < 1$ because, strictly speaking, there is always a finite probability of no defaults in the pool. The probability of zero loss vanishes in the limit of infinitely fine-grained pool, for which we have $G(0) = 1$.

PYKHTIN–DEV MODEL

Loss on a tranche

The model allocates the pool loss to securitisation tranches according to the simple subordination rule. A tranche under consideration is characterised by the attachment point (protection level) s and the detachment point $t \ge s$. The notional amount (thickness) is given by $t - s$. Both s and t are defined per unit of the pool notional and can take values between zero and one. The simple subordination rule means that this tranche experiences no losses if $L \le s$ (pool loss is absorbed by the subordinated tranches), and absorbs pool losses up to the maximum given by $t - s$ when $L \geq s$. Formally, the loss on the tranche can be written as

$$U(s, t) = \int_s^t dl\, 1_{\{L > l\}} \tag{2}$$

where $1_{[\cdot]}$ denotes the indicator function.

Equation (2) can be interpreted as follows. The tranche under consideration can be viewed as an infinite set of infinitesimally thin tranches (ITTs). An ITT characterised by the protection level l and notional dl experiences zero loss if $L \leq l$ and loss equal to dl if $L > l$. This interpretation is often helpful because an ITT is a much simpler object than a tranche of a finite thickness. In many respects, an ITT behaves like a loan with principal dl, probability of default (PD) of $G(l)$ and deterministic LGD of 100%.

Tranche EL and EC

EL for the tranche is obtained by taking the expectation of Equation (2)

$$EL(s, t) \equiv E[U(s, t)] = \int_s^t dl\, G(l) \tag{3}$$

The linearity of the expectation operator ensures that the ITT intuition is preserved in Equation (3): the EL of a tranche is the sum of the ELs of the ITTs composing that tranche. The analogy between ITTs and loans can be easily seen: the EL of an ITT has the same form as the EL of a loan (the product of principal, PD and expected LGD).

EC can be expressed in a similar form. According to Equation (1), EC is given by the EL on the tranche in question conditional on the systematic factor being equal to its $(1 - q)$-th percentile. By taking the expectation of Equation (2) conditionally on event $Z = z_{1-q}$, we obtain the tranche EC as

$$EC_q(s, t) = E\left[U(s, t) | Z = z_{1-q}\right] = \int_s^t dl\, G\left(l | z_{1-q}\right) \tag{4}$$

where $G(l|z) \equiv \Pr[L > l | Z = z]$ is the complementary distribution of loss in the underlying pool conditional on the realisation of the systematic factor. Equation (4) has the same form as Equation (3): the tranche EC is the sum of the ECs of the ITTs composing that tranche. The only difference between the ITT EC and EL is conditioning of the pool loss distribution on $Z = z_{1-q}$.

Tranche PD and LGD

There is an alternative view on tranche EL and EC, based on the notions of tranche PD and LGD. Tranche EL can be represented as the product of tranche PD and expected LGD. For a tranche with protection level s, its PD is given by $G(s)$. Unlike loans and bonds, tranche LGD is driven by the same factor that drives its default: pool loss. Therefore, tranche expected LGD cannot be determined independently of its PD. Expected LGD (defined per unit of pool notional) for a tranche is the expected tranche loss conditional on its default. For a senior tranche with protection level s, this is given by the difference between the pool expected loss conditional on tranche default (ie, $L > s$) and the tranche protection level. Thus, the EL for a senior tranche is

$$EL(s, 1) = G(s)(E[L \,|\, L > s] - s) \qquad (5)$$

The EL for an arbitrary tranche can be calculated as the difference between ELs of two senior tranches:

$$EL(s, t) = EL(s, 1) - EL(t, 1)$$

It is straightforward to establish the equality of the total EL for all tranches in a given securitisation to the pool EL. Indeed, according to Equation (3), the total EL for all tranches equals $EL(0, 1)$. Substituting $s = 0$ into Equation (5), we obtain

$$EL(0, 1) = E[L]$$

regardless of the value of $G(0)$.

According to Equation (1), tranche EC is given by its EL conditional on the extreme value of the systematic risk factor, $Z = z_{1-q}$. Therefore, tranche EC can be represented as the product of its conditional PD and its conditional LGD. For a senior tranche with protection level s, the conditional PD is given by $G(s|z_{1-q})$, while the conditional LGD is given by the difference between the pool EL conditional on *both* $L > s$ *and* $Z = z_{1-q}$ and the tranche protection level. This results in

$$EC_q(s, 1) = G(s|z_{1-q})(E[L|\{L > s\}\&\{Z = z_{1-q}\}] - s) \qquad (6)$$

which differs from Equation (5) by extra conditioning on $Z = z_{1-q}$. The EC for an arbitrary tranche can be calculated as the difference between ECs of two senior tranches:

$$EC_q(s, t) = EC_q(s, 1) - EC_q(t, 1)$$

Similarly to the case of EL, the total EC for all tranches equals $EC_q(0, 1)$ as trivially follows from Equation (4). Substituting $s = 0$ into Equation (6), we obtain

$$EC_q(0, 1) = E[L|Z = z_{1-q}]$$

regardless of the value of $G(0|z_{1-q})$. Thus, the EC for all tranches equals the pool contributory EC (ie, when the pool is viewed as a small part of the investor's portfolio).

Very often, pool loss distribution is unknown in closed form and has to be computed numerically. In such instances, calculation of tranche EL and EC according to Equations (3) and (4) would involve numerical integration of numerically obtained functions. Equations (5) and (6) are equivalent to Equations (3) and (4), respectively, and can be formally derived from them, as shown in Pykhtin (2004). Thus, Equations (5) and (6) allow us to avoid the numerical integration and are, therefore, valuable tools to calculate tranche EL and EC.

While Equations (3) and (5) that we derived for the tranche EL are self-contained and can be calculated for any distribution of pool losses, Equations (4) and (6) for the tranche EC additionally require specification of the relationship between the pool loss and systematic factor Z.

Global and local systematic factors

Very often, assets combined in a pool have more in common than assets in a well-diversified portfolio. For example, the assets in the pool may belong to the same industry. In such cases, correlations between the assets in the pool would on average be higher than the correlations implied by their common dependence on the global systematic risk factor. To describe this effect, we assume that losses in the pool are driven by a local systematic risk factor, appropriate for a given pool. While global systematic risk factor Z can be interpreted as the state of the global economy, the local systematic factor, which we will denote by Y, describes the state of the industry (or other common property) for the assets in the pool. We assume that Y has standard normal distribution and that it is linearly related to Z:

$$Y = \rho_{YZ}Z + \sqrt{1 - \rho_{YZ}^2}\,\varepsilon \qquad (7)$$

where ρ_{YZ} is the correlation between the risk factors and ε is a standard normal variable independent of Z. We assume that higher values of Y correspond to stronger industry and smaller pool losses, which means $\rho_{YZ} > 0$ for cyclical industries. In a multifactor portfolio model, Y would be called a composite factor and ε industry-specific factor.

Fine-grained pools
There is a large class of securitisations based on fine-grained underlying pools. ABSs defined on retail pools (for example, car loans) typically belong to this class. It turns out that the analysis greatly simplifies in such cases due to the fact that most of idiosyncratic risk is diversified away in a fine-grained portfolio. For retail pools, one can safely assume that all idiosyncratic risk is completely diversified away and replace the original loss distribution by a much simpler limiting loss distribution of the infinitely fine-grained portfolio.

When the pool loss is driven by a single systematic factor (Y in our case), one can even relate the EL and EC for ITTs (which are the integrands in Equations (3) and (4)) without making any specific assumptions about the nature of the pool loss distribution. For normally distributed systematic factors, this relation has the form of conditional default probability derived by Vasicek (1987):

$$G(l|z) = N\left(\frac{N^{-1}[G(l)] - \rho_{YZ}z}{\sqrt{1 - \rho_{YZ}^2}} \right) \qquad (8)$$

where $N(\cdot)$ is the cumulative standard normal distribution function and $N^{-1}(\cdot)$ is its inverse.

Vasicek model for the pool

To complete the model, we need to specify the distribution of losses in the underlying pool. It is assumed that the pool contains M loans to distinct borrowers. Losses in the pool occur due to borrowers' defaults and are described by the Vasicek model (Vasicek, 2002). Borrower i will default within one year with probability p_i. Default happens when a continuous ability-to-pay variable X_i describing financial wellbeing of borrower i at the horizon falls below a threshold. This ability-to-pay variable has standard normal distribution and can be interpreted as the standardised log-return on the borrower's assets. The default threshold for borrower i is given by $N^{-1}(p_i)$. The asset return variables depend linearly on the local systematic risk factor Y as

$$X_i = a_i Y + \sqrt{1 - a_i^2}\,\xi_i \tag{9}$$

where a_i is a factor loading determining the sensitivity of borrower i to the local systematic factor Y, and variable ξ_i has standard normal distribution. Variable ξ_i describes the idiosyncratic component of the asset return and is independent across borrowers. Asset correlation between borrower i and borrower j in the pool equals $a_i a_j$.

If borrower i defaults, the amount of loss is determined by its stochastic LGD variable. We assume that these LGD variables are independent between themselves as well as from all the other variables in the model. The pool loss rate, defined as the ratio of the pool loss to the total exposure of the pool, is

$$L = \sum_{i=1}^{M} w_i \text{LGD}_i 1_{\left\{X_i \leq N^{-1}(p_i)\right\}} \tag{10}$$

where w_i is the weight of loan i in the pool, defined as the ratio of the loan principal to the pool principal.

The pool contributory capital can be obtained by taking the conditional expectation of Equation (10):

$$K_C = E\left[L \mid Z = z_{1-q}\right] = \sum_{i=1}^{M} w_i E[\text{LGD}_i]\hat{p}_i(z_{1-q}) \tag{11}$$

where $\hat{p}_i(z)$ is the PD by borrower i conditional on the event $Z = z$ and given by the Vasicek formula

$$\hat{p}_i(z) = N\left(\frac{N^{-1}(p_i) - r_i z}{\sqrt{1 - r_i^2}}\right) \tag{12}$$

where

$$r_i \equiv a_i \rho_{YZ} \tag{13}$$

is the sensitivity of the asset return to the global factor Z.

Unfortunately, it is not possible to obtain complementary loss distribution function $G(l)$ for Equation (10) in closed form. However, there are ways of calculating tranche EL and EC analytically or semi-analytically. These methods are not critical for understanding of the model and are discussed in great detail in Pykhtin (2004).

Examples

A very informative way of analysing risk of various tranches that can be defined on a pool is to plot the ITT capital $G(l|z_{1-q})$ as function of the credit protection level l. The EC for a tranche with the attachment point s and the detachment point t is given by the area under the curve between s and t. The total area under the curve, representing the EC for all tranches, equals pool contributory EC K_C.

We will look at how tranche EC depends upon the granularity of the pool, pool credit quality and correlation between local and global systematic factors. For simplicity, we will look only at homogeneous pools – pools composed of $\bar{M}$ identical loans with PD $\bar{p}$, local factor loading $\bar{a}$, expected LGD $\bar{\mu}$ and standard deviation of LGD $\bar{\sigma}$. Figure 1 shows the ITT capital at $q = 99.9\%$ for homogeneous pools of $\bar{M}$ speculative grade ($\bar{p} = 5.0\%$) loans at two choices of the correlation between the risk factors: $\rho_{YZ} = 0.95$ (a) and $\rho_{YZ} = 0.80$ (b). The global factor loading is kept fixed at $\bar{r} = 0.40$ (corresponding to the global asset correlation of 0.16).[6] Expected LGD for all pools is $\bar{\mu} = 40\%$, and standard deviation of LGD is $\bar{\sigma} = 20\%$. Pool contributory EC computed according to Equation (11) is $K_C = 13.1\%$. Different curves correspond to different values of $\bar{M}$.

The main observation from Figure 1 is that reducing the effective number of loans in the pool reduces the risk of junior tranches and

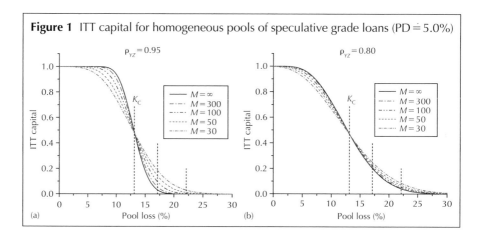

Figure 1 ITT capital for homogeneous pools of speculative grade loans (PD $\doteq$ 5.0%)

increases the risk of senior tranches. This behaviour is very intuitive: lack of diversification in any portfolio leads to increasing risk of very high losses. The crossover region, where the dependence of the ITT capital upon $\bar{M}$ changes its sign, is remarkably small and well defined. The transition happens in a very small vicinity of the pool contributory EC K_C.[7] This rule holds for a very wide range of model parameters, and breaks down only for very coarse-grained pools with low PD, as we will see below.

Reducing the level of correlation between the local and global risk factors reduces the sensitivity of tranche EC to $\bar{M}$, as can be seen from comparison of panels (a) and (b) of Figure 1. An alternative way of describing this effect is that more fine-grained pools are more sensitive to changes in ρ_{YZ}. At the intuitive level, this can be explained as follows. Conditionally on $Z = z_{1-q}$, more fine-grained pools have less uncertainty in the loss rate at given ρ_{YZ}. Therefore, they should be more sensitive to further increase in the pool loss uncertainty resulting from decreasing ρ_{YZ}.

To show these effects quantitatively for tranches of finite size, we have defined a securitisation based on each of the pools. There are four tranches in this securitisation: the first loss piece absorbing pool losses up to $K_C = 13.1\%$ two mezzanine tranches with notionals 4% (more junior) and 5% (more senior) of the pool notional, and the senior tranche taking losses above 22.1%. The tranche bounds are shown in Figure 1. Table 1 shows the EC for these tranches as a fraction of tranche notional for each of the pools.

Table 1 Tranche capital for homogeneous pools of speculative grade loans (PD = 5.0%)

Tranche (%)	M = ∞ (%)	M = 300 (%)	M = 100 (%)	M = 50 (%)	M = 30 (%)
		$\rho_{YZ} = 0.95$			
0–13.1	93.7	92.6	90.8	88.6	86.3
13.1–17.1	20.0	22.7	26.3	29.5	32.1
17.1–22.1	0.57	1.27	3.02	5.79	9.08
22.1–100	0.00	0.00	0.00	0.02	0.08
		$\rho_{YZ} = 0.80$			
0–13.1	85.4	84.9	84.0	82.7	81.1
13.1–17.1	32.6	33.0	33.6	34.4	35.3
17.1–22.1	10.6	11.2	12.4	13.9	15.7
22.1–100	0.11	0.13	0.18	0.26	0.37

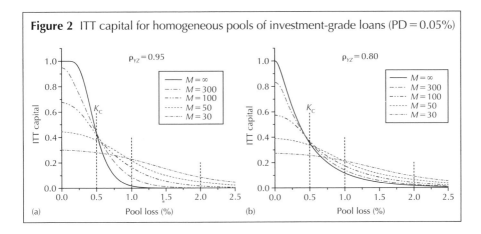

Figure 2 ITT capital for homogeneous pools of investment-grade loans (PD = 0.05%)

Figure 2 shows the ITT capital for investment-grade pools with the PD $\bar{p} = 0.05\%$). All other pool parameters are the same as in the speculative-grade example above. The contributory capital is $K_c = 0.50\%$ for all pools. Most of the observations we have made for the speculative-grade case apply here as well: the main effect of reducing the number of loans $\bar{M}$ in the pool amounts to redistribution of risk from more junior to more senior tranches. However, the magnitude of this effect is much larger than in the speculative-grade case.

This larger magnitude can easily be understood if we recall that the value of the ITT capital at zero loss level is the probability of non-zero loss in the pool, conditional on $Z = Z_{1-q}$. In the speculative-grade examples above, the PD was so high that, conditionally on $Z = z_{0.1\%}$, the probability of no defaults in the pool (and, therefore, zero pool loss) was negligible even for pools with $\bar{M}$ as low as 30. This is why all the curves in Figure 1 start at ITT capital equal to one when pool loss is zero. In contrast, the PD of the investment-grade pools is low enough that the probability of no defaults is significant even when it is conditioned on $Z = z_{0.1\%}$ and $\bar{M}$ is as high as 300. The smaller is $\bar{M}$, the larger is the conditional probability of no defaults, and the lower is ITT capital at zero loss level. Therefore, the dependence of the ITT capital at low pool loss levels upon the number of loans in the pool must be much stronger for investment-grade pools than for speculative-grade pools. Since the total contributory risk of a pool does not depend on $\bar{M}$ (graphically, the total area under each curve must equal the pool contributory EC), the reduction of risk at low loss levels must be compensated by the equal increase of risk at high loss levels.

We have also defined a sample securitisation for the investment-grade case. The first-loss piece absorbs losses up to $K_C = 0.50\%$, the junior and the senior mezzanine tranches take losses between 0.50% and 1.00% and between 1.00% and 2.00%, respectively, and the senior tranche takes losses above 2.00%. The tranche bounds are shown in Figure 2. Table 2 shows the EC for these tranches as a fraction of tranche notional for each of our investment-grade pools.

Table 2 Tranche capital for homogeneous pools of investment grade loans (PD = 0.05%)

Tranche (%)	M = ∞ (%)	M = 300 (%)	M = 100 (%)	M = 50 (%)	M = 30 (%)
		$\rho_{YZ} = 0.95$			
0–0.5	85.2	72.9	58.3	42.0	29.3
0.5–1.0	14.3	22.7	27.3	30.0	25.7
1.0–2.0	0.24	2.14	6.60	11.1	15.4
2.0–100	0.00	0.00	0.01	0.03	0.07
		$\rho_{YZ} = 0.80$			
0–0.5	66.3	60.1	49.9	37.0	26.7
0.5–1.0	21.1	23.4	25.6	27.4	23.7
1.0–2.0	5.13	6.59	9.14	11.9	14.9
2.0–100	0.01	0.02	0.03	0.06	0.10

Tranche rating and EC

From the examples above, we have seen that tranche EC depends on tranche thickness and pool parameters. This suggests that the knowledge of the tranche rating alone is not enough to calculate the EC. While this conclusion holds true generally, there is a special case when EC can be determined from its rating: ITTs defined on infinitely fine-grained pools.

When rating agencies assign ratings to securitisation tranches, one of the most critical inputs to the rating is either tranche EL or tranche PD (see Peretyatkin and Perraudin, 2002). As we have seen above, an ITT with the protection level l is similar to a loan with deterministic LGD of 100% and PD equal to $G(l)$. Therefore, for ITTs, $G(l)$ is the primary input to the rating for both EL- and PD-based rating processes. Thus, Equation (8) essentially relates the ITT rating to its EC for fine-grained pools.

We have mentioned above that Equation (8) is nothing but the Vasicek formula for conditional PD, where the ITT unconditional PD is given by $G(l)$ and asset correlation is given by ρ_{YZ}^2. From Equation (11) we can see that the contributory EC for a loan is given by the expected LGD multiplied by the Vasicek formula. The Vasicek formula here uses the regular asset correlation instead of ρ_{YZ}^2 as an input. This similarity allows for straightforward comparison between ITT and loan EC.

To simplify this comparison, we will assume that the loan has 100% LGD and that to obtain the same rating as the ITT the loan must have the same PD, ie, $G(l)$. Typically, one would expect that ρ_{YZ}^2 will be significantly higher than the typical asset correlation for a loan. If the PD is greater than or equal to one minus the confidence level, the Vasicek formula always gives higher values for higher asset correlations. If, on the other hand, PD $< 1-q$, the Vasicek formula is not monotonic: as asset correlation increases from zero to one, the EC increases, reaches a maximum, and then declines to zero. Thus, if the rating of a thin mezzanine tranche defined on a fine-grained pool is low enough to satisfy $G(l) > 1-q$, this tranche will typically attract higher EC than a correspondingly rated loan. For higher ratings, the tranche EC can be lower or higher than the loan EC, depending on ρ_{YZ} and $G(l)$ (ie, the rating itself).

An ITT based on an infinitely fine-grained pool is the only case when tranche EC can be determined from its rating. While infinitely fine-grained pool is a reasonable approximation for retail pools, real securitisation tranches are usually too thick to be approximated by a single ITT. Thus, EC for real tranches will depend, additionally to the rating, on tranche thickness and pool characteristics. Let us briefly discuss this dependence in qualitative terms.

First of all, tranche EC per unit of notional depends on the tranche thickness.[8] This dependence is different for PD- and EL-based rating systems. Let us consider a set of mezzanine tranches with increasing thickness, all having the same rating. For a PD-based rating, all the tranches in the set will have common attachment point to ensure the same PD. Whatever is the loss in the pool, it will represent a smaller or equal fraction of the tranche notional for thicker tranches than for thinner ones. Therefore, the tranche EC will always decline with the thickness. For a fixed EL-based rating, the answer is not obvious. As the thickness increases, the tranche EC will increase for highly rated thin tranches and decrease for lowly rated tranches and highly rated thick tranches. Regardless of the rating system, the EC for a senior tranche will be less than the one for a mezzanine tranche of the same rating.

Tranche EC also depends on the pool granularity. As we have seen in Figures 1 and 2, this dependence becomes stronger as the pool credit quality improves. As the effective number of exposures in the pool decreases and the pool becomes less granular, the tranche EC increases for highly rated tranches and decreases for lowly rated ones.

Ratings based approach in Basel II

Basel II requires banks to use the Ratings Based Approach (RBA) to determine the regulatory capital for securitisations whenever tranche rating is available. For each credit rating, the RBA has three capital factors: the base factor, somewhat lower factor for highly rated senior tranches, and somewhat higher factor for tranches defined on non-granular pools. These three capital factors attempt to describe the dependence of the EC for a rated tranche upon tranche thickness/seniority and pool granularity. However, this dependence is too rich and complex to be described by only three factors, and the RBA lacks the risk sensitivity. The Supervisory Formula Approach (SFA) based on Gordy – Jones model (see below) is necessarily more risk-sensitive.

On the other hand, a typical situation for an investor into a tranche is that the only information the investor has on the tranche is its rating. The RBA allows one to assign capital to tranches without having much information on the pool. At the same time, the RBA capital factors reflect the fact that, typically, highly rated tranches attract less EC than corresponding highly rated bonds, while lowly rated tranches attract more EC than corresponding lowly rated bonds.

GORDY–JONES MODEL
Loss on a tranche

Gordy–Jones and Pykhtin–Dev models share common foundation: they rely on the ASRF framework and the Vasicek model for the underlying pool. However, apart from this common base, the models are different. Gordy and Jones (2003) do not make a distinction between local and global systematic factors: they assume that $Y = Z$ (or, equivalently, $\rho_{YZ} = 1$) in our notations. On the other hand, they are not satisfied with the simple subordination structure used by Pykhtin and Dev. Gordy and Jones argue that tranche's actual level of protection may differ from the nominal level. This may be due to interaction between the principal and interest cashflows or some other specifics of the cashflow waterfall. Since it is impossible to take into account all the nuances of the waterfall in a simple single-period model, Gordy and Jones made protection levels for all tranches in a securitisation stochastic.

More specifically, they assumed that the actual tranche notionals $\{\tilde{v}_m\}$ for all tranches (m enumerates the tranches) are distributed around the nominal tranche notionals $\{v_m\}$ according to the Dirichlet distribution with parameters $\{\tau v_m\}$, where $\tau > 0$ is the precision parameter. Actual tranche notionals are assumed to be independent of all other stochastic variables in the model. Under this specification, the stochastic tranche notionals always sum up to one. For tranche m, its actual attachment (or detachment) point $\tilde{t}_m$ is distributed around the nominal attachment (or detachment) point t_m according to the beta distribution with parameters τt_m and $\tau(1 - t_m)$. The expectation of $\tilde{t}_m$ equals t_m, and higher values of τ correspond to tighter distributions of $\tilde{t}_m$ around t_m. The limit $\tau \to \infty$ corresponds to the simple subordination rules with deterministic tranche notionals.

Let us consider a first-loss piece with a stochastic detachment point $\tilde{t}$ (the attachment point for a first-loss piece is always zero). There are now two sources of uncertainty in the tranche loss: realisation of the pool loss rate L and realisation of the detachment point $\tilde{t}$. The loss on this tranche will be given by Equation (2) with the uncertain upper limit in the integral:

$$U(0, \tilde{t}) = \int_0^{\tilde{t}} dl\, 1_{\{L > l\}} \tag{14}$$

Tranche EL and EC

EL for this tranche is obtained by taking the expectation of Equation (14)

$$EL(0, t) \equiv E[U(0, \tilde{t})] = \int_0^1 dB(\xi; \tau t, \tau(1 - t)) \int_0^\xi dl\, G(l)$$

where $B(\cdot; a, b)$ is the cumulative beta distribution function with parameters a and b. By changing the order of integration this can be expressed as

$$EL(0, t) = \int_0^1 dl\, G(l)\left[1 - B(l; \tau t, \tau(1 - t))\right] \tag{15}$$

Since the Gordy–Jones model assumes the ASRF framework, the tranche EC can be calculated as the conditional on $Z = z_{1-q}$ expectation of the tranche loss according to Equation (1). By applying this conditional expectation to Equation (14) and repeating the steps we have done for the tranche EL, we obtain

$$EC_q(0, t) = \int_0^1 dl\, G\left(l\,|\,z_{1-q}\right)\left[1 - B(l; \tau t, \tau(1 - t))\right] \tag{16}$$

Equations (15) and (16) define the EL and EC, respectively, for the first-loss piece. The EL for an arbitrary tranche with the nominal attachment point s and detachment point t can be calculated as

$$EL(s, t) = EL(0, t) - EL(0, s)$$

and a similar relation holds for the EC:

$$EC_q(s, t) = EC_q(0, t) - EC_q(0, s)$$

Equations (15) and (16) follow from the uncertainty in the loss prioritisation and are the key results of the Gordy–Jones model. They converge to Equations (3) and (4), respectively, in the limit $\tau \to \infty$. Similarly to Equations (3) and (4), they are valid for any loss distribution in the underlying pool. Gordy and Jones (2003) used the Vasicek model of the pool driven by the global systematic factor, while Gordy (2003b) also used the Vasicek model driven by the local systematic factor, thus combining the Pykhtin–Dev and Gordy–Jones models into a single unified model. Both of these studies concentrate on EC, developing closed-form approximations to Equation (16). The remainder of this chapter will see a discussion of the Gordy–Jones model to EC and a pool driven by the global systematic factor.

Fine-grained pools

Let us consider an infinitely fine-grained pool driven by the global systematic factor Z. This is the case when the integral in Equation (16) can be evaluated analytically. Since all idiosyncratic risk is diversified away in this pool, the pool loss is a deterministic function of Z. If we condition the pool loss on the event $Z = z_{1-q}$, the pool loss rate becomes equal to its conditional expectation, which is pool contributory EC K_C. Therefore, the conditional complementary loss distribution (ie, the conditional probability that pool loss rate exceeds level l) is a step function

$$G\left(l \mid z_{1-q}\right) = 1_{\{l < K_C\}}$$

Substituting this into Equation (16) and calculating the integral (see Gordy and Jones, 2003), we obtain

$$EC_q^\infty(0, t) = K_C \left[1 - B(K_C; \tau t, \tau(1-t))\right] + tB(K_C; \tau t + 1, \tau(1-t)) \quad \textbf{(17)}$$

Equation (17) can be used to calculate EC for securitisations based on retail pools.

Marginal capital

Equation (16) is the Gordy–Jones version of Equation (4). It is even possible to rewrite it in the same form – as an integral of some marginal capital function:

$$EC_q(s, t) = \int_s^t dl\, H_q(l; \tau) \tag{18}$$

This marginal capital is closely related to the conditional complementary loss distribution in the pool $G(l|z_{1-q})$, but also depends upon the "uncertainty parameter" τ. Similarly to $G(l|z_{1-q})$, the marginal capital $H_q(l; \tau)$ is a non-increasing function of the loss level l. Moreover, it has the same value as $G(l|z_{1-q})$ does at $l = 0$ (the probability of non-zero loss, conditional on $Z = z_{1-q}$) and at $l = 1$ (zero). However, the marginal capital declines as l increases in a smoother fashion that $G(l|z_{1-q})$. The uncertainty in loss prioritisation (ie, finite τ) reduces the steepness of the marginal capital function in the vicinity of K_C. The stronger is the uncertainty in loss prioritisation (smaller τ), the smoother is the curve. In the limit of strict loss prioritisation ($\tau \to \infty$), the marginal capital coincides with $G(l|z_{1-q})$.

This dependence of marginal capital upon τ is especially strong in the case of infinitely fine-grained pool, as shown in Figure 3(a) for the case of homogeneous pool with PD $\bar{p} = 0.5\%$, expected LGD $\bar{\mu} = 40\%$, and asset correlation $\bar{a}^2 = 0.16$. Pool contributory capital is $K_C = 2.88\%$. The marginal capital for the strict loss prioritisation is

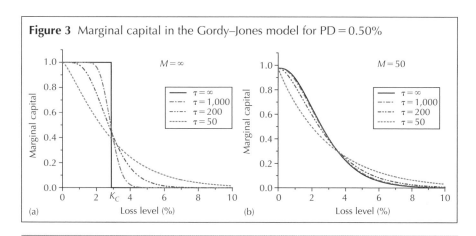

Figure 3 Marginal capital in the Gordy–Jones model for PD $= 0.50\%$

the step function because, as we have discussed above, all idiosyncratic risk in the pool is diversified away and, conditionally on $Z = z_{1-q}$, pool loss is deterministic. It is shown by the solid curve. Three other curves show the marginal capital for $\tau = 1{,}000$, $\tau = 200$ and $\tau = 50$.

As the pool becomes more coarse-grained, the presence of idiosyncratic risk makes the marginal capital function smoother, and the effect of the uncertainty in loss prioritisation is reduced. Figure 3(b) shows the marginal capital curves for a homogeneous coarse-grained pool that differs from the pool above only in the number of borrowers – it has $\bar{M} = 50$.

Mapping between the models

If one compares the marginal capital curves in Figures 1 and 2 with the ones in Figure 3, one might notice a great deal of similarity between them and even wonder whether the Pykhtin–Dev and Gordy–Jones models are all that different. Indeed, the effects of non-perfect correlation ρ_{YZ} between the global and local factors and of uncertainty of loss prioritisation τ on a tranche's EC are very similar.

Gordy (2003b) has shown that one model can even be mapped to the other. This means that, for a given ρ_{YZ} and a set of the pool parameters, one can find such level of τ that the marginal capital curves in the two models are almost indistinguishable. Gordy has also shown that this mapping only weakly depends on most pool characteristics, including "global" asset correlation, number of loans, PD and standard deviation of LGD. Even if we change these pool parameters significantly while keeping ρ_{YZ} fixed, the associated change in the "mapped" τ will be small. The only pool parameter that the mapping is highly sensitive to is the expected LGD.

The reader might wonder why one would need two models if they produce very similar marginal capital functions. Gordy (2003b) answers this concern by stating that

❑ the two models tell different economic stories;
❑ they should be calibrated by different empirical methods; and
❑ when marginal EC is mapped, marginal EL functions will be different.

Thus, the models are not completely redundant, and a unified model may prove to be the best choice overall.

Closed-form approximation

Unfortunately, neither tranche EC nor the marginal capital is available in closed form. Gordy and Jones (2003) have developed an excellent analytical approximation to these quantities. They noticed that the marginal capital function can be written as

$$H_q(l;\tau) = G\left(0\,|\,z_{1-q}\right)[1 - F_q(l;\tau)] \tag{19}$$

where $F_q(l;\tau)$ is a non-decreasing function of loss level l defined on the $[0,1]$ interval and taking value zero at $l = 0$ and value one at $l = 1$. In other words, function $F_q(\cdot;\tau)$ has all the properties of the cumulative distribution function of some random variable with support on the $[0,1]$ interval. Although function $F_q(\cdot;\tau)$ is not available in closed form, Gordy and Jones calculated the mean and the standard deviation of this random variable. Then, they replaced the unknown (in closed form) distribution function $F_q(l;\tau)$ in Equation (19) by the distribution function for the beta distribution, $B(l\,;a_q^\tau, b_q^\tau)$. The parameters a_q^τ and b_q^τ were chosen to match the mean and the standard deviation of the underlying random variable. Gordy and Jones derive these parameters for an arbitrary distribution of pool losses, and then use this general result with the Vasicek model of the pool. Thus the Gordy–Jones approximation to the marginal capital function is

$$\hat{H}_q(l;\tau) = G\left(0\,|\,z_{1-q}\right)\left[1 - B(l;a_q^\tau, b_q^\tau)\right] \tag{20}$$

where the "hat" above the function name indicates approximation. By substituting Equation (20) into Equation (18) and evaluating the integral, Gordy and Jones obtain the EC for a tranche of a finite size in closed form:

$$\widehat{EC}_q(0, t) = G\left(0\,|\,z_{1-q}\right)\left(t\left[1 - B(t;a_q^\tau, b_q^\tau)\right] + \frac{a_q^\tau}{a_q^\tau + b_q^\tau}\,B(t;a_q^\tau + 1, b_q^\tau)\right) \tag{21}$$

Gordy and Jones tested the approximation given by Equations (20) and (21) for the case of Vasicek model of the pool and the confidence level $q = 99.9\%$. They found that the approximation performs extremely well for a very wide spectrum of model

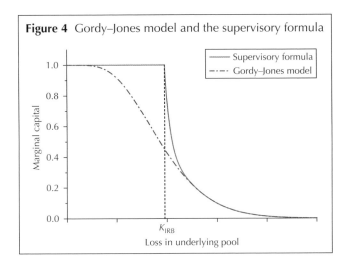

Figure 4 Gordy–Jones model and the supervisory formula

parameters. The interested reader can find further details in Gordy and Jones (2003).

Supervisory formula in Basel II

Used with the Vasicek model of the pool, Equation (21) appears in the Supervisory Formula in Basel (2004) as $K(L)$, where L denotes the detachment point of the first-loss piece (ie, t in our notations). All other parts of the Supervisory Formula represent supervisory overrides imposed on the Gordy–Jones model. These overrides include marginal capital of 100% up to K_{IRB} (K_C in our notations) and the floor of 0.56% of tranche notional for the tranche EC. To avoid a discontinuity of the marginal capital at $L = K_{IRB}$, the regulators have also added an extra term to the Gordy–Jones marginal capital. This term ensures that the regulatory marginal capital equals 100% at K_{IRB}. For loss levels L above K_{IRB}, this term decreases exponentially as one moves to higher L so that the regulatory marginal capital quickly converges to the Gordy–Jones marginal capital, as illustrated in Figure 4.

CONCLUSION

In this chapter there has been a discussion of the allocation of EC to tranches of asset securitisation. Models of EC developed for portfolios of loans and bonds are not directly applicable to securitisation tranches. In other words, credit risk of a securitisation tranche can be very different from that of a similarly rated portfolio of bonds. There two main reasons for this: (i) the proportion of systematic risk is much higher in a tranche than it is in a loan or a bond; (ii) defaults and losses in the event of default are driven by the same random variable (pool loss) for a tranche, but by different, weakly correlated random variables for a loan or a bond. Thus, a dedicated model is necessary to describe the credit risk of securitisations.

We have discussed two models of EC for securitisations: Pykhtin and Dev (2002, 2003) and Gordy and Jones (2003). Both models are rigorous, but simple enough to be implemented analytically or semi-analytically (ie, without use of simulations). They share a set of common assumptions:

❑ a tranche is held in an infinitely fine-grained "super-portfolio" driven by a single systematic risk factor (ASRF framework);
❑ the exposure to the tranche is negligible in comparison with the portfolio notional; and
❑ securitisation is based on a pool of loans driven by the single-factor Vasicek model.

Starting with this common foundation, the two models explore different aspects of the problem. The Pykhtin–Dev model emphasises the potential for a borrower to be more highly correlated with the borrowers in the pool than with the borrowers outside the pool. This is done via introduction of a non-perfect correlation between the global systematic factor driving the "super-portfolio" and the local systematic factor driving the pool. The Gordy–Jones model does not distinguish between global and local factors. Instead, it introduces uncertainty in loss prioritisation to account for possible difference between tranche's nominal and actual levels of protection. Remarkably, the effects of a non-perfect correlation between the global and local factors and of uncertainty of loss prioritisation on a tranche's EC are very similar. It is even possible to map one model to the other.

Both models found their application in Basel II. The Pykhtin–Dev model was used in calibration of the RBA, while the Gordy–Jones model lies in the foundation of the SFA. If calibrated properly, the use of different models in the two approaches should not be a source of inconsistency due to the mapping property. However, the

RBA is necessarily a much cruder approximation to reality than the SFA. This is because, apart from its dependence on the rating, the tranche EC depends on the pool characteristics and on the tranche thickness.

Dependence of the tranche EC on its thickness is different for PD- and EL-based rating systems. For a PD-based rating, the tranche EC will always decline with the thickness. For a fixed EL-based rating, as the thickness increases, the tranche EC will increase for highly rated thin tranches and decrease for lowly rated tranches and highly rated thick tranches. Regardless of the rating system, the EC for a senior tranche will be less than the one for a mezzanine tranche of the same rating. Tranche EC also depends on the pool granularity. As the effective number of exposures in the pool decreases and the pool becomes less granular, the tranche EC increases for highly rated tranches and decreases for lowly rated ones. This dependence becomes stronger as the pool credit quality improves – thus tranche EC also depends on the pool credit quality.

Capital charges for rated securitisation tranches are often compared with the ones for rated corporate bonds. This comparison is difficult to make because, unlike bonds, tranche capital strongly depends on many factors other than rating. On average, highly rated (eg, AAA, AA) tranches require less EC than similarly rated corporate bonds, while lowly rated tranches require more EC than similarly rated bonds (eg, BB, B).

1   Examples include Risk Metrics' CreditMetrics, KMV's PortfolioManager, CSFB's CreditRisk+. See Bluhm, Overbeck and Wagner (2002) for an excellent review of portfolio credit risk models.
2   Models that incorporate this dependence have appeared recently in the literature. See, for example, Frye (2000) and Pykhtin (2003).
3   See Duffie and Gârleanu (2001) for a rigorous dynamic modelling framework for CDOs.
4   See Gordy (2003a) for detailed explanation of the ASRF framework.
5   Vasicek (1991) derived the asymptotic loss distribution for a homogeneous portfolio of loans driven by a single systematic risk factor.
6   Because of Equation (13), it is not possible to vary ρ_{YZ} and, at the same time, keep both local and global factor loadings fixed. We chose to keep the global factor loading fixed because this results in fixed pool contributory capital and, therefore, equal area under all curves.
7   Visually, it appears that all the curves in Figure 1 cross at one point when $l = K_C$. Strictly speaking, this is not case.
8   Tranche EC per unit of pool notional will obviously increase with tranche thickness as follows from Equation (4). In this section we are talking about tranche EC per unit of tranche notional, which can be obtained by dividing Equation (4) by $t - s$. Tranche EC per unit of tranche notional can be interpreted as the average ITT EC between s and t, which can increase or decrease with $t - s$.

REFERENCES

Basel Committee on Banking Supervision, 2004, "International Convergence of Capital Measurement and Capital Standards", A Revised Framework, June.

Bluhm, C., L. Overbeck, and C. Wagner, 2002, *An Introduction to Credit Risk Modeling* (CRC: Chapman & Hall).

Duffie, D., and N. Gârleanu, 2001, "Risk and Valuation of Collateralized Debt Obligations", Working Paper, September.

Frye, J., 2000, "Collateral Damage", *Risk*, pp. 91–4, April.

Gordy, M., 2003a, "A Risk-Factor Model Foundation for Ratings-Based Bank Capital Rules", *Journal of Financial Intermediation,* **12(3)**, pp. 199–232, July.

Gordy, M., 2003b, "Reconciling Two Approaches to Setting Capital for Securitisations", Working Paper, October.

Gordy, M., and D. Jones, 2003, "Random Tranches", *Risk*, pp. 78–83, March.

Peretyatkin, V., and W. Perraudin, 2002, "Expected Loss and Probability of Default Approaches to Rating Collateralised Debt Obligations and the Scope for 'Ratings Shopping'", in Michael K. Ong (ed), *Credit Ratings: Methodologies, Rationale and Default Risk* (London: Risk Books).

Peretyatkin, V., and W. Perraudin, 2003, "Capital for Asset-backed Securities", Working Paper, February.

Pykhtin, M., and A. Dev, 2002, "Credit Risk in Asset Securitisations: Analytical Model", *Risk*, pp. S16–S20, May.

Pykhtin, M., and A. Dev, 2003, "Coarse-Grained CDOs", *Risk*, pp. 113–16, January.

Pykhtin, M., 2003, "Unexpected Recovery Risk", *Risk*, pp. 74–8, August.

Pykhtin, M., 2004, "Asymptotic Model of Economic Capital for Securitizations", in William Perraudin (ed), *Structured Credit Products: Pricing, Rating*, Risk Management and Basel II (London: Risk Books).

Vasicek, O., 1987, "Probability of Loss on Loan Portfolio", KMV Corporation.o

Vasicek, O., 1991, "Limiting Loan Loss Probability Distribution", KMV Corporation.

Vasicek, O., 2002, "Loan Portfolio Value", *Risk*, pp. 160–2, December.

9

Economic Capital for Market Risk

David R. Koenig

PRMIA

In December 1993, Metallgesellschaft AG revealed that a subsidiary has accumulated paper losses of nearly US$1.5 billion from a hedging programme designed to offset the risks of long-dated forward contracts it had sold. Because they were unable to meet the cashflow requirements of the hedges, the positions and programme were liquidated, resulting in the realisation of the losses and a collapse in Metallgesellschaft's stock price.

In 1994, as market prices for mortgage-backed securities changed radically, Askin Capital Management maintained valuations at theoretical levels, substantially above trading prices. Forced liquidations revealed the disparity, spawning the phrase "Askin for mercy" and leading four funds with over US$600 million in assets to bankruptcy.

At end of September 1998, LTCM, a multibillion-dollar hedge fund, was teetering on the brink of default due to continued adverse and extreme market movements. To avoid the threat of a systemic crisis in the world financial system, the Federal Reserve orchestrated a US$3.5 billion rescue package from leading US investment and commercial banks and the unwinding of a substantial portion of the positions held.

It would be difficult to argue that these events were exclusively market risks being realised, but, at their core, market events, and thereby market risk, led to the end results described. In the final analysis, these entities ran out of capital entirely or failed to have sufficient capital to continue operations in any meaning-ful way.

The proper allocation of capital to cover market risks does not mean that events like those above will be prevented in the future. In fact, it may well be that in each of the cases above there was proper capitalisation to the extent desired by the "parent" or controlling entity. Rather, the allocation of capital for market risk is intended both to provide some probabilistic assessment of the like-lihood market risks that will result in a full depletion of capital and to provide a balanced and fair method of rewarding performance across disparate avenues for taking market risk. Perhaps, with proper, well-communicated risk capitalisation in place, such real-isations, while making headlines, will be less surprising and less unsettling.

RISK CAPITAL FOR THE ENTERPRISE

Risk capital, as distinguished from working capital, is that which is held to assure creditors, with some general consensus level of prob-ability, that sufficient reserves exist to meet an entity's obligations to creditors. This is also distinct from regulatory capital. While moving towards a similar definition to risk capital, regulatory capital is held only to satisfy a regulatory requirement, which may not be fully aligned with corporate objectives.

Perhaps the concept is simple enough, but the methods for determining the proper levels and allocation of risk capital are not so simple, nor are they necessarily coherent. In general, the methods used attempt to identify market movements that will result in loss. From these movements, the desired threshold for insolvency is then targeted, say 0.5%, and risk capital is determined to be that at which hypothesised market risks that are realised exceed such an amount only 0.5% of the time.

Risk capital for the subsets of the enterprise

Risk capital is also the amount of "risk" contributed by particular units of a larger entity, be they business units, product lines or individual traders. Used in this context, risk capital provides an objective method for the entity to assess the risk-adjusted perform-ance of subdivisions of the entity and thus to engage in more informed portfolio optimisation decision making.

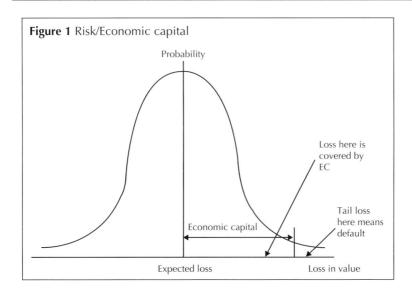

Figure 1 Risk/Economic capital

The calculations for these subsets are even more complex, as each subdivision may result in a need for the assumption of the correlation coefficient with the rest of the units of the entity and allocation of diversification benefits. For example, if the agency desk is short US$100 million GNMA 5.0s and the corporate desk is long US$100 million Daimler 6.5s of 2013, both will uniquely have risk capital assigned to their positions, but the roll-up to the entire trading desk will benefit from the likely negative correlation of these positions. Should the corporate desk benefit from the reduction in total capital that the short GNMA position provides, or the agency desk, or the entity as a whole?

REGULATORY CAPITAL FOR MARKET RISK

Let's start with something a little easier. We begin by exploring a basic approach to assigning capital for market risk. Government and sometime self-regulatory bodies have an interest in maintaining the stability of financial systems. Often this result is targeted to be delivered via a system of oversight and regulation that establishes thresholds for parts of the system to be identified as sound, or well-capitalised, with the theory being that, if all parts are sound, so too is the system.

One of the more developed regulatory frameworks that distinguish different sources of risk that require capital to be allocated against is the Basel Banking Accord. Modified in 1996 to specifically address market risk, the Basel Accord provides for different methods of calculating the amount of regulatory capital needed for market exposures.

As background, in 1988, the BIS adopted a framework for assigning capital for credit risk that simply placed different credit exposures in "buckets". The gradations were advancements on prior methods and introduced the movement of regulatory capital towards that of risk capital. This agreement became known as the Basle Accord.

In 1996, the BIS modified the 1988 agreement and began to incorporate the unique risks presented by market exposures. Substantial derivative losses in the early 1990s helped to stimulate this movement, which, in turn, moved regulatory capital one step closer to being like risk capital.

Banks were thus allowed to start choosing methods they might use to determine the amount of capital that they should allocate for market risk. They could choose a simplified "bucket" approach, like the one that had been implemented for credit risk in 1988, or, under some conditions, adopt a more advanced internal approach to determining market risk capital. Both approaches are discussed below.

Standardised method

This approach allows banks with unsophisticated risk management systems, or with low levels of perceived market risk, to adopt a framework that is more risk-sensitive in terms of calculating regulatory capital, but does not require elaborate modelling or staffing to support the effort.

Market risks are allocated to groupings that include interest rate risk, equity risk, foreign exchange risk, commodities risk and options. Each grouping was then provided with various formulas and buckets for determining the basic capital charge for that type of market risk. Some examples follow.

Interest rates

Under this approach, the capital requirement is calculated by determining both the "*specific risk*" of each security and the

Table 1 Buckets for specific risk

Security type	Remaining time to maturity	Capital charge (%)
Government	All	0.00
Qualifying	6 months or less	0.25
	Between 6 and 24 months	1.00
	More than 24 months	1.60
Others		8.00

portfolio or *"general risk"* that might incorporate some portfolio benefits.

Specific risk is determined by multiplying the face value of the interest rate instrument and bucketing of security type and maturity according to Table 1 (see BIS, 1996).

Government securities are generally those issued by Group of Seven (G7) countries. Qualifying securities include public-sector entities, multilateral guarantee authorities and investment-grade or quality equivalent to investment grade. Each supervisor has some flexibility around these figures, but the general approach is that more capital is assigned for securities that generally should be thought of as having greater price volatility.

General market risk is an additional risk factor that is designed to capture the risk of a general change in market rates. This approach requires banks to hold capital based on either a duration method or maturity method. In each case, the capital charge is the sum of four components: the net short or long position in the whole trading book; a small proportion of the matched positions in each time band; a larger proportion of the matched positions across different time bands; and a charge for any options that may be in the trading book.

As this chapter is using the Basel Accord for illustrative purposes and not an in-depth discussion of the 1996 accord, the following Table 2 illustrates how the duration method is applied and impacts capital charges (see BIS, 1996).

The bank would apply interest rate movements outlined in the table to the net security positions in the zones and time buckets and apply somewhat arbitrary additional charges for basis risk.

Finally, for interest rate derivatives, a rather complex method for converting them into security equivalents uses a table such as

Table 2 Duration method for general market risk

	Assumed change in yield		Assumed change in yield
Zone 1		*Zone 3*	
1 month or less	1.00	3.6 to 4.3 years	0.75
1 to 3 months	1.00	4.3 to 5.7 years	0.70
3 to 6 months	1.00	5.7 to 7.3 years	0.65
6 to 12 months	1.00	7.3 to 9.3 years	0.60
		9.3 to 10.6 years	0.60
Zone 2		10.6 to 12 years	0.60
1.0 to 1.9 years	0.90	12 to 20 years	0.60
1.9 to 2.8 years	0.80	over 20 years	0.60
2.8 to 3.6 years	0.75		

Table 3, which illustrates how they are treated in terms of applying specific and general risk factors (see BIS, 1996).

Equity risk

In a similar fashion, equity risk capital charges are determined by applying specific and general risk factors and use a percentage of face value to determine the charge. For example, the specific risk and general market risk charges are 8% each, except when the portfolio is substantially diversified, in which case the specific risk charge drops to 4%.

Equity derivatives are similarly converted into underlying equivalents and capital charges are applied accordingly.

Foreign exchange risk

Two processes are needed to calculate the capital requirement for foreign exchange risk. The first is to measure the exposure in a single currency position. The second is to measure the risks inherent in a bank's mix of long and short positions in different currencies.

The overall net open position is measured by aggregating the sum of the net short positions or the sum of the net long positions in each single currency and then selecting the greater of the two. The capital charge is 8% of the overall net open position.

If you get a sense that the standard approach seems to have some rather convoluted assumptions, that is because it does. However, it is important to review it for its importance as a first,

Table 3 Treatment of derivatives

Instrument	Specific risk charge[18]	General market risk charge
Exchange-traded future		
– Government: debt security	No	Yes. as two positions
– Corporate debt security	Yes	Yes. as two positions
– Index on interest rates (eg, LIBOR)	No	Yes. as two positions
OTC forward		
– Government debt security	No	Yes. as two positions
– Corporate debt security	Yes	Yes. as two positions
– Index on interest rates	No	Yes. as two positions
FRAs, Swaps	No	Yes. as two positions
Forward foreign exchange	No	Yes. as one position in each currency
Options		*Either*
– Government debt security	No	(a) Carve out together with the associated hedging positions – simplified approach – scenario analysis – internal models (Part B)
– Corporate debt security	Yes	(b) General market risk charge
– Index on interest rates	No	according to the delta-plus
– FRAs, Swaps	No	method (gamma and vega should receive separate capital charges)

very basic attempt to inject risk-sensitivity to the calculation of bank regulatory capital.

Internal models approach

The internal models approach is a more significant step in the direction of aligning regulatory capital charges with risk capital calculations. While many would argue that this approach also contains somewhat random add-ons for capital, the very acceptance of internal models built by the banks themselves for determining regulatory capital adequacy is important. The success of this approach has set the stage for the 2004 Basel II Capital Accord, which extends such an approach to credit and operational risk and will help regulatory capital to even more closely approximate risk capital.

In order for banks to use the internal models approach, they need to obtain regulatory approval first. Such approval is subject to: (i) the bank's risk management system is conceptually sound; (ii) sufficient number of staff are skilled in the use of sophisticated models; (iii) backtesting of the model is done and the results tend to validate the model's *ex ante* assessments and (iv) the bank regularly conducts stress tests of its risks.

The method for determining the capital required for market risk is based upon a value-at-risk (VAR) calculation at a 99th percentile, one-tailed confidence interval using an instantaneous price shock equivalent to a 10-day movement in prices. Banks are able to recognise empirical correlations within broad risk categories when determining VAR.

Banks are expected to use risk factors in their VAR models. Examples include, for interest rates, yield curves and spreads; for equities, index volatility and beta-equivalent measures of risk; for commodities, convenience yield.

The VAR calculation from the internal model is then multiplied by a factor, not below 3, that is determined based upon the backtesting performance of the model's *ex ante* assessments. In addition, a specific risk charge may be added on to the scaled-up VAR figure.

Critics rightly point out that a simple scaling up of a 10-day, 99% confidence VAR number is a less-than-satisfactory translation to get to a realistic estimate of the capital required for market risk. Still, the method represents a further step towards recognition of both the improved abilities to estimate risk and the need for capital charges to be more risk-sensitive.

MARKET RISK CAPITAL CALCULATIONS

While the Basel standard approach is far from being advanced, it gives some gradation and indication that more capital should be held for riskier assets. The internal models approach then recognises that many banks have already developed models that have even finer gradations and more accurately reflect the capital needed to support market risk exposures. The internal models approach, though, has a foundation in short-term VAR, which is not really designed to be used as a capital allocation tool. Hence the need for "fudge" factors such as three-times VAR.

Most firms that use internal models for calculating and allocating capital for market risk will rely on methods that attempt to move further out on the spectrum of modelling unlikely events via Monte Carlo simulation, historic simulation or some other form of stress testing, such as extreme value modelling.

Monte Carlo simulation

By far the most popular and most resource-intensive methods used for the calculation of market risk capital is the use of Monte Carlo simulation. This process uses simulated changes in key risk factors for the price evaluation of specific securities. The simulations are often based on assuming normal distribution of returns or changes in the values of risk factors and the variance of those risk factors.

For example, interest-bearing securities might use the yield curve and yield spreads as key risk factors that affect the value of the security. Equity options might use underlying security values and implied volatility as variables. Literally thousands of simulations of likely combinations of risk factors are run and the corresponding implied security values that come from the random risk factors are rank-ordered. The firm then selects the nth value of the simulation, and the choice of n is determined by the solvency standard at which the firm wishes its credit to be perceived. The difference between the nth value and the current value represents the economic capital at the target confidence level.

Table 4 99.5% confidence value of loss from a Monte Carlo simulation with 10,000 paths

Rank order	Path	Change in value
9,948	4,204	US$(1,035,217)
9,949	35	US$(1,365,272)
9,950	*3,345*	*US$(1,813,710)*
.		
.		
.		
9,997	1,529	US$(3,032,818)
9,998	18	US$(3,055,464)
9,999	9,312	US$(4,009,099)
10,000	8,863	US$(5,001,234)

Monte Carlo simulations are appealing because they inject a certain degree of randomness of future outcomes. However, these outcomes are highly dependent on assumptions about the inputs to the models (correlation, volatility, prepayments and so forth).[1] The computational power required for highly complex simulations can be quite staggering. Computing power has obviously lowered the barrier for many firms, but, as the technology has advanced, so too have the ideas for how to use it. Very simply, firms with more money to spend on technology and human capital will be able to run better simulations and the race will always continue.

Historic simulation

Where Monte Carlo simulations are highly valued for their ability to create a near-infinite set of future outcomes, they do not easily create results that mimic past observed price behaviour in the extreme. In reality, extreme market events tend to happen more frequently than should be expected based on the assumed price distributions used with Monte Carlo methods. This phenomenon is often referred to as the "fat-tail" problem.

One method developed for better mimicking future fat tails is to assume that past fat tails are likely to be good predictors of those that might be seen again. So, rather than create a large set of possible risk-factor levels, systems will value securities based on observed combinations of risk factors from "recent" data.

By so doing, the models will be able to calculate a set of possible values for securities that is utterly defensible as being possible outcomes because their determinants have already been observed. The use of historic data also has the advantage in that fat tails are already built into the method. In other words, one is simply assuming that the fat tails of the past will neither gain nor lose proportion. They will remain equally fat in the future.

Like Monte Carlo simulation, the results of the historic simulation are rank-ordered and the observation that corresponds to the targeted default probability is the capital allocation for market risk.

Historic simulation has shortcomings as well. First, there is no guarantee that the future will mimic the past. We have ample evidence of strong mean-reversion tendencies in many risk factors, but we do not know the pace at which such reversions will occur. The chief shortcoming, though, is the paucity of data available for complex instruments. Where substantial data do exist, lengthening the horizon for analysis of securities implies that there is an even greater reliance on mean-reverting behaviour. Nearly all price data show evidence of serial or autocorrelation that tends to be strongest when measured with the most recent data. The longer the horizon from which the data are gathered, the greater is the loss of information that might be contained in more recent data. On the other hand, if only recent data are used, there are not enough valuations to reliably generate a distribution from which to pull an accurate required capital figure.

Extreme value theory

One of the major drawbacks of distribution assumptions needed for Monte Carlo simulation is that they may not provide for enough clustering of extreme events, or fat tails. While the use of historic simulation is an attempt to create forward-looking fat tails based on past observations, the examination of the distribution of extreme values has taken the maths even further.

In extreme value theory, extreme values are assumed to have a distribution of their own. In essence, the distribution assumptions of Monte Carlo simulations, which are described by mean and variance, are now described with a third parameter, which describes the fatness of the tails. Extreme returns are assumed to converge asymptotically to a known distribution.

Extreme value theory, like the other methods used for estimation of the cost of highly unlikely events, has its drawbacks as well.[2] At the core is an assumption of the independence of observations used to model the distribution of the extreme events. While "normal" market data exhibit autocorrelation, the correlation of extreme events can be very high. For evidence of this, witness the number of extreme market movements in the Nasdaq index in 2000.

Scenario/headline stress testing

Capital allocation has highly material uses, such as ensuring the viability of the firm at some confidence level. It also has a managerial use in the provision of new tools for senior executives and the leaders of groups that originate risk. Quite frankly, most of these people do not care about Monte Carlo or historic simulation methods and the details behind them. They are simply concepts that are too esoteric for their daily business decision making.

Still, those willing to listen to discussions of risk capital have probably experienced a major risk event, know of a peer or competitor that has or have read of cases like those mentioned at the start of this chapter. In other words, there is a tangible way in which they can touch the concepts of extreme events.

Scenario/headline stress testing takes risk factor data from observed extreme events that also made headlines. The Tequila crisis, 1987 or 2000 equity market crashes and even the LTCM-related spread widening are all events that are readily identifiable by most. The actual market conditions and risk factors from these periods can be applied to individual securities to determine what their impact would be today and that figure can be communicated to senior managers.

This is not to be confused with a capital allocation method, but more of an education tool, as there is no way to assign any kind of probability to the repeat of these events. However, one can use them to compare the risk capital figures derived by other methods to those that such headline scenarios would generate. In many ways, such analysis can serve as a reality check for more advanced methods and can serve as a launching board for discussions of whether confidence levels assigned to default are something in which we should have confidence. In other words, despite the industry's relative comfort with market risk, a reasonable amount of scepticism needs to be placed on our ability to calculate probabilities of future market events to the right of the decimal point, as in 99.5% probability versus 99.75% probability. What we can say, though, is that we do have good methods for describing the market risks we face, even if not with exactitude, and when more capital is held by a firm, all else being equal, it is less likely to experience failure because of a market event. We can also say that changes in the level of capital allocated by the methods above should be explainable. This gives risk managers "teaching moments" where the value of our practice can most easily be demonstrated.

Corporate application of market risk capital calculations

Risk capital allocation plays an important role in signalling both an understanding of the risks assumed through market-priced securities and the intended credit-worthiness of the entity holding those positions. It also serves as an educational tool, even beyond the usefulness of scenario/headline stress scenarios.

Ultimately, risk capital calculation and allocation are about making the most efficient use of a scarce and cowardly resource: capital. The chief benefit derived from pursuing the complex analytics and office politicking of implementing a capital allocation framework is that business leaders, who are paid to make decisions, are able to make *better* decisions. They are also able to reward, more accurately, those who report to them and make better decisions.

Consider the case of two business lines, A and B. Each contributed US$100 million in net revenue to their parent company, had equal sales volume and managed to grow their sales volume and expenses in lockstep with each other. In fact, by nearly all accounting and managerial dashboard measures, the two business lines appear identical in input and output.

How might one justify paying the leader of business unit A anything less than business unit B? The most under-reported cost of business is the cost of taking risk. Consider if business line A sold guaranteed hedge funds to senior pensioners, while business line B manufactured foam rubber for use in soft cushions. One could hardly argue that A and B presented their parent firm with equal risks, yet, without any charge for the risk they assume, they would appear to have provided the same return to shareholders.

For simplicity's sake, assume that there are no other forms of risk presented by A and B. Risk capital allows us to distinguish between the market risk of an increase in rubber prices and that of a declining price in hawked hedge funds. Taken in the proper risk-adjusted context, business line A would be suitably recognised for its substantial underperformance relative to business line B and the management of the parent company could take future corrective action by allocating capital away from A and towards B.

As was mentioned earlier, most senior executives care very little about the specifics behind the methods of determining their capital allocation. In fact, most will not know the meaning of the amount of capital that has been allocated to them, regardless of method. In order to communicate the importance of these figures, capital needs to be converted into a cost, just like personnel and office space.

Assume that capital for the parent of A and B can be raised for a cost of 12% per year and that the parent does not wish to charge differentiated rates for capital to its subsidiaries. Now, if business line A was allocated US$700 million in risk capital and business line B was allocated US$300 million, they would, assuming no diversification benefits, in combination, require that the parent company expend US$120 million annually to fund their capital. Of this, 70% could be a line item cost to business line A, resulting in a net economic profit of US$16 million, while business line B would be yielding a net economic profit of US$64 million. Both appear to generate positive value for the firm, but the fact that business line B generates four times the economic profit of business line A signals that resources might be taken from A to grow B and that A's leaders should be less well compensated than the leaders of B. Without a charge for risk, such a conclusion would be hard to reach.

Knowing the market risk of A and B provided the firm with a way to objectively analyse which use of firm capital resulted in the highest benefit to shareholders. Yet, if A's only risk was exposure to the price of a hedge fund and B's only risk was simple exposure to changes in rubber prices, the parent company could use any of the methods detailed above to co-vary hedge fund and rubber prices, and determine a level of market risk capital that is appropriate for the firm as a whole.

CONCLUSION

Market risk capital needs are most accurately calculated by using simulations of future security prices and the covariance of risk factors that determine those prices. Alternative short cuts exist, such as the methods used in the Basel Capital Accord, but leave much to be desired in terms of their reliability. Still, charging for the costs of risk taking, even if such is measured accurately in direction and less accurately in magnitude, provides business leaders with better information on which to make better business decisions and makes the practice of risk management more valuable to the firms that employ risk managers.

1 For a good discussion of Monte Carlo simulations, see Glasserman (2003).
2 Good reference sources for information on extreme value theory in finance include Embrechts, Klüppelberg and Mikosch (1997) and McNeil (1998). See also a series of articles by Professor Kevin Dowd in *Financial Engineering News* at http://www.fenews.com/fen11/extreme.html.

REFERENCES

BIS, 1996, "Amendment to the Capital Accord to Incorporate Market Risks", January.

Embrechts, P., C. Klüppelberg, and T. Mikosch, 1997, *Modelling extremal events for insurance and finance* (Berlin: Springer-Verlag).

Glasserman, P., 2003, *Monte Carlo Methods in Financial Engineering* (Berlin: Springer-Verlag).

McNeil, A. J., 1998, "Calculating Quantile Risk Measures for Financial Return Series Using Extreme Value Theory", mimeo, ETH Zentrum, Zürich.

10

Measuring and Calculating Economic Operational Risk Capital

Anthony Peccia
RCM Risk Management Ltd

This chapter illustrates how an advanced measurement approach (the AMA in BIS terminology) can be constructed that, based on the loss distribution approach (LDA), integrates internal losses, external losses and credible scenario analysis, and incorporates directly into the measurement process the state of the business and controls environments as determined through risk and control self-assessments (RCSAs), key risk indicators (KRIs) and audit assessments. Through this approach, there is no need for ad hoc and most often arbitrary qualitative adjustments. This approach, called the *operational risk ratings approach*, directly measures the risks identified in the RCSA, which then provides management with the insight into which controls to improve in order to achieve or maintain the desired level of operational risk.

Economic operational risk capital: what for?

The New Capital Accord (see BIS, 2004), commonly referred to as Basel II, has spawned a lot of interest in operational risk measurement and management. This interest has in turn spawned a variety of operational risk initiatives, ranging from qualitative self-assessments and various forms of operational risk data collection to some highly sophisticated, and some might say esoteric, discussions of the application of advanced statistics, including using extreme value theory, to measuring operational risk.[1] Unfortunately, all too often, there is only some vague notion that implementing these initiatives will improve the management of operational risk, but there is no clear vision or strategy for what all these initiatives are supposed to achieve. And so, before we can plunge into the measurement of operational risk, we must first develop that vision. Otherwise, we may well have a measure, but the measure will be of limited use.

First we need to recognise that operational risk is already being managed through a variety of means, and therefore any new operational risk initiative, be it data collection or measurement, should leverage or improve existing processes.

The collection, storage and reporting of operational risk information is a massive exercise, which touches all parts of the organisation can become a very costly expenditure in people, process and systems. This is not a trivial cost issue. What is the value added of having risk management implement this costly initiative.

At most banks, most of the information that is being contemplated for collection by these operational risk systems is already originated or collected, stored and reported to business management, senior management and the board of directors by the various organisational units such as finance, audit, legal affairs, corporate security, compliance, operations management, business continuity management, IT management and so on. Likewise, at most banks, all significant operational risk events that occur within an organisation or at major competitors are already reported by the affected party and reviewed, with varying degrees of formality, at management committee meetings. What is the value added of a centralised operational risk group doing the same?

An operational risk manager once complained to a group of other operational risk managers that, at his bank, a major fraud had been detected and reported to senior management. Action plans had been developed and implemented and the operational risk manager responsible was found only several weeks after the fact. The other managers all nodded their heads, sighed in resignation and expressed frustration that it was all too common an occurrence at their respective banks. However, when asked what they would have done with the information if it were given to them at discovery, or how they would have improved the management of risk with that knowledge, none could offer a concrete response.

Some may argue that the existing processes are incomplete and ad hoc on their own. The operational risk group fills the gaps, through standardisation, regularisation and making complete. That may be so, and, if so, it may be much cheaper to fill the gaps within the originating processes rather than implement a new add-on fixing process. It is important to understand that the value of improved operational risk management, as suggested by Basel II, is not being questioned here. What is being suggested is that the development and implementation of the information systems required to support the improved management of operational risk should leverage all existing systems, improve existing them where necessary and avoid duplication. In other words, there should be a concrete value-adding response to the question about what the operational risk manager would do with the information.

Strategic risk management as supported by measurement and operational risk capital is the concrete answer. This is not based on speculation but synthesised by examining successes in other risk disciplines and adapting it to operational risk.

Market risk management is, from many perspectives, the most developed risk management discipline and therefore examining market risk can provide valuable lessons for operational risk management. Market risk management, in its current form, all began with the request by a former JP Morgan chairman to get an independently validated measure of how much money the bank could lose through its numerous trading portfolios from adverse market moves. The request is simple enough. The answer is very difficult to obtain. Sophisticated methodologies had to be developed, sophisticated risk management processes had to be implemented supported by powerful analytic engines and the whole activity had to be managed by sophisticated market risk managers. However, once developed, it had two other highly valuable results. For the first time, the board and senior management could be assured that the market risk taken within the various trading portfolios was within their risk tolerance. This lessened significantly unwelcome surprise effects on the P&L. Second, it permitted portfolio risk management by ensuring that the risk profile of each individual portfolio could be tailored to return the required rate of return on capital, or to disinvest in the portfolio if it could not. Since then, additional substantial value has been extracted, but even the initial two benefits were sufficient to justify the millions of dollars required to implement market risk management.

Imagine, then, a situation in which the operational risk taken within each business unit is measured and is set within certain tolerance levels so that there are very few surprises should losses happen. In addition, the board of directors and senior management are assured that the bank has the capacity to absorb the loss, should it happen, because it has set aside sufficient capital. Furthermore, within those tolerances, business management can decide to either increase the risk by removing expensive controls and adding less expensive capital or decrease the risk by adding less expensive controls and removing more expensive capital. This is the vision and the true value of operational risk management; the function. measurement is the way to realise that value.

To achieve this vision, the measurement model must provide some key results. It should be tied directly to the risks that are identified in the RCSA. It should allow business management to transparently see how the risk measure is affected by their decisions about the business and control environments. It should be an accurate reflection of the actual potential for loss associated with the business and control environments, so all the various types of operational risk receive the same capital for the same amount of risk. And lastly it should satisfy the regulatory requirements of Basel II.

Not all these goals can be achieved to perfection at this stage in the evolution of operational risk management. Nevertheless, incremental progress can be made and substantial value can be created. In other words, even though there may be a long way to go, and some may wish to go only part of the way, they are still better off than if they had not gone at all.

The remainder of the chapter will discuss how such a first-generation measurement model can be built, how to realise some of that value and how greater value can be obtained by pointing the way to future enhancements.

MEASURING OPERATIONAL RISK: AN INTEGRAL PART OF THE MANAGEMENT PROCESS

Where to start? An excellent place to start the development of a measurement of operational risk is the operational risk sound practices document issued by Basel in February 2003 (see BIS, 2003a). This may seem odd since the paper deals mostly with the *management* of operational risk and does not deal with *measurement* at all. Instead, shouldn't we start, as is most often done, with issues around modelling operational risk loss, including statistical techniques for the proper fitting of distributions, how to fill in data gaps and the like? These discussions are no doubt important. However, to build a measurement model that achieves the goals we set out and described in the above, and more specifically one that gives business management the tool for deciding the appropriate business and control environments in which to operate, first we have to establish a coherent operational risk management framework, within which operational risk measurement must fit. The sound practices document deals with such an operational risk management framework.

That paper states ten principles, three of which deal with the role of the board of directors and senior management, four deal with the management of operational risk, two with the supervisory role and one with minimum operational risk disclosure (which by the standards of market and credit risk is truly minimalist!). This document is a great milestone in the evolution of the management of operational risk. It brings together for the first time in a coherent and comprehensive manner all the elements of sound operational risk management.

For the purposes of measuring operational risk, we will focus on the four principles associated with its management. These deal with the identification, assessment, monitoring and control/mitigation of operational risk. Combining these four principles with the qualifying criteria for the advanced measurement approach (AMA) required by Basel II provides us with the integrated operational risk management framework we seek.

Figure 1 graphically illustrates the integrated operational risk management framework in a way that is easy to relate to and easy to remember. Note that the framework refers to measurement within the management framework even though common usage splits measurement and management into two distinct elements. However, better measurement leads to better monitoring and better capital attribution and finally to better control/mitigation, which are all components of managing. Common usage says

Figure 1 Operational risk management: The integrated framework

5 Operational risk control mitigation

1 Operational risk identification

All businesses
All new products
All new initiatives

4 Operational risk capital

2 Operational risk measurement

3 Operational risk monitoring

To be effective and value added to management an integrated approach is required

❏ each component should be *built on* the solid foundation of the previous and through continuous improvement
❏ the succeeding component should *influence* the previous component.

"management" when it actually means "control/mitigation". We will use "management" to refer to all the components, and suggest that to avoid confusion it be widely adopted.

Following the logic of the coherent and integrated operational risk management framework, before the development of the operational risk measurement model can begin, we have to examine the risk identification process and ensure that it is coherent, consistent and supports the vision established for operational risk management.

Too often, the measurement of operational risk is done in isolation of the risk identification process, commonly done through one of the varied approaches to RCSA. Complicating matters further, often the risks identified within the RCSA are different from the risks measured by the measurement model. For example, the RCSA may identify information security risk as a significant risk, whereas many measurement models include information security risk only loosely and implicitly as part of some aggregate measure from which the contribution of information security risk cannot be determined. Not only does this breed confusion, it makes the measurement model largely irrelevant to the manager of information security. Not a good state of affairs. A much better approach is to directly measure the risks identified in the RCSA, which then provides management with the insight to decide which controls to increase/improve or which to remove in order to achieve or maintain the desired level of operational risk.

IDENTIFYING OPERATIONAL RISK:
A COHERENT APPROACH

The first task is to sort out what operational risk is. Basel defines operational risk as the risk of loss resulting from inadequate or failed processes, people and system or from external events.[2] This definition has helped put boundaries around what was previously a residual risk (ie, not market and not credit risk) and it has been immensely helpful. It does, however, remain too high-level to be helpful for managing operational risk. Most banks have drilled down the definition and have developed lists of items to be included. We say items because all the items included are not actually risks, even though they may be called risks. This list often includes such items as key-person risk, information security risk, training risk, complex product risk, system integration risk, regulatory complexity risk, earthquake risk, legal risk, fraud and so on, almost without end. The list is huge because it tends to be a list of all the things that can go wrong, along with a much smaller list of the risks that follow when those things go wrong. Some sort of order is required.

The list is actually composed of three distinct types of item. There are items that describe the characteristics of the business environment. For example, often we hear of key-person risk. Key-person risk is not a risk at all but a contributory factor to the potential for loss (ie, risk). The term "key-person risk" actually describes an environment in which the business activity is highly dependent on a few highly skilled people to carry out a critical activity, where these individuals are in much demand, and the prevailing internal and external circumstances may cause them to leave. Likewise, "regulatory complexity risk" actually describes the characteristic of the regulatory environment in which the business operates, and is not a risk. Carrying out a certain activity that is highly controlled by complex regulations – and the regulations are evolving fast – is much more risky relative to carrying out the same activity in an environment that it is not regulated. There are many similar examples that can be culled from commonly used lists of operational risks. These elements describe the nature of the business environment and should no longer be described as risks but simply as the business environment.

The contribution to the amount of risk resulting from considerations of the business environment is often referred to as the inherent risk.[3]

There are also items that describe controls such as information security risk and training risk. These are not risks: they are controls. When these controls work they reduce the risk and when they fail they increase risk. All these types of item should be aggregated into a separate list of controls, and in aggregate referred to as the control environment.

Finally, there are items in the list that are the actual risk. These are such items as fraud, legal liability and damaged assets. They are distinguished from the other two in that they do not influence the level of risk but rather describe the type of risk and therefore should be exclusively referred to as types of operational risk.

These three elements fit together as follows. The type of activity a business pursues determines the type of operational risk that the business is exposed to. For example, being active in trading market instruments exposes that business to fraud by rogue trading, whereas being active in retail banking does not. The business and control environments in which the business operates determine the amount of the exposure. That is, the business and control environments drive the exposure. Measurement quantifies that exposure.

Having established what we want to measure, (the risk), and what drives the measure (the business and control environments), we can now move on to developing the measurement model. However, a model will require a standardised set of inputs and outputs, ie, the risks and the business and control environments. So before we can proceed to building the model we need to construct these standardised sets.

Standardised operational risks

Basel II has provided a standardised set of seven distinct operational risks. These are summarised in Table 1. These seven Basel operational risk types are not perfect and still contain some of the mixture among risk, business and control environments factors. For example, a system failure is what it says it is. It is a failure that

Table 1 The 7 Basel operational risk types

1. **Internal fraud**
   Losses due to acts of a type intended to defraud, misappropriate property or circumvent regulations, the law or company policy, excluding diversity/discrimination events, which involves at least one internal party.

2. **External fraud**
   Losses due to acts of a type intended to defraud, misappropriate property or circumvent the law, by a third party.

3. **Employment practices and workplace safety**
   Losses arising from acts inconsistent with employment, health or safety laws or agreements, from payment of personal injury claims, or from diversity/discrimination events.

4. **Professional practices**
   Losses arising from an unintentional or negligent failure to meet a professional obligation to specific clients (including fiduciary and suitability requirements), or from the nature or design of a product.

5. **Loss or damage to assets**
   Losses arising from loss or damage to physical assets from natural disaster or other events.

6. **Business disruption and system failures**
   Losses arising from disruption of business or system failures.

7. **Transaction processing risk**
   Losses from failed transaction processing or process management, from relations with trade counterparties and vendors.

can affect the level of internal fraud, external fraud and damage to assets and potentially other operational risk, depending on what the system does. As a result some very complicated decision trees must be invented to ensure proper classification. A good classification should contain categories that are mutually exclusive such as fraud and damage to assets and not be held up by complicated decision trees. Following the grouping of like items discussed above, one could develop a better list of operational risk types. However, that is both beyond the scope of this chapter and at this time the Basel categorisation represents an industry standard.

It is better to proceed with these types, imperfect as they are, and move on rather than spend time perfecting them and postponing measurement to some indefinite time in the future. The whole approach to operational risk management should be one of continuous improvement. This means that working solutions are adopted and implemented for each step of the framework, and improvements are made as required through their actual usage and as new circumstances warrant. This approach ensures quick wins as well as a steady stream of refinements that have the greatest impact on the results, as opposed to refinements, which may be intellectually interesting but have only a marginal impact on actual business results. From time to time the industry and the regulators should come together to refine these risk types.

Next, we require a set of standardised descriptions of the characteristic of the business and control environments, which determine when present, or more accurately the degree to which they are present, the level of operational risk.

RATING THE CONTROL ENVIRONMENT
KEY RISK DRIVERS

In the case of the control environment, there are already a few standards that have been developed by various international industry associations such as Control Objectives for Information Technology (COBiT) by the Information Systems Audit and Control Association, the Internal Control Framework by COSO, and the Capability Maturity Model Software Engineering Institute and others.[4] They are referred to as *maturity models* and segment the state of the control environment into several different classes or ratings, usually five. The rating is determined by the existence of specific and observable conditions about the state of the control environment. The operative words are specific and observable and these should be emphasised, since this is the only way to ensure a repeatable process that yields the same rating regardless of who is involved in the rating process. For example, COBiT assigns the second-highest rating to a control environment where all performance indicators are being recorded and monitored and leading to enterprise-wide improvements, and where most processes are being monitored against baseline metrics, along with many other specified conditions. It is important to emphasise here that, unlike most approaches to control assessments, this one does not ask individuals to determine whether controls are effective or not. Rather it prespecifies what constitutes various degrees of effectives for each control type and then asks individuals (business and support functions) to determine their degree of existence. This has two advantages over the traditional approach. First, it relies on the expertise of audit and other control experts to predetermine what are effective controls for a given set of risks and builds this expertise into the rating methodology. Second, since the determination is based on observation and the process is repeatable and more objective, most other fields that require expert knowledge do pretty much the same. For example a doctor does not ask us whether we are healthy or not, because that is the conclusion to be arrived at based on answers to questions about my condition. So too with the control environment: we should not ask businesses to determine the effectiveness of controls, since that is what is to be concluded. Instead, we should ask for evidence of effectiveness, which is then used to determine the rating.

How is this done in practice? A control environment rating for a given bank is assigned by matching the prevailing control conditions at the bank with the set of observable control conditions, which define each control rating. This is very similar to a credit rating, where each rating is characterised by specific conditions about the balance sheet, income state, quality of management, industry and so on that must be present in order for a specific rating to apply.

The control environment has several dimensions or key risk drivers and sometimes also referred to as KRIs.[5]

Table 2 is an example of the key risk drivers for an operational risk control environment. For certain conditions it may be easy to determine whether the conditions exists or not, while for others there is only a degree of existence, not an either/or.[6] In these situations judgement must be applied to determine whether the degree of existence is sufficient to move it from one rating to another. This is no different in credit. For example, many firms operate in several industries and therefore judgement is used to assign the firm to a specific industry, and consequently to a specific rating. This is also true in many other fields. For example, in health risk one of the conditions for a healthy lifestyle is exercising often. Although one may provide guidance as to what exercising often means, such as doing a thirty-minute workout three times a week, individuals who do a twenty-minute workout every day would also be judged as exercising often, whereas an individual doing five minutes of exercise twice day would not. Wherever possible the criteria

Table 2 The control environment key risk drivers

Control drivers	Characteristics
Policy/directives	Policies/directives current primitive Policies/directives provide adequate guidance Policies/directives are known/followed
Qualified personnel	Turnover Sufficient FTE to execute the control environment described for managing this risk Personnel have the appropriate skill sets to execute and monitor the control environment
Risk measures/limits	Risk measures or limits exist for this activity Risk measures or limits at an appropriate threshold for this activity Risk measures or limits are breached regularly
Process/procedures	Sufficient processes exist to manage this activity Processes documented Documented processes reflect current practices and processes Established process(s) exist to manage this activity
Independent reporting/MIS	Adequate information sources are available to understand what is occurring in your business activities Information is not available when it is needed or is dated Reporting is not clear and concise (ie, complete)
Communication	Communication channels exist for this business activity (ie, Do you know whom to contact when you have a question) When communication channels are used, there is a timely response
Monitoring	Adequate oversight exists for the activities described in the control environment Monitoring activity is independent of the unit that performs the day to day work within the LoB

should be based on specific conditions, but, as the above health example shows, forcing specific conditions where a variety of specific conditions fulfil the general conditions would diminish the value of the rating, not increase it.

The rating is a determination of the degree to which controls are adequate and effective and therefore each rating represents the degree of contribution to the level of operational risk. At this point some might want to construct the rating scheme that correlates best with the actual risk. We suggest that at this stage it is better to proceed with an adequate rating scheme, incorporate that into the measurement model and then adapt and refine the rating scheme through use. Otherwise, seeking the best rating scheme becomes an end it itself, and, in any event, how does one know whether a rating scheme is best until it is actually used in measuring? With time, as industry loss data become available, the ratings and their corresponding determining conditions can be modified to better fit the observed loss experience.

RATING THE BUSINESS ENVIRONMENT
KEY RISK DIVERS

Unlike the case of the control environment, there are no well-established approaches to systematising the relevant operational risk business conditions into risk ratings. Once again, we can turn to observation as the guide. By examining similar business activities carried out in different business environments, we can extract those conditions that affect the level of risk and those that do not. For example, carrying out banking operations in an earthquake zone, flood zone or war zone exposes those operations to more damage to assets and to more operational risk than does carrying those same activities in less dangerous zones. So geographical location is a key risk driver for damage to assets. Delivering and processing a simple product through highly interrelated systems, and therefore complex systems, exposes the bank to more operational risk than delivering and processing the same product through independent systems. This is not simply conjecture. There have been several instances where entire retail banking networks have been brought down by simple programming errors that affected seemingly unrelated systems. System complexity is therefore another business environment key risk driver. An old product offered in a new market with uncharted legal relationships exposes the bank to greater legal risk than the same product offered in a market where the legal relationships have been tested in the courts. Such was the case when banks started to offer plain vanilla swaps to local councils in the UK, and it was later found that the contracts were unenforceable because those local authorities did not have the power to enter into such contracts. So legal environment is also another key risk driver. Many more examples can be drawn from the historical record of operational failures, and after a while a pattern emerges.

Table 3 The business environment key risk drivers

Environmental drivers	Characteristics
Product complexity	Familiar market; P/L complexity Valuation complexity; maturity/uniqueness
Process complexity	Number of processes
Systems complexity	Maturity of technology; complexity of technology Few things through a single system Standalone, centralised/multiple regional points Many things through a single system
Geography	Urban/rural presence; exposure to natural disaster Exposure to terrorism; crime environment Political stability
Legal complexity	Jurisdiction; standardised document and affect on class suits Specialised documentation affect on suits Fiduciary aspect to activity; number of laws governing business
Regulatory complexity	Multiple regulatory bodies; new regulatory bodies New or existing regulatory bodies with evolving mandates Multiple domestic, foreign, or multinational jurisdictions Complex or new regulation
Speed of change	Rapid expansion Rapid downsizing

Table 3 is an illustration of a distillation of those business environment conditions that affect the level of operational risk. The conditions have been organised into seven distinct key risk drivers. These are: product complexity, process complexity, systems complexity, geography, legal complexity, regulatory complexity and speed of change.

Once again, alternative schemes can be proposed. Different schemes will be more suitable to different banks and different situations. What is important for this purpose is not the particular scheme but that a rational scheme for identifying and classifying those business conditions that affects the level operational risk be developed and implemented. Once such a scheme is developed, a similar approach to that used for the control environment is used to classify the business environment into operational risk ratings.

So far we have established that there are the seven types of operational risk, as defined by Basel, and 14 key risk drivers, seven of

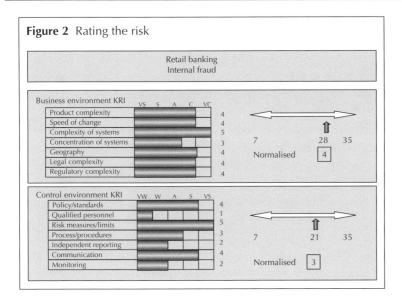

Figure 2 Rating the risk

which reflect the state of the business environment with the other seven reflecting the state of the control environment. These key risk drivers affect the level of exposure to each of the seven operational risks. Clearly, different key risk drivers affect each type of operational risk in different ways. For example, operating in an earthquake zone has a direct impact on the exposure to damage to assets but has a minor, if any, effect on internal fraud. Likewise, detection systems aimed at controlling internal fraud may be well developed, whereas those governing employee practices related to, say, discrimination might not be. To take this into account, a separate rating is required for each type of operational risk.

Figure 2 illustrates such a rating for internal fraud within retail banking. The seven key risk drivers for the business environment were rated, using a five-point scale, ranging from 1 (to indicate a very simple environment) to 5 (to indicate a very complex business environment).

Since each of the seven key risk drivers can range from 1 to 5 the combined rating can range from 7 to 35, and this can then be normalised back to a five-point range by dividing by 7. For this example, each of the key risk drivers has been given equal weighting. This is a simple approach and is a good going-in position where no further knowledge is available. With time, as part of the continuous improvement approach suggested throughout, fact-based weightings can be introduced to reflect that certain key risk drivers of the business environment have different effects on different risks. In this example the overall rating for the business environment has been determined to be 4, which means that there is a high degree of exposure to the internal fraud due to conditions within the business environment. Which conditions? Well, the specific observable elements of each rating, in this case 4, should tell you exactly what those conditions are.

Likewise, the same approach is used for rating the control environment relative to internal fraud in retail banking. The range is from 1 (indicating very week controls) to 5 (indicating very strong controls). In this example, the control environment, as it applies to internal fraud, is rated as 3 and therefore, compared with the business environment rating of 4, the controls are neither sufficiently present nor adequate to balance the effect of the level of risk contributed by the business environment. For the controls to balance the business environment contribution to the risk, a control environment rating of 4 would be required. And, as described above for the business environment, by drilling down into each of the seven key risk drivers for the control environment, and their associated ratings, the control deficiencies can be easily identified.

So far we have a clear picture of the activity we are examining (retail banking), the operational risk under consideration (internal fraud), and, in a qualitative way, have determined that the amount of risk contributed by the specific business environment in which this retail bank is being carried out is more that the risk reduction resulting from the specific control environment in place. Should we wish to reduce the risk, we know that we have to do one of two things. We can reduce contribution to the risk by the business environment, and the rating will tell us exactly what needs to be done. Since many of the business environment conditions are not under our direct control, at least in the short term, we may be limited in how much risk reduction from the business environment is actually achievable. Alternatively, we can increase the reduction in risk by improving controls and once again the rating should tell us which controls to improve. This is a powerful tool for business management and risk management to collaborate on achieving the desired risk level. The desired level should, of course, be determined by

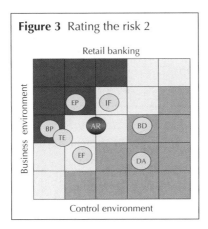

Figure 3 Rating the risk 2

whether the return on capital required supporting that level of risk is being achieved. What does this actually mean? Suppose the return is not being met, because the risk and therefore the capital is too high. Business management can then analyse whether spending more on controls to reduce the risk is offset by the reduction in the cost of capital from the liberated capital.

The process is repeated for the other six operational risks. The results can be summarised into a heat map as illustrated in Figure 3. "IF" represents internal fraud with a control environment rating of 3 and a business environment rating of 4.

This heat map is a graphical representation of the operational risk profile. For ease of illustration the operational risk profile has been segmented into three zones. High risk is associated with the black zone (not enough or effective controls for the risk contributed by the business environment); average risk (the contribution from the business environment is balanced by the reduction in risk by controls) is associated with the white zone; and low risk (the contribution from the business environment is more than balanced by the reduction in risk by controls) is associated with the grey zone. There is nothing to prevent the expansion of the granularity of the risk profile beyond three. However there is a lower limit and this lower limit, as will be seen in the next section, is limited by the number of data available compared with what is required to create credible loss distributions. More on this later. Notice, also, that the individual risks have been aggregated into an aggregate risk denoted by "AR". A description of how this aggregation process is done will have to wait until the measurement model is described, since a meaningful aggregation can be made only through the measurement model.

This approach not only provides a structured, observation-based methodology to operational risk and control assessment, but readily provides the means for a transparent, consistent, aggregatable and drill-down capability to be brought into the business and control environments' key risk drivers that affect the level of risk. Therefore, business management is provided with a valuable tool for (a) determining the level of exposure (in a qualitative way at this time), (b) for understanding why the risk is what it is and (c) determining whether they are unhappy about the level of exposure and the conditions within the business and control environments, which they may change to achieve their desired level of exposure.

Some might say that this is RCSA at its best. Others might object, saying that this is incomplete. The traditional RCSA requires not only an identification of the risk but also a determination of the frequency and severity (financial impact) of the risks. But that is precisely what the measurement process is to deliver. Traditionally, as a part of RCSA, experts are asked to guess (we say "guess" for a reason, on which more later) the frequency of occurrence and then to estimate some characteristic of the potential loss, such as the mean, the most likely or the worst case.

We say "guess" because one of two situations occurs. Either losses happen with sufficient regularity or they do not. In the case of sufficient regularity, expert judgement, based on this rich experience, can be relied upon to estimate credible frequency of occurrence. But, if losses happen with sufficient regularity, then the estimate can be more accurately obtained by a statistical analysis of the historical loss experience and therefore there is no need for a cruder estimate based on the expert judgement. If losses do not happen with sufficient regularity, how can experts possibly estimate a credible frequency? There simply is not sufficient experience for the expertise to develop. Once gain that is where measurement comes in. The measurement model should provide the frequency and severity for the identified risks based on the ratings for the business and control environment.

The remainder of the chapter will show how such a model can be constructed.

THE OPERATIONAL RISK RATING MEASUREMENT
MODEL AND ECONOMIC CAPITAL

Once the operational risk has been identified and rated, using the process described above, measuring the risk is actually a simple exercise – once the elements are in place of course. The measurement process is similar to credit risk. First the loan is rated and then the loss distribution for that rating, which has been determined from the loss experience of a large number of similarly rated loans, is assigned to that loan. In the case of operational risk, instead of the loan, we have the line of business (or, more granularly, the activity within the business line). In addition, operational risk has seven distinct types of risk and therefore the rating applies not only to the line of business but also to each of the different types of risk. What remains to be done is to determine the loss distribution that applies to each operational risk rating associated with each combination of line of business activity and operational risk type. Basel has already pointed the way. Based on the loss experience of 89 banks obtained through the loss collection exercise of 2002 (see BIS, 2003b), Basel calibrated the operational risk for the average bank. It did this by constructing a loss distribution fitted to the set of losses of the 89 banks, and estimated the loss at the 99.9% confidence level to be 15% of gross income.[7]

Basel went further. It segmented the losses according to the different standard lines of business and developed loss distributions for each line of business. In so doing, it determined that, for the average retail bank, the operational risk is 12% of gross income, instead of 15% for the average bank that includes all the eight lines of businesses. For the average trading and sales it is 18% of gross income. The operational risk rate applied to the gross income of the individual line of business is referred to as beta. These betas represent the operational risk rate for each line of business with an average rating for the business and control environment, since the loss data included all various ratings from the different retail bank lines of business included in the sample.

Therefore, if, after identifying and rating the operational risk for our retail banking line of business, the aggregate risk is determined to be in the yellow zone (average risk), the capital required to support the operational risk for our retail bank is 12% of gross income. But what do we do if the aggregate risk is not in the yellow zone? Suppose our retail bank operates in a less risky business

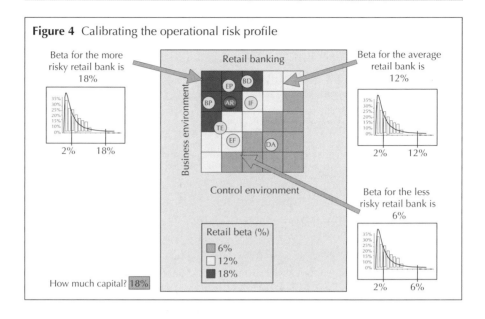

Figure 4 Calibrating the operational risk profile

environment or has better controls so as to place it in the green zone or below average risk. Then what is the required capital? Well, the same process can be applied. The loss data for all retail banking should be segmented into two sets. One set for all losses belong to retail banks that have been rated as a high risk and the other set for all losses belonging to retail banks that have been rated as a low risk, using a particular rating methodology such as the one described in this chapter. Once this is done the same standard statistical techniques, including extreme value theory, can be applied to determine the loss distribution for each set or rating. Suppose that this process is applied and it is determined that low-risk retail banks have a beta of 6% and high-risk retail banks have a beta of 18%, then the required capital for our low-risk rated retail bank is also 6% of its gross income. As in credit risk, once the rating is known, the loss distribution and the capital are also known. Figure 4 illustrates the process in retail banking. The same process can be applied to each of the other seven remaining lines of business.

OPERATIONAL RISK ECONOMIC CAPITAL
To obtain the operational risk capital for the entire bank, first the bank is segmented into the lines of business; then each is rated and

the capital for each is obtained; and finally the capital for each line of business is summed. Three issues can be immediately raised with this approach:

1. where are the data to obtain the loss distribution for each rating to come from?
2. what if we have sufficient internal loss data? Should we not use those data instead?
3. should the capital for the entire bank take into account the less-than-perfect correlations rather than perfect correlation implied by the straight sum?

Let us examine each one in turn.

1. Where are the data to come from?

The loss data have to come from pooling of individual loss experience, but it is insufficient to simply pool loss data. In addition to the loss information, the associated rating or at least the state of both the business and control environments at the time of the loss must be also collected. Without this additional information it will not be possible to derive the loss distributions for each of the ratings, or risk classes. Just as if all losses were pooled without knowing whether it came from retail banking or from any other line of business, it would be impossible after the fact to create loss distribution for different line of business. At present the various industry pooling initiatives have not recognised this and are therefore of very limited use. Hopefully, it will be soon realised that, in addition to risk type and business line, and perhaps some indexes of size such as gross income or assets they are now collecting, addition information about the business and control environments will also have to be collected.

2. What if we have sufficient internal loss data?

If there are sufficient internal data they should be taken into account, and the manner in which they can be taken into account has been well developed by actuaries. Let us see how. Ratings are developed because an individual entity usually does not have sufficient loss experience to be used for deriving credible loss distributions. So, as described above, individual loss experiences that share similar risk characteristics – that is, they have the same rating – are pooled together until there are sufficient data to derive a credible loss distribution for the entire class. No two entities within the pool or risk class have identical risk characteristics, but the similarities are sufficient for the actual loss distribution of any one entity, if it could be calculated, to be similar to the average loss distribution calculated for the risk class. The loss distribution of a particular entity within the class is similar but not identical to the average, and the difference can be determined by combining the limited loss experience of the entity with that of the entire risk class using a methodology called *credibility theory*. The following will illustrate the concept.[8] Suppose an entity does not have sufficient data to calculate its mean loss with great confidence; nevertheless, the mean can be calculated and suppose it is 5. Now supposes the entity belongs to a risk class with a mean loss of 7 and the class has sufficient data to have calculated this mean with great confidence. If we had no confidence in the calculated mean of the entity, because of lack of entity-specific loss data, we would conclude that the actual mean of the entity is 7 and not 5; 5 is simply a reflection of not having sufficient data. On the other, had if there were sufficient data to have the same degree of confidence in the calculation of the mean for the entity as for the class as a whole, we would conclude that the actual mean of the entity is indeed 5. Most of the time the sufficiency of the loss data for the entity is somewhere between the two extremes and therefore our credible-estimate mean for the entity is somewhere in between 5 and 7. Credibility theory says that it is $c5 + (1 - c)7$, where c is the credibility factor, which ranges from 1 to 0, depending on the confidence in the mean of entities calculated from its own loss experience. The same approach can be applied to the entire distribution.

So internal loss data can be used to modify the loss distribution obtained for the entire risk class, in a well-defined way using credibility theory. The modification will depend on how sufficient the internal loss experience is.

3. What about correlations?

Yes, what about correlations? In theory, we all recognise that not all potential losses happen at the same time and therefore summing the individual distributions overstates the actual risk. One could argue that there is no connection between terrorism and fraud since they have different causes. And yet 9/11 showed that the two were indeed connected, not in a causal way but simply because the after-effect of the destruction of the World Trade Center created the conditions that allowed fraud to be more easily committed. Under stress conditions uncorrelated risk becomes correlated. At this time, there simply isn't sufficient empirical evidence to come up with credible estimates of correlations. It is therefore more prudent both for senior management and regulators to default to 100% correlations until credible evidence can be gather to reasonably conclude otherwise.

STRESS TESTING

The methodology allows for the calculation of the operational risk in a stress situation. A stress situation is one in which either the business environment has become much more complex or the controls have severely deteriorated. For example, a stress change in the business environment may be a sudden regime change that introduces very unfriendly laws, a sudden increase in order volumes hitting the Internet discount broker due to a severe market correction, blackouts or a sudden departure of a key trading team. In the case of controls, examples might be a prolonged crash of the fraud detection system or limit monitoring system or a sudden departure of key control personnel. The list can be as large as one's imagination, and this is not particular to operational risk, since all sorts of stress scenarios can be envisaged for both market and credit risk.

However only the plausible scenarios are worth considering. What is a plausible scenario? It is one that has either happened in the past or is a continuation of something that has happened in the past. For example in market risk a one-day 30% decline is stock prices is a plausible stress scenario but a 90% decline is not worth worrying about, even though in theory it could happen. Likewise, for operational risk, it is plausible that there could be a two-week blackout but not one that lasts a year. One need not start from scratch: most banks have developed business continuity plans to deal with such stress situations, and these could be used, at least initially, as the stress scenarios. Once the scenarios have been selected the prevailing operational risk business conditions and the state of the controls under each of these scenarios have to be identified and rated and then a similar process as that described above is followed.

It may be, and probably is, that the rating – say the 1–5 scale previously described – is insufficient to accommodate stress conditions and therefore the scale needs to be expanded or an entirely new stress scale needs to be developed. Once developed, the ratings must be attached to severity distributions and not to loss distributions. The difference is that there is no need to determine frequency since one is interested only in determining the distribution of losses should the scenarios actually happen.

This is the same for market and credit stress scenarios. Stress scenarios are by their very nature even more rare than normal operational risk events, so there is no way to estimate credible frequencies. In any event, the best way to deal with operational risk stress scenarios is not through capital, which would require the estimate of frequency, but through effective business continuity planning and possibly through insurance.

SUMMARY

This chapter has shown that measuring operational risk is important because it is the means to ensure that the operational risk taken every day within each of the operating entities is, individually and in aggregate, within tolerance levels established by the board of directors, and that if a large operational risk loss occurs there is sufficient capital set aside to survive.

The chapter has also illustrated that all the pieces of operational risk measurement (internal loss, external loss, scenario analysis and business and control environments) can be coherently tied together through a ratings-based LDA. This measurement approach is built on a solid foundation of a structured coherent risk and control assessment.

The measure provides not only a capital amount but a valuable tool for business management to determine how much risk to take and how to achieve that level by determining which business and control environments' key risk drivers to change and by how much. There clearly remains much to be done in the area of data collection to put this vision into practice. However, the way forward has been pointed out.

1 Operational risk data may include internal and external loss data, KRIs, near misses, audit score, legal claims, insurance claims, operational risk issues, scenario analysis, etc.
2 Legal risk is included but business, strategic and reputational risks are excluded.
3 Inherent risk is sometimes referred to as the risk without controls or with an average level of controls. This, however, leads to confusion since risk without control is infinite, and what is average is dependent on the business environment. Rather, it is simply the contribution to risk due to the business environment.
4 Details of each of these can be obtained from the Internet by performing a search under their respective names.
5 Key risk indicators are sometimes used to mean any metric of operational performance and capability. What is meant here by KRIs is the metrics associated with key risk drivers.
6 There is a well-developed methodology for dealing with degree of existence. It is known as fuzzy logic and fuzzy clustering. It is beyond the scope of this chapter to elaborate on this topic.
7 It should be noted that this dataset reflects losses over the year 2001 for 89 banks with varying quality and completeness of loss collection ability. Therefore any statistics derived from this dataset is not of high confidence. Nevertheless these are the only relevant data available at this time and the process for deriving the statistics is corrected, and therefore, as more robust loss datasets are created, applying this process will yield statistics of high confidence. Basel probably added a healthy dose of judgement to obtain calibration.
8 For a full exposition of credibility theory and its application see S. W. Phillbrick, 1981, "An Examination of Credibility Concepts", Proceedings of the *Casualty Actuarial Society Journal* LXVII, pp 195–212.

REFERENCES

BIS, 2003a, "Sound Practices for the Management and Supervision of Operational Risk", Basel Committee on Banking Supervision, February.

BIS, 2003b, "The 2002 Loss Collection Exercise for Operational Risk Loss: Summary of the Data Collected", March.

BIS, 2004, "International Convergence of Capital Measurement and Capital Standards", June.

Section 3

Economic Capital Methodologies: Mathematical Treatment

11

A Fundamental Look at Economic Capital and Risk-Based Profitability Measures*

Sebastian Fritz, Michael Kalkbrener, Wilfried Paus

Deutsche Bank AG

Economic capital (EC) and risk-based profitability measures such as risk-adjusted return on capital (RAROC) and economic profit (EP) are widely used throughout the finance industry. As their definitions have evolved over time, they – in our view – appear to lack a formal foundation and, at times, guidance for their application.

In this chapter, we take a step back to look at EC requirements and profitability measures from a slightly more rigid perspective – elaborating on procedures to determine justifiable capital requirements as well as linking their measures to modern portfolio theory.

The chapter is structured as follows:

❑ the next section discusses if and how the right amount of EC for a bank can be determined.
❑ the following section, we present a formal description of the calculation of EC with some focus on its allocation.
❑ the penultimate section deals with the integration of EC into popular risk-based profitability measures.
❑ finally, in the last section, we derive an alternative risk-based profitability measure based on the capital asset pricing model (CAPM) and study how it ties in with profitability measures currently used.

A summary of our main results concludes the chapter.

*The views expressed in this chapter are those of the authors and do not necessarily reflect the position of Deutsche Bank AG.

DETERMINING THE APPROPRIATE LEVEL OF EC

What are the main risks faced by a bank? What is the right amount of capital to cover those risks? How can capital be factored into an overall profitability measure that is applied to transactions, client relationships, business divisions and the bank as a whole?

These are the issues one comes across when implementing a risk-based profitability framework in a bank. Many banks use RAROC or EP based measures (or a combination of both). These measures are based on the assumption that risk is quantifiable and can therefore be used for determining profitability.

However, capital markets seem to tell the following story: the profitability figure often used for public disclosure is net return on equity (ROE), since this concept is independent of in-house definitions of EC requirements. Price over book ratios for many large US-based or European banks can be explained to a large extent by the simple formula:

$$\frac{\text{Price}}{\text{Book}} = \frac{\text{Return on equity}}{\text{Cost of equity}}$$

when applying a cost of equity of $\approx 10\%$. Does that mean, that capital markets simply apply an average risk premium (eg, 10% – Libor) when assessing the profitability of a bank?

Since banks are interested in stable or – even better – steadily increasing ROE numbers, management will usually support any legal method to stabilise earnings. We think that risk-adjusted profitability measures give the right incentives to generate long-term stable ROE numbers. In this chapter, we propose a methodology for determining EC requirements and for integrating EC into risk-adjusted profitability measures.

Any bank faces various uses (and potential misuses) of its EC:

1. preserving the bank's assets against very extreme events (stakeholder view);
2. preserving the bank's assets/deposits against systemic shock (regulatory view);
3. allocating the right amount of capital to a transaction in order to facilitate a risk/return analysis based on the risk appetite of the institution (shareholder view); and

4. giving an indication for line management of the riskiness/loss potential of certain transactions (management view).

It seems to be accepted in the industry that these different requirements can be covered by applying risk measures based on different tolerance levels to the loss distribution of the bank. In consequence, a bank could face more than one capital target and/or ratio to optimise:

1. the stakeholder, potentially backed by rating agencies, may prefer a very high confidence level – eg, 99.99% for a AAA rating.
2. regulators seem to be satisfied with a confidence level of 99.90%.[1]
3. shareholders may be interested in using a level of confidence in line with their risk appetite of the investment – say 99.80% for a BBB-rated bank.
4. line management may rather want to see a level of confidence in the range of 90 to 95% reflecting a 1-in-10–20-years event. Such a number could be seen as an average extreme loss an experienced manager may have come across during their professional career.

But what is a correct tolerance level for EC? According to Bessis (1998), the EC of a bank should reflect its target rating:

> There is a direct link between capital, risk, tolerance level and the bank's default risk. The choice of the level of Economic Capital has to be consistent with the strategy of the bank. The most relevant rule is to choose the capital that provides the desired rating given the risks. Since ratings can be associated to average default rates within each class, the tolerance level should be identical to that associated with the targeted rating.

However, as Matten (1996) explains, "overcapitalisation" driven by a very conservative target rating has potential downsides:

> Against these [the capital requirements] must be set the target return which management wishes to achieve. This will be driven by the market's expectations of returns – exceeding the market's expectations will result in an increase in shareholder value, whereas failing to meet those expectations will result in a destruction of value. The higher the amount of capital which a bank maintains, the higher the profit it will have to earn in order to make the target return.

These conflicting objectives are difficult to balance. We propose the following boundary conditions on EC requirements:

1. the bank-internal tolerance level should be above minimum regulatory requirements, say the 99.90% confidence level.
2. the tolerance level should be above the confidence level associated with the current rating of the bank.[2]
3. if the first two conditions are met, risk tolerance should be at a level which utilises more than 90% of available equity (keeping the rest as a buffer) in order to achieve maximum utilisation of shareholders' money.

Once an adequate tolerance level is defined, should it be held constant or varied over an economic cycle? We favour holding the tolerance level constant since a change in tolerance level will not only change the overall EC requirement, it may also impact capital allocation and therefore the relative profitability of different assets. A lowering of the tolerance level should only be considered as last resort to prevent under-capitalisation. In any disclosure, it would certainly be understood as a material increase in risk appetite of the bank.

If at a given tolerance level the utilisation of shareholders equity drops, a bank is faced with three alternatives:

1. it can invest the released resource into new business (organic growth, acquisitions) in order to increase the revenue base.
2. it can give some of the capital back to the shareholders (share buy-back).
3. it can increase the tolerance level in order to achieve a rating upgrade. This would certainly be interpreted as a reduction in risk appetite of the bank.

In consequence, while regular changes of the tolerance level could be viewed as a means to smooth ROE numbers, we suggest keeping the tolerance level stable as long as the bank does not fundamentally change its strategy.

CALCULATING AND ALLOCATING EC

In the previous section we have discussed EC requirements and tolerance levels of banks. The objective of this section is to identify specific risk measures for the calculation and allocation of EC. The analysis will be done in a portfolio context, ie, we will determine EC for a portfolio $\mathcal{P}$ and allocate EC to its subportfolios $\mathcal{P}_1, \ldots, \mathcal{P}_n$.[3] In this section, portfolios will be represented by their loss variables. More precisely, the loss variable $X_\mathcal{P}$ of portfolio $\mathcal{P}$ is a real-valued function on the probability space $(\Omega, \mathbb{P})$ of all scenarios and $X_\mathcal{P}(\omega)$ specifies the loss of portfolio $\mathcal{P}$ in scenario $\omega \in \Omega$.

EC calculation

EC is a measure designed to state with a high degree of certainty the amount of equity capital needed to absorb unexpected losses. The exact meaning of "high degree of certainty" depends on the risk tolerance of the bank. A popular rule is to choose the tolerance level that reflects the average default rate associated with the rating of the bank. This rule immediately translates into a definition of EC based on value-at-risk (VAR): for example, if the current rating of a bank is AA+ associated with a default rate of 0.02% then the EC is determined by the VAR of the bank's loss distribution at level $\alpha = 99.98\%$.[4]

The simple link between ratings and VAR based EC is one reason why this specific EC methodology has become so popular and has even achieved the high status of being written into industry regulations. The standard procedure for most risk types is to specify the EC of $\mathcal{P}$ as VAR minus expected loss:

$$EC(\mathcal{P}) := VAR_\alpha(X_\mathcal{P}) - E(X_\mathcal{P}) \tag{1}$$

where $E(X_\mathcal{P})$ denotes the mean of the loss variable $X_\mathcal{P}$ of the portfolio $\mathcal{P}$.

It is well known, however, that EC based on VAR has serious disadvantages. As long as the loss variables of portfolios are normally distributed, the VAR methodology encourages diversification, ie,

$$VAR(X + Y) \leq VAR(X) + VAR(Y) \tag{2}$$

for normally distributed loss variables X and Y. For most portfolios the normal distribution assumption is not justified and in this case subadditivity (2) no longer holds for VAR. Diversification, which is commonly considered as a way to reduce risk, may increase VAR and therefore EC.

It has therefore been proposed in a number of papers to replace VAR in (1) by more appropriate risk measures ρ:

$$EC(\mathcal{P}) := \rho(X_{\mathcal{P}}) - E(X_{\mathcal{P}}) \qquad (3)$$

But what are the properties of good risk measures? To answer this question, Artzner *et al* (1997, 1999) presented the following set of axioms.

Coherency axioms for risk measures
Let V denote the linear space of all portfolio loss variables and let ρ be a function from V to $\mathbb{R}$, ie, $\rho(X)$ denotes the risk capital of a portfolio $X \in V$. The risk measure ρ is called coherent if it is

monotonic:	$X \leq Y \Rightarrow \rho(X) \leq \rho(Y)$	$\forall X, Y \in V$
translation invariant:	$\rho(X + a) = \rho(X) + a$	$\forall a \in \mathbb{R}, X \in V$
positively homogeneous:	$\rho(aX) = a \cdot \rho(X)$	$\forall a \geq 0, X \in V$
sub-additive:	$\rho(X + Y) \leq \rho(X) + \rho(Y)$	$\forall X, Y \in V$

The most popular class of coherent risk measures is expected shortfall (ES) (see, for instance, Rockafellar and Uryasev, 2000; Acerbi and Tasche, 2002). For practical purposes, the ES of X at level $\alpha \in (0, 1)$, denoted by $ES_{\alpha}(X)$, can be defined by

$$E\left(X \mid X > VAR_{\alpha}(X)\right) = (1 - \alpha)^{-1} E\left(X \cdot 1_{\{X > VAR_{\alpha}(X)\}}\right) \qquad (4)$$

Intuitively, ES can therefore be interpreted as the average of all losses above a given quantile of the loss distribution. Its exact definition takes care of jumps of the loss distribution at its quantile.[5] More general techniques for specifying coherent risk measures are given in Artzner *et al* (1999), Delbaen (2000, 2002) and Acerbi (2004).

Capital allocation

The coherency axioms provide an excellent framework for the theoretical analysis of risk measures. We now turn to the second problem: the allocation of EC either to subportfolios or to business units. More formally, assume that a risk measure ρ has been fixed and that the EC of $\mathcal{P}$ has been calculated according to (3). The objective is to distribute $EC(\mathcal{P})$ to its subportfolios $\mathcal{P}_1, \ldots, \mathcal{P}_n$.

Again, we propose an axiomatic framework for the analysis and comparison of allocation schemes.[6] A capital allocation is a function Λ from $V \times V$ to $\mathbb{R}$. Its interpretation is, that $\Lambda(X, Y)$ represents the capital allocated to the portfolio X – considered as a subportfolio of portfolio Y. Λ is called a capital allocation with respect to a risk measure ρ if it universally satisfies $\Lambda(X, X) = \rho(X)$, ie, the capital allocated to X (considered as stand-alone portfolio) is the risk capital $\rho(X)$ of X. We propose the following requirements for a capital allocation scheme in a bank.

Allocation axioms
Let Λ be a capital allocation with respect to ρ, ie,

$$\forall X \in V \quad \Lambda(X, X) = \rho(X)$$

Linearity. The capital allocated to a union of subportfolios is equal to the sum of the capital amounts allocated to the individual subportfolios. In particular, the risk capital of a portfolio equals the sum of the risk capital of its subportfolios. More formally, Λ is called linear if

$$\forall a, b \in \mathbb{R}, X, Y, Z \in V \quad \Lambda(aX + bY, Z) = a\Lambda(X, Z) + b\Lambda(Y, Z)$$

Diversification. The capital allocated to a subportfolio X of a larger portfolio Y never exceeds the risk capital of X considered as a stand-alone portfolio: Λ is called diversifying if

$$\forall X, Y \in V \quad \Lambda(X, Y) \leq \Lambda(X, X)$$

Continuity. A small increase in a position does only have a small effect on the risk capital allocated to that position: Λ is called continuous at $Y \in V$ if

$$\forall X \in V \quad \lim_{\epsilon \to 0} \Lambda(X, Y + \epsilon X) = \Lambda(X, Y)$$

It is interesting that a linear and diversifying capital allocation, which is continuous at a portfolio $Y \in V$, is uniquely determined by its associated risk measure, ie, the diagonal values of Λ. More specifically, given the portfolio Y, the capital allocated to a subportfolio X of Y is the derivative of the associated risk measure ρ at Y in the direction of X:

$$\forall X \in V \quad \Lambda(X, Y) = \lim_{\epsilon \to 0} \frac{\rho(Y + \epsilon X) - \rho(Y)}{\epsilon} \tag{5}$$

This result shows that the three axioms are sufficient to uniquely determine a capital allocation scheme. It remains to be shown that capital allocations that satisfy the axioms do exist. It turns out that the existence of linear, diversifying capital allocations is mathematically equivalent to certain properties of the associated risk measure: there exists a linear and diversifying capital allocation with respect to ρ if and only if ρ is sub-additive and positively homogeneous.

So far, we have focused on allocations Λ with respect to arbitrary risk measures ρ. Using (1), Λ can easily be transformed into an allocation scheme for EC: the EC allocated to subportfolio $\mathcal{P}_i$ equals

$$\mathrm{EC}(\mathcal{P}_i, \mathcal{P}) := \Lambda(X_{\mathcal{P}_i}, X_{\mathcal{P}}) - E(X_{\mathcal{P}_i})$$

where $X_{\mathcal{P}_i}$ and $X_{\mathcal{P}}$ are the loss variables of subportfolio $\mathcal{P}_i$ and portfolio $\mathcal{P}$.

Examples
The risk measure ES is coherent and therefore sub-additive and positively homogeneous. Application of the above theorems yields a linear, diversifying allocation scheme with associated risk measure ES: the ES contribution of subportfolio X of Y defined as[7]

$$E\left(X \mid Y > \mathrm{VAR}_\alpha(Y)\right) = (1-\alpha)^{-1} E(X \cdot \mathbf{1}_{\{Y > \mathrm{VAR}_\alpha(Y)\}}) \tag{6}$$

Hence, the ES contribution of a subportfolio can be considered as its average contribution to portfolio losses exceeding the quantile $\mathrm{VAR}_\alpha(Y)$.

VAR, on the other hand, is not a sub-additive risk measure. As a consequence, there do not exist linear diversifying capital allocations for VAR in general. Also, from a practical point of view, the allocation of VAR is a difficult problem. For market risk applications, Hallerbach (1999) suggests allocation based on the directional derivative (5) with $\rho = \mathrm{VAR}_\alpha$. This technique works well in a sufficiently continuous setting (see Tasche (1999) and Gouriéroux et al (2000) for criteria which ensure existence of (5). However, in non-continuous or even discrete models directional derivatives usually do not exist or they are not continuous and highly unstable in α. The standard solution in credit portfolio modelling is to allocate portfolio VAR proportionally to the loss covariances

$$\mathrm{Cov}(X_1, X), \ldots, \mathrm{Cov}(X_n, X)$$

This allocation technique, called volatility allocation, is the natural choice in classical portfolio theory where portfolio risk is measured by standard deviation (or volatility).

In general, combining volatility allocation with VAR works well as long as all loss distributions are close to normal. For credit portfolios, however, it does not: the capital allocated to a subportfolio X of Y may be greater than the risk capital of X considered as a stand-alone portfolio, the capital charge of a loan may even be higher than its exposure (see Kalkbrener *et al*, 2004).

COMMON PROFITABILITY MEASURES

The purpose of the previous section was to develop concepts for calculating and allocating EC. The objective of this section is to use EC for valuing transactions in a portfolio and assessing the shareholder value created by business units.

Profitability assessment by banks is commonly carried out by expressing the risk–return relationship as simple rational functions of risk and return components. The two basic variants of such so-called risk-adjusted ratios are known as RORAC or RAROC, respectively. Both are refinements of the classic ROE ratio.

Reference capital

Before going into more detail, we pick up on the issues previously raised regarding the role of capital in a bank.

While the equity capital is an important and undisputable capital quantity, it does not tell anything about the riskiness of the businesses it is used to support. When measuring profitability from a risk–return perspective, it is therefore important to relate returns to a risk-driven capital measure instead. The natural choice for this is EC. Another option is to use regulatory capital, which, in particular after the refinements under the Basel II accord, is also risk-sensitive. In view of its limitations (eg, not reflecting diversification effects), however, we believe that it should enter any profitability measure rather as a cost than a risk (capital) measure.

Naturally, any capital measure needs to be related to the shareholder's equity capital. A common procedure to achieve this is as follows, taken from Deutsche Bank's Annual Report 2002:

> We rely on our book capital to absorb any losses that result from the risks we assume in our businesses. Book capital is defined as the amount of equity capital that appears in our balance sheet. We use EC as our primary tool to allocate our book capital among our businesses. We also use it to assess their profitability and their relative abilities to employ capital efficiently.

RAROC ratios

The return on risk-adjusted capital (RORAC) measure is a profitability calculated on risk-based capital. In its strict definition RAROC adjusts the return for risk (for instance by calculating margins net of statistical defaults) and relates the result to the equity capital held.

In order to establish a comprehensive risk–return relationship, however, both these adjustments are necessary. Any expected loss should be deducted from anticipated margin income, and the resulting risk-adjusted return should be related to the capital necessary to absorb potential unexpected losses. Consequently, one should merge the two ideas behind RORAC and RAROC into one ratio. Following a general trend throughout the financial industry, we continue to refer to it as RAROC exclusively from now on:

$$\text{RAROC} := \frac{\text{Risk-adjusted return}}{\text{EC}}$$

Herein, the numerator risk-adjusted return comprises the following components:

❑ gross revenues of a transaction/customer relationship,[8]
❑ administration costs (determined by the cost structure and the workflow within the bank),
❑ expected loss (calculated consistently with the EC component given in the RAROC denominator).

It is obvious from the above that, subject to the existence of a suitable allocation of EC, RAROC may be calculated on the portfolio as well as on the transaction level.

Even though the general definition of RAROC given in the above is commonly agreed within the industry, its detailed calculation has not been fixed yet. As work flows, data availability and in particular the business to be evaluated may vary dramatically across institutions, no uniform definitions for these quantities, which may be applicable to all banks alike, exist. Naturally, this bears the risk of mushrooming of different methodological approaches used across banks or even within one institution.

Economic profit

RAROC is a dimensionless risk–return measure. It ranks transactions, customers or business lines by a performance rate (on allocated EC) rather than their performance in monetary terms. But, fixing a minimum level of RAROC required by the bank, the so-called hurdle rate h, automatically gives rise to a profitability measure in currency units. We define the EP by[9]

$$EP = \text{Risk-adjusted return} - h \cdot EC \qquad (7)$$

The product of the hurdle rate and the EC is commonly referred to as the cost of capital, as this quantity may be regarded as the yearly interest one would have to pay for borrowing EC at h. The benchmark for h is the price of risk in the capital market from the shareholder perspective. When employing the equity capital allocation procedure earlier, it can be derived directly from the ROE expectation of the shareholders and the ratio of the bank's EC and its equity capital:

$$h \approx \text{ROE-target} \cdot \frac{\text{Equity capital}}{\text{EC}}$$

The EP thus quantifies the monetary amount in excess (below) the cost of capital generated by a transaction (or a set thereof).

Two transactions may have equal RAROCs while the riskier one generates a higher income or loss, given by their respective EPs. Hence, regarding performance objective setting, EP is the superior measure to RAROC as it quantifies true profits and losses. Therefore, in order to improve an overall profitability rate, it is always possible to eliminate those transactions that are less profitable and to keep only the others. In such cases, the profitability (as a percentage) increases at the expense of size. Usually, both size and profitability should be managed. Using a target value of EP makes explicit the feasibility of such trade-offs and puts some emphasis on the volume of operations.

ALTERNATIVES

While the RAROC/EP concept appears intuitive and is easily communicated due to its cashflow oriented view (all components can be interpreted as individual cashflows), it is not clear whether it covers all aspects of interdependence of these cashflows. Moreover, it does not tell the user what an optimal, yet realistic return of a given portfolio could have been.

In this section, we will therefore focus rather on benchmarking a given portfolio to an optimal portfolio from a risk–return perspective. Hereby, we use the CAPM (see Sharpe, 1964; Lintner, 1965) to derive an alternative profitability measure and subsequently compare it with the EP.

Problems with EP

It is one of the fundamental tenets of modern portfolio theory (the underpinning of all modern financial mathematics) that there is a relationship between the market's expected or required return and the uncertainty surrounding that return. Profitability measures should incorporate this relationship directly alongside the quantification of the loss potential due to defaults or other risk events.

RAROC and EP, being simple financial ratios or a linear combination of the risk-adjusted return and the (allocated) EC, cannot fully recognise the volatility of returns. This is mainly due to the fact that the purpose of EC is to quantify extreme loss events: EC is inevitably focused on the tail and does not adequately reflect the volatility of returns across all scenarios.

A common workaround to still reflect the volatility of earnings is the following: The EC term comprises a term built to assess the so-called business risk. It is designed to capitalise unexpected losses caused by the breakaway of revenue streams in specific business lines. Business risk EC is frequently merged with the EC for operational risk, but its calculation, since driven by modelling P&L

volatility, differs substantially from the approaches used to model operational risk.

In our view it is therefore advisable that, rather than deduct another cost component from the EP, one should take an integrated view of returns and risk.

Capital asset pricing model

A widely accepted approach to modelling the dependency between market return and its uncertainty is given by the CAPM, where uncertainty is expressed in the form of the standard deviation of the return. More precisely, the model states that the required return R_i on an investment can be determined by reference to the historical relationship between the investment and the market:

$$E(R_i) = R_F + \beta_i(E(R_M) - R_F)$$

where R_F refers to the risk-free rate, and R_M to the market return.[10] The expression $E(R_M) - R_F$ refers simply to the excess return of the market over the risk-free rate (the risk premium). The beta is a factor for each individual stock which measures how closely the stock follows the market. It is defined as the covariance of R_i and R_M divided by the variance of R_M.

A CAPM implied profitability measure

Our objective is to integrate the concept of EC into the CAPM and to derive a profitability measure in the extended model.

Let R be the return variable of a portfolio $\mathcal{P}$ which consists of n subportfolios $\mathcal{P}_1, \ldots, \mathcal{P}_n$ with return variables $R_1, \ldots, R_n$, ie, $R = R_1 + \cdots + R_n$. We assume that EC has been calculated and allocated to each of the portfolios using the techniques presented earlier: the EC of the portfolio $\mathcal{P}$ is denoted by $EC(\mathcal{P})$ and the capital allocated to $\mathcal{P}_i$ is denoted by $EC(\mathcal{P}_i, \mathcal{P})$.[11]

As a prerequisite to applying the CAPM, we need to normalise the subportfolios under consideration to unit size. For this, we scale each subportfolio by the factor $EC(\mathcal{P})/EC(\mathcal{P}_i, \mathcal{P})$, such that all subportfolios have the same EC. The return of the i-th scaled subportfolio $\bar{\mathcal{P}}_i$ is then given by

$$\bar{R}_i := \frac{EC(\mathcal{P})}{EC(\mathcal{P}_i, \mathcal{P})} \cdot R_i$$

Note that the contributory EC of $\bar{\mathcal{P}}_i$ equals $\mathrm{EC}(\mathcal{P}) = (\mathrm{EC}(\mathcal{P}) / \mathrm{EC}(\mathcal{P}_i, \mathcal{P})) \cdot \mathrm{EC}(\mathcal{P}_i, \mathcal{P})$. Furthermore,

$$R = \frac{\mathrm{EC}(\mathcal{P}_1, \mathcal{P})}{\mathrm{EC}(\mathcal{P})} \cdot \bar{R}_1 + \cdots + \frac{\mathrm{EC}(\mathcal{P}_n, \mathcal{P})}{\mathrm{EC}(\mathcal{P})} \cdot \bar{R}_n \qquad (8)$$

and

$$1 = \frac{\mathrm{EC}(\mathcal{P}_1, \mathcal{P})}{\mathrm{EC}(\mathcal{P})} + \cdots + \frac{\mathrm{EC}(\mathcal{P}_n, \mathcal{P})}{\mathrm{EC}(\mathcal{P})} \qquad (9)$$

The identities (8) and (9) can be interpreted in the following way: $\mathcal{P}$ is a portfolio consisting of investments $\bar{\mathcal{P}}_1, \ldots, \bar{\mathcal{P}}_n$. The total amount of capital invested in $\mathcal{P}$ is $\mathrm{EC}(\mathcal{P})$, the fraction invested in $\bar{\mathcal{P}}_i$ equals $\mathrm{EC}(\mathcal{P}_i, \mathcal{P}) / \mathrm{EC}(\mathcal{P})$. Following the CAPM, the expected return of $\bar{\mathcal{P}}_i$ is now defined as

$$\left(R_F + (E_R - R_F) \cdot \frac{\mathrm{Cov}(R, \bar{R}_i)}{\mathrm{Var}(R)} \right) \cdot \mathrm{EC}(\mathcal{P})$$

where E_R denotes the normalised mean of the portfolio return R, ie, $E_R = E(R)/\mathrm{EC}(\mathcal{P})$. By multiplying with $\mathrm{EC}(\mathcal{P}_i, \mathcal{P})/\mathrm{EC}(\mathcal{P})$ we obtain the expected return of the (unscaled) portfolio $\mathcal{P}_i$:

$$\left(R_F + (E_R - R_F) \cdot \frac{\mathrm{Cov}(R, \bar{R}_i)}{\mathrm{Var}(R)} \right) \cdot \mathrm{EC}(\mathcal{P}) \cdot \frac{\mathrm{EC}(\mathcal{P}_i, \mathcal{P})}{\mathrm{EC}(\mathcal{P})}$$

$$= R_F \cdot \mathrm{EC}(\mathcal{P}_i, \mathcal{P}) + (E_R - R_F) \cdot \mathrm{EC}(\mathcal{P}) \cdot \frac{\mathrm{Cov}(R, R_i)}{\mathrm{Var}(R)}$$

Our profitability measure is derived from the formula above. More precisely, we propose to replace the expected portfolio return E_R by a target return $\tilde{h}$ set by the bank. Subtraction from $E(R_i)$ yields the profitability measure

$$P(\mathcal{P}_i, \mathcal{P}) := E(R_i) - \left(R_F \cdot \mathrm{EC}(\mathcal{P}_i, \mathcal{P}) + (\tilde{h} - R_F) \cdot \mathrm{EC}(\mathcal{P}) \cdot \frac{\mathrm{Cov}(R, R_i)}{\mathrm{Var}(R)} \right) \qquad (10)$$

with the properties

$$P(\mathcal{P}_i, \mathcal{P}) \begin{cases} =0 \\ >0 \\ <0 \end{cases} \text{if } P_i\text{'s return } R_i \begin{cases} \text{meets} \\ \text{exceeds} \\ \text{falls short of} \end{cases} \text{its expectation.}$$

Observe that this profitability measure comprises two different allocation methods for EC, namely $EC(\mathcal{P}_i, \mathcal{P})$ (an allocation complying with the allocation axioms, eg, ES) and the volatility allocation $EC(\mathcal{P}) \cdot \text{Cov}(R, R_i)/\text{Var}(R)$. In this sense, the CAPM implied profitability measure yields a synthesis of two capital allocation methods commonly thought to be suitable only for different perspectives (see Hall, 2002).

Comparison with EP

We will now investigate the relationship between the CAPM implied profitability measure and EP. Recall from (7), that EP is defined by

$$EP = \text{Risk-adjusted return} - h \cdot EC$$

where the risk-adjusted return comprises the components gross revenues, administration costs and expected loss. Assuming that these components are covered by the return variable R_i, EP can be written as

$$EP(\mathcal{P}_i, \mathcal{P}) = E(R_i) - h \cdot EC(\mathcal{P}_i, \mathcal{P}) \qquad (11)$$

Comparing terms on the right-hand sides of (10) and (11) and choosing $\tilde{h} \equiv h$ (corresponding to setting the return hurdle to covering net capital costs[12]), exposes that the difference between $EP(\mathcal{P}_i, \mathcal{P})$ and $P(\mathcal{P}_i, \mathcal{P})$ boils down to

1. the allocation mechanism applied to the capital cost term; and[13]
2. an additional risk cost term $R_F \cdot (EC(\mathcal{P}_i, \mathcal{P}) - EC(\mathcal{P}) \cdot \text{Cov}(R, R_i)/\text{Var}(R)$ in (10).

Analysis

We now analyse two extreme scenarios in order to illustrate the differences between EP and the CAPM implied profitability measure.

1. "break-even": $h = R_F \Rightarrow EP \equiv P$; and
2. "high ambition": $h \gg R_F \searrow 0 \Rightarrow EP \approx E(R) - h \cdot EC(\cdot, \mathcal{P}), P \approx E(R) - h \cdot EC(\mathcal{P}) \cdot \text{Cov}(\cdot, R)/\text{Var}(R)$.

The "break-even" scenario is likely to hold for banks, which have set a low hurdle rate (state-owned institutions, focus on retail). In this scenario, EP and the CAPM implied profitability measure are identical.

The "high ambition" scenario occurs if either the risk-free rates are very low (ie low interest rates) or the hurdle set by the individual bank is very high. This is usually the case for banks with strong M&A and trading divisions. A high hurdle implies that allocated EC becomes less important for profitability, and that more emphasis is put on the contribution of transactions (subportfolios, business units) to the overall earnings volatility of the bank. In the "high ambition" scenario, the difference between EP and the CAPM-implied profitability measure reduces to the allocation of EC. The latter implies that the banks in question optimise their risk–return best when allocating EC via a volatility allocation rather than an allocation associated with a coherent EC measure.

Under current market conditions (Summer, 2004), risk-free rates around EURIBOR $\approx$ 2.5% and hurdle rates after tax between 10–15% are common for large European banks. That ratio is approximately in line with an allocation of four units of volatility versus VAR/COVAR one unit of ES. In this case, EP based on volatility allocation is a reasonable approximation for optimising and stabilising risk–return.

In conclusion, the bigger the difference between the risk-free rate and the hurdle rate set by the bank the more weight is shifted from ES to volatility allocation when optimising risk–return.

CONCLUSION

In this closing section, we summarise the key messages of this chapter.

Tolerance Level for EC

In order to ensure a sufficient protection from extreme risk events alongside avoiding overcapitalisation at the expense of the bank's shareholders, we suggest deriving a bank's individual EC requirement as follows:

❑ The bank-internal tolerance level should lie above both, the minimum regulatory requirement and the confidence level associated with the current rating of the bank.
❑ If this minimum condition is met, risk tolerance should be at a level, which utilises more than 90% of available equity in order to achieve maximum utilisation of shareholder's money.

Once an adequate tolerance level is defined, it should be held constant – with appropriate action taken should the utilisation of shareholder's equity drop.

Coherent Risk Measures and Allocation

Calculating EC based on VAR has, while being popular with banks and regulators alike, serious disadvantages – the major one being that it does not necessarily recognise diversification. Consequently, one should rather base the calculation of EC on a risk measure with properties matching intuition. The properties are given by the so-called coherency axioms, the most prominent class of risk measure satisfying these axioms is the one of Expected Shortfall measures.

A similarly fundamental approach can be taken in order to allocate EC to subportfolios or to business units compliant with intuition. Requiring basic properties of linearity, continuity and diversification uniquely determines an allocation to any given coherent risk measure.

Refined Profitability Measures

Risk-adjusted profitability measures based on EC give the right incentives to generate long-term stable ROE numbers. The common quantities RAROC and EP, being simple financial ratios or a linear combination of the risk-adjusted return and the (allocated) EC, however, cannot fully recognise the volatility of returns.

In an attempt to take an integrated view of returns and risk, we applied the Capital Asset Pricing Model (CAPM) to derive an alternative profitability measure. Analysis shows that this CAPM implied profitability measure coincides with the classical EP if the bank's return on capital requirement is as low as the risk-free rate. As the bank's return target increases, however, the alternative profitability measure puts more emphasis on the volatility of earnings – a behaviour in line with both, the shareholder and the stakeholder perspective.

1   According to the paper of the Bank of International Settlements – "International Convergence of Capital Measurement and Capital Standards" so-called Basel II Risk Weight Formula – http://www.bis.org/publ/bcbs107.pdf.
2   There may be an issue for banks whose current rating ranks below the regulatory threshold.
3   $\mathcal{P}$ can also be interpreted as a bank with business units $\mathcal{P}_1, \ldots, \mathcal{P}_n$.

4   In this chapter, the $\text{VAR}_\alpha(X)$ at confidence level $\alpha \in (0,1)$ is defined as the smallest α-quantile of X, ie,

$$\text{VAR}_\alpha(X) := \inf\left\{x \in \mathbb{R} \,|\, \mathbb{P}(X \le x) \ge \alpha\right\}$$

5   More precisely: $\text{ES}_\alpha(X) := (1 - \alpha)^{-1}(E(X\,\mathbf{1}_{\{X>\text{VAR}_\alpha(X)\}}) + \text{VAR}_\alpha(X) \cdot (\mathbb{P}(X \le \text{VAR}_\alpha(X)) - \alpha))$. It is easy to see that for most loss distributions the ES_α is dominated by the first term given by (4). The second term is added to ensure coherence.

6   Theoretical and practical aspects of different allocation schemes have been analysed in a number of papers, for instance in Hallerbach (2003), Schmock and Straumann (1999), Delbaen (2000), Denault (2001), Tasche (1999, 2002). The allocation methodology presented in this chapter has been developed in Kalkbrener (2002).

7   Precisely: $\text{ESC}_\alpha(X, Y) := (E(X \cdot \mathbf{1}_{\{Y>\text{VAR}_\alpha(Y)\}}) + \beta_Y \cdot E(X \cdot \mathbf{1}_{\{Y=\text{VAR}_\alpha(Y)\}}))/(1-\alpha)$ with $\beta_Y := (\mathbb{P}(Y \le \text{VAR}_\alpha(Y)) - \alpha)/\mathbb{P}(Y = \text{VAR}_\alpha(Y))$ which again is dominated by (7).

8   Net of refinancing costs.

9   Also widely known as "Value Creation" or "(Shareholder) Value Added".

10 More precisely, R_F (R_M) is the return on an investment of one unit of cash in the risk-free asset (market portfolio).

11 It is assumed that the capital allocation satisfies the linearity axiom.

12 Note that the CAPM is based on the assumption of assets being available at no charge whereas the RAROC/EP framework does not.

13 One must note, however, that this comparison assumes that the risk measure $\text{EC}(\mathcal{P})$ is covering all aspects of risks due to the volatility of earnings. As discussed earlier in this section, this is generally not the case for many economic profit measures used in the industry.

REFERENCES

Acerbi, C., 2004, "Coherent Representations of Subjective Risk-Aversion", in J. Szegö (ed), *Risk Measures for the 21st Century*, Wiley.

Acerbi, C., and D. Tasche, 2002, "On the Coherence of Expected Shortfall", *Journal of Banking and Finance*, **26**, pp. 1487–503.

Artzner, P., F. Delbaen, J.-M. Eber, and D. Heath, 1997, "Thinking Coherently", *Risk*, pp. 68–71, November.

Artzner, P., F. Delbaen, J.-M. Eber, and D. Heath, 1999, "Coherent Measures of Risk", *Mathematical Finance*, **9**, pp. 203-28.

Bessis, J., 1998, *Risk Management in Banking*, Wiley.

Delbaen, F., 2000, "Coherent Risk Measures", Lecture Notes, Scuola Normale Superiore di Pisa.

Delbaen, F., 2002, "Coherent Risk Measures on General Probability Spaces", in Sandmann, K. and Schönbucher, P. J. (eds), *Advances in Finance and Stochastics – Essays in Honour of Dieter Sondermann*, Springer.

Denault, M., 2001, "Coherent Allocation of Risk Capital", *Journal of Risk*, **4(1)**.

Deutsche Bank AG, 2002, Annual Report.

Gouriéroux, C., J. P. Laurent, and O. Scaillet, 2000, "Sensitivity Analysis of Value at Risk", *Journal of Empirical Finance*, **7**, pp. 225–45.

Hall, C., 2002, "Economic Capital: Towards an Integrated Risk Framework", *Risk*, pp. 33–8, October.

Hallerbach, W., 2003, "Decomposing Portfolio Value-at-Risk: A General Analysis", *Journal of Risk*, **5(2)**, pp. 1–18.

Kalkbrener, M., 2002, "An Axiomatic Approach to Capital Allocation", Technical Document, Deutsche Bank AG, Frankfurt.

Kalkbrener, M., H. Lotter, and L. Overbeck, 2004, "Sensible and Efficient Capital Allocation for Credit Portfolios", *Risk*, pp. S19–S24.

Lintner, J., 1965, "Security Prices, Risk and Maximal Gains from Diversification", *Journal of Finance*, pp. 587–615, December.

Matten, C., 1996, *Managing Bank Capital: Capital Allocation and Performance Measurement*. Wiley.

Rockafellar, R. T., and Uryasev S., 2000, "Optimization of Conditional Value-at-Risk", *Journal of Risk*, **2**, pp. 21–41.

Schmock, U., and D. Straumann, 1999, "Allocation of Risk Capital and Performance Measurement", Seminar Presentations at Quantitative Methods in Finance 1999 Conference, University of Technology, Sydney, July and Conference on Risk Theory, Oberwolfach, September, Available at http://www.math.ethz.ch/schmock/ftp/slides/AllocationSlidesOct1999.pdf.

Sharpe, W. F., 1964, "Capital Asset Prices: A Theory of Market Equilibrium Under Conditions of Risk", *Journal of Finance*, pp. 425–42, September.

Tasche, D., 1999, "Risk Contributions and Performance Measurement", Technical Document, Munich University of Technology, Available at http://citeseer.nj.nec.com/tasche99risk.html.

Tasche, D., 2002, "Expected Shortfall and Beyond", *Journal of Banking and Finance*, **26**, pp. 1519–33.

12

A Risk-Factor Model Foundation for Ratings-Based Bank Capital Rules

Michael B. Gordy*

Board of Governors of the Division of Research and
Statistics and Federal Reserve System

Large commercial banks and other financial institutions with significant credit exposure rely increasingly on models to guide credit risk management at the portfolio level. Models allow management to identify concentrations of risk and opportunities for diversification within a disciplined and objective framework, and thus offer a more sophisticated, less arbitrary alternative to traditional lending limit controls. More widespread and intensive use of models is encouraging a more active approach to portfolio management at commercial banks, which has contributed to the improved liquidity of markets for debt instruments and credit derivatives.

Stripped to its essentials, a credit risk model is a function mapping from a parsimonious set of instrument-level characteristics and market-level parameters to a distribution for portfolio credit losses over some chosen horizon. The model output of primary interest, the "economic capital" required to support the portfolio, is derived as some summary statistic of the loss distribution. Once allocated to the individual instruments as capital charges, economic capital provides a shadow price on the cost of holding each position. Directly or indirectly, model applications to portfolio

*The views expressed herein are my own and do not necessarily reflect those of the Board of Governors or its staff. I thank Paul Calem, Darrell Duffie, Paul Embrechts, Jon Faust, Erik Heitfield, David Jones, David Lando, Gennady Samorodnistky, Dirk Tasche, Greg Udell, and Tom Wilde for their helpful comments, and Susan Yeh for editorial suggestions.

management depend on the capacity to assign appropriate instrument-level capital charges.

Model-based assessment of capital charges offers a potentially attractive solution to an increasingly urgent regulatory problem. The current regulatory framework for required capital on commercial bank lending is based on the 1988 Basel Accord. Under the Accord, the capital charge on commercial loans is a uniform 8% of loan face value, regardless of the financial strength of the borrower or the quality of collateral.[1] The failure to distinguish among commercial loans of very different degrees of credit risk created the incentive to move low-risk instruments off balance sheet and retain only relatively high-risk instruments. The financial innovations that arose in response to this incentive have undermined the effectiveness of regulatory capital rules (eg, Jones, 2000) and thus led to current efforts towards reform. It is widely recognised that regulatory arbitrage will continue until regulatory capital charges at the instrument level are aligned more closely with underlying risk.

The Basel Committee on Bank Supervision (1999) undertook a detailed study of how banks' internal models might be used for setting regulatory capital. The Committee acknowledged that a carefully specified and calibrated model could deliver a more accurate measure of portfolio credit risk than any rule-based system, but found that the present state of model development could not ensure an acceptable degree of comparability across institutions and that data constraints would prevent validation of key model parameters and assumptions. It seems unlikely, therefore, that regulators will be prepared in the near- to medium-term to accept the use of internal models for setting regulatory capital. Nonetheless, regulators and industry practitioners appear to be in broad agreement that a revised Accord should permit evolution towards an internal models approach as models and data improve.

At present, it appears virtually certain that a reformed Accord will offer a ratings-based "risk-bucketing" system of one form or another. In such a system, banking book assets are grouped into "buckets," which are presumed to be homogeneous. Associated with each bucket is a fixed capital charge per dollar of exposure. In the latest version of the Basel proposal for an Internal Ratings-Based (IRB) approach (Basel Committee on Bank Supervision, 2001), the bucketing system is required to partition instruments by internal borrower rating; by loan type (eg, sovereign *vs* corporate *vs* project finance); by one or more proxies for seniority/collateral type, which determines loss severity in the event of default; and by maturity. More complex systems might further partition instruments by, for example, country and industry of borrower. Regardless of the sophistication of the bucketing scheme, capital charges are *portfolio-invariant*, ie, the capital charge on a given instrument depends only on its own characteristics, and not the characteristics of the portfolio in which it is held. We take portfolio-invariance to be the essential property of ratings-based capital rules. Throughout this chapter, we will use the term "ratings-based" to refer broadly to portfolio-invariant capital allocation rules with bucketing along multiple dimensions, rather than to constrain the term to schemes in which capital depends only on a traditional univariate credit rating.

Though a ratings-based scheme may be a necessary "second-best" solution under current conditions, it is nonetheless desirable that the capital charges be calibrated within a portfolio model. Consistency with a well-specified model would bring greater discipline and accuracy to the calibration process, and would provide a smoother path of evolution towards a regime based on internal models. This chapter asks how a rigorous models-based calibration of ratings-based capital charges can be achieved? In particular, what modelling assumptions must be imposed so that marginal contributions to portfolio economic capital are portfolio-invariant?

By design, portfolio models do not, in general, yield portfolio-invariant capital charges. To obtain a distribution of portfolio loss, a model must determine a joint distribution over credit losses at the instrument level. The latest generation of widely used models gives structure to this problem by assuming that correlations across obligors in credit events arise due to common dependence on a set of *systematic risk factors*. Implicitly or explicitly, these factors represent the sectoral shifts and macroeconomic forces that impinge to a greater or lesser extent on all firms in an economy. A natural property of these models is that the marginal capital required for a loan depends on how it affects diversification, and thus depends on what other instruments are present in the portfolio.

If economic capital is defined within the value-at-risk (VAR) paradigm, then the problem has a simple answer. Under the VAR paradigm, an institution holds capital in order to maintain a target rating for its own debt. Associated with the target rating is a probability of survival over the horizon (say, 99.9% over one year). To be consistent with its target survival probability (denoted q), the institution must hold reserves and equity capital sufficient to cover up to the qth quantile of the distribution of portfolio loss over the horizon. We show that two conditions are necessary and (with a few regularity conditions) sufficient to guarantee portfolio-invariance under VAR in risk-factor models: First, the portfolio must be asymptotically fine-grained, in the sense that no single exposure in the portfolio can account for more than an arbitrarily small share of total portfolio exposure. Second, there must be at most a single systematic risk factor.

Needless to say, the real world does not give us perfectly fine-grained portfolios. Bank portfolios have finite numbers of obligors and lumpy distributions of exposure sizes. Capital charges calibrated to the asymptotic case, which assume that idiosyncratic risk is diversified away completely, must understate required capital for any given finite portfolio. To assess the magnitude of this bias, we examine the rate of convergence of VAR to its asymptotic limit. As an application, we propose a simple methodology for assessing a portfolio-level add-on charge to compensate for less-than-perfect diversification of idiosyncratic risk. Numerical examples suggest that the method works extremely well, so that moderate departures from asymptotic granularity need not pose a problem in practice for ratings-based capital rules.

Although it is the standard most commonly applied, VAR is not without shortcomings as a risk measure for defining economic capital. Because it is based on a single quantile of the loss distribution, VAR provides no information on the magnitude of loss incurred in the event that capital is exhausted. A more robust risk measure is *expected shortfall* (ES), which is (loosely speaking) the expected loss conditional on being in the tail. From the perspective of an insurer of deposits (eg, the FDIC in the US), an even more relevant risk measure is *expected excess loss* (EEL). Under the EEL paradigm, an institution must hold enough capital so that the expected credit loss in excess of capital is less than or equal to a target loss rate. We consider whether ES and EEL deliver portfolio-invariant capital charges for an asymptotic portfolio in a single-factor setting. Expected shortfall does, but EEL does not, and thus is unsuitable as a soundness standard for deriving risk-bucket capital charges.

The emphasis in this chapter is on generality across portfolios and models. The use of asymptotics to characterise model properties is not new, but all previous analyses have been applied to homogeneous portfolios and with the objective of simplifying computation.[2] Banks vary widely in the size and composition of their portfolios and in the details of their credit risk models. For policy purposes, it is essential that our results be sufficiently general to embrace this diversity. Indeed, our results are shown to apply to quite heterogeneous portfolios and across a broad class of credit risk models.

The first section sets out a general framework for the class of risk-factor models in current use under a book-value definition of credit loss. The second section presents the key results for VAR for this class of models. In the third section, these results are shown to apply equally (with minor additional restrictions) to the case of "multi-state" models in which loss is measured on a market-value basis. A capital adjustment for undiversified idiosyncratic risk is developed in the fourth section. In the fifth section, we examine the asymptotic behaviour of ES and EEL as alternatives to VAR. Concluding remarks focus on the assumption of a single systematic risk factor, which is empirically untenable and yet an unavoidable precondition for portfolio-invariant capital charges. While this assumption ought to be acceptable in the pursuit of achievable and substantive near- to medium-term regulatory reform, it may limit the long-term viability of ratings-based risk-bucket rules for regulatory capital.

A GENERAL MODEL FRAMEWORK UNDER BOOK-VALUE ACCOUNTING

Under a book-value (or *actuarial*) definition of loss, credit loss arises only in the event of obligor default. Change in market value due to rating downgrade or upgrade is ignored. This is the simplest framework for our purposes, because we need only be concerned with default risk and with uncertainty in the recovery value of an asset in the event of obligor default.

An essential concept in any risk-factor model is the distinction between *unconditional* and *conditional* event probabilities.

An obligor's unconditional default probability, also known as its PD or expected default frequency, is the probability of default before some horizon given all information currently observable. The conditional default probability is the PD we would assign the obligor if we also knew what the realised value of the systematic risk factors at the horizon would be. The unconditional PD is the average value of the conditional default probability across all possible realisations of the systematic risk factors.

Let X denote the systematic risk factors (possibly multivariate), which are drawn from a known joint distribution. These risk factors may be identified in some models with specific observable quantities, such as macroeconomic variables or industrial sector performance indicators, or may be left unspecified. Regardless of their identity, it is assumed that all dependence across credit events is due to common sensitivity to these factors. Conditional on X, the portfolio's remaining credit risk is idiosyncratic to the individual obligors in the portfolio. Let $p_i(x)$ denote the probability of default for obligor i conditional on realisation x of X.

This general framework for modelling default is compatible with all of the best-known industry models of portfolio credit risk, including the RiskMetrics Group's CreditMetrics, Credit Suisse Financial Product's CreditRisk$^+$, McKinsey's CreditPortfolio View, and KMV's Portfolio Manager. The similarity to CreditRisk$^+$ is easiest to see because that model is written in the language of conditional default probabilities (Credit Suisse Financial Products, 1977). To obtain CreditRisk$^+$ within our framework, assume that the risk factors $X_1, ..., X_K$ are independent gamma-distributed random variables with mean one and variances $\sigma_1^2, ..., \sigma_K^2$. Let $\bar{p}_i$ denote the PD of obligor i, and specify $p_i(x)$ as

$$p_i(x) = \bar{p}_i \left(1 + \sum_{k=1}^{K} w_{ik}(x_k - 1) \right) \tag{1}$$

where w_i is a vector of factor loadings with sum in $[0, 1]$.[3]

CreditMetrics (Gupton et al, 1997), which is based on a simplified Merton model of default, also can be cast within a conditional probability framework. It is assumed that the vector of risk factors X is jointly distributed $\mathbb{N}(0, \Omega)$. Associated with each obligor is a latent variable R_i which represents the return on the firm's assets. R_i is given by

$$R_i = \psi_i \epsilon_i - X w_i, \qquad (2)$$

where the ϵ_i are iid $\mathbb{N}(0, 1)$ white noise (representing obligor-specific risk). Without loss of generality, the weights w_i and ψ_i are scaled so that R_i is mean zero, variance one.[4] A borrower defaults if and only if its asset return falls below a threshold value γ_i.

To obtain the conditional default probability function $p_i(x)$, observe that default occurs if and only if $\epsilon_i \leq (\gamma_i + X w_i)/\psi_i$. Therefore, conditional on $X = x$, default by i is an independent Bernoulli event with probability

$$p_i(x) = \Pr(\epsilon_i \leq (\gamma_i + x w_i)/\psi_i) = \Phi((\gamma_i + x w_i)/\psi_i) \qquad (3)$$

where Φ is the standard normal cumulative distribution function (cdf). To calibrate the parameter γ_i, note that the unconditional probability of default is $\Phi(\gamma_i)$, so $\gamma_i = \Phi^{-1}(\bar{p}_i)$. See Gordy (2000) for a more detailed derivation of these two models and their representation in terms of conditional probabilities.

In some industry models, it is assumed that loss given default (LGD) is known and non-stochastic. Of the credit VAR models in widespread use, those that do allow for stochastic LGD always take recovery risk to be purely idiosyncratic. In practice, LGD not only may be highly uncertain, but may also be subject to systematic risk. For example, the recovery value of defaulted commercial real estate loans depends on the value of the real estate collateral, which is likely to be lower (higher) when many (few) other real estate projects have failed. Some progress has been made in capturing this effect. Frye (2000) develops an extension of a one-factor CreditMetrics model in which collateral values (and thus recoveries) are correlated with the same systematic risks that drive default rates. Bürgisser *et al* (2001) extend the CreditRisk[+] model to include a systematic factor for recovery risk that is orthogonal to the systematic factors for default risk.

In order to accommodate systematic and idiosyncratic recovery risk, we take *loss*, rather than merely *default status*, as the primitive outcome variable. Let A_i be the exposure to obligor i; these are taken to be known and non-stochastic.[5] Let the random variable U_i

denote loss per dollar exposure. In the event of survival, $U_i = 0$. Otherwise, U_i is the percentage LGD on instrument i, which we permit to be negative to accommodate short positions. The usual assumption of conditional independence of defaults is extended to conditional independence of the U_i. We assume that

($\mathcal{A}$-1) the $\{U_i\}$ are bounded in the interval $[-1,1]$ and, conditional on X, are mutually independent.

For a portfolio of n obligors, define the *portfolio loss ratio* L_n as the ratio of total losses to total portfolio exposure, ie,[6]

$$L_n \equiv \frac{\sum_{i=1}^{n} U_i A_i}{\sum_{i=1}^{n} A_i}. \tag{4}$$

For a given $q \in (0,1)$, VAR is defined as the qth quantile of the distribution of loss, and is denoted $\text{VAR}_q[L_n]$. Let $\alpha_q(Y)$ denote the qth quantile of the distribution of random variable Y, ie,

$$\alpha_q(Y) \equiv \inf\{y : \Pr(Y \leq y) \geq q\}. \tag{5}$$

In terms of this more general notation, we have $\text{VAR}_q[L_n] = \alpha_q(L_n)$.

ASYMPTOTIC LOSS DISTRIBUTION UNDER BOOK-VALUE ACCOUNTING

Suppose that the bank selects its portfolio as the first n elements of an infinite sequence of lending opportunities. To guarantee that idiosyncratic risk vanishes as more assets are added to the portfolio, the sequence of exposure sizes must neither blow up nor shrink to zero too quickly. We assume that

($\mathcal{A}$-2) the A_i are a sequence of positive constants such that
　(a) $\sum_{i=1}^{n} A_i \uparrow \infty$ and
　(b) there exists a $\zeta > 0$ such that $A_n / \sum_{i=1}^{n} A_i = O(n^{-(1/2+\zeta)})$,

where order notation $O(\cdot)$ is defined as in Billingsley (1995, A18). The restrictions in ($\mathcal{A}$-2) are sufficient to guarantee that the share of the largest single exposure in total portfolio exposure vanishes to zero as the number of exposures in the portfolio increases. As a practical matter, the restrictions are quite weak and would be satisfied by any conceivable real-world large bank portfolio. For example, they are satisfied if all the A_i are bounded from below by a positive minimum size and from above by a finite maximum size.

Our first result is that, under quite general conditions, the conditional distribution of L_n degenerates to its conditional expectation as $n \to \infty$. More formally, we can show that

Proposition 1. If ($\mathcal{A}$-1) and ($\mathcal{A}$-2) hold, then, conditional on $X = x$, $L_n - E[L_n|x] \to 0$, almost surely.

The proof, which relies mainly on a strong law of large numbers, is given in Panel 1. Note that there is no restriction on the relationship between A_i and the distribution of U_i, so there is no problem if, for example, high-quality loans tend also to be the largest loans. Also, no restrictions have yet been imposed on the number of systematic factors or their joint distribution.

In intuitive terms, Proposition 1 says that as the exposure share of each asset in the portfolio goes to zero, idiosyncratic risk in portfolio loss is diversified away perfectly. In the limit, the loss ratio converges to a fixed function of the systematic factor X. We refer to this limiting portfolio as "infinitely fine-grained" or as an "asymptotic portfolio." An implication is that, in the limit, we need only know the unconditional distribution of $E[L_n|X]$ to answer questions about the unconditional distribution of L_n. For example, if we wish to know the variance of the loss ratio, we can look to the variance of $E[L_n|X]$:

Proposition 2. If ($\mathcal{A}$-1) and ($\mathcal{A}$-2) hold, then $V[L_n] - V[E[L_n|X]] \to 0$.

The proof is in Panel 1.

A more important result is, in essence, that for any $q \in (0,1)$, the qth quantile of the unconditional loss distribution approaches the qth quantile of the unconditional distribution of $E[L_n|X]$ as $n \to \infty$. Our desired result is to have

$$\alpha_q(L_n) - \alpha_q(E[L_n|X]) \to 0. \tag{6}$$

PANEL 1 PROOF OF PROPOSITIONS 1 AND 2

The proof of Proposition 1 requires a version of the strong law of large numbers for a sequence $\{Y_n\}$ of independent random variables and a sequence $\{a_n\}$ of positive constants:

Lemma 1 (Petrov, 1995, Theorem 6.7). *If, $a_n \uparrow \infty$ and $\Sigma_{n=1}^{\infty}(V[Y_n]/a_n^2) < \infty$, then*

$$\frac{1}{a_n}\left(\sum_{i=1}^{n} Y_n - E\left[\sum_{i=1}^{n} Y_n\right]\right) \to 0 \quad a.s.$$

We also make use of the following lemma.

Lemma 2. If $\{b_n\}$ is a sequence of positive real numbers such that $\{b_n\}$ is $O(n^{-\rho})$ for some $\rho > 1$, then $\Sigma_{n=1}^{\infty} b_n < \infty$.

This lemma is a corollary of Theorem 3.5.2 in Knopp (1956) and the convergence of the harmonic series $1/n^\rho$ for $\rho > 1$ (see Knopp, 1956, Example 3.1.2.3).

We now prove Proposition 1. Let $Y_n \equiv U_n A_n$ and $a_n \equiv \Sigma_{i=1}^{n} A_i$. For any realisation x, conditional independence implies

$$\sum_{n=1}^{\infty}\left(V[Y_n \mid x]/a_n^2\right) = \sum_{n=1}^{\infty}\left(A_n \Big/ \sum_{i=1}^{n} A_i\right)^2 V[U_n \mid x].$$

Under the actuarial definition of loss, $|U_n|$ is bounded in $[0, 1]$, so we must have that $V[U_n \mid x] < 1$ for any $X = x$. For this proposition to hold under the MTM paradigm as well, assumption ($\mathcal{A}$-1) provides a bound on $V[U_n \mid x]$. Therefore, under either definition of loss, there exists a finite constant V^* such that

$$\sum_{n=1}^{\infty}\left(V[Y_n \mid x]/a_n^2\right) \le V^* \sum_{n=1}^{\infty}\left(A_n \Big/ \sum_{i=1}^{n} A_i\right)^2.$$

By part (b) of assumption ($\mathcal{A}$-2), the sequence $\{A_n/\Sigma_{i=1}^{n} A_i\}$ is $O(n^{-(1/2+\zeta)})$ for some $\zeta > 0$, so the sequence $\{(A_n/\Sigma_{i=1}^{n} A_i)^2\}$ is $O(n^{-(1+2\zeta)})$. By Lemma 2, the series sum must be finite. By part (a) of assumption ($\mathcal{A}$-2), we have $a_n \uparrow \infty$. The conditions of Lemma 1 are thus satisfied. The loss ratio L_n is equal to $\Sigma_{i=1}^{n} Y_i/a_n$, so Proposition 1 is proved.

Proposition 2 follows similar logic. We require the following lemma:

Lemma 3. Let $\{b_n\}$ and $\{d_n\}$ be sequences of real numbers such that $a_n \equiv \Sigma_{i=1}^{n} b_i \uparrow \infty$ and $d_n \to 0$. Then $(1/a_n)\Sigma_{i=1}^{n} b_i d_i \to 0$.

This result is a special case of Petrov (1995, Lemma 6.10). If we let $b_n = A_n$ and $d_n = A_n/\Sigma_{i=1}^n A_i$, then assumption ($\mathcal{A}$-2) guarantees that $a_n \uparrow \infty$ and $d_n \to 0$, so apply Lemma 3 to get

$$\frac{1}{\sum\limits_{i=1}^{n} A_i} \sum_{i=1}^{n} \frac{A_i^2}{\sum\limits_{j=1}^{n} A_j} \to 0. \tag{1a}$$

The standard rule for conditional variance gives

$$V[L_n] - V\left[E[L_n \mid X]\right] = E\left[V[L_n \mid X]\right] = \frac{\sum\limits_{i=1}^{n} A_i^2 E\left[V[U_i \mid X]\right]}{\left(\sum\limits_{i=1}^{n} A_i\right)^2}.$$

$E[V[U_i \mid X]]$ must be less than one under the actuarial paradigm. Under the MTM paradigm, we have $E[V[U_i \mid X]] < E\gamma(x)] < \infty$ by assumption ($\mathcal{A}$-1). Therefore, there exists a finite constant V^* such that

$$E\left[V[L_n \mid X]\right] \leq V^* \frac{\sum\limits_{i=1}^{n} A_i^2}{\left(\sum\limits_{j=1}^{n} A_j\right)^2} = V^* \frac{1}{\sum\limits_{i=1}^{n} A_i} \sum_{i=1}^{n} \frac{A_i^2}{\sum\limits_{j=1}^{n} A_j} \leq V^* \frac{1}{\sum\limits_{i=1}^{n} A_i} \sum_{i=1}^{n} \frac{A_i^2}{\sum\limits_{j=1}^{n} A_j} \to 0.$$

As $E[V[L_n \mid X]]$ must be non-negative and is bounded from above by a quantity converging to zero, it too must converge to zero.

For technical reasons, however, we are limited to a slightly restricted variant on this result. Let F_n denote the cdf of L_n. We can show:

Proposition 3. If ($\mathcal{A}$-1) and ($\mathcal{A}$-2) hold, then for any $\epsilon > 0$,

$$F_n\left(\alpha_q(E[L_n \mid X]) + \epsilon\right) \to [q, 1], \tag{7}$$

$$F_n\left(\alpha_q(E[L_n \mid X]) - \epsilon\right) \to [0, q]. \tag{8}$$

The proof is in Panel 2. For all practical purposes, this proposition ensures that Equation (6) will hold.[7] The literal interpretation of Proposition 3 is that if capital is strictly greater than the qth quantile of $E[L_n \mid X]$, then it is guaranteed, in the limit, to cover (or, at least, to come arbitrarily close to covering) q or more of the

PANEL 2 PROOF OF PROPOSITION 3

Almost sure convergence implies convergence in probability (see Billingsley, 1995, Theorem 25.2), so for all x and $\epsilon > 0$,

$$\Pr\left(\left|L_n - E[L_n \mid x]\right| < \epsilon \mid x\right) \to 1. \tag{2a}$$

If F_n is the cdf of L_n, then Equation (2a) implies

$$F_n\left(\left|E[L_n \mid x] + \epsilon \mid x\right) - F_n\left(E[L_n \mid x] - \epsilon \mid x\right)\right) \to 1.$$

Because F_n is bounded in $[0, 1]$, we must have $F_n(E[L_n \mid x] + \epsilon \mid x) \to 1$ and $F_n(E[L_n \mid x] - \epsilon \mid x) \to 0$.

Let S_n^+ denote the set of realisations x of X such that $E[L_n \mid x]$ is less than or equal to its qth quantile value, ie,

$$S_n^+ \equiv \left\{x : E[L_n \mid x] \le \alpha_q(E[L_n \mid X])\right\}.$$

By construction, $\Pr(x \in S_n^+) \ge q$.

By the usual rules for conditional probability, we have

$$
\begin{aligned}
F_n\left(\alpha_q(E[L_n \mid X]) + \epsilon\right) &= F_n\left(\alpha_q(E[L_n \mid X]) + \epsilon \mid X \in S_n^+\right)\Pr(X \in S_n^+) \\
&\quad + F_n\left(\alpha_q(E[L_n \mid X]) + \epsilon \mid X \notin S_n^+\right)\Pr(X \notin S_n^+) \\
&\ge F_n\left(\alpha_q(E[L_n \mid X]) + \epsilon \mid X \in S_n^+\right)\Pr(X \in S_n^+) \\
&\ge F_n\left(\alpha_q(E[L_n \mid X]) + \epsilon \mid X \in S_n^+\right)q. \tag{2b}
\end{aligned}
$$

For all $x \in S_n^+$, we have

$$F_n\left(\alpha_q(E[L_n \mid X]) + \epsilon \mid x\right) \ge F_n\left(E[L_n \mid x] + \epsilon \mid x\right) \to 1$$

so the dominated convergence theorem (Billingsley, 1995, Theorem 16.4) implies that

$$F_n\left(\alpha_q(E[L_n \mid X]) + \epsilon \mid X \in S_n^+\right) \to 1,$$

so from Equation (2b) we have

$$F_n\left(\alpha_q(E[L_n \mid X]) + \epsilon\right) \to [q, 1]$$

as required.

The other half of the proof follows similarly. Define S_n^- as

$$S_n^- \equiv \left\{x : E[L_n \mid X] \ge \alpha_q(E[L_n \mid X])\right\}$$

so that $\Pr(x \in S_n^-) \ge 1 - q$. Then

$$F_n\left(\alpha_q(E[L_n \mid X]) - \epsilon\right) = F_n\left(\alpha_q(E[L_n \mid X]) - \epsilon \mid X \notin S_n^-\right)\Pr(X \notin S_n^-)$$

$$+ F_n\left(\alpha_q(E[L_n \mid X]) - \epsilon \mid X \in S_n^-\right)\Pr(X \in S_n^-)$$

$$\leq q + F_n\left(\alpha_q(E[L_n \mid X]) - \epsilon \mid X \in S_n^-\right)\Pr(X \in S_n^-). \quad \text{(2c)}$$

For all $x \in S_n^-$, we have

$$F_n\left(\alpha_q(E[L_n \mid X]) - \epsilon \mid x\right) \leq F_n\left(E[L_n \mid x] - \epsilon \mid x\right) \to 0$$

so the dominated convergence theorem implies that

$$F_n\left(\alpha_q(E[L_n \mid X]) - \epsilon \mid X \in S_n^-\right) \to 0,$$

so from Equation (2c) we have

$$F_n\left(\alpha_q(E[L_n \mid X]) - \epsilon\right) \to [0, q]$$

as required.

distribution of loss. Similarly, if capital is strictly less than the qth quantile of $E[L_n \mid X]$, then it is guaranteed, in the limit, to fail to cover the qth quantile of the distribution of loss (or, at least, to come arbitrarily close to so failing).

The importance of Proposition 3 is that it allows us to substitute the quantiles of $E[L_n \mid X]$ (which may be relatively easy to calculate) for the corresponding quantiles of the loss ratio L_n (which are hard to calculate) as the portfolio becomes large. It should be emphasised that we have obtained this result with very minimal restrictions on the make-up of the portfolio and the nature of credit risk. The assets may be of quite varied PD, expected LGD, and exposure sizes. Indeed, the portfolio need not be limited to traditional loans or bonds, but could include credit derivatives and guarantees, tranches of structured financial products such as collateralised debt obligations (CDOs) and asset-backed securitisations (ABSs), and so on.[8] We have bounded the support of the U_i, but have otherwise not restricted the behaviour of the conditional expected loss functions (ie, the $E[U_i \mid x]$).[9] These functions may be discontinuous and non-monotonic, and can vary in form from obligor to obligor. More importantly, we have placed no restrictions on the vector of risk factors X. It may be a vector of any finite length and with any distribution (continuous or discrete). The quantiles of $E[L_n|X]$ take on a particularly simple and desirable asymptotic form when we impose two additional restrictions:

($\mathcal{A}$-3) the systematic risk factor X is one-dimensional; and

($\mathcal{A}$-4) there is an open interval B containing $\alpha_q(X)$ and a real number $n_0 < \infty$ such that

  (i)   for all i, $E[U_i|x]$ is continuous in x on B,

  (ii) $E[L_n|X]$ is nondecreasing in x on B for all $n > n_0$, and

  (iii) $\inf_{x \in B} E[L_n|x] \geq \sup_{x \leq \inf B} E[L_n|x]$ and

  $\sup_{x \in B} E[L_n|x] \leq \inf_{x \geq \sup B} E[L_n|x]$ for all $n > n_0$.

Intuitively, assumption ($\mathcal{A}$-3) imposes a single global business cycle as the source of all dependence across exposures. With assumption ($\mathcal{A}$-4), it guarantees that the neighbourhood of the qth quantile of $E[L_n|X]$ is associated with the neighbourhood of the (unique) qth quantile of X. Without ($\mathcal{A}$-4), the tail quantiles of the loss distribution would depend in complex ways on how conditional expected loss for each borrower varies with x. A more parsimonious way to avoid this problem would have been to require that the $E[U_i|x]$ be nondecreasing in x for all i. However, such a requirement would exclude hedging instruments (such as credit derivatives) and obligors with counter-cyclical credit risk. Assumption ($\mathcal{A}$-4) allows for *some* U_i to be negatively associated with X, just so long as, asymptotically and in aggregate, such instruments do not alter the monotonic dependence of losses on the systematic factor when X is near the relevant "tail event." Furthermore, ($\mathcal{A}$-4) allows $E[L_n|X]$ to be discontinuous or locally nonmonotonic in x when x is not in the neighbourhood of $\alpha_q(X)$.

For notational convenience, define functions $\mu_i(x) \equiv E[U_i \mid x]$ and

$$M_n(x) \equiv E\big[L_n|x\big] = \frac{\displaystyle\sum_{i=1}^{n} \mu_i(x) A_i}{\displaystyle\sum_{i=1}^{n} A_i}. \tag{9}$$

We now have

Proposition 4. If ($\mathcal{A}$-3) and ($\mathcal{A}$-4) are satisfied, then $\alpha_q(E[L_n|X]) = E[L_n|\alpha_q(X)] = M_n(\alpha_q(X))$ for $n > n_0$.

Proof. Fix $n > n_0$. If $X \le \alpha_q(X)$, then $M_n(X) \le M_n(\alpha_q(X))$, so

$$\Pr\left(M_n(X) \le M_n(\alpha_q(X))\right) \ge \Pr\left(X \le \alpha_q(X)\right) \ge q.$$

Fix any $y > M_n(\alpha_q(X))$, and let $\hat{x} = \sup\{x : M_n(x) \le y\}$. ($\mathcal{A}$-4) guarantees that $\hat{x} < \alpha_q(X)$, so

$$\Pr(M_n(X) \le y) \le \Pr(X < \hat{x}) < q.$$

Therefore,

$$\inf\left\{y : \Pr(M_n(X) \le y) \ge q\right\} = M_n(\alpha_q(X)) \qquad \square$$

The importance of this result lies in the linearity of the expectations operator. Whereas $\alpha_q(E[L_n|X])$ may in the general case be highly complicated, $E[L_n|\alpha_q(X)]$ is simply the exposure-weighted average of the individual assets' conditional expected losses. Taken together with Propositions 1 and 3, Proposition 4 permits a simple and powerful rule for determining capital requirements. For asset i, allocate capital per dollar book value (inclusive of expected loss) of $c_i \equiv \mu_i(\alpha_q(X)) + \epsilon$, for some arbitrarily small ϵ.[10] Observe that this capital charge depends only on the characteristics of instrument i and thus this rule is portfolio-invariant. Portfolio losses exceed capital if and only if

$$\sum_{i=1}^{n} U_i A_i > \sum_{i=1}^{n} c_i A_i. \qquad (10)$$

Given our rule for c_i and the definition of L_n,

$$\Pr\left(\sum_{i=1}^{n} U_i A_i > \sum_{i=1}^{n} c_i A_i\right) = \Pr\left(L_n > \left(\sum_{i=1}^{n} A_i\right)^{-1} \sum_{i=1}^{n} (\mu_i(\alpha_q(X)) + \epsilon) A_i\right)$$

$$= \Pr\left(L_n > E[L_n|\alpha_q(X)] + \epsilon\right) \to [0, 1-q].$$

Thus, capital is sufficient, in the limit, so that the probability of portfolio credit losses exceeding portfolio capital is no greater than $1 - q$, as desired.

If additional regularity conditions are imposed in order to eliminate the possibility of discontinuities at the desired quantiles, the insolvency probability converges to $1 - q$ exactly for $\epsilon = 0$. A simple way to achieve this would be to require that X be continuous and that the $\mu_i(x)$ functions have bounded derivatives. However, we can be rather less restrictive, as we really need only to guarantee that the asymptotic portfolio loss cdf is smooth and has bounded derivatives in the neighbourhood of its qth quantile value. The following condition is sufficient to circumvent the technical caveats of Proposition 3.

($\mathcal{A}$-5) There exists an open interval B containing $\alpha_q(X)$ on which
    (i)   the cdf of systematic factor X is continuous and increasing,
    (ii) for all i, $\mu_i(x)$ is differentiable, and
    (iii) there are real numbers $\underline{\delta}, \overline{\delta}$ and $n_0 < \infty$ such that
           $0 < \underline{\delta} \leq M_n'(x) \leq \overline{\delta} < \infty$ for all $n > n_0$.

This assumption allows for a non-trivial share of the portfolio to consist of hedged instruments or loans to counter-cyclical borrowers.

In Panel 3, we show that

Proposition 5. If assumptions ($\mathcal{A}$-1)–($\mathcal{A}$-5) hold, then $\Pr(L_n \leq E[L_n|\alpha_q(X)]) \to q$ and $|\alpha_q(L_n) - E[L_n|\alpha_q(X)]| \to 0$.

Therefore, for an infinitely fine-grained portfolio, the proposed portfolio-invariant capital rule provides a solvency probability of exactly q.

The results of this section closely parallel recent developments in techniques for capital allocation in a market risk setting. Gouriéroux *et al* (2000), Tasche (2000) and others show how to take partial first derivatives of VAR.[11] In terms of the notation used here, the first derivative is given by

$$\frac{d\alpha_q(L_n)}{dA_i} = E\left[U_i | L_n = \alpha_q(L_n)\right]. \tag{11}$$

Under the assumptions of Proposition 5, the condition $L_n = \alpha_q(L_n)$ is asymptotically equivalent to $X = \alpha_q(X)$, which implies that marginal VAR is equal to $\mu_i(\alpha_q(X))$. Gouriéroux *et al* (2000) require that the joint distribution of the losses $\{U_i\}$ be continuous, as otherwise VAR need not be differentiable. This presents a problem in application to credit risk modelling, as credit risk is largely driven by discrete events (eg, defaults). The approach taken here in obtaining Proposition 5 allows for the distribution of U_i to be discrete or mixed.[12]

PANEL 3 PROOF OF PROPOSITION 5

The proof of Proposition 5 requires the following lemma:

Lemma 4. Let Y_1 and Y_2 be random variables with cdfs F_1 and F_2, respectively. For all y and all $\epsilon > 0$,

$$|F_1(y) - F_2(y)| \le \Pr\left(|Y_1 - Y_2| > \epsilon\right)$$
$$+ \max\left\{F_2(y + \epsilon) - F_2(y), F_2(y) - F_2(y - \epsilon)\right\}.$$

Proof. Corollary of Petrov (1995, Lemma 1.8). □

To apply Lemma 4, let $Y_1 = L_n$ with cdf F_n and $Y_2 = E[L_n | X]$ with cdf F_n^*. Fix an open set B and real numbers n_0 and $\underline{\delta}, \bar{\delta}$ for which assumptions $(\mathcal{A}\text{-}4)$ and $(\mathcal{A}\text{-}5)$ are satisfied. At every point $\hat{x} \in B$, we have

$$|F_n\left(E[L_n | \hat{x}]\right) - F_n^*\left(E[L_n | \hat{x}]\right)| \le \Pr\left(|L_n - E[L_n | X]| > \epsilon\right)$$
$$+ \max\left\{F_n^*\left(E[L_n | \hat{x}] + \epsilon\right) - F_n^*\left(E[L_n | \hat{x}]\right),\right.$$
$$\left. F_n^*\left(E[L_n | \hat{x}]\right) - F_n^*\left(E[L_n | \hat{x}] - \epsilon\right)\right\} \quad \text{(3a)}$$

for any $\epsilon > 0$.

For $n > n_0$, $(\mathcal{A}\text{-}5)$ guarantees that $M_n(x)$ is strictly increasing on B, so for all $x \in B$, $M_n(X) \le M_n(x)$ if and only if $X \le x$, so $F_n^*(M_n(x)) = H(x)$ where H is the cdf of X.

Fix $\epsilon^* > 0$ such that $(\hat{x} - \epsilon^*, \hat{x} + \epsilon^*) \subset B$. For any positive $\epsilon < \underline{\delta}\epsilon^*$, we then have $\hat{x} + \epsilon/\delta \in B$, so $M_n(\hat{x} + \epsilon/\underline{\delta}) - M_n(\hat{x})$ for all $n > n_0$. As F_n^* is nondecreasing, this implies that

$$F_n^*\left(E[L_n | \hat{x}] + \epsilon\right) \le F_n^*\left(M_n(\hat{x} + \epsilon/\underline{\delta})\right) = H(\hat{x} + \epsilon/\underline{\delta}).$$

Similarly, we have

$$F_n^*\left(E[L_n | \hat{x}] - \epsilon\right) \ge F_n^*\left(M_n(\hat{x} - \epsilon/\underline{\delta})\right) = H(\hat{x} - \epsilon/\underline{\delta}).$$

Thus, for all $n > n_0$,

$$\max\left\{F_n^*\left(E[L_n | \hat{x}] + \epsilon\right) - F_n^*\left(E[L_n | \hat{x}]\right), F_n^*\left(E[L_n | \hat{x}]\right) - F_n^*\left(E[L_n | \hat{x}] - \epsilon\right)\right\}$$
$$\le \max\left\{H(\hat{x} + \epsilon/\underline{\delta}) - H(\hat{x}), H(\hat{x}) - H(\hat{x} - \epsilon/\underline{\delta})\right\}.$$

Assumption $(\mathcal{A}\text{-}5)$ also provides that H is continuous and increasing on B, so for any $\eta > 0$ there exists $\epsilon > 0$ such that

$$\max\left\{H(\hat{x} + \epsilon/\underline{\delta}) - H(\hat{x}), H(\hat{x}) - H(\hat{x} - \epsilon/\underline{\delta})\right\} < \eta. \quad \text{(3b)}$$

By Proposition 1 and the dominated convergence theorem, $L_n - E[L_n | X]$ converges to zero almost surely, which implies convergence in probability as well. Therefore, for any choice of $\epsilon > 0$ and $\eta > 0$, there exists $n_\epsilon < \infty$ such that

$$\Pr\left(|L_n - E[L_n \,|\, X]| > \epsilon\right) < \eta \quad \forall n > n_\epsilon. \tag{3c}$$

Combining these results, we have that for any $\eta < 0$, there exists an $\epsilon > 0$ such that Equations (3b) and (3c) are simultaneously satisfied for $n > \max\{n_0, n_\epsilon\}$. Thus,

$$\lim_{n \to \infty} |F_n(M_n(\hat{x})) - F_n^*(M_n(\hat{x}))| \to 0. \tag{3d}$$

Setting $\hat{x} = \alpha_q(X)$ and observing that $F_n^*(M_n(\alpha_q(X))) = H(\alpha_q(X)) = q$ establishes the first result of Proposition 5.

For any positive $\eta < \bar{\delta}\epsilon^*$ and $n > n_0$, ($\mathcal{A}$-5) implies that $M_n(\alpha_q(X)) - M_n(\alpha_q(X) - \eta/\bar{\delta} \le \eta)$ so $F_n(M_n(\alpha_q(X)) - \eta) \le F_n(M_n(\alpha_q(X) - \eta/\bar{\delta}))$. Because $\alpha_q(X) - \eta/\bar{\delta} \in B$, we have by Equation (3d) that

$$\left| F_n\left(M_n(\alpha_q(X) - \eta/\bar{\delta})) - F_n^*(M_n(\alpha_q(X) - \eta/\bar{\delta})\right) \right| \to 0.$$

For $n > n_0$, $F_n^*(M_n(\alpha_q(X) - \eta/\bar{\delta})) = H(\alpha_q(X) - \eta/\bar{\delta}) < q$, so there exists $\tilde{n}_- < \infty$ such that $F_n(M_n(\alpha_q(X) - \eta/\bar{\delta})) < q$ for all $n > \tilde{n}_-$. Thus, for all $n > \tilde{n}_-$, we have that $F_n(M_n(\alpha_q(X)) - \eta) < q$, which implies that $(M_n(\alpha_q(X)) - \eta < \alpha_q(L_n)$.

By a parallel argument, for all positive $\eta < \bar{\delta}\epsilon^*$ there exists $\tilde{n}_- < \infty$ such that $M_n(\alpha_q(X)) + \eta > \alpha_q(L_n)$ for all $n > \tilde{n}_+$. Thus, for all $n > \max\{\tilde{n}_-, \tilde{n}_+\}$, we have $|\alpha_q(L_n) - M_n(\alpha_q(X))| < \eta$. As η can be made arbitrarily close to zero, the second result of Proposition 5 is established.

Portfolio-invariance depends strongly on the asymptotic assumption and on the assumption of a single systematic risk factor. Portfolios that are not asymptotically fine-grained contain undiversified idiosyncratic risk, which implies that marginal contributions to VAR depend on what else is in the portfolio. As a practical matter, residual idiosyncratic risk need not be an impediment to ratings-based capital allocation. Large internationally active banks are typically (though not invariably) near the asymptotic ideal. Furthermore, the techniques of the fourth section allow for a simple portfolio-level correction.

Assumption ($\mathcal{A}$-3) is much less innocuous from an empirical point-of-view. It can be relaxed only slightly. Say that some group of obligors shared dependence on a "local" risk factor. Conditional on the global risk factor X, the $\{U_i\}$ within the group would no longer be independent, though they would remain independent of the $\{U_j\}$ outside the group. So long as the within-group exposures in *aggregate* account for a trivial share of the total portfolio (ie, they could be aggregated into a single exposure without violating assumption ($\mathcal{A}$-2)), the local dependence can be ignored.

Even the largest banks have geographic and industrial concentrations at some level. If these larger-scale sectors are not perfectly comonotonic, then portfolio-invariance is lost. Say we had two risk factors, and obligors could differ in their sensitivity to each factor. The realisations (x_1, x_2) associated with a given quantile of the loss distribution would then depend on the particular set of obligors in the portfolio. In intuitive terms, the appropriate capital charge for a loan to a heavily X_1-sensitive borrower would depend on whether the other obligors in the portfolio were predominantly sensitive to X_1 (in which case the loan would add little diversification benefit) or to X_2 (in which case the diversification benefit would be larger). To take a simple example, let X_1 represent the US business cycle and X_2 the European business cycle. Consider the merger of a strictly domestic US, asymptotically fine-grained portfolio with another asymptotically fine-grained bank portfolio. If the second portfolio were also exclusively US, then no diversification benefit would ensue, and required capital for the merged portfolio should be the sum of the capital charges on the two portfolios. However, if the second portfolio contained European obligors, then there would be a diversification benefit (as long as X_1 and X_2 were not perfectly comonotonic), and the merger should result in reduced total VAR. Therefore, capital charges could not be portfolio-invariant.

Finally, observe that "bucketing" has not appeared, *per se*, in the derivation. Indeed, the μ_i functions need not even share a common form across instruments. Sorting into a finite number of statistically homogeneous buckets is helpful for purposes of calibration from data, but is not needed for portfolio-invariant capital charges to be obtained.[13]

ASYMPTOTIC LOSS DISTRIBUTION UNDER MARK-TO-MARKET VALUATION

Actuarial models are simple to calibrate and understand, and fit naturally with traditional book-value accounting applied to bank loan books. However, much of the credit risk is missed, especially for long-dated highly rated instruments. Because losses are deemed to arise only in the event of default, no credit loss is recognised when, say, a two-year AA-rated loan downgrades after one year to grade BB. Under a mark-to-market (MTM) notion of loss, credit risk includes the risk of downward (or upward) rating migration, short of default, when the instrument's maturity extends beyond the risk horizon. Even for institutions that report on a book-value basis, it may be desirable to calculate capital charges within a MTM framework in order to capture the additional risk associated with longer instrument maturity.

"Loss" is an ambiguous construct in a MTM setting. We follow one widely used convention in defining the loss rate U_i on asset i as the difference between expected and realised value at the horizon, discounted by the risk-free rate and divided by current market value.[14] For example, $u_i = 0.2$ represents a 20% loss, and $u_i = -0.05$ represents a 5% gain. Other definitions can be applied without changing the results below. We redefine "exposure size" A_i as the current market value.

Credit risk arises due to uncertainty in U. As before, we assume a vector of systematic risk factors X and that the U_i are conditionally independent. The parameterisation and calibration of the $\mu_i(x) \equiv E[U_i|x]$ functions can draw on existing industry models such as CreditMetrics. Say, for example, that we have a rating system with G non-default grades (grade $G + 1$ denoting default), and for each obligor i we have a set of unconditional transition probabilities $\bar{p}_{ig}$ for grade g at the horizon. From these we calculate threshold values γ_{ig} for obligor i's asset return R_i (see Equation (2)), such that obligor i defaults if $R_i \le \gamma_{i,G}$, and transits to "live" grade g if $\gamma_{i,g} < R_i \le \gamma_{i,g-1}$. The variables $(X, \epsilon_1, \epsilon_2, \ldots, \epsilon_n)$ are iid $\mathbb{N}(0, 1)$. Therefore, the conditional transition probabilities are given in CreditMetrics by

$$p_{ig}(x) = \Phi\Big((\gamma_{i,g-1} + xw_i)\big/\sqrt{1 - w_i^2}\Big) - \Phi\Big((\gamma_{i,g} + xw_i)\big/\sqrt{1 - w_i^2}\Big), \quad (12)$$

and the unconditional transition probabilities determine the thresholds as $\gamma_{i,g} = \Phi^{-1}(\bar{p}_{i,g+1} + \cdots + \bar{p}_{i,G+1})$.

Consider a zero-coupon instrument maturing at or after the horizon. Assume the current value A_i is known, and let $v_{ig}(x)$ be the value of instrument i at the horizon conditional on the obligor migrating to rating g. In standard implementations of CreditMetrics, pricing at the horizon is done by discounting future contractual cash flows, where the spreads for each grade are taken as fixed and known. In principle, however, we can allow spreads to be non-stochastic functions of X. The conditional expected MTM value at the horizon is

$$\mathrm{MTM}_i(x) = \sum_{g=1}^{G} v_{ig}(x) p_{ig}(x) + \overline{A}_i \left(1 - E[\mathrm{LGD}_i|x]\right) p_{i,G+1}(x), \quad (13)$$

where $\overline{A}_i$ is the size of the bank's legal claim on the obligor in the event of a default. Coupons can easily be accommodated in this pricing formula as well with some additional notation. The conditional expected loss functions $\mu_i(x)$ are then given by

$$\mu_i(x) = \frac{\exp(-rT)}{A_i} \left(E[\mathrm{MTM}_i(X)] - \mathrm{MTM}_i(x)\right), \quad (14)$$

where T is the time to horizon and r is the risk-free yield for term T.

The results of the previous section can be adapted to a MTM setting without difficulty. In contrast to the actuarial case, the MTM loss rate is not necessarily bounded. To accommodate the MTM case, we modify assumption ($\mathcal{A}$-1) as follows:

($\mathcal{A}$-1) Conditional on X, the $\{U_i\}$ are independent. The conditional second moment of loss exists and is bounded; ie, there exists a function $Y(x)$ such that $E[U_i^2|x] \leq Y(x) < \infty$ for all instruments i and realisations x. Furthermore, $E[Y(X)] < \infty$.

This version of the assumption is strictly weaker than the version of the first section.

For a given portfolio of n assets, L_n, as defined in Equation (4), is the discounted portfolio market-valued credit loss at the horizon as a percentage of current market value. We find that all of the propositions of the second section continue to hold, as stated, under the relaxed version of assumption ($\mathcal{A}$-1). Indeed, the proofs given in the panel explicitly rely only on the relaxed version. The results in no way depend on the assumptions and conventions of CreditMetrics, which are described above for illustrative purposes.[15] By the same logic as before, the appropriate asymptotic capital charge per dollar current market value for asset i is simply $\mu_i(\alpha_q(X))$.

CAPITAL ADJUSTMENTS FOR UNDIVERSIFIED IDIOSYNCRATIC RISK

No portfolio is ever infinitely fine-grained: real-world portfolios have finite numbers of obligors and lumpy distributions of exposure sizes. Large portfolios of consumer loans ought to come close enough to the asymptotic ideal that this issue can safely be ignored, but we ought not to presume the same for even the largest commercial loan portfolios. Unless ratings-based capital rules are to be abandoned for a full-blown internal models approach, we require a methodology for assessing a capital add-on to cover the residual idiosyncratic risk that remains undiversified in a portfolio.

Consider a homogeneous portfolio in which each instrument has the same conditional expected loss function $\mu(x)$ and the same exposure size. Under assumptions ($\mathcal{A}$-3) and ($\mathcal{A}$-4) and suitable regularity conditions,

$$\alpha_q(L_n) = \mu(\alpha_q(X)) + O(n^{-1}). \tag{15}$$

That is, the difference between the VAR for a given finite homogeneous portfolio and its asymptotic approximation is proportional to $1/n$.

One way to obtain this result is through a generalised Cornish–Fisher expansion due to Hill and Davis (1968) for a sequence of distributions converging to an arbitrarily differentiable limiting distribution. The jth term in the expansion of $\alpha_q(L_n)$ is proportional to the difference between the jth cumulants of the distributions for L_n and L_∞. Under very general conditions, the cumulants (for $j \geq 2$) converge at $O(n^{-1})$. The difficulty is in specifying precisely a set of regularity conditions under which the Cornish–Fisher expansion is guaranteed to be convergent.

Building on the results of Gouriéroux *et al* (2000), Martin and Wilde (2002) derive Equation (15) more rigorously as a Taylor series expansion of VAR around its asymptotic value. Although the necessary regularity conditions remain slightly opaque, the main additional requirement is that the conditional variance $V[U|x]$ is locally continuous and differentiable in x. Furthermore, Martin and Wilde show that the $O(n^{-1})$ term is given by β/n where[16]

$$\beta = \frac{-1}{2h(x)} \frac{d}{dx} \left(\frac{V[U \mid x]h(x)}{\mu'(x)} \right) \Bigg|_{x=\alpha_q(X)} \tag{16}$$

and where $h(x)$ is the density of X.

Of course, Equation (15) is in itself an asymptotic result. When we say that convergence is at rate $1/n$, we are saying that *for large enough n* the gap between VAR and its asymptotic approximation shrinks by half when n is doubled. Short of running the credit VAR model, there is no way to say whether a given n is "large enough" for this relationship to hold. To see whether our "$1/n$ rule" works well for realistic values of n and realistic model calibrations, we examine the behaviour of VAR in an extended version of CreditRisk$^+$. The virtue of CreditRisk$^+$ for this exercise is that it has an analytic solution. We not only can execute the model for any n very quickly, but also avoid Monte Carlo simulation noise in the results. However, the standard CreditRisk$^+$ model assumes fixed LGD, and so ignores a potentially important source of volatility.[17] For the special case of a homogeneous portfolio, it is not difficult to augment the model to allow for idiosyncratic recovery risk.

As in the standard CreditRisk$^+$, assume that the systematic risk factor X is gamma-distributed with mean one and variance σ^2. Each obligor has the same default probability $\bar{p}$ and factor loading w. Each facility in the portfolio has identical exposure size, which is normalised to one, and identical expected LGD. The functional form for conditional expected loss function is

$$\mu(x) = E[\text{LGD}] \cdot \bar{p}(1 + w(x - 1)). \tag{17}$$

To introduce idiosyncratic recovery risk, assume LGD for each obligor is drawn from a gamma distribution with mean λ and variance η^2. This specification is convenient because the sum of m independent and identical gamma random variables is gamma-distributed with mean $m\lambda$ and variance $m\eta^2$. Let G_m denote the gamma cdf with this mean and variance. Let π_m denote the probability that there will be m defaults in the portfolio; these probabilities are calculated in the usual way in CreditRisk$^+$. The cdf of L_n can then be obtained as

$$\Pr(L_n \leq y) = \sum_{m=0}^{\infty} \pi_m G_m(ny).$$

Long before m approaches n, the π_m become negligibly small, so numerical calculation of Equation (18) presents no difficulty. A minor disadvantage of this specification is that it allows LGD to exceed one. However, so long as η is not too large, aggregate losses in the portfolio will be well-behaved, so the problem can be ignored.

For this model, the asymptotic slope β is given by

$$\beta = \frac{1}{2\lambda}(\lambda^2 + \eta^2)\left(\frac{1}{\sigma^2}\left(1 + \frac{\sigma^2 - 1}{\alpha_q(X)}\right)\left(\alpha_q(X) + \frac{1-w}{w}\right) - 1\right). \quad \textbf{(19)}$$

This formula generalises a formula derived in Wilde (2001) under the specific parameter values used in the Basel proposal.

Calibration is intended to be qualitatively faithful to available data. When CreditRisk$^+$ is calibrated to rating agency historical performance data, as in Gordy (2000), one finds a negative relationship between $\bar{p}$ and w. By contrast, when a Merton model such as CreditMetrics is calibrated to these data, there is no strong relationship between PD and factor loading. This makes sense, as there is no strong reason to expect that average asset-value correlation should vary systematically across rating grades. To make use of this stylised fact in our calibration, we choose a constant asset-value correlation of 15% in CreditMetrics, and calculate a within-grade default correlation for each grade. Shifting back to CreditRisk$^+$, we set a conservative but reasonable value of $\sigma = 2$ for the volatility of X, and then calibrate w for each rating grade so that the within-grade default correlation matches the value from CreditMetrics.[18] The remainder of the calibration exercise is straightforward. We choose stylised values for the default probabilities, and assume that LGD has mean 0.5 and standard deviation 0.25. The chosen coverage target is $q = 0.995$ of the loss distribution.

Results are shown in Table 1 for five rating grades. The final column ($n = \infty$) provides the asymptotic capital charge, so the difference between each column and the final column represents

Table 1 Convergence of VAR

Rating	$\bar{p}$	w	$VAR_q[L_n]$ for values of n					
			200	**500**	**1,000**	**2,000**	**5,000**	∞
A	0.06	1.011	0.723	0.521	0.445	0.406	0.381	0.364
BBB	0.20	0.836	1.425	1.190	1.106	1.064	1.038	1.020
BB	1.25	0.602	5.217	4.947	4.856	4.810	4.783	4.764
B	6.25	0.415	17.881	17.584	17.485	17.435	17.405	17.385
CCC	17.50	0.295	37.663	37.335	37.226	37.172	37.139	37.117

Note: Default probabilities and VAR expressed in percentage points. Simulations assume $q = 0.995$, $\sigma = 2$, $\lambda = 0.5$, and $\eta = 0.25$.

the "true" granularity add-on. Even for portfolios of only $n = 200$ homogeneous obligors, granularity add-ons are small in the absolute sense (under 60 basis points). However, the add-ons can be large relative to the asymptotic capital charge for investment grade obligors. For a homogeneous portfolio of 200 A-rated loans, the granularity add-on is roughly equal to the asymptotic charge.

Figure 1 demonstrates the relationship between the theoretical granularity add-on and $1/n$ for three homogeneous portfolios. For an extremely low-quality portfolio (CCC rating), the predicted linear relationship holds down to $n = 200$.[19] For the medium-quality (BB rated) portfolio, there are visible but negligible departures from the predicted linear relationship when $n < 500$. For a high-quality portfolio (A-rated), departures from linearity are visible at $n = 1,000$ and become significant at lower values of n. Because departures from linearity are in the concave direction, a granularity adjustment calibrated to the asymptotic slope β would slightly overshoot the theoretically optimal add-on for smaller high-quality portfolios.

In the case of a non-homogeneous portfolio, determining an appropriate granularity add-on is only slightly more complex. The method of Wilde (2001) accommodates heterogeneity (the $V[U|x]$ and $\mu(x)$ terms in Equation (16) become $V[L_n|x]$ and $M_n(x)$, respectively). An alternative two-step method also appears to work quite well and may be better suited to a regulatory setting. The first step is to map the actual portfolio to a homogeneous "comparable portfolio" by matching moments of the loss distribution. The second step is to determine the granularity add-on for the comparable

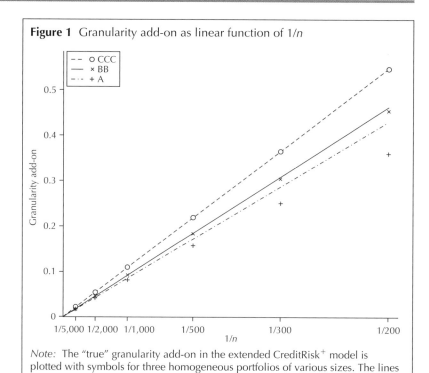

Figure 1 Granularity add-on as linear function of $1/n$

Note: The "true" granularity add-on in the extended CreditRisk$^+$ model is plotted with symbols for three homogeneous portfolios of various sizes. The lines show the corresponding theoretical add-on for this model.

portfolio. The same add-on is applied to the capital charge for the actual portfolio.

Consider a heterogeneous portfolio of n lending facilities divided among B buckets. Within each bucket b, every facility has the same PD $\bar{p}_b$, factor loading w_b, expected LGD λ_b and LGD volatility η_b. Exposure sizes A_i are allowed to vary across facilities in a bucket. To measure the extent to which bucket b exposure is concentrated in a small number of facilities, we require the within-bucket Herfindahl index given by[20]

$$H_b \equiv \frac{\sum_{i \in b} A_i^2}{\left(\sum_{i \in b} A_i \right)^2}.$$

The higher is H_b, the more concentrated is the exposure within the bucket, so the more slowly idiosyncratic risk is diversified away. The matching methodology takes bucket-level inputs $\{\bar{p}_b, w_b, \lambda_b, \eta_b, H_b\}$ and total bucket exposure. This data structure may be especially convenient in a regulatory setting with bucket-level reporting requirements.

The goal is to construct the comparable portfolio as a portfolio of n^* equal-sized facilities with common PD $\bar{p}^*$, factor loading w^*, and LGD parameters λ^* and η^*. In principle, a wide variety of moment restrictions could be used to do the mapping, but it seems best to choose moments with intuitive interpretation. Panel 4 develops a matching procedure based on five moments:[21]

❑ exposure-weighted expected default rate,
❑ expected portfolio loss rate,
❑ contribution of systematic risk to loss variance,
❑ contribution of idiosyncratic default risk to loss variance, and
❑ contribution of idiosyncratic recovery risk to loss variance.

Under this methodology, each of the parameters of the comparable portfolio is given by an explicit linear equation that can be interpreted as a weighted average of the characteristics of the heterogeneous portfolio. Most interestingly, the number of loans n^* can be interpreted as an inverse measure of weighted exposure concentration. Finally, the asymptotic slope β^* for the comparable homogeneous portfolio is given by Equation (19).

The portfolio data needed for the mapping method should pose minimal additional reporting burden for regulated institutions. Default probability, expected LGD and total bucket exposure would need to be reported by the bank to calculate the asymptotic capital charge. Factor loadings and LGD volatilities would likely be assigned as functions of the $\bar{p}_b$ and λ_b; this is indeed the case in the proposed IRB approach (Basel Committee on Bank Supervision, 2001). The only new required inputs, the within-bucket Herfindahl indices, are easily calculated from the individual exposure sizes.

Matching lower-order moments gives no guarantee that the loss distribution for the comparable portfolio will display higher-order moments very close to those of the original heterogeneous portfolio. Tail quantiles of the loss distribution are sensitive to higher-order moments, so the performance of the methodology needs to be confirmed on a range of empirically plausible portfolios. As an example, we construct a portfolio of 600 obligors divided equally

PANEL 4 CONSTRUCTION OF THE COMPARABLE HOMOGENEOUS PORTFOLIO

Moment restrictions provide a convenient and intuitive way to map the heterogeneous portfolio into a homogeneous portfolio of n^* equal-sized facilities with common PD $\bar{p}^*$, factor loading w^*, and LGD parameters λ^* and η^*.

Let s_b denote the share of total portfolio exposure held in bucket b, ie,

$$s_b \equiv \frac{\sum_{i \in b} A_i}{\sum_i A_i}.$$

The first two restrictions equate exposure-weighted expected default rate and expected portfolio loss rate:

$$\bar{p}^* = \sum_{b=1}^{B} \bar{p}_b s_b \quad \text{and} \quad \lambda^* \bar{p}^* = \sum_{b=1}^{B} \lambda_b \bar{p}_b s_b. \tag{4a}$$

Thus, λ^* is the expected loss rate divided by the expected default rate; ie,

$$\lambda^* = \frac{\sum_{b=1}^{B} \lambda_b \bar{p}_b s_b}{\sum_{b=1}^{B} \bar{p}_b s_b}. \tag{4b}$$

The remaining moment restrictions equate across the actual and comparable portfolios the contribution to loss variance from different sources of risk. The contribution of systematic risk (ie, $V[E[L \,|\, X]]$) takes the simple form

$$V[E[L_n \,|\, X]] = \sigma^2 \left(\sum_{b=1}^{B} \lambda_b \bar{p}_b w_b s_b \right)^2, \quad V[E[L^* \,|\, X]] = \sigma^2 (\lambda^* \bar{p}^* w^*)^2,$$

which implies

$$w^* = \frac{\sum_{b=1}^{B} \lambda_b \bar{p}_b w_b s_b}{\sum_{b=1}^{B} \lambda_b \bar{p}_b s_b}. \tag{4c}$$

Note that w^* is simply an expected loss-weighted average of the w_b.

The contribution of idiosyncratic risk to loss variance (ie, $E[V[L_n \,|\, X]]$) works out to

$$E[V[L_n \mid X]] = \sum_{b=1}^{B} \left(\lambda_b^2 \left(\bar{p}_b(1-\bar{p}_b) - (\bar{p}_b w_b \sigma)^2 \right) + \bar{p}_b \eta_b^2 \right) H_b s_b^2,$$

$$E[V[L^* \mid X]] = \frac{1}{n^*} \left(\lambda^{*2} \left(\bar{p}^*(1-\bar{p}^*) - (\bar{p}^* w^* \sigma)^2 \right) + \bar{p}^* \eta^{*2} \right).$$

Terms containing $\lambda^2(\bar{p}(1-\bar{p}) - (\bar{p}w\sigma)^2)$ represent the contribution of idiosyncratic default risk, and terms containing $\bar{p}\eta^2$ represent the contribution of idiosyncratic recovery risk. By matching these two contributions separately, we get the final two restrictions needed for identification. The number of exposures in the comparable portfolio works out to

$$n^* = \left(\sum_{b=1}^{B} \Lambda_b H_b s_b^2 \right)^{-1} \tag{4d}$$

where

$$\Lambda_b \equiv \frac{\lambda_b^2(\bar{p}_b(1-\bar{p}_b) - (\bar{p}_b w_b \sigma)^2)}{\lambda^{*2}(\bar{p}^*(1-\bar{p}^*) - (\bar{p}^* w^* \sigma)^2)}.$$

Finally, the variance of LGD for the comparable portfolio is given by

$$\eta^{*2} = \frac{\eta^*}{\bar{p}^*} \sum_{b=1}^{B} \eta_b^2 \bar{p}_b H_b s_b^2. \tag{4e}$$

across four buckets. The buckets represent high investment grade, low investment grade, high speculative grade and moderate-to-low speculative grade. Factor loadings are calibrated as in Table 1. Expected LGDs for the buckets are set to 0.3, 0.2, 0.6, and 0.5, respectively, and the LGD volatility is set to $\eta_b = 0.5\sqrt{\lambda_b(1-\lambda_b)}$. Table 2 displays the bucket-level parameters.

Exposure size for facility i is set to i^4; ie, A_i is US\$1 for the first exposure, US\$16 for the second, US\$81 for the third, and so on. The exposures are assigned to buckets by turn. The first exposure is assigned to Bucket 4, the second to Bucket 3, the third to Bucket 2, the fourth to Bucket 1, the fifth to Bucket 4, and so on. Looking at the portfolio as a whole, we find that the largest 10% of exposures account for roughly 40% of total exposure, which matches the empirical rule of thumb reported by Carey (2001) for concentration of outstandings. Also, portfolio exposure is roughly split between investment and speculative grades, which appears to be typical of a commercial loan portfolio at a large bank (see Treacy and Carey, 1998, Chart 3).

Table 2 Bucket-level parameters of stylised portfolio

	$\bar{p}$	w	λ	η
1	0.05	1.040	0.3	0.229
2	0.50	0.715	0.2	0.200
3	1.00	0.629	0.6	0.245
4	5.00	0.440	0.5	0.250

Note: Default probabilities in percentage points.

We first obtain parameters for the comparable homogeneous portfolio. The comparable portfolio has $n^* = 218.7$ obligors, which is under 40% of the obligor count of the original portfolio.[22] Each obligor has PD of 1.64% and factor loading $w^* = 0.487$. LGD has expected value 0.491 and volatility 0.247.[23] By construction, the comparable portfolio matches the original portfolio in its expected loss rate of 0.804%. For each portfolio, the standard deviation of the loss rate is 0.918%. Once the comparable portfolio is determined, the asymptotic slope β is calculated for the target quantile q. Finally, we approx imate VAR_q for the original portfolio as its asymptotic VAR plus β_q^*/n^*.

Results are shown in Table 3 for three tail values of q. Row (i) presents estimates of VAR obtained by direct simulation of the original portfolio. Row (ii) presents the asymptotic VAR for the original portfolio given by $E[L_n|\alpha_q(X)]$. Row (iii) shows VAR for the comparable portfolio obtained using the cdf in Equation (18). The granularity add-on β_q^*/n^* is shown in row (iv). Row (v) sums the asymptotic VAR and granularity add-on to get our approximation. Tracking error between rows (v) and (i) is shown in the final row.

The procedure works well for all values of q. Despite the relatively small obligor count in the comparable portfolio, the error due to linear approximation of the "$1/n$ rule" is minimal. At $q = 99.5\%$, our approximated VAR overshoots its target by 2.2 basis points.

It should be emphasised that the theoretical underpinnings for the granularity adjustment apply equally to MTM models. The simple linear formulae for parameters of the comparable homogeneous portfolio depend on the linear functional forms assumed in CreditRisk$^+$. Specifications based on more complex models, eg,

Table 3 Direct and approximated estimates of VAR

Estimates	Target quantile, q		
	99.0	99.5	99.9
(i) "True" VAR	4.577	5.522	7.872
(ii) Asymptotic VAR	4.220	5.109	7.260
(iii) VAR for comparable portfolio	4.570	5.535	7.872
(iv) Granularity add-on	0.357	0.435	0.627
(v) Approximated VAR	4.578	5.544	7.886
(vi) Tracking error	0.001	0.022	0.014

Note: All quantities expressed in percentage points. "True" VAR estimated by simulation with 300,000 Monte Carlo trials.

KMV Portfolio Manager or CreditMetrics, imply more complex mapping formulae whose inputs need not be reducable to bucket-level summary statistics (eg, Herfindahl indices). However, it seems reasonable to conjecture that one can achieve tolerable accuracy using crude rules based on the CreditRisk$^+$ formulae. What is most important is that there be a reasonably accurate measure for the "effective" obligor count in a heterogeneous portfolio. Most bank portfolios are heavy-tailed in exposure size distribution, and thus may have an effective n^* that is an order of magnitude smaller than the raw obligor count in the portfolio.

ASYMPTOTIC PROPERTIES OF ALTERNATIVE RISK MEASURES

Industry application of credit risk modelling to capital allocation appears almost invariably to equate soundness with a coverage target for VAR. However, because it ignores the distribution of losses beyond the target quantile, VAR has significant theoretical and practical shortcomings. As has been emphasised in recent literature on risk measures, VAR is not sub-additive. That is, if L_A and L_B are losses on bank portfolios A and B, then we need not have $VAR_q[L_A + L_B] \leq VAR_q[L_A] + VAR_q[L_B]$, which would imply that a merger of bank A and bank B could *increase* VAR; see Frey and McNeil (2002, Section 2.3) for an example based on credit risk measurement. Sub-additivity is one of the four requirements for a "coherent" risk measure as set forth by Artzner *et al* (1999).

Under the assumptions needed to achieve portfolio-invariance, $VAR_q[L_A + L_B] = VAR_q[L_A] + VAR_q[L_B]$, so sub-additivity is preserved in mergers of asymptotically fine-grained portfolios. Even in this case, however, VAR can be manipulated by splitting the portfolio. Under an actuarial definition of loss, for example, a portfolio consisting of a single loan with default probability under $1 - q$ has $\text{VAR}_q = 0$, but the same loan has positive contribution (assuming positive dependence of U on X) to VAR in an asymptotically fine-grained portfolio. Segregating this loan from the larger portfolio does not change the VAR contributions of the remaining loans, so VaR is unambiguously reduced.

Another problem is that a mean-preserving spread of the loss distribution can decrease VAR. This results in a counterintuitive non-monotonic relationship between within-portfolio correlation and VAR. Correlations increase with factor loadings, and, when factor loadings are low to moderate, VAR does as well. However, as factor loadings are pushed higher and higher, the loss distribution becomes increasingly long-tailed. VAR then shrinks towards the median, while the probability of a cataclysmic loss increases. In the limiting case of perfectly comonotonic losses, the default rate is either zero (with probability $1-\bar{p}$) or one (with probability $\bar{p}$). If $\bar{p} < 1-q$, then $\text{VAR}_q = 0$. For a survey discussion of the potential pitfalls of VAR, see Szegö (2002).

As an alternative to VAR, Acerbi and Tasche (2002) propose using generalised ES, defined by

$$\text{ES}_q[Y] = (1-q)^{-1} \left(E\left[Y \cdot 1_{\{Y \geq \alpha_q(Y)\}} \right] + \alpha_q(Y)(q - \Pr(Y < \alpha_q(Y))) \right). \quad (20)$$

The first term is often used as the definition of ES for continuous variables. It is also known as "tail conditional expectations." The second term is a correction for mass at the qth quantile of Y. Under this definition, Acerbi and Tasche (2002) show that ES is coherent and equivalent to Rockafellar and Uryasev's (2002) CVAR.

ES offers some important advantages as a soundness standard. By Acerbi and Tasche (2002, Corollary 3.3), ES_q is continuous and monotonic in q, so small increases in the "stringency" of the capital rule (as controlled by q) lead to small increases in required capital. ES is nondecreasing with any mean-preserving spread in the loss distribution, so ES cannot decrease as factor loadings rise.

In Panel 5, we show that

PANEL 5 PROOF OF PROPOSITION 6

ES is the sum of expected loss in the tail and a correction term for mass at the VAR boundary. Under the given assumptions, the latter term disappears asymptotically both in $ES_q[L_n]$ and $ES_q[M_n(X)]$. For $n > n_0$, the variable $M_n(X)$ is continuous in the neighbourhood of $M_n(\alpha_q(X))$ and, by Proposition 4, $\alpha_q(M_n(X)) = M_n(\alpha_q(X))$; this implies $\Pr(M_n(X) < M_n(\alpha_q(X))) = q$. By Chebyshev's inequality and assumption $(\mathcal{A}\text{-}1)$, we have

$$M_n(\alpha_q(X))^2 \le \frac{E[M_n(X)^2]}{\Pr(M_n(X) > M_n(\alpha_q(X)))} \le \frac{E[\gamma(X)]}{1-q} < \infty,$$

so the sequence $\{M_n(\alpha_q(X))\}$ is bounded from above. Therefore,

$$\alpha_q(M_n(X))(q - \Pr(M_n(X) < \alpha_q(M_n(X)))) = 0 \quad \forall n > n_0,$$

Although L_n need not be continuous, arguments parallel to those used in the proof of Proposition 5 show that $\Pr(L_n \ge \alpha_q(L_n)) \to 1 - q$. That proposition also provides that $|\alpha_q(L_n) - M_n(\alpha_q(X))| \to 0$, so $\alpha_q(L_n)$ is asymptotically bounded from above. This implies

$$\lim_{n \to \infty} |\alpha_q(L_n)(q - \Pr(L_n < \alpha_q(L_n)))| = 0.$$

To complete the proof, we now only need show that

$$\left| E\left[L_n \cdot 1_{\{L_n \ge \alpha_q(L_n)\}} \right] - E\left[M_n(X) \cdot 1_{\{M_n(X) \ge \alpha_q(M_n(X))\}} \right] \right| \to 0. \tag{5a}$$

Let $Y_n \equiv (L_n - \alpha_q(L_n))$ and let $\hat{Y}_n \equiv (M_n(X) - M_n(\alpha_q(X)))$. The terms of Equation (5a) can be re-written as

$$E\left[M_n(X) \cdot 1_{\{M_n(X) \ge \alpha_q(M_n(X))\}} \right] = E\left[M_n(X) - M_n(\alpha_q(X))) \cdot 1_{\{M_n(X) - M_n(\alpha_q(X)) \ge 0\}} \right]$$
$$+ M_n(\alpha_q(X)) E\left[1_{\{M_n(X) \ge M_n(\alpha_q(X))\}} \right]$$
$$= E[\max\{\hat{Y}_n, 0\}] + M_n(\alpha_q(X)) \Pr(M_n(X) \ge M_n(\alpha_q(X)))$$

and similarly

$$E\left[L_n \cdot 1_{\{L_n \ge \alpha_q(L_n)\}} \right] = E[\max\{Y_n, 0\}] + \alpha_q(L_n) \Pr(L_n \ge \alpha_q(L_n)).$$

As $|\alpha_q(L_n) - M_n(\alpha_q(X))| \to 0$ and

$$\lim_{n \to \infty} \Pr(L_n \ge \alpha_q(L_n)) = \lim_{n \to \infty} \Pr(M_n(X) \ge M_n(\alpha_q(X))) = 1 - q,$$

we have

$$|\alpha_q(L_n) \Pr(L_n \ge \alpha_q(L_n)) - M_n(\alpha_q(X)) \Pr(M_n(X) \ge M_n(\alpha_q(X)))| \to 0.$$

For all $y, \hat{y} \in \mathfrak{R}, |\max(y,0) - \max(y,0)| \le |y - \hat{y}|$. Therefore,

$$|E[\max\{Y_n, 0\}] - E[\max\{\hat{Y}_n, 0\}]|$$

$$\le E[|Y_n - \hat{Y}_n|] \le E[|L_n - M_n(X)|] + |\alpha_q(L_n) - M_n(\alpha_q(X))|.$$

As each of these terms converges to zero, Equation (5a) is established.

Proposition 6. If assumptions $(\mathcal{A}\text{-}1)$–$(\mathcal{A}\text{-}5)$ hold, then $|ES_q[L_n] - ES_q[M_n(X)]| \to 0$.

An immediate implication is that ES-based capital charges are portfolio-invariant under the same assumptions as VAR-based capital charges. The asymptotic ES, $ES_q[M_n(X)]$, can be decomposed as $(\Sigma_i c_i A_i)/(\Sigma_i A_i)$, where the capital charge per dollar of exposure to i is $c_i = E[U_i | X \ge \alpha_q(X)]$. Observe that c_i depends only on how U_i depends on X, and so is portfolio-invariant. Under a variety of model specifications, c_i has an analytical solution, so there is no operational difficulty in calibrating ratings-based capital charges to an ES soundness standard.

Another alternative to VAR is EEL. For a random variable Y and target loss rate $\theta > 0$, EEL is defined by

$$EEL_\theta[Y] \equiv \inf\{y: E[(Y-y)^+] \le \theta\} \tag{21}$$

where Y^+ denotes $\max(Y, 0)$. Under the EEL paradigm, an institution holds capital (plus reserves) so that the expected credit loss in excess of capital is less than or equal to the target loss rate. That is, the required total capital is given by $EEL_\theta[L_n]$ per dollar of total exposure.

EEL is sensitive to the tail of the loss distribution, so shares many of the advantages of ES. More importantly, the target rate θ represents the expected loss borne by the depository insurance agency (such as the FDIC in the US), so EEL-based capital has a natural policy interpretation. Unlike ES, however, EEL cannot be reconciled with portfolio-invariant capital charges. Some intuition for this problem can be gained by writing the asymptotic EEL for homogeneous portfolios in terms of the distribution of the systematic risk factor. Assume we have loans of two types, denoted "a" and "b". Let $\mu_a(x)$ denote the expected loss for bucket a loans conditional on $X = x$. By reasoning very similar to that of Proposition 6, we can show that

$$E[(L_a - y)^+] \to E[(\mu_a(X) - y)^+]$$

for any y. Therefore, the asymptotic EEL capital charge c_a is set so that $E[(\mu_a(X) - c_a)^+]$ equals the desired target θ. Similar analysis for bucket b gives c_b.

Now say we have a mixed portfolio containing equal numbers of loans from a and b. For simplicity, the exposures are equal-sized. Asymptotic EEL capital for the mixed portfolio is given by $EEL_\theta[\mu_m(X)]$. By construction of the mixed portfolio, we have $\mu_m(X) = (\mu_a(X) + \mu_b(X))/2$. If asymptotic EEL were portfolio-invariant, then $c_m \equiv (c_a + c_b)/2$ would satisfy

$$\theta = E[(\mu_m(X) - c_m)^+]. \tag{22}$$

We now require the following triangle inequality:

Lemma 5. If Y_1 and Y_2 are integrable random variables on a common probability space, then

$$E[(Y_1 + Y_2)^+] \le E[Y_1^+] + E[Y_2^+].$$

If $\Pr((Y_1 < 0 < Y_2) \vee (Y_2 < 0 < Y_1)) > 0$, then the inequality is strict.

Proof is given in Panel 6.

The conditions of Lemma 5 apply to $Y_j \equiv (\mu_j(X) - c_j)/2$, which gives us

$$E[(\mu_m(X) - c_m)^+] \le E[((\mu_a(X) - c_a)/2)^+] + E[((\mu_b(X) - c_b)/2)^+] = \theta. \tag{23}$$

In general, the threshold realisation of X at which $\mu_a(x) = c_a$ does not equal the corresponding threshold for portfolio b, so for some interval of x values we will have either $\mu_a(x) - c_a < 0 < \mu_b(x) - c_b$ or $\mu_a(x) - c_a > 0 > \mu_b(x) - c_b$. Therefore, the inequality in Equation (23) will in most situations be strict, which implies that c_m is too strict a capital requirement for the asymptotic mixed portfolio.

To provide a rough idea of how much we overshoot required capital in a mixed portfolio, we apply EEL to an asymptotic, single

PANEL 6 PROOF OF LEMMA 5

Let $(\Omega, \mathcal{F}, P)$ be the probability space for Y_1 and Y_2. Divide Ω into two subsets

$$B_1 = \left\{ \omega: 0 \leq \min(Y_1(\omega), Y_2(\omega)) \bigvee \max(Y_1(\omega), Y_2(\omega)) \leq 0 \right\},$$

$$B_2 = \left\{ \omega: (Y_1(\omega) < 0 < Y_2(\omega)) \bigvee (Y_2(\omega) < 0 < Y_1(\omega)) \right\}.$$

Observe that $B_1 \cup B_2 = \Omega$ and $B_1 \cap B_2 = \varnothing$. If Y is an integrable random variable on $(\Omega, \mathcal{F}, P)$, we can write

$$E[Y^+] = \int_\Omega \max(Y(\omega), 0) P(d\omega)$$

$$= \int_{B_1} \max(Y(\omega), 0) P(d\omega) + \int_{B_2} \max(Y(\omega), 0) P(d\omega).$$

The set B_1 contains all ω for which Y_1 and Y_2 are either both positive or both negative. Under both these circumstances, $\max(Y_1(\omega) + Y_2(\omega), 0)$ equals $\max(Y_1(\omega), 0) + \max(Y_2(\omega), 0)$, so

$$\int_{B_1} \max(Y_1(\omega) + Y_2(\omega), 0) P(d\omega)$$

$$= \int_{B_1} \max(Y_1(\omega), 0) P(d\omega) + \int_{B_1} \max(Y_2(\omega), 0) P(d\omega). \qquad \text{(6a)}$$

The set B_2 contains all ω for which Y_1 and Y_2 are of opposite sign, so

$$\int_{B_2} \max(Y_1(\omega) + Y_2(\omega), 0) P(d\omega)$$

$$\leq \int_{B_2} \max(Y_1(\omega), 0) P(d\omega) + \int_{B_2} \max(Y_2(\omega), 0) P(d\omega). \qquad \text{(6b)}$$

Summing left and right hand sides of Equations (6a) and (6b), we obtain

$$E\left[(Y_1 + Y_2)^+ \right] \leq E[Y_1^+] + E[Y_2^+]. \qquad \text{(6c)}$$

If $P(B_2) > 0$, then the inequality in Equation (6b) is strict, and therefore the inequality in Equation (6c) is strict as well.

---

systematic factor version of CreditRisk$^+$. In Panel 7, we show that asymptotic EEL takes on a relatively simple form in this model. Table 4 presents EEL- and VAR-based capital requirements for homogeneous asymptotic portfolios of different credit ratings. Parameters for each rating grade and the volatility of X are taken

PANEL 7 ASYMPTOTIC EEL IN CREDITRISK$^+$

We derive the asymptotic EEL for a homogeneous portfolio under a single-systematic-factor version of CreditRisk$^+$. Let $\bar{p}$ denote default probability, λ denote LGD, w denote factor loading, and σ denote the volatility of systematic factor X. The conditional expected loss rate in the CreditRisk$^+$ specification is given by Equation (17). As $n \to \infty$, L_n converges to $\mu(X)$, so asymptotic EEL is equal to the value of c solving

$$\theta = E\left[(\mu(X) - c)^+ \right] = \int_{\mu^{-1}(c)}^{\infty} (\mu(x) - c)h(x)\,dx, \qquad (7a)$$

where $h(\cdot)$ is the gamma density with mean one, variance σ^2. Using Abramowitz and Stegun (1968, 6.5.1, 6.5.21) to solve this integral, we obtain

$$\theta = (EL - c)(1 - H(\mu^{-1}(c)))$$

$$+ \frac{EL \cdot w}{\Gamma(1 + 1/\sigma^2)} (\mu^{-1}(c)/\sigma^2)^{1/\sigma^2} \exp\left(\frac{-\mu^{-1}(c)}{\sigma^2} \right), \qquad (7b)$$

where $H(\cdot)$ denotes the gamma cdf, EL is expected loss ($\lambda\bar{p}$), and

$$\mu^{-1}(c) = \frac{c - (1 - w) \cdot EL}{w \cdot EL}.$$

The gamma cdf is available in nearly all numerical packages. Standard software for solving nonlinear equations quickly finds the capital ratio c which covers EEL target θ. In the special case of $\sigma = 1$, the gamma distribution reduces to the exponential distribution, and Equation (7b) simplifies to

$$\theta = w \cdot EL \cdot \exp(-\mu^{-1}(c)).$$

This yields the closed-form solution

$$EEL_\theta[L_\infty] = c = EL - w \cdot EL \cdot (1 + \ln(\theta) - \ln(w \cdot EL)).$$

from Table 1. The "EEL" and "VAR" columns in Table 4 report required capital charges (gross of reserves) for an EEL target of $\theta = 0.00002$ (ie, 0.2 basis points) and a VAR target of $q = 99.5\%$, respectively. The value of θ was chosen to equate capital requirements under the two standards for an obligor at the border of investment and speculative grades (ie, between BBB and BB).

Table 4 Asymptotic EEL and VAR capital charges

	EEL	VAR
AA	0.050	0.135
A	0.131	0.248
BBB	0.571	0.709
BB	4.135	3.397
B	19.352	12.657
CCC	45.550	27.390

Note: Capital in percentage points.

Table 5 Asymptotic EEL for mixed portfolios

Bucket *a*	Bucket *b*	c_m	$(c_a + c_b)/2$	Error (%)
AA	A	0.088	0.090	+2.7
A	B	8.378	9.741	+16.3
BBB	BB	2.210	2.353	+6.5
AA	CCC	19.658	22.800	+16.0

Note: Capital charges expressed in percentage points.

In this example, the EEL standard produces lower (higher) capital requirements than VAR for the higher (lower) grades.

We next form mixed portfolios. In each case, we assume an asymptotic portfolio of equal-sized loans, half of which are in one bucket and half in another bucket. It is straightforward to show that the conditional expected loss rate for a mixed portfolio is

$$\mu_m(x) = \frac{1}{2}\mu_a(x) + \frac{1}{2}\mu_b(x) = \lambda \bar{p}_m(1 + w_m(x-1)) \tag{24}$$

where $\bar{p}_m$ and $(\bar{p}_a + \bar{p}_b)/2$ and $w_m = (\bar{p}_a w_a + \bar{p}_b w_b)/(2\bar{p}_m)$. The $\mu_m(x)$ take on the same form as for homogeneous portfolios, so the tools of Panel 7 apply without modification. Results for four different mixed portfolios are presented in Table 5. The third column shows the EEL for the mixed portfolio, while the fourth column shows the average of the EELs for homogeneous portfolios of the two constituent buckets. The final column shows the "tracking error" as a percentage of the third column. As one would expect, the average of the homogeneous capital charges overshoots the correct mixed-portfolio capital charge by a relatively small (though non-negligible) amount when the two buckets are adjacent. For a mix of grades AA and A, we overshoot by under 3%. For a mix of BBB and BB, we overshoot by 6.5%. If distant buckets are mixed, the overshoot is much larger (over 16% for the two examples in the table).

DISCUSSION

Ratings-based assignment of capital charges offers significant advantages in regulatory application. The current Accord is itself a simple ratings-based framework. The proposed new Accord will introduce additional bucketing criteria and make better use of information in borrower ratings, yet still be viewed as a natural extension of the current regime. Because the capital charge for a portfolio is simply a weighted sum of the dollars in each bucket, ratings-based systems are relatively simple to administer and need not impose burdensome reporting requirements. Validation problems are also limited in scope. As the new Accord is currently envisioned, the most significant empirical challenge facing supervisors would likely concern the quality of default probability estimates for internal grades.

Though not often recognised in the debate on regulatory reform, in practice many (if not most) large banks apply ratings-based rules for allocation of capital at the transaction level. Even at institutions that have implemented models for portfolio management and portfolio-level capital assessment, there may be reluctance to apply the implied marginal capital requirements to assess hurdle rates for individual transactions. Computational and information systems burdens may be substantial. More important perhaps, line managers are likely to oppose any performance monitoring system in which a loan that could be booked one day at a profitable credit spread becomes unprofitable the next due only to changes in the composition of the bank's overall portfolio. The need for stability in business operations thus favors portfolio-invariant capital charges at the transaction level.

This chapter shows how risk-factor models of credit VAR can be used to justify and calibrate a ratings-based system for assigning capital charges for credit risk at the instrument level. Ratings-based systems, by definition, permit capital charges to depend only on the characteristics of the instrument and its obligor, and not the characteristics of the remainder of the portfolio. Risk-factor models deliver this property, which we call *portfolio-invariance*, only if two conditions are satisfied. First, the portfolio must be asymptotically fine-grained, in order that all idiosyncratic risk be diversified away. Second, there can be only a single systematic risk factor.

Violation of the first condition, which occurs for every finite portfolio, does not pose a serious obstacle in practice. Analysis of rates of convergence of VAR to its asymptotic limit leads to a robust and practical method of approximating a portfolio-level adjustment for undiversified idiosyncratic risk.

The second condition presents a greater dilemma. The single risk-factor assumption, in effect, imposes a single business cycle on all obligors. A revised Basel Accord must apply to the largest international banks, so the risk factor should in principle represent the global business cycle. By assumption, all other credit risk is strictly idiosyncratic to the obligor. In reality, the global business cycle is a composite of a multiplicity of cycles tied to geography and to prices of production inputs. A single-factor model cannot capture any clustering of firm defaults due to common sensitivity to these smaller-scale components of the global business cycle. Holding fixed the state of the global economy, local events in, for example, France are permitted to contribute nothing to the default rate of French obligors. If there are indeed pockets of risk, then calibrating a single-factor model to a broadly diversified international credit index may significantly understate the capital needed to support a regional or specialised lender.

Would empirical violation of the single-factor assumption necessarily render a risk-bucket capital rule unreliable and ineffective? The answer depends on the scope of application and the sophistication of debt markets. Regulators will need to use caution and judgment in applying risk-bucket capital charges to institutions that are less broadly diversified. One should note that the current Basel Accord, which is itself a risk-bucket system, is applied to an enormous range of institutions, so it seems unlikely that a reformed Accord would bring about any greater harm.

More generally, the ability of banks to subvert ratings-based capital rules by exploiting the inadequacy of the single-factor assumption depends on the capacity of debt markets to recognise and price different risk factors. At present, such capacity appears to be lacking. Partly because markets do not yet provide precise information on correlations of credit events across obligors, many (perhaps most) of the institutions that actively use credit VAR models effectively impose the single-factor assumption.[24] In the near- to medium-term, therefore, the implausibility of the single-factor assumption need not present an obstacle to the implementation of reformed ratings-based risk-bucket capital rules. In the long run, however, the need to relax this assumption may impel adoption of a more sophisticated internal-models regulatory regime.

1 The so-called 8% rule takes a rather broad definition of "capital." In effect, roughly half this 8% must be in equity capital, as measured on a book-value basis. A very limited degree of risk-sensitivity is achieved through discounts to the standard 8% that are applied to certain special classes of lending, eg, to OECD member governments, to other banks in OECD countries, and for residential mortgages.

2 Large-sample approximations have been applied to homogeneous portfolios under single risk-factor versions of the RiskMetrics Group's CreditMetrics (Finger, 1999) and KMV Portfolio Manager (Vasicek, 1997) in order to obtain computational shortcuts. Bürgisser *et al* (2001) characterise the asymptotic behaviour of a generalised CreditRisk$^+$ model on a sequence of portfolios with n statistically identical copies of a fixed heterogeneous portfolio.

3 Strictly speaking, this functional form is invalid because it allows conditional probabilities to exceed one. In practice, this problem is negligible for high- and moderate-quality portfolios and reasonable calibrations of the σ_k^2.

4 The usual specification has Xw_i added, not subtracted. The change in sign here is convenient because it implies that the $p_i(x)$ function will be increasing in x, but does not otherwise change the statistical properties of the model. The scaling of R_i implies that the weight on the idiosyncratic factor is given by $\psi_i = (1 - w_i' \Omega w_i)^{1/2}$.

5 In practice, it need not be so simple. If the instrument is a coupon bond, book-value expos- ure is simply the face value. Much bank lending, however, is in the form of lines of credit which give the borrower some control over the exposure size. Borrowers do tend to draw down unutilised credit lines as they deteriorate towards default. If we assume that uncer- tainty in A is idiosyncratic conditional on the state of the obligor and is of bounded variance, then all the conclusions of this chapter continue to hold. In this case, we interpret A_i as the *expected* dollar exposure in the event of obligor default.

6 For simplicity, we assume that the portfolio contains only a single asset for each obligor. Under actuarial treatment of loss, multiple assets of a single obligor may be aggregated into a single asset without affecting the results.

7 The difference has to do with the possibility that the unconditional distributions for the $\{E[L_n|X]\}$ will permit jump points (or arbitrarily steep slope) at the quantiles $\alpha_q(E[L_n|X])$ as $n \to \infty$.

8 For extensions of the results of this chapter to determining economic capital requirements on CDO and ABS tranches, see Pykhtin and Dev (2002, 2003) and Gordy and Jones (2003).

9 Technically, the CreditRisk$^+$ model allows U_i to exceed one, because it approximates the Bernoulli distribution of the default event as a Poisson distribution. To accommodate CreditRisk$^+$, we could loosen this restriction to a requirement that the U_i have bounded variance. See the modified version of ($\mathcal{A}$-1) introduced in the third section.

10 In most practitioner discussions, it is assumed that expected loss is charged against the loan loss reserve and that "capital" refers only to the amount held against unexpected loss. In this chapter, "capital" refers to the gross amount set aside.

11 This problem was solved independently by several authors. See references in Tasche (2002, Section 4).

12 Tasche (2000) provides slightly less stringent conditions for differentiability. Tasche (2001) applies Equation (11) to a discrete model (CreditRisk$^+$), and discusses the technical issues that arise.

13 Multi-state models such as CreditMetrics and CreditPortfolioView typically calibrate PDs to a finite set of rating grades, but the factor loadings w_i may be set at the individual obligor level. In this case, each obligor would comprise its own "bucket." In the KMV model, there is a continuum of "rating grades," so buckets do not arise in any natural way.

14 Coupon payments, if any, are assumed to be accrued to the horizon at the risk-free rate. Some convention also must be imposed on which intra-horizon cashflows are received on defaulting assets. In practice, how coupons are handled has little effect on the loss distribution, and no qualitative effect on the asymptotics.

15 In the spirit of KMV Portfolio Manager, for example, one could replace Equation (12) with the conditional density function for the default probability at the horizon. The summation in Equation (13) would be replaced by an integral, and the v_{ig} would be obtained using risk-neutral valuation. Valuation in the default state in Equation (13) also would be modified.

16 Equation (16) is obtained through less formal arguments in Wilde (2001).

17 The standard model also implies a discrete loss distribution. As n increases, the "steps" in the loss distribution are realigned, which causes local violations of monotonicity in the relationship between n and VAR.

18 See Gordy (2000) for more details on the choice of σ and on using within-grade default correlations for consistent calibration across the two models.

19 The slope between each plotted point is constant to six significant digits for both B (not shown) and CCC portfolios.

20 The Herfindahl index is a measure of concentration in very widespread use in antitrust analysis, and should be familiar to many practitioners.

21 The matching procedure specified in the proposed granularity adjustment of Basel Committee on Bank Supervision (2001, Chapter 8) is based on a different set of moments but follows similar intuition.

22 Note that the procedure for calculating the granularity add-on does not require n^* to be an integer.

23 In practice, as in this exercise, LGD volatility is often assumed to be a simple function of expected LGD. Reporting requirements and computations could be simplified by setting $\eta^* = \mathrm{VLGD}(\lambda^*)$. While this ignores the effect of nonlinearity in VLGD, the difference is typically small. In our example, $\mathrm{VLGD}(\lambda^*)$ would have been 0.250.

24 Users of KMV Portfolio Manager and CreditMetrics often impose a uniform asset-value correlation across obligors. Users of CreditRisk$^+$ typically assume a single-factor and a factor loading of $w = 1$ for all obligors. In both these examples, the user is implicitly imposing both a single systematic factor and a uniform value for the factor loading.

REFERENCES

Abramowitz, M., and I. A. Stegun, 1968, *Handbook of Mathematical Functions*, National Bureau of Standards.

Acerbi, C., and D. Tasche, 2002, "On the Coherence of Expected Shortfall", *J. Banking Finance*, **26**, pp. 1487–1503.

Artzner, P., F. Delbaen, J.-M. Eber, and D. Heath, 1999, "Coherent Measures of Risk", *Math. Finance*, **9**, pp. 203–28.

Basel Committee on Bank Supervision, 1999, "Credit Risk Modelling: Current Practices and Applications", Technical report, Bank for International Settlements.

Basel Committee on Bank Supervision, 2001, "The Internal Ratings-Based Approach: Supporting Document to the New Basel Capital Accord", Technical report, Bank for International Settlements.

Billingsley, P., 1995, "Probability and Measure", Third Edition, (New York: Wiley).

Bürgisser, P., A. Kurth, and A. Wagner, 2001, "Incorporating Severity Variations into Credit Risk", *Risk*, **3**, pp. 5–31.

Carey, M., 2001, "Dimensions of Credit Risk and their Relationship to Economic Capital Requirements", in F. S. Mishkin (ed), *Prudential Supervision: What Works and What Doesn't*, University of Chicago Press.

Credit Suisse Financial Products, 1977, "CreditRisk+: A Credit Risk Management Framework", Credit Suisse Financial Products.

Finger, C. C., 1999, "Conditional Approaches for CreditMetrics Portfolio Distributions", *CreditMetrics Monitor*, pp. 14–33.

Frey, R., and A. J. McNeil, 2002, "VAR and Expected Shortfall in Portfolios of Dependent Credit Risks: Conceptual and Practical Insights", *J. Banking Finance*, **26**, pp. 1317–34.

Frye, J., 2000, "Collateral Damage: A Source of Systematic Credit Risk", *Risk*, p. **13**.

Gordy, M. B., 2000, "A Comparative Anatomy of Credit Risk Models", *J. Banking Finance*, **24**, pp. 119–49.

Gordy, M., and D. Jones, 2003, "Random Tranches", *Risk*, **16**, pp. 78–83.

Gouriéroux, C., J. Laurent, and O. Scaillet, 2000, "Sensitivity Analysis of Values at Risk", *J. Empirical Finance*, **7**, pp. 225–45.

Gupton, G. M., C. C. Finger, and M. Bhatia, 1997, "CreditMetrics – Technical Document", (New York: JP Morgan).

Hill, G., and A. Davis, 1968, "Generalised Asymptotic Expansions of Cornish–Fisher Type", *Ann. Math. Statist*, **39**, pp. 1264–73.

Jones, D., 2000, "Emerging Problems with the Basel Capital Accord: Regulatory Capital Arbitrage and Related Issues", *J. Banking Finance*, **24**, pp. 35–58.

Knopp, K., 1956, *Infinite Sequences and Series*, (New York: Dover).

Martin, R., and T. Wilde, 2002, "Unsystematic Credit Risk", *Risk* **15**, pp. 123–28.

Petrov, V. V., 1995, "Limit Theorems of Probability Theory", Oxford University Press.

Pykhtin, M., and A. Dev, 2002, "Credit Risk in Asset Securitisations: Analytical Model", *Risk*, **15**, pp. S16–S20.

Pykhtin, M., and A. Dev, 2003, "Coarse-grained CDOs", *Risk*, **16**, pp. 113–16.

Rockafellar, R. T., and S. Uryasev, 2002, "Conditional Value-at-Risk for General Loss Distributions", *J. Banking Finance*, **26**, pp. 1443–71.

Szegö, G. P., 2002, "Measures of Risk", *J. Banking Finance*, **26**, pp. 1253–72.

Tasche, D., 2000, "Conditional Expectation as Quantile Derivative", Working Paper, TU München.

Tasche, D., 2001, "Calculating Value-at-Risk Contributions in CreditRisk^{+}", Working Paper, ETH Zentrum.

Tasche, D., 2002, "Expected Shortfall and Beyond", *J. Banking Finance*, **26**, pp. 1519–33.

Treacy, W. F., and M. S. Carey, 1998, "Credit Risk Rating at Large US Banks", *Fed. Reserve Bull*, **84**, pp. 897–921.

Vasicek, O. A., 1997, "The Loan Loss Distribution", Technical report, KMV Corporation.

Wilde, T., 2001, "Probing Granularity", *Risk*, **14**, pp. 103–6.

13

Allocating Portfolio Economic Capital to Sub-Portfolios

Dirk Tasche*

Deutsche Bundesbank

From an economic point of view, the risks that arise in a bank's portfolio need to be covered by a corresponding amount of capital to absorb potential losses. This capital commonly is referred to as economic capital. It mainly represents the value of the company's stock capital and comprises all reserves the bank is holding to cover occurring losses.[1] In Matten (see 1996, p. 9), the role of capital is described as acting "as a buffer against future, unidentified, even relatively improbable losses, while still leaving the bank able to operate at the same level of capacity".

In a situation of intensifying competition and decreasing return margins banks need to ensure an efficient use of their economic capital. It is becoming a core objective of risk management to ensure that the economic capital is invested efficiently in business lines yielding highest risk-adjusted performance. As a fundamental competitive necessity risk managers need to identify risk return efficient portfolios and to break them down into operational keys for the ongoing operative business management.

Recent developments in the regulatory environment enforce the importance of allocating economic capital in a reasonable way. Within the supervisory review of financial institutions that apply

*The opinions expressed in this chapter are those of the author and do not necessarily reflect views shared by the Deutsche Bundesbank or its staff.

or want to apply the internal-ratings-based approach provided by the Basel II framework, supervisors will in particular examine whether the institutions have installed adequate procedures for dealing with economic capital (see BCBS, 2004).

Risk and return contribution of sub-portfolios or business lines represent basic management information for an integrated risk return management of the bank portfolio. On the one hand, return contributions of single assets or sub-portfolios can easily be determined by expected return margins that add up straight forward to target returns on any portfolio level. On the other hand, it seems a more complex problem to determine risk contributions of single assets or sub-portfolios in the overall portfolio. Portfolio effects and benefits of diversification have to be taken into account adequately, yielding *risk-adjusted risk contributions.* As any risk contribution in the portfolio needs to be covered by the corresponding amount of economic capital, the question of measuring risk contributions can be considered equivalent to the problem of allocating economic capital.

Comprehensive work has been done to develop methods of how to calculate risk contributions in an appropriate way (see eg, Denault, 2001; Kalkbrener, 2002; Stoughton and Zechner, 2004). However, from a practical point of view, the allocation problem, ie, the question of how the single assets contribute to the overall portfolio risk, and how this information is used in risk return bank management, cannot be considered as completely solved, yet. Instruments need to be implemented to use the information of capital allocation appropriately in the ongoing business. Major issues in this context are the definition of adequate limit systems and of risk-adjusted pricing and risk-adjusted performance measurement, based on efficient economic capital allocation. In this chapter we examine how to conduct capital allocation for a financial institution's portfolio in a manner that is compatible with portfolio optimisation. We present major findings on theoretical concepts of capital allocation, that prove that there is only one definition for the risk contributions which is suitable for performance measurement, namely as a derivative of the underlying risk measure in the direction of the asset weight in question. We will then review for some examples how risk contributions, ie, capital allocation can be calculated.

This chapter is organised as follows: after presenting a portfolio model in the section "Background and Model" running examples of risk measures are given in the section "Examples of Risk Measures". The section "Risk Contributions and Differentiable Risk Measures" contains the above-mentioned result on suitableness for performance measurement (Theorem 1). The section "Examples of Risk Contributions" gives the results on differentiation. The section "Conclusions" completes this chapter.

In the following text we will make use of the following notation. For a positive integer d the set N_d is defined by $N_d \stackrel{\text{def}}{=} \{1, \ldots, d\}$. For a vector $x \in \mathbb{R}^d$, x_i denotes its i-th component. For $x, y \in \mathbb{R}^d$ we denote by $x'y \stackrel{\text{def}}{=} \Sigma_{i=1}^d x_i y_i$ the Euclidean scalar product of x and y. For $i \in N_d$ the vector $e^{(i)} \in \mathbb{R}^d$ denotes the i-th canonical unit vector, ie,

$$e_j^{(i)} = \begin{cases} 1, & \text{if } i = j \\ 0, & \text{if } i \neq j \end{cases}$$

BACKGROUND AND MODEL

We are going to study a model for the cashflow generated by an investment consisting of several assets $1, \ldots, d \geq 2$. We use the term asset as an abbreviation for "asset or liability" or the difference of these two. Thus, the cashflow of an asset may be positive and negative.

Examples for such assets are a risky loan granted by a bank and refinanced with deposits and a credit derivative on the default of the loan that the bank bought with borrowed money in order to reduce its risk. For the first asset the expected cashflow should be positive whereas for the second asset it might be negative.

Mathematically we describe the cashflow C_i of asset i by its expected profit/loss margin m_i and by (-1) times the deviation of the cashflow from its margin. This means

$$C_i = m_i - X_i \tag{1}$$

where X_i is an integrable random variable with $E[X_i] = 0$. We call X_i the *fluctuation* caused by asset i. The cashflow from the investment now is

$$C(u) = \sum_{i=1}^d u_i C_i = \sum_{i=1}^d m_i u_i - \sum_{i=1}^d u_i X_i \tag{2}$$

for an investment portfolio consisting of u_i units of asset $i, i = 1, \ldots, d$. The random variable

$$Z(u) = \sum_{i=1}^{d} u_i X_i \qquad (3)$$

is the *portfolio (cashflow) fluctuation.*

In case of a negative cashflow $C(u)$ the investor will go bankrupt unless he has allocated some capital from his equity in order to prevent insolvency. The amount of capital allocated for this reason is called *economic capital.* This is the way equity contributes to the investment (see Matten, 1996, p. 32). Hence the expected return on equity for the investment has to be calculated as a RORAC by the ratio of the expected cashflow and the economic capital. This shows that the economic capital is crucial for the performance of the investment. If it is low, the expected performance will be good but the probability of insolvency might also be high. If the economic capital is high the investor's creditors will be happy but the performance of the investment may be poor.

Thus the fact that there are a lot of suggestions for the definition of the economic capital is not astonishing. Each proposal has its advantages and disadvantages (see the discussions for risk measures under various aspects in Artzner *et al*, 1999, or Schröder, 1996).

We will distinguish the risk and the economic capital of a portfolio. The risk will be a quantity measuring the portfolio fluctuation as defined by Equation (3) whereas the economic capital will depend on the portfolio fluctuation *and* on the profit/loss margins.[2] In other words, while the risk will tell us only something about the deviations of the portfolio cashflow from its expected value, the economic capital will also take into account the expected value itself.

We do not need a formal definition of the notion *risk*. As seen above, a portfolio is represented by a vector $u = (u_1, \ldots, u_d) \in U \subset \mathbb{R}^d$. The u_i may be interpreted as weights or numbers of pieces of the assets. The set U contains the portfolios that are currently under consideration. A *risk measure* then is simply a function $r : U \to \mathbb{R}$, and $r(u)$ is the *risk* of portfolio u. We do not impose any special property on the function r to be a risk measure, but we will often assume the risk measures to be differentiable functions. Also, when examining which risk measure to use for a portfolio in practice one might be well-advised to take care of some or of all the properties discussed in Artzner *et al* (1999).

We need not define formally the economic capital of a portfolio either. Example 2 below will show that the choice $r(u) - \sum_{i=1}^{d} u_i m_i$ for the economic capital is reasonable since with an appropriate risk measure r the probability of the cashflow to fall short of (-1) times this quantity will be low.

EXAMPLES OF RISK MEASURES

Mapping the riskiness of a set U of portfolios by a single function $r : U \to \mathbb{R}$ is not a simple task. Some knowledge about the portfolio is needed. Examples for the necessary knowledge are worst-case scenarios based on human expertise or statistical models of the portfolio cashflow which might be built from historical data. We will focus on the following three examples of risk measures from practice which all need a statistical model of the cashflow. Note that in these examples from a technical point of view the assumption $E[X_i] = 0$ is not necessary. Nonetheless, it might be reasonable in an economic context (see previous section).

Example 1. (Standard deviation)
Assume that $(X_1, \dots, X_d)$ is a random vector such that $\text{var}(X_i) < \infty$ for each $i \in N_d$. Fix $c > 0$.

With $Z(u)$ as in Equation (3),

$$r(u) \overset{\text{def}}{=} c\sqrt{\text{var}(Z(u))}, \quad u \in \mathbb{R}^d \qquad (4)$$

defines the usual standard deviation risk measure which is very popular in practice. The constant c is often chosen as the 95%- or the 99%-quantile of the standard normal distribution, ie, $c = 1.65$ and $c = 2.33$ respectively. $\qquad\qquad\square$

Example 2. (Value-at-risk (VAR))
Let $(X_1, \dots, X_d)$ be any random vector in $\mathbb{R}^d$. Fix $\alpha \in (0, 1)$ and denote by

$$Q_\alpha(u) \overset{\text{def}}{=} \inf \left\{ z \in \mathbb{R} : P[Z(u) \le z] \ge \alpha \right\}, \quad u \in \mathbb{R}^d \qquad (5)$$

the α-*quantile* of the portfolio fluctuation $Z(u)$, defined by Equation (3). Then

$$r(u) \overset{\text{def}}{=} Q_\alpha(u), \quad u \in \mathbb{R}^d \tag{6}$$

defines the risk measure VAR. □

There does not seem to be any common view in the literature whether for the definition of VAR one should take the "pure" quantile or the quantile minus some benchmark. In Definition 2 below we will use for arbitrary risk measures the expected profit/ loss margin as a benchmark when defining our notion of return. The reason for doing so is the fact that

$$P[C(u) < m'u - Q_\alpha(u)] \le 1 - \alpha$$

with $C(u)$ being the portfolio cashflow as in Equation (2). Hence $Q_\alpha(u) - m'u$ is just the amount of capital to be allocated in order to prevent insolvency with probability α or more. Often, α is chosen with a view on the intended rating of the institution.

Example 3. (Expected shortfall)
Fix an $\alpha \in (0,1)$. Assume that $(X_1, \ldots, X_d)$ is a random vector such that $E[|X_i|] < \infty$ for each $i \in N_d$.
    Observe that for all $u \in R^d$ we have by definition of $Q_\alpha(u)$ in Equation (5)

$$P[Z(u) \ge Q_\alpha(u)] \ge 1 - \alpha \tag{7}$$

Hence the risk measure

$$r(u) \overset{\text{def}}{=} E\big[Z(u)|Z(u) \ge Q_\alpha(u)\big], \quad u \in \mathbb{R}^d \tag{8}$$

is well defined. It corresponds to the shortfall risk measure well known from literature (see Schröder, 1996). □

Acerbi and Tasche (2002) and Rockafellar and Uryasev (2002) discuss a *coherent* (see Artzner *et al*, 1999) modification of the short-fall measure (*expected shortfall or conditional value-at-risk, CVAR*) that does not differ too much from Equation (8) in general. In order to create more flexibility in expressing the investor's degree of risk-aversion, *spectral risk measures* are introduced as a further coherent generalisation of expected shortfall (see Acerbi, 2002). Tasche (see 2002, Remark 3.8) presents an example of a spectral measure that takes into account higher moment effects while guarantueeing a fixed probability of solvency. Fischer (2003) describes coherent risk measures that generalise the notion of semi-deviation.

In the Markowitz portfolio theory (see Markowitz, 1952; Tucker *et al*, 1994) the fact that the standard deviation risk measure has nice differentiation properties is heavily exploited. In the section "Examples of Risk Contributions" we will see that the VAR and shortfall risk measures are differentiable in a rather general context as well.

From general mathematical analysis it is clear that the derivatives of a function play the most important role when we study the effects of changing the values of one or more of its arguments. For the class of homogeneous risk measures this connection is particularly close as the subsequent proposition (well known as *Euler's theorem*) shows. We need a slightly more general notion of homogeneity.

Definition 1.

(i) a set $U \subset \mathbb{R}^d$ is *homogeneous* if for each $u \in U$ and $t > 0$ we have $tu \in U$.

(ii) let τ be any fixed real number. A function $r : U \to \mathbb{R}$ is *τ-homogeneous* if U is homogeneous and for each $u \in U$ and $t > 0$ we have $t^\tau r(u) = r(tu)$. □

Proposition 1 tells us in Equation (9) that differentiable τ-homogeneous functions can be represented as a weighted sum of their derivatives in a canonical manner.

Proposition 1.

Let $\emptyset \neq U$ be a homogeneous open set in $\mathbb{R}^d$ and $r : U \to \mathbb{R}$ be a real-valued function. Let $\tau \in \mathbb{R}$ be fixed.

(a) if r is τ-homogeneous and partially differentiable in u_i for some $i \in N_d$ then the derivative $\partial r / \partial u_i$ is $(\tau - 1)$-homogeneous.

(b) if r is totally differentiable then it is τ-homogeneous if and only if for all $u \in U$

$$\tau r(u) = \sum_{i=1}^{d} u_i \frac{\partial r}{\partial u_i}(u) \tag{9}$$

(c) assume $d \geq 2$. Let r be τ-homogeneous, continuous, and for $i = 2, \ldots, d$ partially differentiable in u_i with continuous derivatives $\partial r / \partial u_2, \ldots, \partial r / \partial u_d$. Then on the set $U \setminus (\{0\} \times \mathbb{R}^{d-1})$ the function r is also partially differentiable in u_1 with a continuous derivative and satisfies Equation (9).

RISK CONTRIBUTIONS AND DIFFERENTIABLE RISK MEASURES

Equation (9) is appealing because it suggests a natural way to apportion the portfolio risk to the single assets while simultaneously respecting their weights. There are good reasons for such an apportionment; see Litterman (1996) or Zöller (1996) for some of them. The most important might be risk-adjusted performance measurement. In this section we show that careful assignment of risk contributions of the assets can be useful in optimising performance measured as ratio of expected cashflow and economic capital. On the contrary, a thoughtless assignment may result in a rather misleading indication for the portfolio management.

As with the notions of risk and economic capital we do not need any formal definition for *risk contribution*. Finding meaningful risk contributions corresponds to deciding from which vector field $a = (a_1, \ldots, a_d) : U \to \mathbb{R}^d$ most information can be inferred about a certain function $r : U \to \mathbb{R}$, the risk measure. In a differentiable context the answer seems clear: from the gradient of r.

Nonetheless, examining the problem more closely is instructive. We begin by defining the return function corresponding to a risk measure seen as an ordinary function. Examples for return functions in the sense of Definition 2 are the well known RARORAC (risk-adjusted return on risk-adjusted capital) or the Sharpe Ratio.

Definition 2.
Let $\emptyset \neq U$ be a set in $\mathbb{R}^d$ and $r : U \to \mathbb{R}$ be some function on U. Fix any $m \in \mathbb{R}^d$.

Then the function $g = g_{r,m} : \{u \in U : r(u) \neq m'u\} \to \mathbb{R}$, defined by

$$g(u) \overset{\text{def}}{=} \frac{m'u}{r(u) - m'u} \tag{10}$$

is called return function for r. $\qquad\square$

As we see the economic capital as a reserve to compensate unexpected losses in the future it should be discounted with some factor when the portfolio return is calculated. The factor should depend on the length of the time interval under consideration and the risk-free interest rate. We do not care about this factor because we are not primarily interested in absolute performance but in performance relative to those of other portfolios or assets.

If the economic capital $r(u^{(i)}) - m'u^{(i)}$ of portfolios $u^{(i)}$, $i = 1, 2$, is positive then it is clear that the performance of $u^{(1)}$ is better than that of $u^{(2)}$ if and only if $g(u^{(1)}) > g(u^{(2)})$. But we also allow negative values for the economic capital. This may be reasonable when considering a portfolio of guarantees or derivatives which are held in order to reduce economic capital.

Observe that the case of opposite signs in the denominator and the numerator of the quotient in Equation (10) is unrealistic. On the one hand, the case of a positive numerator and a negative denominator means that someone gives us a present of a guarantee and even pays for being allowed to do so. On the other hand, the case of a negative numerator and a positive denominator means that we are so kind to pay for being allowed to bear someone else's risk.

More interesting is the case where both the denominator and the numerator in Equation (10) are negative. In this case $g(u)$ depicts the profit of a counterparty and should therefore be – from the investor's point of view – hold as small as possible.

Keep the meanings of the signs in Equation (10) in mind when interpreting the following definition. It translates the postulate that a risk contribution should give the right signals for portfolio management into a mathematical formulation.

Definition 3.
Let $\emptyset \neq U$ be a set in $\mathbb{R}^d$ and $r : U \rightarrow \mathbb{R}$ be some function on U.

A vector field $a = (a_1, ..., a_d) : U \rightarrow \mathbb{R}^d$ is called *suitable for performance measurement* with r if it satisfies the following two conditions:

(i) for all $m \in \mathbb{R}^d$, $u \in U$ with $r(u) \neq m'u$ and $i \in N_d$ the inequality

$$m_i r(u) > a_i(u)m'u \qquad (11)$$

implies that there is an $\epsilon > 0$ such that for all $t \in (0, \epsilon)$ we have

$$g_{r,m}(-te^{(i)} + u) < g_{r,m}(u) < g_{r,m}(te^{(i)} + u) \tag{12}$$

(ii) for all $m \in \mathbb{R}^d$, $u \in U$ with $r(u) \neq m'u$ and $i \in N_d$ the inequality

$$m_i r(u) < a_i(u)m'u \tag{13}$$

implies that there is an $\epsilon > 0$ such that for all $t \in (0, \epsilon)$ we have

$$g_{r,m}(-te^{(i)} + u) > g_{r,m}(u) > g_{r,m}(te^{(i)} + u) \tag{14}$$

$\square$

Remark 1.

(i) the quantity $a_i(u)$, $i \in N_d$, may be regarded as the risk contribution of one unit or one piece of asset i or as *normalised* risk contribution of asset i.

(ii) evidently, Equation (11) is equivalent to

$$m_i(r(u) - m'u) > (a_i(u) - m_i)m'u \tag{15}$$

and similarly for Equation (13). Inequality (15) indicates the relation between the portfolio return $g(u)$ and the return $m_i/(a_i(u) - m_i)$ of asset i as part of the portfolio which ensures that the portfolio return will increase when the weight of asset i in the portfolio is increased.

(iii) we will see in Proposition 3 that suitableness for performance measurement as in Definition 3 often implies a similar property for sub-portfolios consisting of more than one asset.

The following result shows that for a "smooth" function the only vector field which is suitable for performance measurement with the function is the gradient of the function. With a view on the additivity relation Equation (9), in case of one-homogeneous-risk measures capital allocation by means of the gradient is called *Euler allocation* (see Patrik *et al*, 1999).

Theorem 1.
Let $\emptyset \neq U \subset \mathbb{R}^d$ be an open set and $r : U \to \mathbb{R}$ be an function that is partially differentiable in U with continuous derivatives. Let $a = (a_1, \ldots, a_d) : U \to \mathbb{R}^d$ be a continuous vector field.

Then the vector field a is suitable for performance measurement with r if and only if

$$a_i(u) = \frac{\partial r}{\partial u_i}(u), \quad i = 1, \ldots, d, \quad u \in U \tag{16}$$

Proof. Observe that for $u \in U$ with $r(u) \neq m'u, m \in \mathbb{R}^d$, and $i = 1, \ldots, d$ we get

$$\frac{\partial g_{r,m}}{\partial u_i}(u) = (r(u) - m'u)^{-2}$$

$$\times \left(m_i r(u) - a_i(u)m'u + \left(a_i(u) - \frac{\partial r}{\partial u_i}(u) \right) m'u \right) \tag{17}$$

If Equation (16) is satisfied then the suitableness for performance measurement follows immediately from Equation (17).

For the necessity of Equation (16) fix any $i \in N_d$ and note that by continuity we only need to show Equation (16) for $u \in U$ such that $u_i \neq 0$ and $u_j \neq 0$ for some $j \neq i$. Now, the proof is simple but requires some care for several special cases. These cases are:

(i) $a_i(u) \neq 0, r(u) \neq 0, r(u) \neq u_i a_i(u)$,
(ii) $a_i(u) \neq 0, r(u) \neq 0, r(u) = u_i a_i(u)$,
(iii) $a_i(u) = 0, r(u) \neq 0$,
(iv) $r(u) = 0$, each neighbourhood of u contains some $v \in U$ such that $r(u) \neq 0$,
(v) $r(v) = 0$ for all v in some neighbourhood of u.

We will only give a proof for case (i) because the proofs for (ii) and (iii) are almost identical, (iv) follows by continuity and (v) is trivial.

Choose any $j \in N_d \setminus \{i\}$ with $u_j \neq 0$ and define $m(t) \in \mathbb{R}^d$ by

$$m_i(t) \stackrel{\text{def}}{=} 1$$

$$m_j(t) \stackrel{\text{def}}{=} \frac{t}{u_j} \left(\frac{r(u)}{a_i(u)} - u_i \right)$$

and

$$m_l(t) \stackrel{\text{def}}{=} 0 \quad \text{for } l \neq i, j$$

Then

$$m(t)'u = t\,\frac{r(u)}{a_i(u)} + (1-t)u_i$$

and

$$m_i(t)r(u) - a_i(u)m(t)'u = (1-t)(r(u) - u_i a_i(u))$$

Hence by suitableness and Equation (17) we can choose sequences (t_k) and (s_k) with $t_k \to 1$ and $s_k \to 1$ such that for all $k \in \mathbb{N}$ we have $m(s_k)'u \neq r(u) \neq m(t_k)'u$ as well as

$$(1-t_k)(r(u)-u_i a_i(u)) + \left(a_i(u) - \frac{\partial r}{\partial u_i}(u)\right)\left(t_k\,\frac{r(u)}{a_i(u)} + (1-t_k)u_i\right) \geq 0$$

and

$$(1-s_k)(r(u)-u_i a_i(u)) + \left(a_i(u) - \frac{\partial r}{\partial u_i}(u)\right)\left(s_k\,\frac{r(u)}{a_i(u)} + (1-s_k)u_i\right) \leq 0$$

Now $k \to \infty$ yields Equation (16). $\qquad\qquad\Box$

Denault (see 2001, Section 5) shows by arguments from game theory that in case of a one-homogeneous risk measure its gradient is the only *allocation principle* that fulfils some *coherence* postulates. His results apply to coherent risk measures only. Similarly, Kalkbrener (2002) proves that in case of sub-additive and one-homogeneous risk measures only derivatives yield risk contributions that do not exceed the corresponding stand-alone risks.

By Theorem 1 we know that, if a risk measure is smooth, we should use its partial derivatives as risk contributions of the assets in the portfolio. Otherwise we run the risk of receiving misleading informations about the profitability of the assets. Let us review the concept of marginal risk, known from literature, under this point of view.

Example 4.
Let $r : U \to \mathbb{R}$ be any risk measure for some portfolio with assets $1,\ldots,d$. Some authors (see Matten, 1996, chapter 6 or CreditMetrics, 1997) suggest the application of the so-called *marginal risk* for

determining the capital required by an individual business or asset.[3] Formally, the marginal risk r_i of asset i, $i = 1, ..., d$, is defined by

$$r_i(u) \stackrel{\text{def}}{=} r(u) - r(u - u_i e^{(i)}), \quad u \in \mathbb{R}^d \tag{18}$$

ie, by the difference of the portfolio risk with asset i and the portfolio risk without asset i. Setting for $i = i, ..., d$

$$a_i(u) \stackrel{\text{def}}{=} \frac{r_i(u)}{u_i}, \quad u \in \mathbb{R}^d, \ u_i \neq 0 \tag{19}$$

creates a vector field $a = (a_1, ..., a_d)$ measuring normalised risk contributions of the assets in the sense of Remark 8 (i) (see also Finger, 1999).

If r is differentiable then, in general, a will not be identical with the gradient of r. To see this, note that by the mean value theorem for $u \in \mathbb{R}^d$ there are numbers $\theta_i(u) \in [0, 1]$, $i = 1, ..., d$, such that

$$r_i(u) = u_i \frac{\partial r}{\partial u_i} (u - \theta_i(u) u_i e^{(i)}) \tag{20}$$

By Equations (20) and (19) in general we have

$$a_i(u) \neq \frac{\partial r}{\partial u_i} (u)$$

and hence by Theorem 1 the vector field a will not be suitable for performance measurement with r. If r is also 1-homogeneous then by Proposition 1 (b) it has the nice feature that

$$r(u) = \sum_{i=1}^{d} u_i \frac{\partial r}{\partial u_i} (u)$$

Equation (20) now reveals that the equality $\sum_{i=1}^{d} r_i(u) = r(u)$ is unlikely. □

Actually, it can be shown that the risk contributions according to the marginal risk principle in the sense of Example 4 do not add up to the full economic capital if the risk measure r is sub-additive, 1-homogeneous, and differentiable.

Proposition 2. Let $r : U \to \mathbb{R}$ with $U \subset \mathbb{R}^d$ be a sub-additive (ie, $r(u + v) \leq r(u) + r(v)$), 1-homogeneous, and differentiable risk measure. Then the sum of the risk contributions $r_i(u)$, $i = 1, \ldots, d$, as defined by Equation (18) underestimates the total risk, ie,

$$\sum_{i=1}^{d} r_i(u) \leq r(u), \quad u \in U \tag{21}$$

Proof. Fix any $u \in U$ and $i \in \{1, \ldots, d\}$. By Proposition 1 (b) we then obtain

$$r(u) = \sum_{j=1, j \neq i}^{d} u_j \frac{\partial r}{\partial u_j}(u) + u_i \frac{\partial r}{\partial u_i}(u) \tag{22}$$

Proposition 2.5 of Tasche (2002) implies

$$\sum_{j=1, j \neq i}^{d} u_j \frac{\partial r}{\partial u_j}(u) \leq r(u - u_i e^{(i)}) \tag{23}$$

Inserting Equation (23) in Equation (22) yields

$$r_i(u) = r(u) - r(u - u_i e^{(i)}) \leq u_i \frac{\partial r}{\partial u_i}(u) \tag{24}$$

The assertion follows now by adding up the terms $u_i \, \partial r / \partial u_i(u)$ over i and applying Proposition 1 (b). $\qquad\square$

Observe that Theorem 1 suggests a more appropriate way for calculating a meaningful marginal risk of asset i: simply use the difference quotient

$$h^{-1}\left(r(u + he^{(i)}) - r(u)\right) \approx \frac{\partial r}{\partial u_i}(u) \tag{25}$$

with some suitable small $h \neq 0$. However, practical experience shows that reaching numerical stability with an approach like Equation (25) is a subtle problem. Therefore, alternative methods as described in the section "Examples of Risk Contributions" below are of high interest.

The notion of suitableness for performance management is based on the consideration of single assets. The following proposition says that the gradient of a risk measure also provides useful information about the profitability of sub-portfolios consisting of more than one asset.

For any vector $v \in \mathbb{R}^d$ with $v \neq 0$ denote by $\partial \phi / \partial v$ the directional derivative

$$\frac{\partial \phi}{\partial v}(u) = \sum_{i=1}^{d} v_i \frac{\partial \phi}{\partial u_i}(u)$$

of the function ϕ in direction v.

See Remark 1 (ii) for the interpretation of the following Equations (26) and (27).

Proposition 3.
Let $\emptyset \neq U \subset \mathbb{R}^d$ be an open set and $r : U \to \mathbb{R}$ any function which is partially differentiable in U with continuous derivatives. Let $v \in \mathbb{R}^d \setminus \{0\}$ be an arbitrary weight vector.

(i) for all $m \in \mathbb{R}^d$, $u \in U$ with $r(u) \neq m'u$ and

$$m'vr(u) > m'u \frac{\partial r}{\partial v}(u) \tag{26}$$

there is an $\epsilon > 0$ such that the mapping

$$t \mapsto g_{r,m}(u + tv), (-\epsilon, \epsilon) \to \mathbb{R}$$

is strictly increasing.

(ii) for all $m \in \mathbb{R}^d$, $u \in U$ with $r(u) \neq m'u$ and

$$m'vr(u) < m'u \frac{\partial r}{\partial v}(u) \tag{27}$$

there is an $\epsilon > 0$ such that the mapping

$$t \mapsto g_{r,m}(u + tv), (-\epsilon, \epsilon) \to \mathbb{R}$$

is strictly decreasing.

Proof. Proposition 3 is an immediate consequence of the following equality:

$$\frac{dg}{dt}(u + tv)\bigg|_{t=0} = (r(u) - m'u)^{-2} \left(m'vr(u) - m'v \frac{\partial r}{\partial v}(u) \right) \qquad \square$$

From Definition 3 and Theorem 1 the reader will expect that the returns of all sub-portfolios are equal if a portfolio is optimal in the sense of a maximal return $g_{r,m}(u)$. Formally, this is stated in the following theorem.

Theorem 2.
Let $\emptyset \neq U \subset \mathbb{R}^d$ be an open set and $r : U \rightarrow \mathbb{R}$ a function that is partially differentiable in U with continuous derivatives.
Let $\emptyset \neq I \subset N_d$, $m \in \mathbb{R}^d$ and $v \in U$ with $r(v) \neq m'v$ be fixed.
Assume that there is an $\epsilon > 0$ such that for all $u \in U$ with $|u_i - v_i| < \epsilon$ for $i \in I$ and $u_i = v_i$ for $i \notin I$ we have $r(u) \neq m'u$ and

$$g_{r,m}(v) \geq g_{r,m}(u) \tag{28}$$

Then

$$m_i r(v) = m'v \frac{\partial r}{\partial u_i}(v), \quad i \in I \tag{29}$$

If moreover, r is 1-homogeneous and $I \neq N_d$ then we also have

$$\left(\sum_{j \notin I} m_j v_j \right) r(v) = m'v \sum_{j \notin I} v_j \frac{\partial r}{\partial u_j}(v) \tag{30}$$

Proof.
Equation (29) is obvious from Equation (17) in the proof of Theorem 1.

Assume now that r is 1-homogeneous. Then by Proposition 1 (b)

$$\sum_{j \notin I} v_j \frac{\partial r}{\partial u_j}(v) = r(u) - \sum_{j \in I} v_j \frac{\partial r}{\partial u_j}(v)$$

Together with Equation (29) this implies

$$\left(\sum_{j \notin I} m_j v_j \right) r(v) = r(v) m'v - \sum_{j \in I} m_j r(v) v_j$$

$$= m'v \left(r(v) - \sum_{j \in I} v_j \frac{\partial r}{\partial u_j}(v) \right)$$

$$= m'v \sum_{j \notin I} v_j \frac{\partial r}{\partial u_j}(v)$$

$\square$

Remark 2.

If $m_i \neq \partial r/\partial u_i(v)$ then Equation (29) says that the return

$$\frac{m_i}{\dfrac{\partial r}{\partial u_i}(v) - m_i}$$

of asset i equals the optimal portfolio return $g_{r,m}(v)$.

Similarly, if $\sum_{j \notin I} m_j v_j \neq \sum_{j \notin I} v_j\, \partial r/\partial u_i(v)$ then Equation (30) states that the sub-portfolio return

$$\frac{\displaystyle\sum_{j \notin I} m_j v_j}{\displaystyle\sum_{j \notin I} v_j \frac{\partial r}{\partial u_j}(v) - \sum_{j \notin I} m_j v_j}$$

equals the portfolio return $g_{r,m}(v)$ as well.

EXAMPLES OF RISK CONTRIBUTIONS

In this section we compute the derivatives of the risk measures introduced as examples in the section "Examples of Risk Measures". The resulting risk contributions have appealing interpretations as predictors of the asset cashflows given a worst case scenario for the portfolio cashflow. For the VAR the risk contributions obtained by differentiation differ from the covariance-based contributions that are widely used in practice.

Covariance-based risk contributions

Let us briefly recall the notion *best linear predictor*. Assume that Y and Z are square-integrable real random variables on the same probability space. If $\mathrm{var}(Z) > 0$ then we can compute the projection $\pi_Z(z, Y)$ of $Y - E[Y]$ onto the linear space spanned by $Z - E[Z]$ via

$$\pi_Z(z,Y) = \frac{\mathrm{cov}(Y,Z)}{\mathrm{var}(Z)} z, \quad z \in \mathbb{R} \tag{31}$$

$\pi_Z(z, Y)$ is the best linear predictor of $Y - E[Y]$ given $Z - E[Z] = z$ in the sense that the random variable $\pi_Z(Z - E[Z], Y)$ minimises the L_2-distance between $Y - E[Y]$ and the linear space spanned by

$Z - E[Z]$. Choosing a value for z corresponds to defining a worst-case scenario for the portfolio cashflow. We first consider the case $z = c\sqrt{\mathrm{var}(Z)}$ in Equation (31).

Example 5. (Continuation of Example 1)
Define $U \subset \mathbb{R}^d$ by

$$U \overset{\text{def}}{=} \left\{ u \in \mathbb{R}^d \,|\, \mathrm{var}(Z(u)) > 0 \right\} \tag{32}$$

and suppose $U \neq \emptyset$. Then U is a homogeneous open set. For $u \in U$ define the vector field $a = (a_1, \dots, a_d) : U \to \mathbb{R}^d$ by

$$a_i(u) \overset{\text{def}}{=} \pi_{Z(u)}(r(u), X_i) = c\,\frac{\mathrm{cov}(X_i, Z(u))}{\sqrt{\mathrm{var}(Z(u))}}, \quad i = 1, \dots, d \tag{33}$$

Thus $a_i(u)$ is the best linear predictor of the cashflow fluctuation of asset i given that the portfolio fluctuation is just the risk $r(u)$ defined in Example 1. In $u \in U$ we have for $i = 1, \dots, d$

$$2r(u)\,\frac{\partial r}{\partial u_i}(u) = \frac{\partial r^2}{\partial u_i}(u)$$

$$= c^2\,\frac{\partial}{\partial u_i}\left(\sum_{j=1}^{d} \sum_{l=1}^{d} u_j u_l \,\mathrm{cov}(X_j, X_l) \right)$$

$$= 2c^2\,\mathrm{cov}(X_i, Z(u))$$

and hence

$$\frac{\partial r}{\partial u_i}(u) = c^2\,\frac{\mathrm{cov}(X_i, Z(u))}{r(u)} = a_i(u) \tag{34}$$

By Theorem 1, the vector field a is thus suitable for performance measurement with r. Moreover, since r is 1-homogeneous we know from Proposition 1 (b) without computation that

$$r(u) = \sum_{i=1}^{d} u_i a_i(u), \quad u \in U$$

$\square$

Another appealing choice for the value of z in Equation (31) is $z = Q_\alpha(u)$. This leads us to the situation of Example 2.

Example 6. (Continuation of Example 2)

Define again $U \subset \mathbb{R}^d$ by Equation (32) and suppose $U \neq \emptyset$. For $u \in U$ define analogously to Example 5 the vector field $a = (a_1, ..., a_d)$: $U \to \mathbb{R}^d$ by

$$a_i(u) \stackrel{\text{def}}{=} \pi_{Z(u)}(r(u), X_i) = \frac{\text{cov}(X_i, Z(u))}{\text{var}(Z(u))} Q_\alpha(u), \quad i = 1, ..., d \quad (35)$$

Then we have again $r(u) = \sum_{i=1}^{d} u_i a_i(u), u \in U$. This method for determining the contributions of the assets is proposed for instance in Section 6.1 of Overbeck and Stahl (1998) or in Appendix A13 of CSFP (1997). We will see in the next subsection that in general we have $a_i \neq \partial r / \partial u_i$, and hence a is not suitable for performance measurement with r.[4] □

Observe that in case of an elliptically (and in particular of a normally) distributed random vector $(X_1, ..., X_d)$ Equations (33) and (35) lead to the same result when the constant c is chosen as the α-quantile of the standardised univariate marginal distribution (see Embrechts *et al*, 2002, Theorem 1). If the distribution of $(X_1, ..., X_d)$ is not an elliptical distribution, the a_i and the $\partial r / \partial u_i$ in Example 6 can considerably differ. In particular, this may be the case in credit portfolios (see CreditMetrics, 1997, Section 1.1.2, or Kalkbrener *et al*, 2004).

Quantile based risk contributions

In this subsection we will compute the risk contributions that are associated with the VAR risk measure from Example 2 via differentiation. However, in general the quantile function $Q_\alpha(u)$ from Equation (5) will not be differentiable in u. In order to guarantee that differentiation is possible we have to impose some technical assumptions on the joint distribution of the fluctuation vector $(X_1, ..., X_d)$. The most important one among these could roughly be stated as: at least one among the fluctuations X_i must have a continuous density.

Assumption (S).

For fixed $\alpha \in (0, 1)$, we say that an $\mathbb{R}^d$-valued random vector $(X_1, ..., X_d)$ satisfies Assumption (S) if $d \geq 2$ and the conditional distribution of X_1 given $(X_2, ..., X_d)$ has a density

$$\phi : \mathbb{R} \times \mathbb{R}^{d-1} \to [0, \infty), (t, x_2, ..., X_d) \mapsto \phi(t, x_2, ..., X_d)$$

which satisfies the following four conditions:

(i) for fixed $x_2, \ldots, x_d$ the function $t \mapsto \phi(t, x_2, \ldots, X_d)$ is continuous in t.

(ii) the mapping

$$(t, u) \mapsto E\left[\phi\left(u_1^{-1}\left(t - \sum_{j=2}^{d} u_j X_j\right), X_2, \ldots, X_d\right)\right],$$

$$\mathbb{R} \times \mathbb{R} \setminus \{0\} \times \mathbb{R}^{d+1} \to [0, \infty)$$

is finite-valued and continuous.

(iii) for each $u \in \mathbb{R} \setminus \{0\} \times \mathbb{R}^{d-1}$

$$0 < E\left[\phi\left(u_1^{-1}\left(Q_\alpha(u) - \sum_{j=2}^{d} u_j X_j\right), X_2, \ldots, X_d\right)\right]$$

with $Q_\alpha(u)$ defined by Equation (5).

(iv) for each $i = 2, \ldots, d$ the mapping

$$(t, u) \mapsto E\left[X_i \phi\left(u_1^{-1}\left(t - \sum_{j=2}^{d} u_j X_j\right), X_2, \ldots, X_d\right)\right],$$

$$\mathbb{R} \times \mathbb{R} \setminus \{0\} \times \mathbb{R}^{d+1} \to \mathbb{R}$$

is finite-valued and continuous. □

Note that (i) in general implies neither (ii) nor (iv). Furthermore, (ii) and (iv) may be valid even if the components of the random vector $(X_1, \ldots, X_d)$ do not have finite expectations. Before turning to the next result let us just present some situations in which Assumption (S) is satisfied:

1. $(X_1, \ldots, X_d)$ is normally distributed and its covariance matrix has full rank.

2. $(X_1, \ldots, X_d)$ and ϕ satisfy (i) and (iii) respectively and for each $(s, v) \in \mathbb{R} \times \mathbb{R} \setminus \{0\} \times \mathbb{R}^{d-1}$ there is some neighbourhood V such that the random fields

$$\left(\phi\left(u_1^{-1}(t - \sum_{j=2}^{d} u_j X_j), X_2, \ldots, X_d\right)\right)_{(t,u) \in V}$$

and for $i = 2, \ldots, d$

$$\left(X_i \phi \left(u_1^{-1} \left(t - \sum_{j=2}^{d} u_j X_j \right) \right), X_2, \ldots, X_d \right)_{(t,u) \in V}$$

are uniformly integrable.

3. $E[|X_i|] < \infty, i = 2, \ldots, d$, and ϕ is bounded and satisfies (i) and (iii).

4. $E[|X_i|] < \infty, i = 2, \ldots, d$. X_1 and $(X_2, \ldots, X_d)$ are independent. X_1 has a continuous density f such that

$$0 < E \left[f \left(u_1^{-1} \left(Q_\alpha(u) - \sum_{j=2}^{d} u_j X_j \right) \right) \right]$$

5. there is a finite set $M \subset \mathbb{R}^{d-1}$ such that

$$P[(X_2, \ldots, X_d) \in M] = 1$$

and (i) and (iii) are satisfied.

Note that situation 3 is a special case of situation 2 and that situations 4 and 5 respectively are special cases of situation 3. Four shows that $Q_\alpha(u)$ can be forced to be differentiable by disturbing the portfolio cashflow fluctuation $Z(u)$ with some small independent noise.

Proposition 4.

For some given $\alpha \in (0,1)$, let $(X_1, \ldots, X_d)$ be an $\mathbb{R}^d$-valued random vector satisfying Assumption (S). Set $U \overset{\text{def}}{=} \mathbb{R} \setminus \{0\} \times \mathbb{R}^{d-1}$ and define the random field $(Z(u))_{u \in U}$ by

$$Z(u) \overset{\text{def}}{=} \sum_{i=1}^{d} u_i X_i, \quad u \in U$$

Then the function $Q_\alpha : U \to \mathbb{R}$ with

$$Q_\alpha(u) \overset{\text{def}}{=} \inf\{z \in \mathbb{R} : P[Z(u) \leq z] \geq \alpha\}, \quad u \in U$$

is partially differentiable in U with continuous derivatives

$$\frac{\partial Q_\alpha}{\partial u_1}(u)$$

$$= u_1^{-1}\left(Q_\alpha(u) - \frac{E\left[\left(\sum_{j=2}^d u_j X_j\right)\phi\left(u_1^{-1}\left(Q_\alpha(u) - \sum_{j=2}^d u_j X_j\right), X_2, ..., X_d\right)\right]}{E\left[\phi\left(u_1^{-1}\left(Q_\alpha(u) - \sum_{j=2}^d u_j X_j\right), X_2, ..., X_d\right)\right]}\right)$$

(36)

and

$$\frac{\partial Q_\alpha}{\partial u_i}(u) = \frac{E\left[X_i\phi\left(u_1^{-1}\left(Q_\alpha(u) - \sum_{j=2}^d u_j X_j\right), X_2, ..., X_d\right)\right]}{E\left[\phi\left(u_1^{-1}\left(Q_\alpha(u) - \sum_{j=2}^d u_j X_j\right), X_2, ..., X_d\right)\right]},$$

(37)

$$i = 2, ..., d$$

Proof. See Tasche (2000). □

Remark 3.
Equations (37) and (36) allow an interesting interpretation. Fix $u \in \mathbb{R}\setminus\{0\} \times \mathbb{R}^d$ and set for $z \in \mathbb{R}$

$$g_u(z) \overset{\text{def}}{=} E\left[\phi\left(u_1^{-1}\left(z - \sum_{j=2}^d u_j X_j\right), X_2, ..., X_d\right)\right]$$

It is not hard to see that $g_u/|u_1|$ is a continuous density of the random variable $Z(u)$. As a consequence, for $i = 2, ..., d$ the functions $h_u^{(i)}$ with

$$h_u^{(i)}(z)$$

$$\overset{\text{def}}{=} \begin{cases} 0, & \text{if } g_u(z) = 0 \\ g_u(z)^{-1} E\left[X_i\phi\left(u_1^{-1}\left(z - \sum_{j=2}^d u_j X_j\right), X_2, ..., X_d\right)\right], & \text{otherwise} \end{cases}$$

provide versions of $E[X_i|Z(u) = \cdot]$, the conditional expectation of X_i given $Z(u)$.[5] Similarly we have

$$E[X_1|Z(u) = z] = u_1^{-1}\left(z - \sum_{j=2}^{d} u_j h_u^{(j)}(z)\right)$$

Hence Proposition 4 says nothing else than

$$\frac{\partial Q_\alpha}{\partial u_i}(u) = E[X_i|Z(u) = Q_\alpha(u)], \quad i = 1, \ldots, d \tag{38}$$

Equation (38) has been presented in Hallerbach (2003) without examination of the question whether Q_α is differentiable and in Gouriéroux *et al* (2000) for the case of $(X_1, \ldots, X_d)$ with a joint density.

Recall that the conditional expectation of X_i given $Z(u)$ essentially may be seen as the best predictor of X_i by elements of the space $M \overset{\text{def}}{=} \{f(Z(u)) \mid f : \mathbb{R} \to \mathbb{R} \text{ measurable}\}$.

As mentioned above the best linear predictor of X_i given $Z(u)$ is the best predictor of X_i by elements of the space $\{mZ(u) \mid m \in \mathbb{R}\} \subset M$.

We are now in a position to discuss Examples 2 and 6 again.

Example 7. (Continuation of Example 2)
By Proposition 4 under Assumption (S) for $i = 1, \ldots, d$ the mappings $b_i : \mathbb{R} \setminus \{0\} \times \mathbb{R}^{d-1} \to \mathbb{R}$ with

$$b_i(u) \overset{\text{def}}{=} \frac{\partial r}{\partial u_i}(u) = \frac{\partial Q_\alpha}{\partial u_i}(u) \tag{39}$$

are well defined. They provide a vector field of risk contributions $b = (b_1, \ldots, b_d)$ which by Proposition 1 (b) satisfies

$$r(u) = \sum_{i=1}^{d} u_i b_i(u), \quad u \in U$$

and is suitable for performance measurement with r by Theorem 1. By Equation (38) we see that in general the vector fields a from

Example 6 and b are not identical unless the random vector $(X_1, ..., X_d)$ is elliptically distributed (see Embrechts *et al*, 2002, Section 3.3). ☐

In practice, estimating or calculating the conditional expectation in Equation (38) turns out to be difficult (see Yamai and Yoshiba, 2001). The CreditRisk$^+$ portfolio model (see CSFP, 1997) represents a notable exception to this rule (see Tasche, 2004). Martin *et al* (2001) suggest approximating the VAR contributions by means of the saddle-point methodology.

Shortfall based risk contributions

As in the previous subsection for the quantile-based risk we calculate here the risk contributions which are associated to the shortfall-based risk (see Example 3) via differentiation. Again there is the problem that the quantile function in general might not be differentiable. Nevertheless, the following proposition shows that we may differentiate the shortfall measure under almost the same assumptions as those for the quantile.

Proposition 5.
Let $X_1, ..., X_d$ and α be as in Proposition 4 and assume

$$E\big[|X_i|\big] < \infty, \quad i = 1, ..., d$$

Define U, $Z(u)$ and $Q_\alpha(u)$ as in Proposition 4 and set

$$S_\alpha(u) \stackrel{def}{=} E\big[Z(u)|Z(u) \ge Q_\alpha(u)\big], \quad u \in U$$

Then S_α on U is continuous and partially differentiable in u_i, $i = 1, ..., d$, with continuous derivatives

$$\frac{\partial S_\alpha}{\partial u_i}(u) = E\big[X_i|Z(u) \ge Q_\alpha(u)\big], \quad i = 1, ..., d \tag{40}$$

Proof. See Tasche (2000). ☐

Proposition 5 leads to the proposal in Overbeck and Stahl (1998), Section 7, for the shortfall risk contributions.

Example 8. (Continuation of Example 3)

By Proposition 5 under Assumption (S) for $i = 1, \ldots, d$ the mappings $a_i : \mathbb{R} \backslash \{0\} \times \mathbb{R}^{d-1} \to \mathbb{R}$ with

$$a_i(u) \stackrel{\text{def}}{=} \frac{\partial r}{\partial u_i}(u) = \frac{\partial S_\alpha}{\partial u_i}(u) \tag{41}$$

are well defined. They provide a vector field of risk contributions $a = (a_1, \ldots, a_d)$ which by Proposition 1 (b) satisfies

$$r(u) = \sum_{i=1}^{d} u_i a_i(u), \quad u \in U$$

and is suitable for performance measurement with r by Theorem 1. Moreover, the $a_i(u)$ can also be calculated via

$$a_i(u) = E[X_i | Z(u) \geq Q_\alpha(u)] \tag{42}$$

□

Yamai and Yoshiba (2001) observe that estimations of risk contributions to the shortfall measure tend to be unstable. When the portfolio loss distribution is determined with Monte-Carlo simulation, this instability problem can be solved with importance sampling (see Kalkbrener *et al*, 2004; Merino and Nyfeler, 2004). An analytical solution is available for the CreditRisk$^+$ portfolio model (see Tasche, 2004).

Observe that, even if Assumption (S) does not hold, in the cases of quantile and shortfall based risk measures we can define risk contributions by Equations (38) and (42) respectively. The contributions defined in this way might also have a good chance to being suitable with their corresponding risk measures.

CONCLUSIONS

Allocating economic capital to the sub-portfolios or single assets in a portfolio is a fundamental task for the portfolio managers. In this chapter, we have shown that the choice of the adequate methodology for this breakdown of the economic capital is crucial for reaching sensible results. It has turned out that the allocation procedure has to be based on the derivatives of the applied risk measure with respect to the weights of the sub-portfolios or assets. Otherwise there is a high risk of ending up with counterintuive effects on the performance of the portfolio. The derivatives methodology (or Euler allocation) is numerically more demanding than some of the more traditional methods. However, the past three or four years have seen considerable progress in the corresponding computational procedures. As a consequence, in a modern financial institution there is no reason to dispense with a methodology of economic capital allocation that is intuitive and suitable for performance measurement.

1   Depending on accounting standards, the economic capital may differ distinctively from the stock capital. For instance, in some European countries, hidden reserves play a crucial role in the definition of economic capital. See eg, Theiler (2004).

2   Banks tend to define economic capital as the amount of capital that is needed to cover *unexpected loss* (UL). This corresponds rather to the notion of *risk* as used in this chapter. We do not follow the banks' convention because the simultaneous examination of unexpected losses and expected margins is crucial for some of the results of this chapter. Nevertheless, these results hold also for the case that economic capital is based on unexpected losses only.

3   This methodology is also called *with-without principle* by some authors.

4   Kalkbrener *et al* (2004) discuss the deficiencies of the so-called *variance-covariance* allocation in detail.

5   Since under Assumption (S) the events $\{Z(u) = z\}$ have probability 0, the conditional expectation here must be understood in the non-elementary sense (see eg, Durrett, 1995).

REFERENCES

Acerbi, C., 2002, "Spectral Measures of Risk: A Coherent Representation of Subjective Risk Aversion", *Journal of Banking & Finance*, **26(7)**, pp. 1505–18.

Acerbi, C., and D. Tasche, 2002, "On the Coherence of Expected Shortfall", *Journal of Banking and Finance*, **26(7)**, pp. 1487–503.

Artzner, P., F. Delbaen, J. Eber, and D. Heath, 1999, "Coherent Measures of Risk", *Mathematical Finance*, **9(3)**, pp. 203–28.

BCBS, 2004, *International Convergence of Capital Measurement and Capital Standards: A Revised Framework*, Basel Committee on Banking Supervision (BCBS), http://www.bis.org/publ/bcbs107.htm, June.

CreditMetrics, 1997, *CreditMetrics™ – Technical Document*, in JP Morgan & Co. Incorporated, http://www.creditmetrics.com/creditdocs.html.

CSFP, 1997, *CreditRisk+, A Credit Risk Management Framework*, Credit Suisse Financial Products (CSFP), http://www.csfb.com/creditrisk/.

Denault, M., 2001, "Coherent Allocation of Risk Capital", *Journal of Risk*, **4(1)**, pp. 1–34.

Durrett, R., 1995, *Probability: Theory and Examples*, 2nd edition (Belmont: Wadsworth).

Embrechts, P., A. McNeil, and D. Straumann, 2002, "Correlation and Dependency in Risk Management: Properties and Pitfalls", in M. Dempster (ed), *Risk Management: Value at Risk and Beyond*, Cambridge University Press.

Finger, C., 1999, *Risk-Return Reporting*, RiskMetrics Group, CreditMetrics Monitor, http://www.creditmetrics.com/creditdocs.html, April.

Fischer, T., 2003, "Risk Capital Allocation by Coherent Risk Measures Based on One-Sided Moments", *Insurance: Mathematics and Economics*, **32(1)**, pp. 135–46.

Gouriéroux, C., J. P. Laurent, and O. Scaillet, 2000, "Sensitivity Analysis of Values at Risk", *Journal of Empirical Finance*, **7**, pp. 225–45.

Hallerbach, W., 2003, "Decomposing Portfolio Value-at-Risk: A General Analysis", *Journal of Risk*, **5(2)**, pp. 1–18.

Kalkbrener, M., 2002, "An Axiomatic Approach to Capital Allocation", Technical Document, Deutsche Bank AG.

Kalkbrener, M., H. Lotter, and L. Overbeck, 2004, "Sensible and Efficient Allocation for Credit Portfolios", *Risk*, **17(1)**, pp. S19–S24.

Litterman, R., 1996, "Hot Spots™ and Hedges", *The Journal of Portfolio Management*, **22**, pp. 52–75.

Markowitz, H., 1952, "Portfolio Selection", *Journal of Finance*, **7**, pp. 77–91.

Martin, R., K. Thompson, and C. Browne, 2001, "VAR: Who Contributes and How Much?", *Risk*, **14(8)**.

Matten, C., 1996, *Managing Bank Capital* (Chichester: Wiley).

Merino, S., and M. A. Nyfeler, 2004, "Applying Importance Sampling for Estimating Coherent Credit Risk Contributions", *Quantitative Finance*, **4**, pp. 199–207.

Overbeck, L., and G. Stahl, 1998, "Stochastische Modelle im Risikomanagement des Kreditportfolios", in A. Oehler (ed), *Credit Risk und Value-at-Risk Alternativen*, pp. 77–110 (Stuttgart: Schäffer-Poeschel Verlag).

Patrik, G., S. Bernegger, and M. Rüegg, 1999, "The Use of Risk-Adjusted Capital to Support Business Decision Making", *Casualty Actuarial Society Forum*, http://www.casact.org/pubs/forum/99spforum/99spftoc.htm.

Rockafellar, R. T., and S. Uryasev, 2002, "Conditional Value-at-Risk for General Loss Distributions", *Journal of Banking & Finance*, **26(7)**, pp. 1443–71.

Schröder, M., 1996, "Ein verallgemeinerter Value-at-Risk-Ansatz", in M. Schröder (ed), *Quantitative Verfahren im Finanzmarktbereich*, pp. 81–98, Nomos-Verl.-Ges.

Stoughton, N. M., and J. Zechner, 2004, "Optimal Capital Allocation using RAROC and EVA", CEPR Discussion Paper No. 4169, http://www.cepr.org/, January.

Tasche, D., 2000, "Conditional Expectation as Quantile Derivative", Working Paper, Technische Universität München, http://arxiv.org/abs/math.PR/0104190.

Tasche, D., 2002. "Expected Shortfall and Beyond", Working Paper, Technische Universität München, http://arxiv.org/abs/cond-mat/0203558.

Tasche, D., 2004, "Capital Allocation with Creditrisk+, in V. M. Gundlach and F. B. Lehrbass (ed), *CreditRisk+ in the Banking Industry*, pp. 25–44, Springer.

Theiler, U., 2004, "Risk Return Management Approach for the Bank Portfolio", in G. Szegö (ed), *Risk Measures for the 21st Century*, pp. 403–30 (Chichester: John Wiley & Sons).

Tucker, A., K. Becker, M. Isimbabi, and J. Ogden, 1994, *Contemporary Portfolio Theory and Risk Management* (Minneapolis/St. Paul: West Publishing).

Yamai Y., and T. Yoshiba, 2001, "Comparative Analyses of Expected Shortfall and VAR: Their Estimation Error, Decomposition, and Optimization", IMES Discussion Paper No. 2001-E-12, Bank of Japan.

Zöller, R., 1996, "Marginal Value-at-Risk", in M. Schröder (ed), *Quantitative Verfahren im Finanzmarktbereich,* pp. 115–32, Nomos-Verl.-Ges.

14

Spectral Capital Allocation

Ludger Overbeck

University of Giessen

Portfolio modelling has two main objectives: the quantification of portfolio risk, which is usually expressed as the economic capital of the portfolio, and its allocation to subportfolios and individual transactions. The standard approach in credit portfolio modelling is to define the economic capital in terms of a quantile of the portfolio loss distribution. The capital charge of an individual transaction is usually based on a covariance technique and called volatility contribution.[1]

Since the work by Artzner *et al* (1997) coherent risk measures are discussed intensively in finance and risk management. More recent is the question of a more coherent capital allocation. Especially the use of expected shortfall allocation as an allocation rule that is recommend in Overbeck (1999), Denault (2001), Bluhm, Overbeck and Wagner (2002), Kurth and Tasche (2003), Kalkbrener, Lotter and Overbeck (2004).

Expected shortfall measures are the building blocks of more general coherent risk measures, the spectral risk measure. These are convex mixtures of expected shortfall measures where the mixture can be represented as a probability measure on the confidence level from 0 to 1 or as an increasing weight function for the confidence level. It is known that the only substantial restriction on this weight function is that higher confidence level should have larger weights. Already in the original paper by Acerbi (2002) the interpretation of the weight function in terms of risk aversion is given. In terms of that the requirements just mean that higher losses have higher awareness and aversion.

In this chapter it is known that the axiomatic approach to capital allocation (Kalkbrener, 2002; Kalkbrener *et al*, 2004) can also be carried out easily for spectral risk measures. This approach is strongly related to the capital allocation based on derivatives or sensitives. The only result which is necessary for this is an explicit formula of the density of the probability describing the scenario associated with the weight function. This is given in Theorem 1.

The chapter will then focus on the study of spectral allocation in a Merton-type credit portfolio model accompanied by concrete examples.

SPECTRAL RISK MEASURES AND ALLOCATION

It is well known that the following four conditions define a coherent risk measure, Artzner *et al* (1997, 1999), Delbaen (2000).

Formally, a risk measure is nothing else but a positive real valued function r defined on the set V of random variables X, representing potential losses in "portfolio X" (portfolios are identified with their loss variables). The number $r(X)$ denotes the risk in portfolio X. r is called coherent if it obeys the following four rules.

❑ subadditivity (Diversification)

$$r(X + Y) \le r(X) + r(Y)$$

❑ positive homogeneous (Scaling)

$$r(aX) = ar(X), \quad a > 0$$

❑ monotone

$$r(X) \le r(Y) \quad \text{if } X < Y \text{ (almost surely)}$$

❑ translation property

$$r(X + a) = r(X) - a$$

Convex analysis already gives that a sub-additive positive homogeneous function r can be point wise written as the maximal value of all linear functions which are below r (Delbaen, 2000; Kalkbrener, 2002; Kalkbrener *et al*, 2004). For risk measures this means that already axioms 1 and 2 lead to the following representation

$$r(X) = \max \left\{ l(X) \mid l \le r, l \text{ linear function} \right\} \tag{1}$$

The risk measure evaluated at a loss variable X takes the same value as the largest value of all linear function which lies below r on V evaluated on X.

Conceptually, this is similar to the gradient of the function r evaluated at the point X or as the best linear approximation of r which coincides with r at the point X. We will later see that this intuition gives rise to a sensible capital allocation.

A typical linear function for random variable is the expectation operator. Hence the basic result by Artzner *et al* (1997), Delbaen (2000)

$$r(X) = \sup\left\{E_Q[X] \mid Q \in \mathcal{Q}\right\} \qquad (2)$$

$\mathcal{Q} = \mathcal{Q}_r$, a suitable set of probability measures of absolutely continuous probability measures $Q \ll P$ with density dQ/dP, is similar to the representation (1).

The set $\mathcal{Q}$ is called the generalised scenarios associated with r. If the supremum is actually taken at some probability measure, this probability measure or its density with respect to P is called the generalised scenario associated with r. This approach also fits into the intuitive feature of risk measurement, namely scenario or stress analysis. For the interpretation in terms of scenarios the formulation with probability measure is more natural, but for the axiomatic approach to capital allocation the representation (1) is very useful.

The most prominent example of a coherent risk measure is expected shortfall (sometimes called conditional VAR/tail conditional expectation). It is denoted by ES_α and measures the average loss above the α-quantile of the loss distribution. The associated generalised scenarios can be explained as follows: to each loss variable Y define the scenario as the "historical" calibrated objective scenario constraint on the condition that the loss variable exceeded its quantile. The expected shortfall coincides with the largest mean loss in these scenarios. Intuitively,

$$E\left[L \mid L > q_\alpha(L)\right] = \max\left\{E[L \mid Y > q_\alpha(Y)] \mid \text{all } Y \in L_\infty\right\}$$

Even if generalised scenarios are defined as a supremum, in the case of expected shortfall we can identify the density of the maximal "scenario". For this we need the formally correct definition of expected shortfall at level α. The problem with the intuitive definition above is the possible positive mass at the quantile itself. The exact definition of the expected shortfall at level α is therefore (see Acerbi and Tasche, 2002; Kalkbrener *et al*, 2004):

Definition 1.

$$\mathrm{ES}_\alpha := (1-\alpha)^{-1} \left(E\left[L\,\mathbf{1}_{\{L > q_\alpha(L)\}} \right] + q_\alpha(L) \cdot \left(\mathbb{P}\left[L \leq q_\alpha(L) \right] - \alpha \right) \right)$$

Here we take the quantile defined by

$$q_u(L) = \inf\left\{ x \mid P[L \leq x] \geq u \right\}$$

the smallest u-quantile

Since $\mathrm{ES}_\alpha = E[L g_\alpha(L)]]$ with the function

$$g_\alpha(Y) := (1-\alpha)^{-1} \left(\mathbf{1}_{\{Y > q_\alpha(Y)\}} + \beta_Y \mathbf{1}_{\{Y = q_\alpha(Y)\}} \right) \tag{3}$$

where β_Y is a real number and

$$\beta_Y := \frac{\mathbb{P}(Y \leq q_\alpha(Y)) - \alpha}{\mathbb{P}(Y = q_\alpha(Y))} \quad \text{if } \mathbb{P}(Y = q_\alpha(Y)) > 0$$

the density of the associated maximal scenario turns out to be the function g_α.[2]

For the interpretation of this density function in terms of risk aversion as outlined in Acerbi (2002), let us reformulate the expected shortfall as an integral over the quantile function, the inverse of the distribution of L. It is well known that

$$\mathrm{ES}_\alpha = (1-\alpha)^{-1} \int_\alpha^1 q_u(L)\, du$$

The implicit risk aversion with expected shortfall is, that all quantiles below α or all losses below the α quantile have no weights, ie, there is no risk aversion and all losses above the α-quantile have the same risk aversion. Therefore the risk aversion weight function associated with ES_α turns out to be

$$w_{\mathrm{ES}_\alpha}(u) = (1-\alpha)^{-1} \mathbf{1}_{\{u > \alpha\}} \tag{4}$$

From a risk management point of view there might be many other weights given to some confidence levels u. If the weight function is increasing, which is reasonable since higher losses should have larger risk aversion weight, then we arrive at spectral risk measures.

Definition 2. Let w be an increasing function from $[0,1]$ such that $\int_0^1 w(u)\,\mathrm{d}u = 1$, then the map r_w defined by

$$r_w(L) = \int_0^1 w(u)q_u(L)\,\mathrm{d}u$$

is called a spectral risk measure with weight function w.

The name spectral risk measure comes from the representation

$$r_w(X) = \int_0^1 \mathrm{ES}_\alpha(1-\alpha)\mu_u(\mathrm{d}a) \tag{5}$$

$$\text{with the spectral measure } \mu((0,b]) = w(b) \tag{6}$$

This representation is very useful when we want to find the scenario function representing a spectral risk measure r_w.

Theorem 1. The density of the scenario associated with the risk measure equals

$$L_w := g_w(L) := \int_0^1 g_\alpha(L)(1-\alpha)\mu(\mathrm{d}\alpha) \tag{7}$$

Here $g_\alpha(L)$ is defined in formula (3). In particular

$$r_w(L) = E[LL_w] \tag{8}$$

Proof. We have

$$r_w(L) = \int_0^1 \mathrm{ES}_\alpha(L)(1-\alpha)\mu(\mathrm{d}\alpha)$$

$$= \int_0^1 E[LL_\alpha](1-\alpha)\mu(\mathrm{d}\alpha)$$

$$= \int_0^1 \max\left\{ E[Lg_\alpha(Y)] \,|\, Y \in L_\infty \right\}(1-\alpha)\mu(d\alpha)$$

$$\geq \max\left\{ \int_0^1 E\left[L\int_0^1 g_\alpha(Y)(1-\alpha)\mu(d\alpha) \right] \,\middle|\, Y \in L_\infty \right\}$$

$$= \max\left\{ E[Lg_w(Y)] \,|\, \forall Y \in L_\infty \right\}$$

$$\geq E[Lg_w(L)]$$

Hence

$$r_w(L) = \max\left\{ E[Lg_w(Y)] \,|\, \forall Y \in L_\infty \right\} = E[Lg_w(L)] \qquad \square$$

Spectral capital allocation

Let us recall the approach in Kalkbrener (2002) and Kalkbrener *et al* (2004). Starting with the representation (1) one can now find for each Y a linear function $h_Y = h_Y^r$ which satisfies

$$r(Y) = h_Y(Y) \quad \text{and} \quad h_Y(X) \leq r(X), \quad \forall X \qquad (9)$$

A "diversifying" capital allocation associated with r is given by

$$\Lambda_r(X, Y) = h_Y(X) \qquad (10)$$

The function Λ_r is then *linear* in the first variable and *diversifying* in the sense that the capital allocated to a portfolio X is always bounded by the capital of X viewed as its own subportfolio[3]

$$\Lambda(X, Y) \leq \Lambda(X, X) \qquad (11)$$

In general we have the following two theorems: A linear and diversifying capital allocation Λ, which is continuous at a portfolio Y, is uniquely determined by its associated risk measure, ie, the diagonal values of Λ.[4] More specifically, given the portfolio Y then the capital allocated to a subportfolio X of Y is the derivative of the associated risk measure ρ at Y in the direction of X.

Theorem 2. Let Λ be a linear, diversifying capital allocation. If Λ is continuous at $Y \in V$ then for all $X \in V$

$$\Lambda(X, Y) = \lim_{\epsilon \to 0} \frac{r(Y + \epsilon X) - \rho(Y)}{\epsilon}$$

The following theorem states the equivalence between positively homogeneous, sub-additive risk measures and linear, diversifying capital allocations.

Theorem 3. (a) If there exists a linear, diversifying capital allocation Λ with associated risk measure r, ie, $r(X) = \Lambda(X, X)$, then r is positively homogeneous and sub-additive.
(b) If r is positively homogeneous and sub-additive then Λ_r as defined in (10) is a linear, diversifying capital allocation with associated risk measure r.

Since in the case of spectral risk measures r_w the maximal linear functional in (9) can be identified as an integration with respect to the probability measure with density (7) from Theorem 1, we obtain $h_Y(X) = E[Xg_w(Y)]$ and therefore the following capital allocation

$$\Lambda_w(X, Y) = E[Xg_w(Y)] \tag{12}$$

Intuitively, the capital allocated to transaction or subportfolio X in a portfolio Y equals its expectation under the generalised maximal scenario associated with w.

Examples
1. As a first step in the application of spectral risk measures one might consider giving different weight to different loss probability levels. This is a straight-forward extension of expected shortfall. One might view expected shortfall at the 99%-level view as a risk aversion which ignores losses below the 99%-quantile and all losses above the 99%-quantile have the same influence. From an investor's point of view this means that only senior debts are cushioned by risk capital. One might on the other hand also be aware of losses which occur more frequently, but of course with a lower aversion than those appearing rarely.
   As a concrete example one might set that losses up to the 50% confidence level should have zero weights, losses between 50% and 99% should have a weight w_0 and losses above the 99%-quantile should have a weight of k_1w_0 and above the 99.9% quantile it should have a weight of k_2w_0. The first tranch from 50% to 99% correspond to an investor in junior debt, and the tranch

from 99% to 99.9% to a senior investor and above the 99.9% a super senior investor or the regulators are concerned. This gives a step function for w:

$$w(u) = w_0 \mathbf{1}_{\{0.99 > u > 0.5\}} + k_1 w_0 \mathbf{1}_{\{0.999 > u > 0.99\}} + k_2 w_0 \mathbf{1}_{\{1 > u > 0.999\}}$$

The parameter w_0 should be chosen such that the integral over w is still 1.

2. A more continuous form of this is an exponential function starting at a point u_0 between 0 and 1 and then increasing up to 1

$$w(u) = \mathbf{1}_{\{u > u_0\}} \exp(\kappa u)$$

with some constant κ.

Remarks.

1. Expected shortfall allocation which allocates the average loss of transaction i in all cases where the overall portfolio capital exceeds a certain quantile can be interpreted as a causal capital allocation. Literally the actual contribution of the transaction to the overall capital is allocated if the conditional expectation is used. In the same way the spectral allocation – at least when the weight function is a step function – is a causal allocation. Here, of course, the future loss for which the capital is needed gets a different weight from those obtained by a simple conditional expectation, as in the expected shortfall contribution.

2. Also from the point of view that all actual losses have different impact or subsequent losses. A large loss which is reported in the press might have consequent losses – due to reputational impacts – exceeding the first actual loss by far, and might even damage the capital basis. On the other hand small losses are directly covered by income and won't affect the capital. Therefore a different weighting of different loss sizes might be useful.

3. In the case of a continuous distribution one can rewrite

$$\int_0^1 w(u) q_u(L) \, du = E[w(U) q_u(L)] = E[w(F(L)) L]$$

Then the calibration of the weight function can be done in terms of portfolio loss itself instead of the quantiles of the loss distribution.

However, the new weight function, now defined on the range of the loss variable L, has to be transformed $w_F(x) := w(F(x))$

IMPLEMENTATION

There are several ways to implement a spectral contribution in a portfolio model. According to Acerbi (2002) a Monte Carlo-based implementation of the spectral risk measure would work as follows:

Let L^n be the n-th realisation of the portfolio loss. If we have generated N loss distribution scenario, let us denote by $n : N$ index of the n-th largest loss which itself is then denote by $L^{n:N}$, ie, the indices $1 : N, 2 : N, ..., N : N \in \mathbb{N}$ are defined by the property that

$$L^{1:N} < L^{2:N} < \cdots < L^{N:N}$$

The approximative spectral risk measure is then defined by

$$\sum_{n=1}^{N} L^{n:N} w(n/N) \Big/ \sum_{k=1}^{N} w(k/N)$$

Therefore a natural way to approximate the spectral contribution of a transaction L_i is

$$\sum_{n=1}^{N} L_i^{n:N} \frac{w(n/N)}{\sum_{k=1}^{N} w(k/N)}$$

It is then expected that

$$E[L_i L_w] = \lim_{N \to \infty} \sum_{n=1}^{N} L_i^{n:N} \frac{w(n/N)}{\sum_{k=1}^{N} w(k/N)}$$

Another possibility is to rely on the approximation of the expected shortfall contribution as in Kalkbrener et al (2004) and to integrate over the spectral measure μ:

$$E[L_i L_w] = \lim_{N \to \infty} \int_0^1 \left(\sum_{n=1}^{N} L_i^{n:N} \frac{w_\alpha(i/N)}{\sum_{k=1}^{N} w_\alpha(k/N)} (1-\alpha) \right) \mu(da) \qquad (13)$$

If L has a continuous distribution than we have that

$$E[L_i L_w] = E\left[L_i \int_0^1 L_\alpha \mu(d\alpha)\right]$$

$$= \int_0^1 E[L_i \mathbf{1}_{L > q_\alpha(L)}](1-\alpha)^{-1} \mu(d\alpha)$$

$$= \lim_{N \to \infty} N^{-1} \sum_{n=1}^{N} L_i^n \int_0^1 \mathbf{1}_{L^n > q_\alpha(L)} (1-\alpha)^{-1} \mu(d\alpha) \qquad \textbf{(14)}$$

If L has not a continuous distribution we have to use the density function (7) and might approximate the spectral contribution by

$$E[L_i L_w] \sim N^{-1} \sum_{n=1}^{N} L_i^n g_w(L^n) \qquad \textbf{(15)}$$

The actual calculation of the density g_w in (15) might be quite involved. On the other hand the integration with respect to μ in (13) and (14) is also not easy. If w is a step function as in the Example 1 above, then μ is a sum of weighted Dirac-measure and the implementation of spectral risk measure is straightforward.

---

1   We refer to Bluhm *et al* (2002) and Crouhy *et al* (2000) for a survey on credit portfolio modelling and capital allocation.
2   Note that $ES_\alpha(Y) = E(Y \cdot g(Y))$ and $ES_\alpha(X) \geq E(X \cdot g(Y))$ for every $X, Y \in V$.
3   $\Lambda(X, X)$ can be called the standalone capital or risk measure of X.
4   $\lim_{\epsilon \to 0} \Lambda(X, Y + \epsilon X) = \Lambda(X, Y) \forall X$.

REFERENCES

Acerbi, C., 2002, "Spectral Measures of Risk: A Coherent Representation of Subjective Risk Aversion", *Journal of Banking and Finance*, **26**, pp. 1505–18.

Acerbi, C., and D. Tasche, 2002, "On the Coherence of Expected Shortfall", *Journal of Banking and Finance*, **26**, pp. 1487–503.

Artzner, P., F. Delbaen, J.-M. Eber, and D. Heath, 1997, "Thinking Coherently", *Risk*, pp. 68–71, November.

Artzner, P., F. Delbaen, J.-M. Eber, and D. Heath, 1999, "Coherent Measures of Risk", *Mathematical Finance*, **9**, pp. 203–28.

Bluhm, C., L. Overbeck, and C. Wagner, 2002, *An Introduction to Credit Risk Modeling* (CRC Press: Chapman & Hall).

Crouhy, M., D. Galai, and R. Mark, 2000, "A Comparative Analysis of Current Credit Risk Models", *Journal of Banking and Finance*, **24**.

Delbaen, F., 2000, "Coherent Risk Measures", Lecture Notes, Scuola Normale Superiore di Pisa.

Denault, M., 2001, "Coherent Allocation of Risk Capital", *Journal of Risk*, **4(1)**.

Kalkbrener, M., 2002, "An Axiomatic Approach to Capital Allocation", Technical Document, Deutsche Bank AG, Frankfurt.

Kalkbrener, M., H. Lotter, and L. Overbeck, 2004, "Sensible and Efficient Capital Allocation", *Risk*, January.

Kurth, A., and D. Tasche, 2003 "Contributions to Credit Risk", *Risk*, pp. 84–8, March.

Overbeck, L., 1999, Allocation of Economic Capital in Loan Portfolios, Proceedings, "Measuring Risk in Complex Stochastic Systems", in Stahl/Härdle (eds), *Lecture Notes in Statistics* (Berlin: Springer).

Overbeck, L., and G. Stahl, 2003, "Stochastic Essentials for the Risk Management of Credit Portfolios", *Kredit und Kapital 1*.

Rockafellar R. T., and S. Uryasev, 2000, "Optimization of Conditional Value-at-Risk", *Journal of Risk*, **2**, pp. 21–41.

15

Evaluating Design Choices in Economic Capital Modelling: A Loss Function Approach*

Nicholas M. Kiefer, C. Erik Larson

Cornell University, OCC

Economic capital models are complex, and by their design usually take as input the output of several other modelling exercises, including but not limited to the estimation of asset-level default probabilities (PD), loss-given default (LGD) rates, and cross-asset correlations of these same parameters.

Due to their inherent complexity, it is imperative that financial institutions develop an assessment of the model risk associated with the use of economic capital models, as well as their associated driver models. Model risk is defined for this purpose as incorrect predictions or incorrect decisions resulting from the misuse of models. Model risk is assessed in the context of the intended use of models and best-known practices used to build models. Credit-risk decision models are evaluated with respect to sample design, modelling techniques, validation procedures and revalidation procedures. Since all models are imperfect, model risk is best thought of as losses that might be sustained due to the overly broad interpretation or use of a model beyond the scope of application for which it was developed.

*The statements made and views expressed herein are solely those of the authors, and do not represent official policies, statements or views of the Office of the Comptroller of the Currency, the US Department of the Treasury or its staff.

This chapter considers issues relating to the segmentation or grouping of credit exposures and the potential impact upon economic capital allocation and attribution. This type of evaluation plays a key role in the first stage of economic capital model validation, namely that of assessing the logical structure of a model's design relative to its intended application.

In most quantitative approaches to assessing expected loss and reserves, or the appropriate amount of economic capital to support a portfolio of assets, the risk ratings of the individual asset and the associated estimates of PD and LGD are key inputs. PD and LGD can be estimated using a variety of techniques including simple descriptive statistical analysis, statistical and econometric regression models and structural finance models. Whatever approach, these metrics are almost impossible to estimate uniquely for each asset – there is simply not enough available information. Assets are therefore grouped, or segmented, into categories – buckets – and PDs are estimated by bucket. This results in PD estimates that are actually average PDs for assets within categories.

Since models that yield estimates of economic capital requirements are typically nonlinear in PD, the degree of grouping or bucketing in a PD rating system has implications for economic capital. There is a trade-off in the estimation problem, in that grouping allows higher precision in estimating the group average as the size of the group increases, but large groups tend to combine heterogeneous assets and thus the average is less relevant. Similarly, groups that are too small yield estimated PD with large estimation error.

This chapter analyses exactly this trade-off in the context of economic capital allocation and attribution. We employ the Basel II specification in our analysis since it is built upon a very simplified economic capital model that allows for marginal portfolio capital charges to be computed based upon exposure-level characteristics (see Vasicek, 1997; Gordy, 2000, for a detailed discussion). As a tool for setting minimum regulatory capital charges, the Asymptotic Single Risk Factor model has the desirable administrative property that total portfolio credit risk capital can be computed as the sum of exposure-level capital charges, which in turn are functions only of PD, LGD and a single portfolio-level asset correlation coefficient. However, this simplicity does not come without cost, since one can justify computing portfolio capital charges in this way only if (i) there is a single systematic risk factor driving correlations across obligors, and (ii) no exposure in a portfolio accounts for more than an arbitrarily small share of total exposure.

The Basel II implementation process is devoting considerable resources to defining standards and procedures by which to judge the readiness and ability of financial institutions to estimate loan characteristics including PD and LGD. Supervisory authorities are developing detailed specifications of the validation standards for these drivers. We do not focus on issues relating to the validation of models used to estimate the drivers of, or inputs to, economic capital models. Our focus is instead on the application of the economic capital model, and we emphasise that a loss or value function must be specified so as to quantify the gains and losses from choosing a more or less granular asset segmentation scheme. The numbers and types of alternate loss functions that could be specified are great, and varying with the ultimate business uses of the capital estimates. Nevertheless, a natural starting point is to consider the mean-square error implications (MSE) of alternate segmentations or groupings of assets for economic capital. We illustrate the implications with several numerical examples.

PARAMETER ESTIMATION

Consider first the case of two assets, of differing types 1 and 2, with 2 the riskier (higher PD) asset. The question of segmentation is whether or not to combine assets 1 and 2 into the same risk bucket for purposes of estimating PD and capital. Suppose there is a sample of experience on loans of each type, n_1 observations on loans of type 1 and n_2 on loans of type 2. Presumably (but not necessarily) $n_1 > n_2$, so that there are fewer of the riskier type of asset. Let x_1 and x_2 be the observed average default rates of assets 1 and 2. Now, suppose that x_1 and x_2 are normally distributed with mean vector θ and variance matrix Σ. This makes sense if n_1 and n_2 are fairly large, or if x_1 and x_2 are suitable transformations of the default rates, for example logits. We proceed with the actual rates, so that the situation is one of estimation of two binomial probabilities, noting that the results easily apply more generally. In this case the variance has a simple structure, with

$$\Sigma_{11} = \theta_1(1 - \theta_1)/n_1, \quad \Sigma_{22} = \theta_2(1 - \theta_2)/n_2$$

To simplify matters, we will assume here that $\Sigma_{12} = \Sigma_{21} = 0$.

The single "restricted" estimator, x_r, that results from combining type 1 and type 2 assets into one group is given by

$$x_r = (n_1 x_1 + n_2 x_2)/n, \quad \text{where } n = n_1 + n_2$$

Its expectation is

$$E[x_r] = (n_1 \theta_1 + n_2 \theta_2)/n$$

The biases of x_r as an estimator of θ_1 and θ_2 are

$$E(x_r - \theta_1) = n_2(\theta_2 - \theta_1)/n, \quad E(x_r - \theta_2) = -n_1(\theta_2 - \theta_1)/n$$

These are sensible: the higher-risk asset has an underestimated PD and the lower-risk an overestimated PD, and the position of the average between these two PDs depends on the relative sample sizes. The gain from allowing this bias is a variance reduction relative to the unrestricted estimator. The variance of x_r is

$$V(x_r) = (n_1^2/n^2)\Sigma_{11} + (n_2^2/n^2)\Sigma_{22}$$
$$= \left(n_1\theta_1(1 - \theta_1) + n_2\theta_2(1 - \theta_2)\right)/n^2$$
$$= \left(n_1\theta_1(1 - \theta_1) + n_2\theta_2(1 - \theta_2)\right)/n^2$$

ESTIMATING CAPITAL REQUIREMENTS

Rather than simply consider the variability or bias in estimation of PD, we want to focus on the variability in estimation of risk capital. As mentioned earlier, we will consider capital as determined by the risk weight formula for corporate, sovereign and bank (CSB) exposures specified in the proposed revisions to the Basel Accord (BIS, 2004). Actually, we will use a somewhat simplified version of the Basel II function, considering the case where asset maturity is fixed at one year and LGD = 100%.

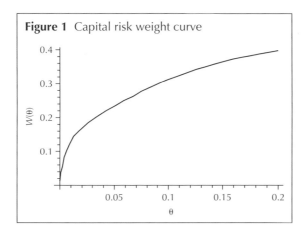

Figure 1 Capital risk weight curve

Let $W(\theta)$: $[0, 1] \to [0, 1]$ denote the curve giving the capital risk weight (in fractions of LGD) as a function of the probability of default. We have that

$$W(\theta) = N\left[G(\theta)(1 - R)^{-0.5} + G(0.999)(R/(1 - R))^{-0.5}\right] - \theta$$

where $R = 0.12(1 + \text{EXP}(-50\theta))$, $N(x)$ denotes the cumulative distribution function for a standard normal random variable, and $G(z)$ denotes the inverse cumulative normal distribution. We have made a further simplification by approximating the term $\text{EXP}(-50)$ appearing in the published formula by zero. The actual value is less than 10^{-20}. Note that this risk weight curve is generally a concave function in PD, as illustrated in Figure 1.

It is interesting to note at the outset that, while in general the unrestricted observed default rate is an unbiased estimator for the true group default probability θ, *the risk weight corresponding to the observed default rate, $W(x)$, does not yield an unbiased estimate of the risk weight corresponding to the true default probability, $W(\theta)$.* Indeed, since the risk curve is concave, we have $E[W(x)] < W(E[x]) = W(\theta)$, by Jensen's inequality. Thus "plugging in" an unbiased estimator for PD and evaluating the risk curve there leads to a higher than appropriate capital estimate.[1]

LOSS FUNCTIONS

We are now at a point where we can discuss the alternative loss functions that could be considered in assessing the consequences of bucketing decisions on economic capital estimates. We will want to make a distinction between capital allocation and capital attribution. When discussing capital allocation, we will be referring to the assessment of total capital at the portfolio level; the corresponding loss function will focus on the variation in the average risk weight across buckets. In contrast, the capital attribution process focuses on getting capital assigned appropriately at the bucket level, and consequently, a loss function for assessing attributed capital will be driven by a weighted average of variations in bucket-level capital risk weights.

Capital allocation

The average capital risk weight for our portfolio containing n_1 assets of type 1 and n_2 assets of type 2 is given by:

$$\left(n_1 W(\theta_1) + n_2 W(\theta_2)\right)/n$$

It will also be useful to use a quadratic approximation to the concave $W()$ function:

$$W(x) = ax - bx^2 + k$$

Using this approximation, the average capital risk weight, when evaluated using the unrestricted estimates x_1 and x_2, has expected value

$$
\begin{aligned}
(n_1/n)&\left(aE[x_1] - bE[x_1]^2 - b\Sigma_{11} + k\right) \\
&+ (n_2/n)\left(aE[x_2] - bE[x_2]^2 - b\Sigma_{22} + k\right) \\
&= (n_1/n)(a\theta_1 - b\theta_1^2 - b\Sigma_{11}) \\
&\quad + (n_2/n)(a\theta_2 - b\theta_2^2 - b\Sigma_{22}) + k
\end{aligned}
$$

If the default probabilities θ were known, the average capital risk weight would be correctly calculated as

$$(n_1/n)\left(a\theta_1 - b\theta_1^2\right) + (n_2/n)\left(a\theta_2 - b\theta_2^2\right) + k$$

Hence the bias in the average capital risk weight is negative and equal to

$$-b(n_1\Sigma_{11} + n_2\Sigma_{22})/n$$

Similarly, we calculate the variance of the average portfolio risk weight to be

$$E\left[n_1\left(a(x_1 - \theta_1) - b(x_1^2 - \theta_1^2)\right) + n_2\left(a(x_2 - \theta_2) - b(x_2^2 - \theta_2^2)\right)\right]^2 / n^2$$

Using the assumed independence of x_1 and x_2, and noting that the normal third moments are zero and fourth moments are $3\Sigma_{jj}^2$, this simplifies to

$$\left(n_1^2\left(a^2\Sigma_{11} + b^2(3\Sigma_{11}^2)\right) + n_2^2\left(a^2\Sigma_{22} + b^2(3\Sigma_{22}^2)\right)\right) / n^2$$

We now have enough information to show that when risk weights are calculated by plugging the unbiased, unrestricted estimators into the W function (as envisioned by Basel II), the MSE in the average risk weight is given by

$$\begin{aligned} \mathrm{MSE}_u = \big(&b^2(n_1\Sigma_{11} + n_2\Sigma_{22})^2 \\ &+ n_1^2\left(a^2\Sigma_{11} + 3b^2\Sigma_{11}^2\right) + n_2^2\left(a^2\Sigma_{22} + 3b^2\Sigma_{22}^2\right)\big) / n^2 \end{aligned}$$

We now turn to the average capital risk weight that is obtained from using the restricted estimator that combines assets into a single bucket. We consider the calculation of W at x_r. Again using our quadratic approximation to W, taking expectations yields

$$E[W(x_r)] = \left(aE[x_r] - b(E[x_r]^2 - bV(x_r) + k\right)$$

Recall that $E[x_r] = (n_1\theta_1 + n_2\theta_2)/n$ and that $V(x_r) = (n_1^2/n^2)\Sigma_{11} + (n_2^2/n^2)\Sigma_{22}$.

Thus the bias in using the restricted estimator $W(x_r)$ for $W(\theta)$ is given by

$$\begin{aligned} &a\left((n_1\theta_1 + n_2\theta_2)/n\right) - b\left((n_1\theta_1 + n_2\theta_2)^2/n^2\right) \\ &\quad - b\left((n_1^2/n^2)\Sigma_{11} + (n_2^2/n^2)\Sigma_{22}\right) \\ &\quad - (n_1/n)(a\theta_1 - b\theta_1^2) - (n_2/n)\left(a\theta_2 - b\theta_2^2\right) \end{aligned}$$

The variance of $W(x_r)$ is given by

$$\begin{aligned} V(W(x_r)) &= a^2V(x_r) + b^2(3V(x_r)^2) \\ &= a^2\left((n_1^2\Sigma_{11} + n_2^2\Sigma_{22})/n^2\right) + b^2\left(3\left((n_1^2/n^2)\Sigma_{11} + (n_2^2/n^2)\Sigma_{22}\right)^2\right) \end{aligned}$$

and the MSE$_r$ is of course the variance plus the squared bias.

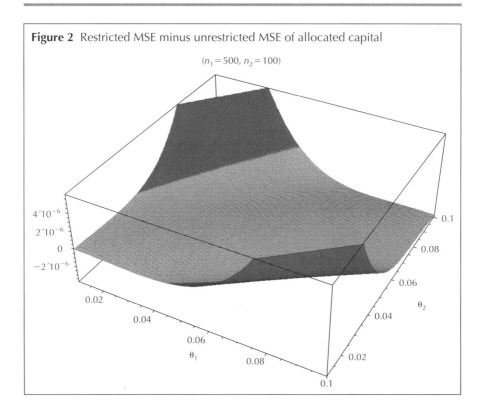

Figure 2 Restricted MSE minus unrestricted MSE of allocated capital

$(n_1 = 500, n_2 = 100)$

The best quadratic approximation to $W(\theta)$ around $\theta = 0.05$ is given by

$$W(\theta) = 0.130922 + 2.33006\,\theta - 5.17491\,\theta^2$$

Note that this quadratic approximation is quite accurate, with a maximum absolute relative error of less than 0.2% for $0.015 < \theta < 0.1$ (ie, the maximum error as a fraction of the actual $W(\theta)$ is less than 0.002)

Figures 2 and 3 illustrate the impact of choosing to combine or segment asset classes for the purpose of allocating economic capital. The figures graph the difference between the two mean square error measures of the average risk weight as functions of θ_1 and θ_2, the true rates of default for the two asset classes in the portfolio. The surface has been shaded to illustrate the regions where, for the indicated portfolio sizes, the difference between θ_1 and θ_2 results in

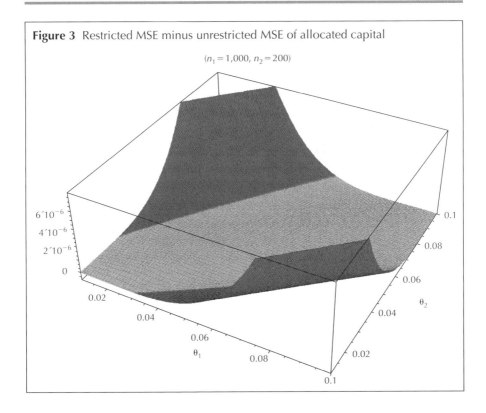

Figure 3 Restricted MSE minus unrestricted MSE of allocated capital

$(n_1 = 1,000, n_2 = 200)$

either positive (dark grey) or negative (light grey) differences in restricted less unrestricted MSE. When the difference is positive, a granular bucketing system is to be preferred to one that pools asset types for the purposes of minimising MSE in total capital allocation. Similarly, when the difference is negative, a pooling of asset types results in lower MSE. Comparing Figures 2 and 3 illustrates the impact of larger sample sizes. We see that, as expected, the restriction is better when the values of PD across the buckets are closer together. Larger sample sizes lead to restrictions being less desirable.

Capital attribution
Capital attribution is concerned with bucket- or segment-level accuracy in estimation. We therefore want to formulate a loss function that is sensitive to variation in bucket-specific estimates of risk weights.

When attributing capital to each of our two assets, using the unrestricted estimators, the expected value of the bucket-specific risk weights is given by

$$E[W(x_1)] = \left(aE[x_1] - bE[x_1]^2 - b\Sigma_{11} + k\right)$$
$$= \left(a\theta_1 - b\theta_1^2 - b\Sigma_{11} + k\right)$$

$$E[W(x_2)] = \left(aE[x_2] - bE[x_2]^2 - b\Sigma_{22} + k\right)$$
$$= \left(a\theta_2 - b\theta_2^2 - b\Sigma_{22} + k\right)$$

If the true segment-specific default rates are known, then the risk weights would be computed as

$$W(\theta_1) = a\theta_1 - b\theta_1^2 + k$$

$$W(\theta_2) = a\theta_2 - b\theta_2^2 + k$$

Which allows us to compute the unrestricted estimate bucket-level risk weight biases as

$$E[W(x_1) - W(\theta_1)] = -b\Sigma_{11}$$

$$E[W(x_2) - W(\theta_2)] = -b\Sigma_{22}$$

The variances of the bucket-level risk weight estimates are given by

$$V[W(x_1)] = E\left[\left(a(x_1 - \theta_1) - b(x_1^2 - \theta_1^2)\right)^2\right]$$
$$V[W(x_2)] = E\left[\left(a(x_2 - \theta_2) - b(x_2^2 - \theta_2^2)\right)^2\right]$$

Since the normal third moments are zero and fourth moments are $3\Sigma_{jj}^2$, these simplify to

$$V[W(x_1)] = \left(a^2\Sigma_{11} + b^2(3\Sigma_{11}^2)\right)$$

$$V[W(x_2)] = \left(a^2\Sigma_{22} + b^2(3\Sigma_{22}^2)\right)$$

By adding the bias-squared, the bucket-level unrestricted MSE are given by

$$\text{MSE}_{u1} = a^2\Sigma_{11} + 4b^2\Sigma_{11}^2$$

$$\text{MSE}_{u2} = a^2\Sigma_{22} + 4b^2\Sigma_{22}^2$$

Which allows us to compute the weighted-average unrestricted MSE across buckets as

$$\text{MSE}_u = (n_1/n)(a^2\Sigma_{11} + 4b^2\Sigma_{11}^2) + (n_2/n)(a^2\Sigma_{22} + 4b^2\Sigma_{22}^2)$$

Turning to the restricted estimator, we have from our previous work that

$$E[W(x_r)] = a\big((n_1\theta_1 + n_2\theta_2)/n\big) - b\big((n_1\theta_1 + n_2\theta_2)/n\big)^2 \\ - b\big((n_1^2/n^2)\Sigma_{11} + (n_2^2/n^2)\Sigma_{22}\big) + k$$

and

$$V(W(x_r)) = a^2\big((n_1^2\Sigma_{11} + n_2^2\Sigma_{22})/n^2\big) \\ + b^2\big(3\big((n_1^2/n^2)\Sigma_{11} + \big(n_2^2/n^2\big)\Sigma_{22}\big)^2\big)$$

We compute the restricted estimate bucket-level risk weight biases as

$$E[W(x_r) - W(\theta_1)] = a\big((n_1\theta_1 + n_2\theta_2)/n\big) - b\big((n_1\theta_1 + n_2\theta_2)/n\big)^2 \\ - b\big((n_1^2/n^2)\Sigma_{11} + (n_2^2/n^2)\Sigma_{22}\big) - (a\theta_1 - b\theta_1^2)$$

$$E[W(x_r) - W(\theta_2)] = a\big((n_1\theta_1 + n_2\theta_2)/n\big) - b\big((n_1\theta_1 + n_2\theta_2)/n\big)^2 \\ - b\big((n_1^2/n^2)\Sigma_{11} + (n_2^2/n^2)\Sigma_{22}\big) - (a\theta_2 - b\theta_2^2)$$

Again, by adding the variance and the squared bias, the bucket-level MSEs from using the restricted estimator are given by

$$\text{MSE}_{r1} = a^2\big((n_1^2\Sigma_{11} + n_2^2\Sigma_{22})/n^2\big) \\ + b^2\big(3\big((n_1^2/n^2)\Sigma_{11} + (n_2^2/n^2)\Sigma_{22}\big)^2\big) \\ + \big(a\big((n_1\theta_1 + n_2\theta_2)/n\big) - b\big(((n_1\theta_1 + n_2\theta_2)/n\big)^2 \\ - b\big((n_1^2/n^2)\Sigma_{11} + (n_2^2/n^2)\Sigma_{22}\big) - (a\theta_1 - b\theta_1^2)\big)^2$$

$$\text{MSE}_{r2} = a^2\big((n_1^2\Sigma_{11} + n_2^2\Sigma_{22})/n^2\big) \\ + b^2\big(3\big((n_1^2/n^2)\Sigma_{11} + (n_2^2/n^2)\Sigma_{22}\big)^2\big) \\ + \big(a\big((n_1\theta_1 + n_2\theta_2)/n\big) - b\big(((n_1\theta_1 + n_2\theta_2)/n\big)^2 \\ - b\big((n_1^2/n^2)\Sigma_{11} + (n_2^2/n^2)\Sigma_{22}\big) - (a\theta_2 - b\theta_2^2)\big)^2$$

Figure 4 Restricted MSE minus unrestricted MSE of attributed capital

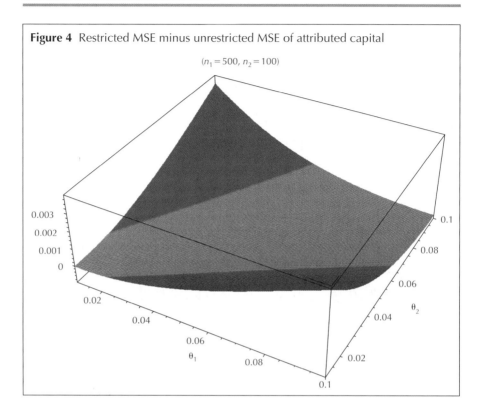

$(n_1 = 500, n_2 = 100)$

The weighted-average restricted MSE across buckets is

$$
\begin{aligned}
\mathrm{MSE_r} = {} & (n_1/n)\Big(a^2\big((n_1^2\Sigma_{11} + n_2^2\Sigma_{22})/n^2\big) \\
& + b^2\big(3\big((n_1^2/n^2)\Sigma_{11} + (n_2^2/n^2)\Sigma_{22}\big)^2\big) + \\
& + \big(a\big((n_1\theta_1 + n_2\theta_2)/n\big) - b\big(((n_1\theta_1 + n_2\theta_2)/n)^2 \\
& - b\big((n_1^2/n^2)\Sigma_{11} + (n_2^2/n^2)\Sigma_{22}\big) - (a\theta_1 - b\theta_1^2)\big)^2\Big) \\
& + (n_2/n)\Big(a^2\big((n_1^2\Sigma_{11} + n_2^2\Sigma_{22})/n^2\big) \\
& + b^2\big(3\big((n_1^2/n^2)\Sigma_{11} + (n_2^2/n^2)\Sigma_{22}\big)^2\big) \\
& + \big(a\big((n_1\theta_1 + n_2\theta_2)/n\big) - b\big(((n_1\theta_1 + n_2\theta_2)/n)^2 \\
& - b\big((n_1^2/n^2)\Sigma_{11} + (n_2^2/n^2)\Sigma_{22}\big) - (a\theta_2 - b\theta_2^2)\big)^2\Big)
\end{aligned}
$$

Figures 4 and 5 illustrate again the difference between MSEs in risk weights that arise for various combinations of θ_1 and θ_2.

Again, we see that the restrictions are desirable only when the PDs are close. Here, in contrast to the case of total capital, it is not

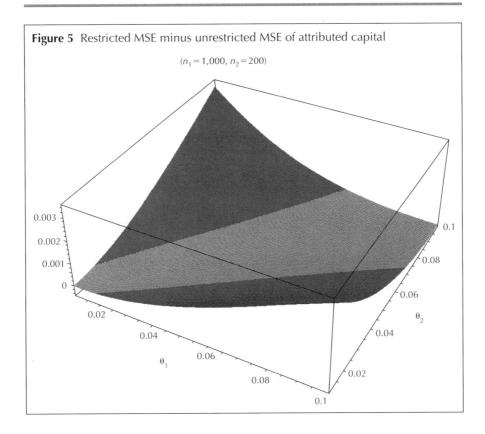

Figure 5 Restricted MSE minus unrestricted MSE of attributed capital

$(n_1 = 1,000, n_2 = 200)$

only the difference between the PDs that matters. When PDs are small, restrictions are less desirable for a given distance between them. Concern for bucket-level accuracy will lead to less combining of estimators.

CONCLUSIONS

This chapter illustrates an approach to capital model assessment by considering the trade-off between the decrease in sampling variance obtained by combining data to increase sample size and the bias resulting from characterising unlike assets with the same default probability.

We considered accuracy in the estimation of both portfolio- and asset-level capital requirements using a specification from the proposed revisions to the Basel Accord. Our suggested technique can be used to quantify whether a loss in accuracy from grouping or segmentation is outweighed by the decrease in variance of estimated capital. Although these numbers are specific to the example, it is likely that the relative ranking of the criteria holds more generally. That is, the "loss" from grouping is small when the evaluation criterion is the accuracy of estimation of the required total capital; grouping is of more concern when we are interested in getting capital attributed correctly at the bucket level.

Note that we have not here suggested practical methods for deciding the granularity of a bucketing procedure. We have simply considered the effects of using different criteria to judge the effects of pooling buckets. A classical approach is to "pretest", perhaps with a t-test for differences in means, and then decide whether to pool on the outcome of such a test (see Mosteller, 1948). Classically, the pretest is done on the difference between parameter estimates. The pretest, if desired, might be better done on the estimated capital requirements directly.

---

1 To see this, take a Taylor series expansion of $W(x_1)$ around the true default rate θ_1. This yields

$$W(x_1) = W(\theta_1) + \partial W(\theta_1)/\partial x_1 \times (x_1 - \theta_1) + (1/2)\partial^2 W(\theta_1)/\partial x_1^2 \times (x_1 - \theta_1)^2 + r$$

where r is small (with a maximum order of $(x_1 - \theta_1)^3$). Taking expectations gives

$$E[W(x_1)] = W(\theta_1) + (1/2)\partial^2 W(\theta_1)/\partial \theta_1^2 \times V(x_1)$$

since $E(x_1 - \theta_1) = 0$. Since W is concave, the second term is negative and the random variable $W(x_1)$ has expectation smaller than $W(E[x_1]) = W(\theta_1)$. Kiefer and Larson (2003) investigate this bias in detail and propose corrections.

REFERENCES

Basel Committee on Banking Supervision, 2004, "International Convergence of Capital Measurement and Capital Standards: A Revised Framework" (Basel: Bank for International Settlements).

Gordy, M. B., 2000, "A Risk-Factor Model Foundation for Ratings-Based Bank Capital Rules", Working Paper, Board of Governors of the Federal Reserve System.

Kiefer, N. M., and **C. E. Larson,** 2003, "Biases in Default Estimation and Capital Allocations Under Basel II," Cornell Working Paper, June.

Mosteller, F., 1948, "On Pooling Data", *Journal of the American Statistical Association*, **43**, pp. 231–42.

Vasicek, O. A., 1997, "The Loan Loss Distribution", Technical Report, KMV Corporation.

Index